THE LAWS OF INDO-EUROPEAN

BENJAMINS PAPERBACKS

2

BENJAMINS
BP
PAPERBACKS

THE LAWS OF
INDO-EUROPEAN

N.E. COLLINGE
University of Manchester

JOHN BENJAMINS PUBLISHING COMPANY
Amsterdam/Philadelphia

1985

Library of Congress Cataloging in Publication Data

Collinge, N.E.
 The laws of Indo-European.

(Benjamins Paperbacks; 2)
Bibliography
Includes index.
1. Indo-European languages -- Phonology, Historical. 2. Indo-European languages --
Grammar, Historical. I. Title. II. Series.
P577.C64   1985   410   85-9192
ISBN 90-272-2102-2 (European) / 0-915027-75-5 (U.S.) (alk. paper)

FOR MILDRED, TOM AND ANNA

Les loix...ont des rapports entre elles; elles en ont avec leur origine, avec l'objet du législateur, avec l'ordre des choses sur lesquelles elles sont établies. C'est dans toutes ces vues qu'il faut les considérer.

Montesquieu: *De l'esprit des lois* 1.3.

The worst I wish the law is, that his eye may be opened by experience.

Dickens: *Oliver Twist* ch.51.

PREFACE

On first embarking on the stormy waters of Indo-European studies — as often since — I wished I had a guide to those named 'laws' of history which scholars seemed to treat as old friends, thinking them too familiar to need introduction. This work is the report of a personal voyage of exploration around those 'laws'. In compiling the log of the voyage I know I have not shed the enthusiasms or the dislikes which attach themselves like limpets to the long-term traveller. But the record, however subjective, may serve as an initial chart for other explorers.

The blame for what is not said as it should be (or said when it should not be) must be mine only. But my sincere thanks are due — and have been given — to those who have contributed to my understanding on various hypotheses. By their repeated helpfulness, the late Alan S.C. Ross, and more recently Greville Corbett, Harry Leeming, John Payne, and Patrick Stiles have deserved a particular record here of my grateful appreciation. The editor of the CILT Series, Konrad Koerner, has been stalwart in kindly guidance and generous with helpful information; and the house of Benjamins is a model of encouragement.

The initial typing of an awkward and much-corrected manuscript has been nobly done by Nola Bowden and Irene Pickford. The Universities of Birmingham and Manchester allowed me study leave at crucial stages of research. Finally, I am grateful to the Mont Follick Trust for financial assistance towards the production of the final copy of the whole work.

Warts and all, here it is.

Manchester.   NEC
December 1983

CONTENTS

ABBREVIATIONS AND ACRONYMS

ACil	*Amsterdam Classics in Linguistics* (series I of *Studies in the Theory and History of Linguistic Science*). Amsterdam & Philadelphia: Benjamins.
ADA	*Anzeiger für deutsches Altertum und deutsche Literatur*. Wiesbaden. (Suppl. to *ZDA*)
AGI	*Archivio Glottologico Italiano*. Turin/Florence.
AJP	*American Journal of Philology*. Baltimore, Maryland.
AL (Haf)	*Acta Linguistica Hafniensia*. International journal of structural linguistics. Copenhagen.
AL (Hun)	*Acta Linguistica Academiae Scientiarum Hungaricae*. Budapest.
ALL	*Archiv für lateinische Lexicographie und Grammatik*. Leipzig.
ArchL	*Archivum Linguisticum.* Glasgow/Leeds.
ASAW	*Abhandlungen (usw.) der Sächsichen Akademie der Wissenschaften zu Leipzig (Phil-Hist. Klasse).* Berlin.
ASlPh	*Archiv für slavische Philologie.* Berlin.
AVP	*Archiv für vergleichende Phonetik.* Berlin. (See *ZPhon*)
BB	*Beiträge zur Kunde der indogermanischen Sprachen* (ed. by A. Bezzenberger). Göttingen. (Merged with *KZ*)
BDG	*Grundriss der vergleichenden Grammatik der indogermanischen Sprachen.* (K. Brugmann (vols.I, II_1, II_2), B. Delbrück (vols.III-V).) 1st ed. 1886-1900; 2nd ed. (of vols.I, II_1, II_2 only) 1897-1916. Strassburg: Trübner.
BL/LB	*Bibliographie Linguistique/Linguistic bibliography.* Utrecht & Antwerp; since 1976: The Hague.
BPTJ	*Biuletyn polskiego towarzystwa językoznawczego.* Wrocław/Kraków.
BSL	*Bulletin de la Société de Linguistique de Paris.* Paris.
BSOAS	*Bulletin of the School of Oriental and African Studies.* University of London: London.
CIL	*Corpus Inscriptionum Latinarum.* Berlin.

CILT	*Current Issues in Linguistic Theory* (series IV of *Studies in the Theory and History of Linguistic Science*). Amsterdam & Philadelphia: Benjamins.
CJL/RCL	*Canadian Journal of Linguistics/Revue Canadienne de Linguistique*. Toronto/Ottawa.
CFS	*Cahiers Ferdinand de Saussure*. Geneva.
CLS	(Papers from the sessions of the) Chicago Linguistic Society, Chicago.
CQ	*The Classical Quarterly*. London.
CR	*The Classical Review*. London.
CS	(Curtius') *Studien zur griechische und lateinische Grammatik*. Leipzig: Hirzel.
CTL	*Current Trends in Linguistics* (Series title) (ed. by T.A. Sebeok). The Hague: Mouton, 1963-1976.
DLZ	*Deutsche Literaturzeitung für Kritik der internationalen Wissenschaft*. Berlin.
DU	*Der Deutschunterricht*. Stuttgart.
EG	*Etudes Germaniques*. Revue de la Société des Etudes Germaniques. Paris.
FoL	*Folia Linguistica*. Acta Societatis Linguisticae Europaeae. The Hague.
FoLH	*Folia Linguistica Historica*. Acta Societatis Linguisticae Europaeae. The Hague.
GL	*General Linguistics*. University Park, Pennsylvania.
GQ	*Germanic Quarterly*. Lancaster, Pennsylvania.
GR	*The Germanic Review*. New York.
HL	*Historiographia Linguistica*. Amsterdam.
HL (A&J)	*Historical Linguistics (I, II)*, ed. by J.M. Anderson & C. Jones, 1974. Amsterdam: North Holland.
HSCP	*Harvard Studies in Classical Philology*. Cambridge, Massachusetts.
IF	*Indogermanische Forschungen*. Zeitschrift für Indogermanis-

	tik und allgemeine Sprachwissenschaft. Berlin.
IIJ	*Indo-Iranian Journal.* Dordrecht/Boston.
IJAL	*International Journal of American Linguistics.* Chicago.
IJb	*Indogermanisches Jahrbuch.* Berlin/Leipzig.
IJSLP	*International Journal of Slavic Linguistics and Poetics.* Since vol. 23: Columbus, Ohio.
IORJS	*Izvestija otdelenija russkogo jazyka i slovestnosti.* Akademija Nauk. St. Petersburg (Leningrad). From 1896 to 1927; then:
IpRJS	*Izvestija po russkomu jazyku i slovestnosti.* Leningrad.
JAOS	*Journal of the American Oriental Society.* New Haven, Conn.
JEGP	*The Journal of English and Germanic Philology.* Urbana, Illinois.
JGP	*Jahresbericht über die Erscheinungen auf dem Gebiete der germanischen Philologie.* Berlin.
JIES	*Journal of Indo-European Studies.* Since 1976: Washington, D.C.
JIPA	*Journal of the International Phonetic Association.* London. (Formerly: *Le Maître Phonétique.*)
JL	*Journal of Linguistics.* London.
KZ	(A. Kuhn's) *Zeitschrift für vergleichende Sprachforschung auf dem Gebiete der indogermanischen Sprachen.* Berlin, later Göttingen.
Lg	*Language.* Journal of the Linguistic Society of America. Baltimore, Maryland.
LI	*Linguistic Inquiry.* Cambridge, Massachusetts.
MDU	*Monatshefte für deutschen Unterricht.* Madison, Wisconsin.
MLN	*Modern Language Notes.* Baltimore, Maryland.
MLR	*The Modern Language Review.* Cambridge.
Mn	*Mnemosyne.* Leiden.
MPh	*Modern Philology.* Chicago.
MSL	*Mémoires de la Société de Linguistique de Paris.* Paris.
MSOS	*Mitteilungen des Seminars für orientalische Sprachen an der Königlichen Friedrich-Wilhelm-Universität zu Berlin.* Berlin.
MSS	*Münchener Studien zur Sprachwissenschaft.* Munich.

MU   *Morphologische Untersuchungen auf dem Gebiete der indo-germanischen Sprachen*, ed. by K. Brugmann and H. Osthoff, 6 vols. Leipzig, 1878-1910.

NAWG   *Nachrichten (usw.) der Akademie der Wissenschaften in Göttingen (Phil.-Hist. Klasse).* Göttingen.
NJL   *Nordic Journal of Linguistics.* Oslo. (Continuation of *NTS*).
NTF   *Norsk Tidsskrift für Filologi.* Copenhagen.
NTS   *Norsk Tidsskrift für Sprogvidenskap.* Oslo.

OLZ   *Orientalische Literaturzeitung.* Berlin

PedS   *Sprogvidenskaben i det nittende Aarhundrede: Metoder og resultater.* By H. Pedersen. Copenhagen, Gyldendalske Boghandel, 1924. (Cited after the English transl. by John Webster Spargo, *Linguistic Science in the Nineteenth Century*, Cambridge, Mass.: Harvard Univ. Press, 1931; repr. under the new title of *The Discovery of Language*, Bloomington: Indiana Univ. Press, 1962).
PBB   (H. Paul & W. Braune's) *Beiträge zur Geschichte der deutschen Sprache und Literatur.* Halle.
PBB(T)   Parallel edition of *PBB* 77 →. Tübingen.
P(1)ICHL   *Historical Linguistics: Proceedings of the First International Conference on Historical Linguistics (Edinburgh, 1973).* Ed. by J.M. Anderson & C. Jones. 2 vols. Amsterdam: North Holland, 1974.
P(4)ICHL   *Papers from the 4th International Conference on Historical Linguistics (Stanford, 1979).* Ed. by E.C. Traugott, R. LaBrum & S. Shepherd. Amsterdam: Benjamins, 1980.
P(5)ICHL   *Papers from the 5th International Conference on Historical Linguistics (Galway, Ireland, 1981).* Ed. by A. Ahlqvist. Amsterdam: Benjamins, 1982.
P(6)ICHL   *Papers from the 6th International Conference on Historical Linguistics (Poznań, 1983).* Forthcoming.
P(8)ICL   *Proceedings of the 8th International Congress of Linguists* (Oslo, 1957). Ed. by Eva Sivertsen et al. Oslo Univ. Press, 1958.
P(9)ICL   *Proceedings of the 9th International Congress of Linguists*

(Cambridge, Mass., 1962), Ed. by Horace G. Lunt. The Hague: Mouton, 1964.

P(10)ICL   *Actes du Xe Congrès internationale des Linguistes.* (Bucharest, 1967). Académie de Roumanie, 1969.

P(11)ICL   *Proceedings of the 11th International Congress of Linguists.* (Bologna-Florence, 1972). Ed. by L. Heilman. Società editrice il Mulino, 1974.

P(12)ICL   *Proceedings of the 12th International Congress of Linguists* (Vienna, 1977). Ed. by W. Dressler et al. Innsbruck: Inst. für Sprachwissenschaft, 1979.

RBPhH/BTFG   *Revue Belge de Philologie et d'Histoire/Belgisch Tijdschrift voor Filologie en Geschiedenis.* Brussels.

REA   *Revue des Etudes Anciennes.* Bordeaux/Paris.

REIE   *Revue des Etudes Indo-Européennes.* Bucharest.

REL   *Revista Española de Lingüistica.* Madrid.

RES   *Revue des Etudes Slaves.* Paris.

REV   *Russkij filologičeskij vestnik.* Warsaw.

RFIC   *Rivista di filologia e di istruzione classica.* Turin.

RHA   *Revue Hittite et Asianique.* Paris.

RPh   *Revue de Phonétique.* Paris.

SB   *Studi Baltici.* Rome.

SEEJ   *Slavic and East European Journal.* Madison, Wisconsin/Urbana-Champaign, Illinois.

SEER   *The Slavonic and East European Review.* London.

SEinf   *Einführung in die vergleichende Sprachwissenschaft.* By O. Szemerényi. Darmstadt: Wissenschaftliche Buchgesellschaft. 1970; 2nd ed. 1980.

SiHoL   *Studies in the History of Linguistics.* (Series II of *Studies in the Theory and History of Linguistic Science*). Amsterdam & Philadelphia: Benjamins.

SL   *Studia Linguistica.* Lund.

SLS   *Studies in the Linguistic Sciences.* Urbana-Champaign, Illinois.

SMEA   *Studi Micenei ed Egeo-anatolici.* Rome.

TAPA   *Transactions (and Proceedings) of the American Philological*

	Association. Cleveland, Ohio.
TCLP	*Travaux du Cercle Linguistique de Prague.* Prague.
TPS	*Transactions of the Philological Society.* Oxford.
VJa	*Voprosy Jazykoznanija.* Moscow.
VSJa	*Voprosy slavjanskogo jazykoznanija.* Moscow.
WPZ	*Wiener Prähistorische Zeitschrift.* Vienna.
WS	*Wörter und Sachen.* Heidelberg.
ZDAL	*Zeitschrift für deutsches Altertum und deutsche Literatur.* Wiesbaden.
ZDL	*Zeitschrift für Dialektologie und Linguistik.* Wiesbaden. (Supersedes *ZMf*)
ZDMG	*Zeitschrift der Deutschen Morgenländischen Gesellschaft.* Wiesbaden.
ZDP	*Zeitschrift für deutsche Philologie.* Halle.
ZMf	*Zeitschrift für Mundartforschung.* Halle / Wiesbaden. (Continued as *ZDL*)
ZPhon	*Zeitschrift für Phonetik, Sprachwissenschaft und Kommunikationsforschung.* Berlin. (Supersedes *AVP*)
ZRPh	*Zeitschrift für Romanische Philologie.* Tübingen.
ZSlPh	*Zeitschrift für Slavische Philologie.* Leipzig/Heidelberg.

FESTSCHRIFTEN

(Noted as 'Fs' + surname of honorand)

Fs Beeler:	(K. Klar, M. Langdon & S. Silver, ed.) *American Indian and Indoeuropean Studies offered to Madison S. Beeler.* The Hague: Mouton. 1980.
Fs Benveniste:	(F. Bader et al., ed.) *Mélanges linguistiques offerts à Emile Benveniste.* (SL Paris). Louvain: Peeters. 1975.
Fs Buyssens:	(J. Dierickx & Y. Lebrun, ed.) *Linguistique contemporaine: hommage à Eric Buyssens.* Brussels, Univ. Libre. 1970.
Fs Fourquet:	(P. Valentin & G. Zink, ed.) *Mélanges pour Jean Fourquet.* Paris; Klincksieck; Munich: Hueber. 1969.

Fs Greenberg: (A. Juilland, et al. ed.) *Linguistic Studies offered to Joseph Greenberg.* 3 vols. (paged consecutively). Saratoga, Calif.: Anma Libri, 1976.

Fs Halle: (S.R. Anderson & P. Kiparsky, ed.) *A Festschrift for Morris Halle.* New York; Holt, Rinehart & Winston. 1973.

Fs Hamm: (K. Sturm-Schnabl, ed.) *Bereiche der Slavistik.* Vienna, Austrian Academy. 1975.

Fs Jakobson (1): (M. Halle, H.G. Lunt et al. ed.) *For Roman Jakobson.* The Hague: Mouton. 1956.

id(2) *To honor Roman Jakobson.* 3 vols. The Hague: Mouton. 1967.

id(3) (C.E. Gribble, ed.). *Studies presented to R. Jakobson by his students.* Columbus, Ohio: Slavica. 1968.

Fs Lehmann: (P.J. Hopper, ed.) *Studies in descriptive and historical linguistics.* (For Winfred P. Lehmann.) Amsterdam: Benjamins. 1977.

Fs McIntosh (1): (M. Benskin & M.L. Samuels, ed.) *So many people longages and tonges.* (For Angus McIntosh). Edinburgh: Middle English Dialect Project. 1981.

Fs Maurer (1): (S. Gutenbrunner et al, ed.) *Die Wissenschaft von deutscher Sprache und Dichtung.* Stuttgart: Klett. 1963.

Fs Niedermann: (M. Renard & G. Redard cur.) *Hommages à Max Niedermann.* Brussels: Collection Latomus. 23. 1956.

Fs Palmer: (A.M. Davies & W. Meid, ed.) *Studies in Greek, Italic, and Indo-European Linguistics offered to L.R. Palmer.* Innsbruck: Inst. für Sprachwissenschaft. 1976.

Fs Penzl: (I. Rauch & G.F. Carr, ed.) *Linguistic method: essays in honor of Herbert Penzl.* The Hague: Mouton. 1979.

Fs Roth: *Festgruss an Rudolf von Roth.* Stuttgart. 1893.

Fs Saussure: *Mélanges de linguistique offerts à M. Ferdinand de Saussure.* Paris: Champion. 1908.

Fs Schneider: (K. Jankowsky & E. Dick, ed.) *Festschrift for K. Schneider,* Amsterdam: Benjamins. 1982.

Fs Sehrt: (E.A. Raven, W.K. Legner & J.C. King, ed.) *Germanic Studies in honor of Edward Sehrt.* Coral Gables: Miami Ling. Ser. 1. 1968.

Fs Seiler: (G. Brettschneider & C. Lehmann, ed.) *Wege zur Universalienforschung.* (For Hansjakob Seiler.) Tübingen: Narr. 1980.

Fs Stang: (V. Rūķe-Draviņa, ed.) *Donum Balticum.* (For C.S. Stang.) Stockholm: Almqvist & Wiksell. 1970.

Fs Starck: *Taylor Starck Festschrift.* The Hague: Mouton. 1964.

Fs Streitberg: *Streitberg Festgabe.* Leipzig: Markert & Petters. 1924.

Fs Szemerényi: (B. Brogyanyi, ed.) *Studies in diachronic, synchronic, and typological linguistics.* (For Oswald Szemerényi.) 2 vols. Amsterdam: Benjamins. 1980.

Fs Thieme: (G. Budd & A. Wezler, ed.) *Studien zur Indologie und Iranistik,* 5/6 (for P. Thieme). 1980.

MEMORIALS

(noted as 'Mem' + surname of memorand)

Mem Chatterji: (B.P. Mallik, ed.) *Suniti Kumar Chatterji Commemoration volume.* Burdwan Univ., West Bengal, India. 1981.

Mem Firth: (C.E. Bazell et al, ed.) *In memory of J.R. Firth.* London: Longmans. 1966.

Mem Foerste: (D. Hoffman & W. Sanders, ed.) *Gedenkschrift für William Foerste.* Cologne/Vienna: Böhlau. 1970.

Mem Kerns: (Y.C. Arbeitman & A.R. Bomhard, ed.) *Bono homini donum: essays in historical linguistics in memory of J. Alexander Kerns).* 2 vols. Amsterdam: Benjamins. 1981.

Mem Mossé: *Mélanges de linguistique et de philosophie Fernand Mossé in memoriam.* Paris: Didier. 1959.

SIGLA LINGUISTICA

$	syllable boundary
=	minimal boundary in root→stem formation
+	inflexional boundary
#	derivational boundary
# #	word boundary
-	general sign of combining of components
/ /	enclose systematic phonological segments
[ ]	enclose phonetic symbols
>	"is historically replaced by"
<	"is historically the successor to"
→	"undergoes derivation into"
←	"is derived from"
~	"is genetically cognate with"
*	reconstructed form
* *	improbable reconstruction
†	non-existent form
—	long vowel or heavy syllable
∪	short vowel
∩	light syllable

INTRODUCTION

What follows is basically a work of reference. It seems essential to make accessible the basic provisions of each named Indo-European law and the substantial revisions it has suffered over the years. What the term 'law' means, and how a pronouncement qualifies for the title, are issues better left to philosophers of language history. The analogy for what is offered here might be the sort of explanation one gives to enigmatic place-names, especially parts of cities, like the 'Annexe' in Toronto or the 'Bull Ring' in Birmingham or the 'Shambles' in Manchester. No terminology can be more handy; but newcomers find it interesting to learn the origin of the name and the changes in the area to which each refers, and they need to be informed of the current confines (and whether the place still exists) as accurately as possible.

The convenience of having named laws is reduced if, as often, (a) different pronouncements are accorded the same title, and (b) a single law is variously awarded different names. The first difficulty is offered a cure here by writing of, for instance, 'Sievers' Law I' and 'Sievers' Law II', and so forth; the second problem is handled, in respect of such laws as Brugmann's, Dolobko's, and others, by noting and evaluating rival claims. Sometimes a dual nomenclature is suggested where it has not been used before; after all, scholars should be given their just deserts.

Various considerations have been borne in mind in preparing this catalogue:
1) Laws are often quoted nowadays as if their contents are widely and precisely known — but this is sometimes not so;
2) a version is commonly presented as an orthodoxy — where there may in fact be widely variant readings of the law;
3) contemporary theorists often cite as gospel a law about which historians have fought bitterly and on which there remains many an honest doubt;
4) ordinances are repeatedly attacked, or revised, in ways which ignore similar offensives in the past or variations which were observed by their inventor in the first place; and lastly
5) much sterling work prompted by these laws deserves not to be forgotten, perhaps as as a paradigm of diachronic scholarship or possibly because of fruitful findings on the side.

By no means all the laws treated here have been as useful as their authors hoped or are as healthy now as they should have liked. Some have sickened for years and may be beyond salvation: those of Fortunatov (I), Lachmann and Thurneysen are cases in point. Grimm's may be close to expiry; Brugmann's, on the other hand, seems to have risen from the dead. Again, the coverage here is only too clearly uneven. This is not entirely because of the difference in the scope or implications of each law. Frankly, there is here a deliberate subjectivity, and no doubt some arbitrary judging of contributions; indeed, there are some instances of simple liking and dislike. Exhaustivity is always an *ignis fatuus*; real exhaustivity is hardly to be claimed here, as deserving comments may be embedded in seemingly irrelevant works, and some relevant works may be in languages whose unfamiliarity makes the contents inaccessible. Above all, some economic limit has seemed desirable; and in any case 1983 has generally been a closing date for reference. But one hopes that a nominal exhaustivity has been achieved. On the majority of the laws more has been put together here than ever before, and what is included should infallibly lead both to a full understanding of the law's provisions in each case and to instructive bibliographies in works themselves quoted. So that enquirers are at least set on the long but inviting path of further discovery; on which, personal travel is quite essential.

The material has been divided, some laws being assigned to mainline treatment and some relegated to an appendix. The reasons for the distinction should be fairly clear. To qualify for a main article the law should be either of wide scope or continuing appeal, or at least it should have elicited a quantity of comment and stirred the excitement (or perhaps the irritation) of scholars during its career. Or else, especially if among those created in the recent fashion of reviving the named law as a tool of the trade, it must look as if it will stir some excitement. It must also be a succinct statement of a recognized historical Indo-European event. The appendix (Appendix I) houses laws of lesser moment, and those rulings which give, instead, procedural guidelines to diachronic and other linguists, or virtually proverbial expressions of tendency in human language and its users. It is, even so, folly to pretend that the assignment here of laws to various categories is either thoroughly defensible now or not likely to be quite radically changed before long.

With which in mind, let us propel each law for its moment into the limelight.

AITKEN'S LAW

This law's domain is a regional variety of a single language, Scots English. Yet it has been the cause of wider ideological differences and must have some significance in general phonology. Its name honours a contemporary scholar, (Adam) Jack Aitken, who has laboured long on *A Dictionary of the Older Scottish Tongue*. His researches into vowel length in Scots English and its evolution (the major data-source being Wettstein 1942: 6-11) have led him to identify two diachronic processes of the late 16th or early 17th century: on which, consult Aitken 1962, 1965, 1977, 1979, 1981. The processes are these:

(1)   all long vowels and diphthongs shortened, except before /r v z d/ or / # # /;

(2)   non-high short vowels lengthened when before /r v z d/ or / # # /

The combination of (1) and (2) — with /dz/ and /#/ and 'hiatus' added to the context — is now called by its author 'the Scottish vowel-length rule' (SVLR). It is restricted in its pure form to end-stressed syllables; and is located in time and space as a Central Scotland shift clearly later than the Great Vowel Shift of the 15th century (e.g. Aitken, 1977:8-9). Awareness of the phenomena may be attributed as far back as William Grant in 1914 or even Karl Luick in 1896: see (Vaiana) Taylor, 1975:423n1.

There are two dimensions of relevance: the first is that of phonological explanation. Herein process (2) has met with little disagreement. A formalization probably recognisable by Lass, Pullum and other commentators is:

$$
\begin{bmatrix} V \\ \text{- high} \\ \text{- long} \end{bmatrix} \rightarrow [\text{+ long}] \Bigg/ \left\{ \begin{matrix} \# \# \\ \begin{bmatrix} C \\ \text{+ continuant} \\ \text{+ voice} \\ \text{- lateral} \end{bmatrix} \end{matrix} \right\}
$$

— allowing for personal preferences over the use of 'long' (as opposed to *VV)* and so forth. The grouping of processes (1) and (2) together, however, rests on the identity of the context specified in each. Vaiana 1972 (cf. (Vaiana) Taylor 1974:406) — following David Murison — gave to the complex so established the title 'Aitken's Law'. On the other hand Lass (1974:320 and passim) simply calls the common context 'the Aitken environment'.

The intriguing fact is that the conditioning context of process (2) is the inhibiting context of process (1). Phonologists have to decide whether or not to treat the Aitken environment as the same dynamic element in both shifts (which both occurred at more or less the same historical period and both concerned length in vowels). If the environment is so treated, then the concept of a conditioned *absence* of change in (1) presents itself: i.e., the shift-type 'A → A/B'. If it is *not* so treated, then the device of negative or blocking context (or 'sheltering environment') is being used. Each strategy affronts somebody. Indeed, the whole question arose appropriately again in the mid-1970s, just a century after the larger question of exceptions to rules (and their treatment) had exercised the neogrammarians; for the debates, old and new, see Collinge (1978, esp.62-63.). Lass (1973, 1974) and Pullum (1974) are on opposite sides here, and would respectively formalize process (1) as (where the first part of the rule is a 'does not happen' case):

$$\begin{bmatrix} V \\ +\text{long} \end{bmatrix} \rightarrow \begin{cases} [+\text{long}] \\ [-\text{long}] \end{cases} \Bigg/ \text{——— AE}$$

and

$$\begin{bmatrix} V \\ +\text{long} \end{bmatrix} \rightarrow [-\text{long}] \Big/ \neg \text{——— AE}$$

($\neg$ means NOT, and AE means 'the Aitken environment'.)

Pullum (1974) gives a careful theoretical evaluation of the merits and defects of the alternative treatments. Lass (1974:323-75) is more practically concerned with the Aitken environment's dynamism not only in its different effects in Scots but also elsewhere, where it is far from its inventor's domain, such as in 14th century Northern Middle English. This detachment leads him to see the law itself as one late chapter in an evolutionary conspiracy to Scandinavize northern forms of English (cf. (Vaiana) Taylor 1974). Not that the Scandinavian and Scots length distribution is identical, however. The aim now becomes to have (a) shortness as the lexical quality of *all* vowels and (b) a lengthening rule wherever the context demands 'strengthening' (Lass 1974:336; (Vaiana) Taylor 1974:417). On which last point, more in a moment.

Ewen (1977:307) accepts that the outcome of the law is that, for all Scots non-high vowels, length is predictable once the context is known. He goes further in arguing that the Aitken environment constitutes a natural phonological class for the relevant dialects; and that the law is best considered in terms of a 'lenition hierarchy'. The former point is somewhat counter-intuitive, one must protest; and the declaration seems unhappily circular. As for the second, although the framework and technical notation advised is that of a 'dependency' phonology rather than a 'distinctive feature' phonology, the teleological explanation is much the same as (in fact, the inversion of) the sonorance reinforcement proposed by (Vaiana) Taylor in 1974, or what Anderson & Jones (1974:25) term a 'vowel strengthening schema'.

One sees how use is being made of the linked concepts of inherent strength of phonological entities and of strengthening (the strong) to offset more marked-ly the weak. The former notion comes from Grammont; but the latter (and the combining of the ideas) has had many champions in recent times. Among the most notable is Foley (1977); but several are discussed in Appendix I Section B, under 'Grammont's laws'. Grimm's and Lachmann's laws (q.v.) have likewise been subjected to explanations which calculate strengthening conspiracies or strength/weakness intensifyings. Lass & Anderson (1975, chap.5) specifically discuss this approach in relation to English. Yet, as applied to Aitken's law, the 'sonorance scale' of (Vaiana) Taylor (1974:406-407), based on acoustic energy (like the exactly reversed 'lenition scale', or 'strength scale' of articulatory resistance), has a weak-to-strong range which agrees with the usual orthodoxy in respect of vowels but not in respect of consonants (/t, s, d, z, l, j, i, ii/). Thus, a rather too subjective employment of the notion of strength is presently deployed on Aitken's discovery.

The second dimension of the shift(s) is that of diffusion, both areal and morphonological. Aitken himself admits (1981:137) that 'simple, clear-cut' operation of the law is not found in all dialects. In particular, 'long' has to mean 'fully long', and not merely 'non-short', if a cross-dialectal generalization is to be made. If the formalization used above has '+' added to its right, the consistency of the law's application is notably increased (Aitken 1981:139). Aitken gives a thorough dialectal-diachronic survey of the law's progress, through time and place and phonetic environments.

REFERENCES

Aitken, A.J. 1962. *Vowel length in Modern Scots.* Edinburgh; Dept. of English Language, Univ. of Edinburgh. Mimeo.

—————. 1975. *The Scottish vowel-length rule.* Edinburgh; Dept. of English Language, Univ. of Edinburgh. Mimeo.

—————. 1977. How to pronounce Older Scots. In *Bards and Makars* (ed. by A.J. Aitken, M.P. McDiarmid, and D.S. Thomson). Glasgow; Glasgow Univ. Press, 1-21 (esp.8-10).

—————. 1979. Scottish speech: a historical view with special reference to the Standard English of Scotland. In *Languages of Scotland* (ed. by A.J. Aitken and T. McArthur) 85-118. Edinburgh: Chambers. (Reports of conferences of 1975 and 1976 organised by Univ. of Glasgow.)

—————. 1981. The Scottish vowel-length rule. In *Fs McIntosh*, 131-57.

Anderson, J.M. & Jones, C. 1974. Three theses concerning phonological representations. *JL* 10.1-26.

Collinge, N.E. 1978. Exceptions, their nature and place — and the Neogrammarians. *TPS* 1978.61-86.

Ewen, C.J. 1977. Aitken's law and the phonatory gesture in dependency phonology. *Lingua* 41.307-29.

Foley, J. 1977. *Foundations of theoretical phonology.* Cambridge, Univ. Press.

Lass, R. 1973. A case for making phonological rules state things that don't happen. Edinburgh; *Working Papers in Linguistics* 3. 10-18.

—————. 1974. Linguistic orthogenesis? Scots vowel quantity and the English length conspiracy. *HL (A&J)* 2. 311-52, esp. 319-26.

————— & Anderson, J.M. 1975. *Old English phonology.* Cambridge, Univ. Press.

McClure, J.D. 1977. Vowel duration in a Scottish accent. *JIPA* 7.10-16.

Pullum, G.K. 1974. Sheltering environments and negative contexts: a case against making phonological rules state things that don't happen. Edinburgh; *Working Pap. Ling.* 4.31-41.

Taylor, M.E. (Vaiana) 1974. see Vaiana 1974.

Vaiana, M.E. 1972. *A study in the dialect of the southern counties of Scotland.* Diss. Indiana Univ., Bloomington.

—————. 1974. The great southern Scots conspiracy: pattern in the development of Northern English. *HL (A&J)* 2. 403-26.

Wettstein, P. 1942. *The phonology of a Berwickshire dialect.* Diss., Univ. Zurich. Bienne: Schüler.

BARTHOLOMAE'S LAW

Christian Bartholomae lived from 1855 to 1925. By the time he was thirty he had proposed and codified an observation on an assimilation process in Indo-Iranian, operative on consonant clusters over a morphological boundary; this, essentially, is still known to the world as Bartholomae's law. In 1882 he examined sequences like /-gh+t-/ and /-gh+s-/ in that branch of IE. His conclusion is thereafter presented compendiously, across Indic, Old Persian and Avestan, in his 1883 handbook (48, § 124). It is further cited at 1885:206, by way of smoothing the path of those who relate the Iranian forms of the 'daughter' word to congeners in various IE languages, especially to the curious Greek form. The law's formula there is:

> ... wenn in der wortbildung oder −flexion ein tönender aspirirter mit einem tonlosen geräuschlaut zusammentrifft, so wird letzterer tönend und unternimmt des ersten aspiration.

This is usually understood to mean that, e.g., *labh+ta-* will give *labhda-* in the perfect participle, a true result for Sanskrit although the aspiration is lost in Iranian. The presence of /+/ (*wortflexion*) or even / # / (*wortbildung*) is noteworthy; so is the apparent collapsing of /-t/ and /-s/ under the general term 'geräuschlaut' (cf. Bartholomae 1883:48). This latter is traditional; it is not, however, an assertion of identity between stops and continuants in reflexes. Yet a common element is provided by the presumption of an interim presibilantizing of the second (dental) of contiguous plosives. Thus $/dht/ > /d^Zdh/$, and no doubt $/ght/ > /g^Zdh/$, after which Indic and Old Persian lose the sibilant and Avestan loses the prior stop (except for the labial, which is a special case: $/bht/ > /wd/$, according to Bartholomae). Equally special, even in Indic, is the result of palatal $/g'h+t/$: so *lig´h+to- > *liẓdha-´> līḍha-* [*li:q^ha-*].

Gray (1964) adduces Hittite (*azteni*), Greek (πύστις) and Latin (*-sessus*) in support of the presibilant; but the prior stop must also be dental and need not be (indeed, is not) an aspirate. Gray faces the odder aspects of Bartholomae's pronouncement (of which the etymological and morphological justifying is quite straightforward): namely, the *progressive* assimilation of voicing and (in Indic) the apparent rightward shift of aspirate-release. As to the latter, Gray assumes that a mid-cluster breath effect is not to be considered and that only aspirate throw-back is a feasible alternative view of the process (on which, much is said on Grassmann's law). But thirty or more common roots (like *labh-*) cannot be subject to ATB, and so aspirated, in Indic. Therefore, while in this theory the type *dhatta-* (which is quite irregular for Bartholomae himself) is the 'correct' version, for Gray *labdha-* typifies the desperate remedy applied to the intransigents, so to speak. In support of this, we learn that the *dhatta-* type outnumbers the *buddha-* type (which on this basis must have been analogically attracted to the *labdha-* group, one presumes) in the R̥gveda by a ratio of 10 to 7.

Some take the law to be of PIE date, even so. Kuryłowicz regularly opines so, and denies that the aspirated segments had yet become 'phonemic' (1935: 51; 1956:379ff.; 1964:13; 1968. 339 – even suspecting a widespread phenomenon with Akkadian connections). Bartholomae (1895:20) himself suggested a wider domain (cf. Wackernagel 1895: 32-33). So does Szemerényi (*SEinf* 95), for whom the limitation to Indo-Iranian is a secondary accident and arises from a revised treatment in Greek and Latin for instance (λέκτρον, *lectus* < *legh-*, cf. λέχος). He insists (136) that Bartholomae offers no ground for opposing 'mediae aspiratae' (see his doubts in Szemerényi 1967: 89) and 'tenues aspiratae', so that the latter must be an innovation rather than an archaism in Indo-Iranian. Yet he speaks of the law as 'Aryan' only, in 1972 (146). Bennett (1966) is quite sceptical about traces of the law in Germanic (against Kluge and Brugmann). Indeed, Hittite is perhaps the only other happy hunting ground; so Szemerényi hints (1966: 206n84), for /dh+t/, and Puhvel (1972) asserts it for the sequence /gh+t/ > /gd/ (*gd, kt*), as in *egdu* < *eygh+tu* (cf. Tocharian B *yku*). He even supposes a spread to /g+/ after Anatolian loss of the aspirated stops.

Miller (1977a) had the bright idea that even the PIE root structure rejection of **/tegh/ (or **/ghet/) was simply the 'root-as-domain' aspect of a general and natural process which also operated across morpheme boundaries (/+/): the glottal difference in the consonants had to be severely reduced by one means or another (although it was tolerated within *words*, even compounds: so *bhr̥ti-* — /bhr̥ # ti-/ — despite the usual reverse strength relation of / # / to /+/). In another paper Miller (1977b) takes the further step of 'solving' the root constraint in terms of the new glottal theory of PIE stops. To this our Appendix II is devoted; and there consideration is given to the rather more shattering (because splendidly simple) view of Gamkrelidze (1981) that Bartholomae's law, even though accepted as special to Indic (rather than general (P)IE), is in large part not a shift-process at all. Anderson (1970:388) saw 'BL' as having two stages:

(1)   /bh+t/ → /bhdh/

(2)   /bhdh/ → /bdh/

and (2) at least, for Gamkrelidze, is simply a matter of phonotactic choice between positional variants of /b^h/ (etc.). An even simpler view is that of Ejerhed (1981:146), namely that BL is just a movement of /h/, which is a separate *segment* in Sanskrit; that goes no way to solving the matter.

Bartholomae was always vulnerable after honestly setting out the idiosyncratic reflex-patterns within the Indo-Iranian sub-groups (1883:48); equivalence is only once attested there (/dh+t/ → /zd/ in both Iranian sub-groups). Anderson's chopping up of the law allows an attempted slotting of its parts into the more radical discussions of Indic aspiration-processes; these are ventilated below under Grassmann's law, where the thoughts of Whitney (1879), Vennemann (1979), and others are considered. It is hard to discuss one of these laws without the other, in fact.

But such chopping up is less hostile than Mey's exterminating zeal (1972). He presupposes the demise of Grassmann's ordinance and sets about interring Bartholomae's in the same grave. Reinterpreting the facts of Sanskrit (and correcting Anderson *en passant*), Mey collapses deaspiration with devoicing at word-end, and both with a 'voice and aspiration assimilation constraint' before a consonant (assuming that '#' – our # # – is just a consonantal segment bereft of a plus value for any feature). His 'rule', where both /dh+t/ and /d+t/ are supposed to be phonotactically handled by means of inter-exclusive (a) and (b) operations respectively, is scarcely a model of perspicuity (especially as to 'γvoi'):

$$
\begin{bmatrix} +\text{obst} \\ \langle \overset{+\text{asp}}{\underset{a\ \text{voi}}{}} \rangle a \end{bmatrix}_{1} \begin{bmatrix} +\text{obst} \\ \langle \overset{\beta\ \text{asp}}{\underset{\gamma\ \text{voi}}{}} \rangle b \end{bmatrix}_{2} \rightarrow \begin{bmatrix} {}^{1} \\ \langle \overset{\beta\ \text{asp}}{\underset{\gamma\ \text{voi}}{}} \rangle b \end{bmatrix} \begin{bmatrix} {}^{2} \\ \langle \overset{+\text{asp}}{\underset{a\ \ \text{voi}}{}} \rangle a \end{bmatrix}
$$

Schindler (1976) has made perhaps the most determined effort, within the traditional IE phonetic framework, to evolve a combined diachronic and synchronic derivation for the forms – in effect, only the Indic forms, in any detail – which surface after the array of phonological processes of which 'BL' is just one phase (636). His version of the law is for Proto-Indo-Iranian; it is not of

PIE vintage but is clearly pre-Iranian:

$$\begin{bmatrix} +\text{obst} \\ \\ -\text{asp} \end{bmatrix} \rightarrow \begin{bmatrix} +\text{voice} \\ \\ +\text{asp} \end{bmatrix} \Big/ \begin{bmatrix} +\text{voice} \\ \\ +\text{asp} \end{bmatrix} \text{——— *(mirror image, iterative)}$$

By this, not only /dht/ but also /tdh/ and /ddh/ all become /dhdh/ — the 'first stage' (and the really Bartholomaic part) of BL. (Oddly, Schindler accepts *rundh+ thas* as giving the same result as *rundh+tas*, and as very old in attestation (624); but his rule cannot handle it; and the root *dhā* also remains unexplained in behaviour.) Schindler has, of course, a prior rule of *s*-insertion to cope with Bartholomae's ideas, and a later rule to excise the *s*. But his further rule which removes voice and aspiration from word-final obstruents or the prior obstruent in a final cluster will not take us to medial /-ddh-/ as is on the face of it required: hence recourse is had to a very generalized sort of Grassmann's law (and cyclically, as GL precedes BL by several 'rules', in his view). This version of GL (Schindler 1976:625) — cf. Miller (1977a) — allows an *optional* syllabic nucleus between the inter-affecting consonants. (As to Schindler's notions of GL, something is said on that law, below.)

Magnusson's (1969) general theory of the manipulation of oppositions of plosives says much, but illuminates little, on the law (among others). But the big caveat is the radical reinterpretation of the PIE plosive system, set out in Appendix II. Bartholomae's is one of the numerous laws susceptible thereby to disfiguring, if not to extinction.

REFERENCES

Anderson, S.R. 1970. On Grassmann's law in Sanskrit. *LI* 1.387-96.

Bartholomae, C. 1882. Die arische Vertretung von med. asp. *+t* und med. asp. *+s*. *Arische Forschungen* I.3-24. Halle: Niemeyer.

———. 1883. *Handbuch der altiranischen Dialekte.* Leipzig; Breitkopf & Härtel. (Repr., Wiesbaden; Sandig, 1968.)

———. 1885. Θυγάτηρ. *KZ* 27.206-207.

———. 1895. *Vorgeschichte der iranischen Sprachen.* In *Grundriss der iranischen Philologie* I, ed. by W. Geiger and E. Kuhn. Strassburg; Trübner.

Bennett, W.H. 1966. The Germanic evidence for Bartholomae's law. *Lg* 42.733-37.

Ejerhed, E.I. 1981. The analysis of aspiration in Sanskrit phonology. *NJL* 4. 139-59.

Gamkrelidze, T.V. 1981. See Appendix II.

Gray, J.E.B. 1964. Aspirate Sandhi. *BSOAS* 27.615-19.

Kuryłowicz, J. 1935. *Etudes indoeuropéennes* I. Kraków: Prace Komisji Językowej Polskiej Akademji Uniejętposci, 21.

—————. 1956. *L'apophonie en indoeuropéen.* Wrocław: Polska AN.

—————. 1964. On the methods of internal reconstruction. *P(9)JCL* 9-31.

—————. 1968. *Indogermanische Grammatik* II. Heidelberg: Winter.

Magnusson, W.L. 1969. Occludent orders in IE. *Linguistics* 54.86-112.

Mey, J.L. 1972. Was Bartholomae really a Grassmann? *NTS* 26.81-90.

Miller, D.G. 1977a Bartholomae's law and an IE root structure constraint. *Fs Lehmann*, 365-92.

—————. 1977b. Some theoretical and typological implications of an IE root structure constraint. *JIES* 5. 31-40.

Puhvel, J. 1972. Bartholomae's law in Hittite. *KZ* 86.111-15.

Schindler, J. 1976. Diachronic and synchronic remarks on Bartholomae's and Grassmann's laws. *LI* 7.622-37.

Szemerényi, O. 1966. Iranica II. *Die Sprache* 12.190-226.

—————. 1967. The New Look of Indo-European. *Phonetica* 17.65-99.

—————. 1972. Comparative linguistics. *CTL* 9.119-95.

Vennemann, T. 1979. Grassmann's law, Bartholomae's law, and linguistic methodology. *Fs Penzl*, 557-84.

Wackernagel, J. 1895. Miscellen zur griechischen Grammatik. *KZ* 33.1-62.

Whitney, W.D. 1889. *A Sanskrit grammar.* 2nd rev. ed., Boston: Ginn. (1st. ed., Leipzig; Breitkopf & Härtel, 1879.) (12th unchanged ed., Cambridge, Mass.: Harvard Univ. Press, 1972.)

BRUGMANN'S LAW

Towards the close of the nineteenth century opinion was divided as to the non-high vowels ascribable to Proto-Indo-European. Sanskrit offered /a/ where other languages suggested a reconstruction of the triad /e,o,a/. Some interfering incidences of /a/ with odd cognates were, so to speak, sterilized by Brugmann's own hypothesis of derivation from 'sonant nasals'. But for the remaining occurrences of non-high vowels the question remained: had there been a conditioned split outside Indic or a merger inside? General principles, irritatingly but not unusually, prompted no solution. The traces, once discovered, of obstruent palatalization in prehistoric Indic before a presumable /e/ were seen as a godsend, and 'the law of the palatals' entered history. Its story is recorded in its place. But before this had occurred to several scholars, and before PIE had been securely accorded its three lower vowels, Karl Brugman(n) (1849-1919) – the spelling of his surname changed in his lifetime – famous among the *Junggrammatiker*, had pardonably backed both sides. In 1876 (363ff. see also 1879:2ff.) he set up a non-high PIE vowel of indeterminate oral position on the front-back axis and allowed (at least implicitly) three significant alternants: /a_1, a_2, a_3/, reflecting distinctively elsewhere as /e, o, a/. (It is a nuisance that Hübschmann, [1879:409], has /a_1, a_2, a_3/ reflecting as /a, e, o/.)

It was, of course, essential to establish that though they seemed alike they did not behave alike; Collitz (1878:303-304) insisted that the difference was fully there, as /e, a, o/, in PIE – and one should be brave and say so. In both 1876 and 1879 Brugmann drew on earlier hints by Bopp and Schleicher to elaborate his law and to highlight the individuality of his /a_2/. Whereas /a_1/, he said, is found as $e(a)$ in the European and Armenian systems but as a in Indo-Aryan, /a_2/ is more various. It surfaces as o in Armenian, Hellenic, Italic and Slavic; as a in Celtic, Germanic and Baltic; but – and this is the nub – as $\bar{a}$ in Indo-Aryan in all open syllables (though as $\breve{a}$ in closed syllables). As a partial explanation he conceived a_2 as 'half-long'. For this exposition the author himself claimed the status of law: "als gesetz lässt sich aufstellen ..." (1879:2). His examples include (for open syllables) *bhár-ā-masi* (sic) (= φέρομεν), *dā̆r-u* (= δόρυ), *pā̆d-am* (= πόδα), and (for closed syllables) *dadárśa* (= δέδορκε) and *ábhă̆ram* (= ἔφερον, < *é+bher+om #). (But there is *bhară̆mā̆ṇa-*, φερόμενος).

Opinion was not united by this thesis. Support of a kind came soon from

Saussure (1879 passim, with evidence from Armenian), though presented as independent thought; and more tardily from Streitberg, more or less converted by 1894 (365). But when Osthoff loyally and speedily (*MU* 1. 1878:207ff.) had canonized it as 'Brugmann's law', he had stirred yet again the disgust of Schmidt (1881:7-60). Möller, also hostile, characteristically saw a parallel in Hebrew (1879:519n.). But Möller could not then understand why a_1 (as well as i and u) did not react similarly. Schmidt (1881:7ff.) credited Brugmann (with a nod in the direction of Amelung [1874:369], who saw a convergence in Indic of PIE /a/ and /e/) with rightly acknowledging three PIE vowels *de facto*. But Schmidt pointed to some very obvious exceptions as to length: *ặpas-* (Lat. *opus*), *ặvi-* (Lat. *ouis*), *pặti-* (πόσις) etc. Thereafter Brugmann limited his own input to apophonic **o* (or, more correctly, **o* in metaphony with **e*). Presumably the *-μενος/-mặna-* equation is then typical, but uncomfortable. Collitz (1878: 291ff.; 1886a: 2ff. and 1886b: 215), Fick (1880: 423-33), Bechtel (1892: 46ff.) – and even Delbrück (1894: 132) – were unhappy over the law's apparent short-comings. Indeed, Collitz, Schmidt and finally Hirt (1913) accumulated a list of no less than 67 etyma offensive to Brugmann's creed.

The inventor was loyal to his own brainchild at least as late as the second edition of the first volume of the *Grundriss* (1897; cf. I 139, 153). But increasing unease led to apostasy a few years later; and so a footnote in 1913 (Brugmann 1913: 191n.2) locates his surrender at sometime "seit Grundr. 2^2.1. (1906)". At any time after Leskien's 1876 statement of neogrammarian tenets, exceptions could be declared to be merely apparent or analogy could be invoked to make such deviance respectable. But to justify analogy in principle is not to prove its operation, or its direction, in given cases. Defence seemed vain. So Hirt in 1920(19) said roundly, of Brugmann's ordinance, "the law is dead" – and added that it had been nothing but a nuisance.

Resurrection would now have to depend on modification of the dogma. Yet, despite the author's own renunciation, fighters on the law's side (and a lively general interest in it) continued to emerge – and still so continue. Bloomfield (1897:56) was scornful about the 'repeatedly announced demise' of the law. Current belief seems to be with him. Debrunner (1957:8), like Buck (1917 passim) for an earlier epoch, lines up the warriors in the battle. By 1957, they amount to those mentioned fully above and below, and (less crucially) Bartholomae, Fay, Hübschmann, Kronasser, Meillet, Pisani, Thumb, Uhlenbeck, Wüst, and Zubatý (with references).

As to the sufficiency of the open syllable condition, forms like *pặd-ā* (quite apart from the *ặpas-* type) put it always at risk. Some rescue came in 1893. On

22 July of that year the Swiss Edmund Kleinhans (1870-1934) wrote privately to Holger Pedersen and proposed a revision of the law which found public expression only in Pedersen's *KZ* article of seven years later (1900:87). The shift 'PIE $\breve{o}$ > I-Ar. $\bar{a}$' was now to be limited to those open syllables where the consonantal onset of the next syllable was a nasal or a liquid; otherwise, the reflex is $\breve{a}$. Ever since, the law's quaint appellation has been 'Brugmann's law in the Kleinhans formulation' (or some say 'the Kleinhans-Pedersen formulation'): cf. Mayrhofer 1964:178 and 1965:18 (= Ford's transl. 1972: 21). But now *pā̆dam* and *vā̆cam* become awkward (and simply to point to Got. *fōtu* or Lat. *uōcem* is scarcely an answer, unless PIE 'wild-card' length variety as in **wīro-* 'man' or **wīso-* 'poison' or **wē̆* 'or', is felt to be a comfortable recourse – and even there V.A. Dybo saw an Italo-Celtic shortening at *VSJa* 5; (1961). 9-34). In Buck's view (1917) it may be, after all, a quite different sort of history: namely that IE has widespread and rather uncontrolled vṛddhi of /e/, and the Indo-Iranian effect is really of $\bar{a}$ < $\bar{e}$. Even so, it is intriguing that Pāṇini's sutra 7.3.101 (*ato dīrgho yañi*) already handles non-high vowel lengthening in conjugation as being sensitive to following /m, n, r, l/ (cf. Kleinhans), and to /y, w/ (added to Brugmann's law by Lehmann 1952:13) – and (by the rules of notation) also to *jh, bh*. Many apparent Brugmannian forms must be subsumed here; and it is very tempting to suggest that the contextual anubandha be emended (to *yami*) so as to exclude the last two items.

The necessity of the syllabic openness condition was reaffirmed much more recently by Kuryłowicz. He also removed a crowd of exceptions by adroit use of the PIE laryngeal segment. This was in 1927. At that time he was credibly locating the Saussurean 'sonant coefficients' in the contexts indicated, at least partly, by Hittite *h* (1927a). To use a later notation, *-oRV-* submits to the law, *-oRHV-* closes the prior syllable and must be rejected as input: hence, in the original perfect, 1sg. *cakā̆ra* but 3sg. *cakā̆ra*.

But the history of opinions, even more than that of deeds, repeats itself. By 1956 (some say, by 1948; see Szemerényi 1972: 165) Kuryłowicz too had lost confidence, and abjured his own phonetic explanation, for all its brilliance. In his later years he pressed for a morphological, and often analogical, explanation of several laws: those of Hirt and Mikkola (as he calls it) of Lachmann, of Saussure. Brugmann's is then (Kuryłowicz 1956: 322, 324, 337) seen as a restitution of morphologically significant (but eroded) contrast within a 'formation fondée' or 'motivée' (see Appendix I, Section B). So when the PIE pair *sed-/sod-* had confusingly become *sad-/sad-* it was amended to *sā̆d-/sād-*; but that happened only in open syllables (which is rather curious, is it not?). Yet Kuryłowicz's own enthusiastic laryngealist disciples maintained faith in the *cakắra* 'proof'. Indeed, Kuiper (1959) chides Hauschild (1958), who actually rejects Brugmann's law, for even trying to solve the question without the aid of *H.* (See also Kuiper 1947: 198-199). Thus Skt. *ắnas,* Lat. *onus,* may be from *$*H_3en$*: so Viredaz 1983. (It is odd, though, that Kuiper feels constrained to suggest a non-etymological status for the *o* of Lat. *opus,* so as to neutralize *ắpas-*; is this the sign of the end of Kleinhans' influence?) Kuryłowicz's dismantling approach (cf. 1977: 163-79) allows Gonda to call Brugmann's law "long disputed and now refuted" (1971: 25-26, 102). But that rouses the ire of Sihler (1980:873-75) who strongly reasserts the law's validity (apparently in its pre-Kleinhans form) by appealing to the testimony of causative/frequentative verb stems in the Ṛgveda (or, anyway, those with a 'clear pedigree'). If a laryngeal-conscious interpretation is employed, then the lengthened vowel in the stem of the derived form not merely occurs in 95% of the incidences of the 27 clearly aniṭ roots, as it should, but also fails to occur if and only if the root has a postvocalic segment with the features [+ sonorant, - syllabic] — specifically /r, m, y, w/ — which is the characteristic phonotactic profile of most seṭ roots. The return for 'correct' Brugmannian quantity (short) in the seṭ root verbs is also 95%. That the picture becomes quickly less clear in later Vedic and classical Sanskrit is claimed to be the natural result of the attractiveness of *CáCắyắ-* as a marked formation. The apparent vagaries of *pắtaya-* at all stages are nullified by the convenient assumption, of a kind so dear to generative synchronists, of *two* semantically close but distinct verbal roots (*$*petH_1$* and *$*petH_2$*) — although the exceptional nature of the reflexes of the latter is still not easily to be denied. But non-laryngealists also abound, and they too feel they can save Brugmann's face, if only by tinkering with details, or with chronology. Debrunner (1957:8) cites wide acceptance. Mayrhofer (1952), as he discouragingly said, brought out "the mummy into the light" and offered in its stead a live working hypothesis: that an early shift of *ŏ* to *ă* produced a paradigm in *-ŏr, -ăram* which needed partial levelling to *-ŏr, -ăram.* Well, Brugmann had argued for original Latin **datŏrem* in 1876:367. (But Meillet 1906/8:191, sees the type as the victim of rhythmic and/or analogical patterning.). Later Mayrhofer, in any case, retracted his opposition (cf. 1964:178).

After Kuryłowicz came a hiatus. The law was perhaps still alive, but, failing new therapy, had no great promise of health. But recently a radical new treatment has been applied by the pen of Burrow (1975). It deserves both notice and evaluation. Burrow had observed in 1971 (546) that a shift 'PIE *ŏ* > Skt *ā*' seemed to occur unexpectedly in the context /-nd (as in *kāṇḍa-,* Gk κονδύλος).

Four years later he proposed more generally that the Brugmann reflex is a matter of regularity, in Indic at least, and that its true environment is actually *all*, including closed, syllables. The only general exceptions admitted are the cases where the length has been subsequently removed from the vowel under the influence of conjugational or derivational pressures. Otherwise *ā* is always (at least in Sanskrit) the outcome of PIE *ŏ*, provided only that the latter is in metaphony with *ĕ*. Gone now is the restriction to open syllables (Brugmann); gone is the condition of non-obstruence on the following consonant (Kleinhans); gone is the influence of morphology (Kuryłowicz). Charpentier's old connection of *mārga-* with Gk. *ἀμορβός* is reinstated as one typical instance, and **(sm+)-mŏrg^Wo-* is declared to be expected input to the law. Scorn is poured on the invokers of PIE lengthened ('extended') grade (who had indeed been careless over parity of morphological conditions). Apart from the *mārga-*type, the causatives (or class X̄ verbs) like *sādayati* fall once again into the law's clutches, and the restriction to metaphonic *ŏ* handles the apparent exceptions (1) */–CV: ắpas-, ắvi-* Lat. *opus, ouis*) etc., (2) */– CCV: ăṣṭáu, sắrva-* (Gk. *ὀκτώ, ὅλϜο-*) etc. Or else some rather arbitrary loss of length has occurred at a late period: that is why *vārtaka-* (rare but expected) gives way to *vắrtaka-*, Gk *ὄρτυξ*).

Question: if the perfect is another favourable domain for the law (*cakắra* etc.), why now do we not find †*vavārta*? Answer: because of paradigmatic levelling exerted from e.g. *vắrtate*. Question: then why does not *cakắra* (3 sg) revert to **cakắra* in view of *kăroti*? Answer: because this would alter the syllabic weight (although the reasons for its being protected are left obscure, beyond a suggestion that this particular rhythm is somehow especially suitable for perfects). Question: but now that *-CH-* (*-RH-*) is no longer, on the face of it, an inhibiting environment, why is the 1.sg. result not (†) *cakắra*? (it is only so by levelling, later; the inherited form is **Ce-CŎC+HV*). Answer: because the laryngeal is neither a full consonant – a fashionable doctrine again, to the chagrin of some of us – nor yet a vowel; it is an articulatory oddity as a medial segment, showing affinities with glottal or speech pause. So this context is held in some obscure way to be the cause of *V̆*. Apparently *rătha-* is then from **rotH+o-* [rot?o]?

Problems remain. Burrow accepts (1975:70) that *năgná-, năkti-* are aberrant; they cannot be pronounced clearly non-metaphonic, in view of Hitt. *nekumant-, nekut-*. He does not admit to any other such anomaly, despite the *pād-, păd-* alternation in the 'foot' word (cf. Lat. *pĕd-*). One can believe that Sanskrit has pushed word-forms around rather, on the way to establishing its characteristic 2- or 3-strength stem-alternation. But even so the equation *păḍaḥ ~πόδας* is noteworthy. Burrow allows analogy of his own choosing, not of others'. For example: it seems that (as Kuryłowicz said) the *cakắra, cakā́ra* (1sg, 3sg) pattern moulds other perfects to the same regularity: so *tatắpa, tatā́pa*. But then, is not the 2sg form (for instance) uncomfortably *jagắntha, cakắrtha*, etc. instead of *-gān-, -kār-*, as analogy might, and Burrow's version of the law should, make it? The argument from metrics, justifying *vavắrta* but *cakā́ra* can hardly be applied in inverted fashion; †*cakā́rtha* would spoil nothing. Worst of all, the behaviour of clusters involving *H* is said to instantiate that of those with *C*ʔ or *C#*. Therefore, Burrow must find phonetic evidence of the former, or a prior reason for examples of the latter (like the shortness of the last vowel in, e.g., *ábharăm*). Brugmann could handle *ábharăm* by pointing to the syllable-closing final consonant: that can be no inhibitor for Burrow. The vowel of this affix is usually seen as metaphonic. This is actually not beyond dispute; but Burrow does not dispute it. The point is not parried, or even met at all.

Even so, this article remains a courageous revival and a notable clarification. Moreover, it closes (80) with the by no means novel hint that the Brugmannian shift — which Burrow stoutly believes in, in *some* form — perhaps somehow depends on the absence of accent on the affected syllable. Greek δώτορα (as against δοτῆρα) seems to confirm the relation of the grade to the accent position which was long since suggested for metaphony by δαίμων versus ποιμήν. But *dātăram* is awkward for Burrow's idea (unless, horrid thought, it really answers to δοτῆρα and confirms Brugmann's *first* formulation of the law in the *first* syllable). Equally tiresome would then be the *cakā́ra*-type phenomena; indeed, if the law affects unaccented syllables in the majority of incidences (as Burrow claims), that majority is certainly less than overwhelming.

Burrow's administering of the second kiss of life to the law has an interesting dividend. It nullifies the main effect of the Kleinhans formulation, the concentrating of dynamic on the following consonant. If we are free to look again at the vowel it is possible to speculate on, for example, an inherently greater duration in a back mid (than a front mid) vowel. Then — and this was Brugmann's own idea — the law has a ready-made motivation. True, only one IE stock would then preserve the feature; but after all the original value of PIE /w/ is only kept in English (*work, wet* etc.). Still, supporting evidence is needed, and possibly it may come from an odd source: Viredaz (1983) links PIE /e, o/ with North West Caucasian /ă, ā/, suggestively, as the basic minimal vocalism in each case. Possibly it is not so. But the question is at least re-opened.

REFERENCES

Amelung, A. 1874. Erwiderung. *KZ* 22.361-71. (Reply to Leo Meyer, *KZ* 21.241-49 [1873].)

Bartholomae, C. 1891. Arm. *a* > griech. o und die indogermanische vokalreihen. *BB* 17.91-133.

Bechtel, F. 1892. *Die Hauptprobleme der indogermanischen Lautlehre seit Schleicher.* Göttingen: Vandenhoeck & Ruprecht.

Bloomfield, M. 1897. IE notes. *TAPA* 28.55-57.

Brugmann, K. 1876. Zur geschichte der stammabstufenden declinationen. *CS* 9.361-406. (Sec. I: Die nomina auf *-ar-* und *-tar-*.)

—————, 1879. Zur geschichte der nominalsuffixe *-as-*, *-jas-* und *-vas-*. *KZ* 24.1-99. (= Habilitationsschrift of 1877.)

—————, 1897. Second edition of Volume 1 of *BDG* (see Abbrevs.).

—————, 1913. Zu den Ablautverhältnisse der sogenannten starken Verba des Germanischen. *IF* 32.179-95.

Buck, C.D. 1896. Brugmann's law and the Sanskrit vṛddhi. *AJP* 17. 445-72.

Burrow, T. 1971. Spontaneous cerebrals in Sanskrit. *BSOAS* 34.538-59.

—————, 1975. A new look at Brugmann's law. *BSOAS* 38.55-80.

Collitz, H. 1878. Ueber die annahme mehrerer grundsprachlicher *a*-laute. *BB* 2.291-305.

—————. 1886a. Die flexion der nomina mit dreifacher stammabstufung in altindisch und in griechisch. *BB* 10.1-71.

—————. 1886b. Die neueste Sprachforschung und die Erklärung des idg. Ablautes. *BB* 11.203-42. (Repr. in Wilbur 1977.)

Debrunner, A. 1957. See Wackernagel 1896.

Delbrück, B. 1894. Der Typus φέρω-φορέω im Arischen. *IF* 4.132-33.

Fay, E.W. 1892. Studies in etymology. *AJP* 13.463-82.

Fick, A. 1880. Review of Saussure 1879. *Göttingische Gelehrte Anzeiger,* Stück 14 (7 April 1880), 417-39.

Gonda, J. 1971. *Old Indian* = Handbuch der Orientalistik, ed. by B. Spuler et al. Abt.II, Bd.I, Abschnitt 1. Leiden / Cologne: Brill.

Hauschild, R. 1958. Revision of 3rd edn. of A. Thumb, *Handbuch des Sanskrit.* Heidelberg: Winter.

Hirt, H. 1913. Fragen des Vokalismus und der Stammbildung im Indogermanischen. *IF* 32.236-47.

—————, 1920. *Indogermanische Grammatik II.* Heidelberg: Winter.

Hübschmann, H. 1879. Iranische Studien. *KZ* 24.322-411.

————, 1885. *Das indogermanische Vokalsystem.* Strassburg: Trübner.

Kleinhans, E. 1893. See Pedersen 1900.

Kuiper, F.B.J. 1947. *India Antiqua.* Leiden: Brill.

————, 1959. rev. of Hauschild 1958. *Lingua* 8.424-41.

Kuryłowicz, J. 1927a. ə indo-europeen et ḫ hittite. *Symbolae Rozwadowski* 1.95-104. Kraków: Drukarnia Universytetu Jagiellońskiego.

————, 1927b. Les effets du ə en indo-iranien. *Prace filologiczne* 11.201-43. (cf. ibid. 9.206-207.)

————, 1947/8. Le degré long en indo-iranien. *BSL* 44.42-63.

————, 1949. La loi de Brugmann. *BSL* 45.57-60.

————, 1951. Tzw. prawo Brugmann w indoiranskim. *Rozprawy Kom. Orient.* 58-62.

————, 1956. L'apophonie en indo-européen. Wrocław: Polska AN(§§ 41-43).

————, 1968. *Indogermanische Grammatik* II. Heidelberg: Winter.

————, 1977. *Problèmes de linguistique indo-européenne.* Wrocław: Polska. AN

Lehmann, W.P. 1952. *Proto-Indo-European phonology.* Austin: Univ. of Texas Press.

Mayrhofer, M. 1952. Zur Restproblematik des 'Brugmannschen Gesetzes'. *KZ* 70.8-19.

————, 1964. 'Hethitisch und Indogermanisch'. Gedanken zu einem neuen Buche. *Die Sprache* 10.174-97.

————, 1965. *Sanskrit-Grammatik.* Berlin: W. de Gruyter. 2nd ed. (1st ed., 1964.) (Trans. by Gordon B. Ford Jr., Univ. of Alabama Press, 1972.)

Meillet, A. 1896. *Varia. MSL* 9.138-59.

————, 1905/6. *Varia. MSL* 13.237-53; cf.1906/8, *MSL* 14.190-92.

Meyer, G. 1896. *Griechische Grammatik.* 3rd ed. Leipzig: Breitkopf & Härtel. (1st ed. 1880.)

Möller, H. 1879. Epenthese vor k-lauten im germanischen. *KZ* 24.427-522.

Paul, H. 1877. Die vocale der flexions- und ableitungssilben in den altesten germanischen dialecten. *PBB* 4.315-475.

Pedersen, H. 1900. Wie viel laute gab es im indogermanischen? *KZ* 36.74-110.

Saussure, F. de 1879. *Mémoire sur le système primitif des voyelles dans les langues indo-européennes.* Leipzig: Teubner. (Publ. December 1878.) Repr. in *Recueil des publications scientifiques de Ferdinand de Saussure,* ed. by C. Bally & L. Gautier. 1-268. Geneva: Sonor; Lausanne: Payot, 1922.

Schmidt, J. 1881. Zwei arische *a*-laute und die palatalen. *KZ* 24.2-179, esp. 7-60.

Sievers, E. 1926. Vedisches und Indogermanisches III. *IF* 43.129-206.

Sihler, A.L. 1980. Review of Kuryłowicz 1977. *Lg* 56.870-77.
Streitberg, W. 1894. Die Entstehung der Dehnstufe. *IF* 3.304-416.
Szemerényi, O. 1972. Comparative linguistics. *CTL* 9.119-95.
Uhlenbeck, C.C. 1897. Zur lautgeschichte. *PBB* 22.543-47.
Viredaz, R. 1983. The PIE and the N-W. Caucasian vowel system. (Paper given at Hull, July 1983; unpubl.; to appear.)
Wackernagel, J. 1896. *Altindische Grammatik I.* (Revised by L. Renou, with *Nachträge* (194 pp.] by A. Debrunner, 1957.) Göttingen: Vandenhoeck & Ruprecht.)
Wilbur, T.H., ed. 1977. *The Lautgesetz controversy: A documentation.* (= *ACiL* 9.)
Zubatý, J. 1892. Zum baltischen *u. BB* 18.241-66.

CALAND'S LAW

The status of law was not dreamt of by the eponymous originator of this observation on IE suffixal patterning, nor has it been universally accorded since. In 1892 and 1893, in successive issues of Kuhn's *Zeitschrift*, Wilhelm Caland (1859-1932) first noted a convenient explanation for a small problem in one language and then suspected its wider relevance. In 1892 he discusses the structure of the Avestan adjective *khr̥vidru-*; he decides on the division *khr̥vi+dru-* and adduces the forms *khrūra-, khrūma-*. A common base element thus appears to offer three morphological alternants as its extenders: that is,

$$\text{*khrw+} \begin{cases} i\text{-} \\ ra\text{-} \\ ma\text{-} \end{cases} .$$

Other evidential forms are *tighra-* (cf. Skt. *tigma-*) beside *tižyaršti*, and *dərəzra-* beside *dərəzi.ratha*. It seems then that positives and comparatives, or simple forms and compounds, systematically alternate in their prime suffixation. In 1893 some additional Sanskrit testimony emboldened Caland to surmise an Indo-European rule; but he thought only in terms of the special behaviour of a limited set of adjectives in Indo-Iranian.

Recognition that here was a morphological discovery of some usefulness came when Wackernagel lent his imprimatur, first in 1897 — extending the domain to include Greek — and then in his grammar (1905, §24). Indeed, in Europe the finding has been called 'the law of Caland and Wackernagel'; but English-speaking usage is against the appellation, which is certainly inconvenient, considering the existence of Wackernagel's own laws (q.v.). Due notice of it was taken, as by Fraenkel (1909: 124n.2), Güntert (1910:26-27) and Hirt (1913: 284-86; 1927: 274). Sporadic citations as of an accepted process are then encountered (Benveniste 1935:80; Schwyzer 1939:447-48, Szemerényi 1964: 395-98 and now Palmer 1980: 37, 98). But it is not until comparatively recent years that further *theoretical* progress has been made.

The contribution of Kuryłowicz (1964:232) is oddly confusing for so eminent and clear a thinker; but in effect he is pulling together the views of Hirt and Schwyzer. He appears to invert Caland's order of events, in that he sees

Vedic *śuci- (for example) as the base, whence attested śukra- is the derived adjectival form. An original -i suffix is preserved in compounds; from this arises a new but reversed simple-versus-compound system, namely of +ra/u versus +i. This is like Szemerényi's view, though that is special in physical detail, in that -rV- derives from -i-rV- — itself a cumulation of formants — by syncope (1964: 397; 1972:159-60). Householder & Nagy (1972:41) agree on the priority, giving credit to Wackernagel, and use the law's constraints to explain the origin of circumventory expressions like ἱερὸν μένος in Epic formulae. But then this -i- is available as a novel and spare component for fresh formations, such as adjectives in -ios. This derivational process presumes a *tertiary* detaching of already *secondary* -ra- or -ma- or -u-. The -i- element returns to the stage with the determination of an ageing repertory actor — which is also Schwyzer's view of what happens in Greek (1939:448). Watkins (1971:64-65) follows this path into Vedic morphology, but he is more Caland-like in vision. For him, positive degree śukra- passes to comparative degree śocīyas (cf. κυδρός → κυδι-; or αἰσχρός → αἰσχίων might be cited) and -i- is (synchronically, at least) secondary. But kṣudra- seems a secondary formation, with kṣodīyas (to root kṣud) neither more nor less derived. Pinault (1982:267-68) also links the Sanskrit comparative to the Caland system (craftily defined as simply "mutual implication between various derivatives").

Gonda (1971:52) sees the Indic evidence as simply continuing to display a 'curious survival', namely, the derivational process +ra → +i in the prior members of compounds. The connexion with -u- is noted, as is the link with comparative and superlative adjectival forms. In novel fashion, the neuter noun-formant -as- (*ᵉ/os-) is tied in: so ug-rá-, 'energetic' alternates with ój-as-, 'creative energy'. In fact the whole grouping is called a 'Suffixverband' (a term invented in 1968 by Leumann).

In 1975 Bader concentrated on Greek as a test-bench for Caland's law. She inclines to agree with Hirt, Schwyzer, and Kuryłowicz on the conserved nature of -i-, giving reasons for seeing -mo- and like suffixes as secondary in history (cf. Hirt 1913:288n.). Though -i- is at home in compounds, it is credited (as by Schwyzer, 1939:450) with more basic occurrence, in the adverbial and conjunctional range (μόγις, μέχρι(ς), χωρίς etc.). Alone of the linked suffixes it is freely nominal or adjectival. It associates readily with the r/n extension (though Benveniste 1935:28, would rather say that fundamentally -u- and -r- show closest attachment), and then gains a range of alternants — with r, n, m, l, u, and the neuter noun-formant *-ᵉ/os(-). So that Bader is ready to exemplify thus: αἰθι-, αἰθήρ, αἴθων, αἰθάλη, αἰθύσσω, -αυθής from the root *aidh-, 'be bright'.

But there is here an air of pride in the suffixal nimbleness of Indo-European, rather than a controlled analysis of incidence, function and constraints. Bader inclines to allow even a Caland variant in -ti-, on the evidence of forms like βωτι- άνειρα.

Nussbaum's thesis (1976) is entirely devoted to the problem. His view of the matter is that there is no 'law' involved at all. This is not to be interpreted as accusing a regularity of having been supposed where it does not really exist (as some attacks on Brugmann's or Lachmann's or Grassmann's laws actually do); nor does it amount to a correcting of the placing of the regularity. It is rather a matter of establishing a set of correlated morphological properties of considerable regularity, but recognizing their quite limited distribution (as a set). A PIE root may, or may not, possess a 'Caland system'. For instance, a stative verb formed by suffixal -e- (cf. Watkins 1971) is one member of a set of derivatives of its root. In the nominal sector the root should possess a neuter in $-^e/os$-. In the adjectival scatter there will be a choice among suffixes — all equally original — in -ro- or -u- or -i- or -ont-, with further possible combinations or extensions. Distributional rules can and should be supplied. For instance, in Indic the -i- form is the regular choice for the first element of a compound. No diachronic priority can be stated, as between the alternants; the mere discovery and distributional statement of the set is the essence of the Caland affair. There are further subtleties, though. Suffixes may be central or marginal, a distinction which permits their co-functioning: so in Latin the central element -i- combines with the marginal -dh- to produce adjectives in -idus (cf. rubidus ~ ruber): cf. Hamp (1981).

But Latin -d- is often quasi-participial (cf. rapidus, splendidus); and a parallelism with -n- participles (pᵣná- etc.) is possible; so Hamp (1980:271n.14 — cf. FoLH. 20:149-50 (1981)) who remarks on $*nog^w(e) + d/n$-, > Skt nagná-, Lat. nŭdus. As -n- is already a relevant suffix, the domain of 'Calandism' (so to call it) is thus made potentially enormous.

Tucker (1979 and 1981:25-30) uses a systematic, Nussbaum-type patterning, to explain Greek conjugational formation of the -ῡνω, -αινω kinds. From roots in final nasal, metanalysis extracts the extensions -nyō and ᵣᵣyō (cf. Sievers' law?). Forms with a Caland -u- favour the former (βαρύς → βαρυ+νιω → βαρῡνω) — as Fraenkel first noted — while other Caland varieties replace it with the latter (κυδι- → κυδ' + ανιω → κυδαίνω) — but one cannot but note that ἀρτῡνω is related to ἀρτι - (πους, etc), and καλλῡνω to κάλλος, while Tucker supposes (29) that morphological loss of +u- induces -αινω. Hittite -(a)nu is called as a verbal formant witness: so tepnu from tep-u-, 'small', or palḫanu-formed on *palhi-*, 'wide', each of which indicates a nasal infixation applied to a Caland form with *-u* (whereas Sanskrit has that effect, in *dahbnoti*, only where a Caland *alternation* in *-ro* occurs; so *dabhra-*). These forms had been already adduced by Mayrhofer (1964:196).

If anything is clear from these excursions it is that much more work is needed on Caland roots in order to clarify the morphological processes. Are they language-specific? Is the *-i-* formant the basic, common suffix? What role does nasal reshaping play? Has the central-marginal distinction any validity? Hamp has recently (1983) suggested a 'morphological law', in the shape of a complex regularity in language-specific replacements of PIE formant-suffixes; if this is so, we are not dealing with cognate lexemes, and the alternants go well beyond Caland's − so PIE +*u* gives way to Toch. +*ro* but Slav. +*ko* etc. Even so, some Caland evidence may turn out just to be part of that wider pattern. And so on. It would be a pity to lose our footing on this slippery but useful path towards a real understanding of the Indo-European morphological inventory and the ingenuity which informs it.

REFERENCES

Bader, F. 1975. La loi de Caland et Wackernagel en grec. *Fs. Benveniste*, 19-32.

Benveniste, E. 1935. *Origines de la formation des noms en indo-européen.* 2nd ed. Paris: Adrien-Maisonneuve. (1st ed., 1948.)

Caland, W. 1892. Beiträge zur Kenntnis des Avesta, No.19. *KZ* 31.266-68.

−−−−−, 1893. Beiträge [. . .], No.26. *KZ* 32. 592.

Fraenkel, E. 1909. Zur Frage der idg. *r-n*-Stämme. *KZ* 42.114-30.

Gonda, J. 1971. *Die Indischen Sprachen* (1er Abschnitt: *Old Indian*) ed. by J. Gonda., = Vol.1.1 of *Handbuch der Orientalistik*, ed. by B. Spuler. (2er Abt., *Indien*). Leiden/Cologne: Brill.

Güntert, H. 1910. Zur Geschichte der griechischen Gradationsbildungen. *IF* 27.1-72.

Hamp, E.P. 1980. On participial **-do-* and verbs and adjectives and colours. In *Fs Seiler*, 268-73.

−−−−−. 1981. Vicus Cuprius. *AJP* 102.149-50.

−−−−−, 1983. A morphological law. *Lingua* 61.1-8.

Hirt, H. 1913. Fragen des Vokalismus und der Stammbildung im idg. *IF* 32.209-318.

−−−−−, 1927. *Indogermanische Grammatik* vol. 3. Heidelberg: Winter.

Householder, F.W. & Nagy, G. 1972, *Greek: A survey of recent work*. The Hague: Mouton.

Kuryłowicz, J. 1964. *The inflectional categories of Indo-European*. Heidelberg: Winter.

Mayrhofer, M. 1964. 'Hethitisch und Indogermanisch': Gedanken zu einem neuen Buche. *Die Sprache* 10.174-97.

Nussbaum, A. 1976. *Caland's 'law' and the Caland system*. Unpubl. diss. Cambridge, Mass.; Harvard Univ.

Palmer, L.R. 1980. *The Greek language*. London; Faber & Faber.

Pinault, G.J. 1982. A neglected phonetic law. *P(5) ICHL*, 265-72.

Schulze, W. 1892. *Quaestiones epicae*. Gütersloh: Bertelsmann.

Schwyzer, E. 1939. *Griechische Grammatik* I. (2). Munich; Beck.

Specht, F. Beiträge zur griechischen Grammatik. *KZ* 59.31-131.

—————, Eine Eigentümlichkeit indogermanischer Stammbildung. *KZ* 62. 216-35.

Szemerényi, O.1964, *Syncope in Greek and Indo-European and the nature of the Indo-European accent*. Naples: Istituto Universitario Orientale di Napoli (Sez. ling., 3).

—————, 1972. Comparative linguistics. *CTL* 9.119-95.

Tucker, M.E. 1979. *Secondary ablaut: The development of a regular conjugation in early Greek*. Diss., Oxford Univ.

—————, 1981. Greek factitive verbs in -οω, -αυνω, and -υνω. *TPS* 1981.15-34.

Wackernagel, J. 1897,. *Vermischte Beiträge zur griechischen Sprachkunde*. Rektoratsfeier Univ. Basel. 3-62 (esp.8-14). (Repr. in *Kleine Schriften* I. 764-823 [esp.769-75], 1953.)

—————, 1905. *Altindische Grammatik* 2.1. Göttingen: Vandenhoeck & Ruprecht.

Watkins, C. 1971. Hittite and IE studies: The denominative statives in -*ē*. *TPS* 1971.51-93.

DOLOBKO'S LAW*

This stands among the numerous laws of accent-shift in Slavic. The chief originator was Milyj Gerasimovič Dolobko, writing in 1927 about the accent on encliticized adjectives in Slavic after the break-up of Balto-Salvic unity. His topic is limited and his title is quite explicit. Even so, the law was adumbrated in respect of a mediaeval Muscovite dialect by L.L. Vasil'ev possibly by 1905 (cf. Vasil'ev 1929); and it is sometimes called by the joint name, especially by Dybo whose doctoral dissertation and 1981 book have really so canonized it. Many laws of Slavic accentuation concern various instances of retraction; refreshingly, here is one of rightward movement. (In a sense, its leftward counterpart is Pedersen's law II.)

The pronouncement applies to forms where the enclitic pro-nominal particle has become a regular adjectival suffix, and this in words with paradigmatically mobile accent — on which see Appendix III. (Again, it is the corresponding proclitic effect which is covered by applications of Pedersen's law II.) For Dolobko, in the basic barytone form the accent moved from the initial syllable towards the end of the word. Of the four lexemic pairs in his title, the first two show the shift and the others do not. The change precedes the loss of intervocalic /j/, and is clear enough as being a movement. What is debatable is the length of the movement: that is, just how far to the right the accent goes. For some, it shifts to the preclitic syllable: so Stang (1957:103) and Ebeling (1967: 587). Others assign it to the suffixal syllable itself: so Dybo (1962:26-27;1971) and Kortlandt (1975:39; 1978:275).

A similar shift occurs clearly much later in Middle Bulgarian. It is presumably independent, but one recalls the problematic relation of Grassmann's law in Indic to like phenomena in Greek). On this, see Bulaxovskij 1921:286, Kodov 1929:88, and Stang 1957:103. Dybo too writes on the shift (1977), having earlier considered Old Russian and Middle Bulgarian verb-forms in the light of the law (1971).

Dolobko's law appears to be of much the same date as Pedersen's law II.

* See Appendix III

REFERENCES*

Bulaxovskij, L.A. 1921. K bolgarskomu udarenija. *Južnoslevenski filolog.* 2.285-94.

Dolobko, M. 1927. Nóč'-nočés', ósen'-osenés', zimá-zimús', léto-létos'. *Slavia* 5.678-717.

Dybo, V.A. 1962. O rekonstrukcii udarenija v praslavjanskom glagole. *VSJa* 6.3-27.

————, 1971a. O frazobyx modifikatsijax udarenija v praslavjanskom. *Sovjetskoe slavjanovedenije* 1971. 6. (See also the reference to his work in this area at 1981:52.)

————, 1971b. Zakon Vasil'eva-Dolobko i akcentuacija form glagola v drevnerusskom i srednebolgarskom. *VJa* 20:2.93-114.

————, 1975. Zakon Vasil'eva-Dolobko v drevnerusskom. *IJSLP* 18.7-81.

————, 1977. Imennoje udarenije v srednebolgarskom i zakon Vasil'eva-Dolobko. *Slavjanskoe i balkanskoe jazykoznanije* ed. by I.A. Gindin & G.P. Klepikova. Moscow, 189-272.

Kodov, H. 1929. *Podvižnoto bălgarsko udarenie i negovoto otnošenie kăm praslavjanskoto udarenie I.* Sofia.

Vasil'ev, L.L. 1929. *O značenii kamory v nekotoryx drevnerusskix pamjatnikax xvi-xvii vekov.* Leningrad: (Repr. in *Trudy po istorii russkogo i ukrainskogo jazykov.* Munich: Fink. 465-628, 1972.)

* Also quoted or relevant are:
Dybo 1981*; Ebeling 1967*; Garde 1976*; Kortlandt 1975*, 1978*; Stang 1957*.
– on which see Appendix III.

DYBO'S LAW*

This ordinance is normally assigned to the credit of the contemporary scholar Vladimir Antonovič Dybo. Like Dolobko's, it provides for a rightward shift of Slavic word-accent — not too frequent an occurrence. At some time after the split between Baltic and Slavic, vowels in the Slavic languages found themselves in open syllables and with an intonational distinction between circumflex and acute. Short vowels, if they were accented but were non-acute, then lost their accent to the following syllable. Such was Dybo's own formula (1962), writing in particular on the verb, other than *e*-verbs: so *nòsiti* > *nosìti*. The law was soon extended to noun paradigms (as *bloxú*); so that barytone paradigms gave way to ending-stressed forms. Some claim that the law's effect was to restore distinctive length to pre-tonic vowels.

Illič-Svityč (1963; cf. the joint work of the same year) regards the law as indeed the origin of predominantly end-stressed nouns in Slavic (cf. Stang's *b*-stressed types — on which see Appendix III, and Kortlandt 1983a:34). Vermeer (forthcoming), after Ebeling (1967:586- 590) appears to speak of the law as applying, in the case of mobile words, to those whose stress is not on the first syllable: this thesis deserves critical comment from the experts. Dybo (1962:8-9) reckoned to observe a third kind of 'intonation' which he supposed to originate in mobile acute paradigms and spread to those of the mobile circumflex type. But the positional shift then becomes obscure in its motivation.

Ebeling (1967:578, 585-86) analyses the law into two stages. First — after Dybo — the third type of intonation is established in those syllables which have short, stressed, vowels in columnar paradigms (and perhaps falling vowels, also); these syllables then differ from equivalent initial syllables in the mobile paradigms. Secondly, the accent shifted its position rightwards, away from (and perhaps deleting?) this new type of syllable. The reason is not clear.

Dybo's law seems to feed Stang's law. That is, many words undergo first rightward and then leftward shift at a fairly late stage of Proto-Slavic. That is how the *b*-stressed words gain their stem-stressed forms, and why *b*-stressed masculine *o*-stems appear to surface quite late; the latter are really original

*See Appendix III

neuters which were not *b*-stressed, so they were not removed by the law of Illič-Svityč, as were original masculine *o*-stems.

Kortlandt's major exploitation of Dybo's law has long been (and still is in 1983:36-37 and 1983b:180-81) as an indicator, by the conditions of its *non*-occurrence with acutes, of the presence of inherited laryngeal consonant segments. These, in his view, survived until late in Slavic (cf. Illič-Svityč 1963, on Hirt's law I). Kortlandt believes Stang's law to be of the ninth century (1975:34), and not too distant in time from Dybo's (of course). Then the latter looks like a child of the early ninth, or late eight, century. The obvious inference then is that Baltic too might, after all, show traces of the shift; and Garde (1976:16-17, 208ff.) thinks that Lithuanian does indeed oblige (via Saussure's law?) where the target syllable is acute. (But Dybo's law is not, except perhaps in Lithuanian itself, a true parallel to Saussure's, which always requires an acute landing site.)

The law's authorship is a trifle obscure. Some would rather call it 'Illič-Svityč's law' (as Garde 1976:16-17., who restricts it to 'strong stems'). Doubtless this nomenclature arises from the deductions made by Illič-Svityč (1963); cf. also Dybo & Illič-Svityč (1963). But (1) Kortlandt, like most people, uniformly uses the title 'Dybo's law' – see especially 1975:87; 1983a:35); and (2) Illič-Svityč has his own law (q.v.).

Some issues remain unsolved:*

(a) Were the West Slavic languages susceptible to the law or not?
    – Kortlandt says 'yes' (1975:34ff.; 1978:279; 1983a:38-39; 1983b:180-181); Garde (1973:161) says 'non liquet' (and 1976:16 implies 'no'); Halle & Kiparsky (1981:177) say 'only in short stems'.

(b) Does van Wijk's law feed Dybo's?
    – Kortlandt (1975:7) believes it does, at least for Serbo-Croat; thus *nósienu* > (by van Wijk's law) *nòšēnъ* > (by Dybo's law) *nošén* > (by Stang's law) *nòšen*.

(c) Is the law a mirage?
    – so Johnson (1980), who replaces it with a four-stage process of shifts (494). This attack has received firm counter-fire: e.g., from Vermeer. A contest is, no doubt, about to develop.

---

* See also Dybo 1968, for some related issues.

REFERENCES*

Dybo, V.A. 1962. O rekonstrukcii udarenija v praslavjanskom glagole. *VSJa* 6.3-27.

—————, 1968. Akcentologija i slovo-obrazovanije v slavjanskom. In *VI*th Int. Cong. of Slavists (Prague): Russian contributions. *Slavjanskoe jazy-koznanije* 6. (Moscow: AN SSSR), 148-224.

—————, & Illič-Svityč, V.M. 1963. K istorii slavjankoj sistemy akcentnacionnyx paradigm. *Slavjanskoe jazykoznanije* 5.70-87.

Garde, P. 1973. Le paradigme accentuel oxyton, est-il slave commun? *RES* 49.159-71.

Halle, M., & Kiparsky, P. 1981. Rev. article on Garde 1976. *Lg* 57:150-81.

Johnson, D.J.L. 1980. Dybo's law and metatony in the present tense of the Slavonic verb. *SEER* 58.481-99.

Kortlandt, F.H.H. 1983a = 1983*

—————. 1983b. On final syllables in Slavic. *JIES* 11.167-85 (esp. 180-81).

Vermeer, W.R. (forthcoming in *FolH)* On clarifying some points of Slavonic accentology: the quantity of the thematic vowel in the present tense and related issues. (Opposes Johnson 1980.)

* Quoted or relevant also are:
Dybo 1981*; Garde 1976*; Ebeling 1967*; Illič-Svityč 1963* (=1979*); Kortlandt 1975*, 1978*, 1983*; Stang 1957*.
− on which see Appendix III.

EBELING'S LAW*

The Dutch scholar Carl Ebeling put forward, in 1963 and again in 1967, what was in effect a unified theory of verbal paradigmatic accentuation in Slavic and possibly in Balto-Slavic (so Kortlandt 1975:5; 1977:322). The relevant inheritance from PIE was of a verbal accent which was not always realized on the verb itself; and, if mobile, it was not systematically so realized in the immediate pre-Slavic period. Hence, according to Ebeling, Slavic verbs must have made a regularizing choice. This must have been conditioned by their own syllabic count in different forms: the disyllables tended to adopt an initial accent, the polysyllables to accent the final syllable. The verbal polysyllables underwent no subsequent leftward movement, although the nominal paradigms had it (cf. Pedersen's law II). But the disyllabic verb-forms were slower at becoming initially stressed, and may be considered to have had an interim final-accent phase, with a later discernible shift to the left. Discerning that last movement, and identifying it as an example of a wider 'law of maximal contrasts' (1967: 580), is Ebeling's major specific contribution to that largish sector of accent-diachrony known as Slavic 'retraction'.

Ebeling himself admits exceptions to his law in its crude form, and offers at least one motivated constraint upon it: if leftward accent movement would increase the incidence of homonymy, then it does not occur (1967:584). Other awkward non-occurrences (where either syllable is checked) are explained by Kortlandt (1974:300-301, and 1975:5), characteristically, as inhibited by interfering laryngeals which were still segmentally realized at the crucial time (see on Dybo's and Hirt's laws). His stock (noun) example is *golHváH > galvà but *golHvaí > gálvai. This entails an early date for Ebeling's law which puts it close to, but without doubt after, that of Hirt's (for other reasons see also Kortlandt, 1977:322); it must precede that of Dybo's This makes it at least possible that Ebeling's treatment (pace its author) can refer to Balto-Slavic — and Kortlandt himself offers for that field a revised version of the law, which might be formalized thus:-

* See Appendix III.

$$\# \# \underline{\quad\quad} C_o \left[\overset{2}{\underset{+stress}{\underline{\quad\quad}}} \right] \# \# \longrightarrow \# \# \left[\overset{1}{\underset{+stress}{\underline{\quad\quad}}} \right] C_o \underline{\quad\quad} \# \#$$

Condition: in syllable 2 the vowel is short or circumflexed.

REFERENCE*

Ebeling, C.L. 1963. Questions of relative chronology in Common Slavic and Russian phonology. *Dutch contributions to the Fifth Intern. Congress of Slavicists*, 27-42. The Hague: Mouton.

* Quoted or relevant also are:
Ebeling 1967*; Kortlandt 1974*, 1975*, 1977*, 1978*.
— on which see Appendix III.

ENDZELIN'S LAW

The reflexes of PIE diphthongs vary considerably in the derived languages – even under Schmalstieg's recent ideas. Greek seems to have maintained */ei, ai, oi/ from the traditional array, and Sanskrit to have collapsed them into a single monophthong (as it has similarly treated the series with a back glide offset). The Baltic experience has been warmly debated.

In 1892 Hirt – following hints by Brugmann at *MU* 5:57 – suggested (33ff., esp.37) that both 'ei' and 'oi' (this latter collapsing with 'ai' in Baltic) became '*ë*', whence *ie*, if under main stress and not followed by a palatalized consonant (so *deivỹs* was protected on two counts). This view is supported by Brugmann in *BDG*, 191, by Nieminen in 1922 (74ff.) and by Torbiörnsson in 1931. But Ivan Martinovič Endzelin – or, in native Latvian form, Jānis Endzelīns (1873-1961) – offered a more limited version of the shift in 1907 (and 1908). He maintained it in his Lettish grammar (1922 – cf. 1971:34) and in 1927:58ff., and repeated it in 1948 in a work which now has a wider dissemination since its 1971 translation into English.

For Endzelin, only PIE /ei/ passed via /ḗ/ to Baltic /íe/ (the accent being accepted as an essential condition). The obvious example is **deĩwos* > **dḗvas* > Lith. *diẽvas*, Latv. *dièvs*. The accent here is in the correct place probably only because of Nieminen's law (cf. Skt. *deváḥ*); and the PIE form could be a late secondary development (see Szemerényi, *SEinf*, 126). More serious is the unchanged Old Prussian reflex: *deiw-*. So the questions which arise are:

(1)   How many diphthongs are affected?
(2)   Is the accent-condition needed?
(3)   Are there exceptions – or surprising reflexes caused by analogy?
(4)   Is the shift Common Baltic?
(5)   What is its date?

These should be borne in mind in what follows: on the last, see already Hirt (1892:38).

Torbiörnsson (1931) defends the Hirtian version as the source of *-íe(s)* endings in noun-paradigms in Lithuanian; these forms were both generalized to cases without end-stress and subjected to blocking by counteranalogy (as in *bõtais*). The law is, for him, at least earlier than Saussure's law (by which the input, of accented final syllables, would have been greatly increased), but that still leaves it far from common to the Baltic group. But generalization is not so easy to motivate elsewhere: the most-quoted lexeme in this affair is Lith. *dieverìs*, where the testimony of Armenian *taigr*, Sanskrit *devár-*, Greek δᾱήρ, Latin *lēuir*, OHG *zeihhur* and OCS *děvěrĭ* suggests PIE **daiwér-*; and then unaccented *ai* > *ie*. Besides, Hirt's citing of unchanged *laikýti* ignores the earlier form *laĩkyti* (see on Saussure's law). It is not too surprising that Mahlow in 1879 had the bold notion that /ei/ was not changed but /ai/ always became Baltic *ie*. (Osthoff denounced this idea at *MU* 4:112.)

According to Hjelmslev (1932), a cross-syllabic effect was suggested by Pedersen in lectures in Copenhagen in 1920; namely, that vowel harmony was here at work and caused a leftward extension of a feature's domain – a virtually 'prosodic' answer. But against Brugmann's choice of the feature palatal quality – with a spreading, leftwards, domain – Pedersen preferred 'closeness': that is, the crucial presence of the feature [+high] in the following syllabic nucleus overrode distinctions of front versus back, or long versus short. Hjelmslev adopts this blocking idea (1932:100ff., 234), despite believing that Lithuanian *i* and *u* were soon to become 'relatively open' (237). His version of what became known as Endzelin's law is that /ai, ei/ regularly become /ie/ *except* where the closeness of the next occurring vowel maintains the high offset of the preceding diphthong, and so blocks all change. Hjelmslev restricts the law to Latvian and Lithuanian. He can quote *steigiù* (PIE **steigh-*, Gk. στείχ-) with the harmony operating, against *diẽvas*, as expected, where it is absent. Unhappily, there are dozens of non-conforming sequences; and Hjelmslev's discussion resolves into a series of saving explanations, usually of a morphological sort. For example, *véidas*, 'face', would seem to reflect exactly what Greek (*F*)εἶδος does; but the reflex-form is irregular and needs rescue.

Hjelmslev is, however, able to bring in /oi/ (cf. Hirt). This is after all reasonable, considering that /eu, au, ou/ certainly seem to act alike in Baltic history: cf. respectively Lith. *laũkas* "white-spotted" (Gk. λευκός); *augti* "grow" (Lat. *augeo*); and *laũkas* "field","clearing"(OLat. *loucos*). So *piéva* "meadow", presumably reflects PIE **poiwā*, as does West Greek ποία, 'grass'; and the long debated alternation *snaĩgė, sniẽgas* may rest on **snoig^wh-* (OE *snāw*) with following front and back vowel, respectively, and no interfering analogy.

Kortlandt (1974:301) agrees that the law covers all three diphthongs: for /oi/ he adds *piemuõ, píemeni* (with immaterial accent mobility) where Greek has ποιμήν, ποιμένα. He also proposes that the interim stage with /ē/ caused a major, if temporary, restructuring of the Baltic vowel system(s), whereby:

(1) $\begin{aligned} &\ddot{e} \;/\; \bar{e} \\ &\phi \;/\; \bar{a} \\ &\ddot{o} \;/\; \bar{o} \end{aligned}$ (2) $\begin{aligned} &\ddot{e} \;/\; \bar{\rho} \;(</Vi/) \\ &(\ddot{o}>)\,\ddot{a} \;/\; \bar{e} \\ &\bar{a} \;/\; \bar{o} \;(?\text{whence} > \bar{o}/uo) \end{aligned}$

While such speculation can be prompted by it, Endzelin's law still retains power; but really it has been reshaped beyond recognition.

REFERENCES*

Endzelin, I.M. 1907. O proisxoždenij litovsko-latyšskogo *ie. IORJS* 12.40-66. (Cf. *Lietuvią Tauta* 2:2. 284ff., 1908.)

———, 1922. *Lettische Grammatik.* Riga: Gulbis; also Heidelberg; Winter, 1923. (Revised as *Latviešu valodas gramatika*, Riga: 1951.)

———, 1927. *Lekcijas par baltu valodu salīdzināmo gramatika.* Riga: Latvijas vidusskolu skolotaja kooperativa izdevums.

———, 1948. *Baltu valodu skaņas un formas.* Riga: Latvijas valsts izdevniectba.

———. 1971. Transl. of Endzelin 1948 by W.R. Schmalstieg and B. Jēgers, as *Comparative phonology and morphology of the Baltic languages.* The Hague: Mouton. (A transl. into Lithuanian was made in 1957: *Baltų kalbų garsai ir formos.* See, e.g. *Lg* 50.586-91 [1974].)

Hirt, H. 1892. Vom schleifenden und gestossenen Ton in den indogermanischen Sprachen I. *IF* 1.1-42.

Hjelmslev, L. 1932. *Etudes baltiques.* Copenhagen: Levin & Munksgaard.

Mahlow, G.H. 1879. *Die langen vocale A E O in den europäischen sprachen: Ein Beitrag zur vergleichenden Lautlehre der idg. Sprachen.* Berlin: Hermann.

Nieminen, E. 1922. See on Nieminen's law.

Torbiörnsson, T. 1931. Einige litauische Kasusformen und der Lautübergang *ai* > *ie. IF* 49. 119-126.

* Relevant or quoted also are:
Kortlandt 1974*, 1977*
– on which see Appendix III.

FORTUNATOV'S LAW I

F.F. Fortunatov (1848-1914), leader of the old Moscow school of linguists, had a share in the law which more normally bears only Saussure's name. He was, however, the first to enunciate another regularity of shift − this time in the sector of Old Indic consonantism. The law is usually cited as his alone; yet even here he shares the credit to some extent with another.

In 1881 he stated a law, at the outset of an article and with enviable clarity: "In der gruppe '*l*+dental' im Altindischen schwindet das *l* und der dental geht in lingual über" (215). That is, the cluster loses its lateral segment and the apical stop is retroflexed. Then some thirty-five etyma were paraded in testimony; and the paper closed with a brief denial of any like occurrence when the liquid in such a cluster is /r/; for the assimilating shift $rC_\alpha > C_\alpha C_\alpha$, as in *vaṭṭai* from *vartate*, is as much a Prakritism as is, say, $rC > aC$ in *naṭa-* from **nr̥ta-*. Among the typical and better exempla were these:

kuṭhāra-	"axe"	: **kult-*; Lat. *culter*; Lith. *kùlti, kálti*; cf. Skt. *kuliśa-*
ghaṭa-	"jar"	: **ghelt-*; Lith. *gélda*; OPr. *galda* (if not a loan); Germ. *Gelte*
jaṭhara-	"belly"	: **gélt-*; Got. *kilþei* (but see below); OE *cild*; OSwed. *kulder*
paṭa-	"linen cloth"	: **polt-*; Got. *falþan.*; OCS *platĭno*; Russ. *polotnó*; (Arm. *partak*; Pers. *pardah*?)
vaṭa-	"fig tree"	: **we/₀lt-*; Lith. *váltis, vélti*; (OCS *valiti, valjati*; ORuss. *volotĭ*).
hāṭaka-	"gold"	: **gʰe/₀lt-*; PreSlav. **zolto*; OCS *zlato;* Lith. *zelts*; Got. *gulþ*.

Fortunatov's most powerful weapon is the strange rarity of the perfectly natural sequence /-ld-/ in Indic (although it does also seem to be avoided in Latin; cf. Collinge 1976:57). Vedic offers instrumental *gáldayā* (*RV* 8.1.20), along with *gard-* forms. But any *l* is problematic in Vedic; and Fortunatov later argues (1900:12), somewhat sophistically, that as nobody really knows what the word means nobody can plot its history; but now see Hamp 1981.110. (Some forms of *phult-* occur in such grammarians as Pāṇini and Vopadeva, but they are late and not ad rem.)

Certainly the law seeks proof of its triggering segment outside Indic; that sort of external search encouragingly likens it to such accepted edicts as Verner's law or the 'law of the palatals'. Besides, /1/ and /d/ are often phonetically close in realization and historically linked: cf. von Bradke 1887:298. We have Latin *lacruma, leuir, olet* against δάκρυ, δᾱήρ, *odor*. Hence a sort of intersegmental transfer of features is likely enough. But, for all that, the law has had a disappointingly mixed reception and has often come close to bankruptcy.

Its immediate supporters were Windisch (1885), Froehde (1886:298-99.), von Bradke (1887; 1897:156ff.), Johansson (1890:442; 1893:42, 64), Bezzenberger (1890: 240-41), Hoffmann (1892:286-87.), Persson (1895:288 and n.3), and Uhlenbeck (1898: 54-56). Most added fresh evidence; the last-named chose good examples. Fick and Hübschmann approved (on them see Fortunatov 1900: 3). Petersson (1911) rejects Fortunatov's unwise idea that PIE had a second /1/ segment (12-13.); but he offers some new words in evidence (e.g., *pīṭha-*, 79-80.; *ghāṭā-*, 82-83; *piṭhara-*, 85-86), and regards the aberrant type *mardhati* (< *maldh-*), *jartu-* as 'dialectal' (106). On balance, but only on balance, he accepts the law (109). Finally, in 1927, Hirt could not find that the law had been disproved (cf. his comment at Thumb 1930 I.489); and he gave it the sanctuary, and sanctity, of a paragraph in his Indo-European grammar (1927: 205, § 174), with nineteen exampla. Since then, many scholars have referred to it by Fortunatov's name, as a matter of course: so, for example, recently Allen (1973: e.g., 103-104 and n. 17; 105 and n.19), regarding it as the diachronic counterpart to some of the descriptive phonotactics of Sanskrit as stated by Zwicky (1965. 66 ff.).

Scheftelowitz (1925) upbraids the law as not facing the facts, but does not say why. Instead, he offers a new version, omitting clusters with obstruents in second position. His version is restricted to nasals and sibilants:

$$[\text{-V}l \, {}^{n}_{n} / \, {}_{n}^{s} \text{-}] \quad \rightarrow \quad [\text{-V: } {}^{n}/_{s}\text{-}]$$

as in *meln(ak)-* (μέλλαξ; OPr. *melnijks*) > *māṇava-*. This is tantamount to pillaging a house to build a cabin. But vague doubts about the stability of the house are just detectable in Hirt; and in Pokorny's dictionary similar forms are sometimes explained by the law and sometimes excused as Prakritisms (as Burrow [1972:532] adroitly points out). Undoubtedly, Prakrit forms are rife in Sanskrit. So Scheftelowitz is simply 'tra color che son sospesi'. More committed sceptics soon emerged.

The opponents of the law were spurred into protest less by Fortunatov's original suggestion than by Bechtel's powerful support of it in 1892 (and the author's own renewed defence in 1900). Bechtel devoted the closing pages (382-90; ch.10, § 2) of his well-known *Hauptprobleme* (a) to substantiating fourteen of the original witness lexemes (or sixteen, if one counts the added *kiṇa-* and *kuṇi-*, never strongly urged but often accepted, as by Burrow 1972: 543), and (b) to using the law to prove that Indic inherited separate PIE /r/ and /l/, even if dialects collapsed the latter with the former (as did Vedic) — or even vice versa. The law therefore need have only /l/ as its triggering and disappearing liquid, and is pan-Indic. By this exposition it became known for some time as 'the law of Fortunatov and Bechtel', and sometimes simply as 'Bechtel's law'.

The first counterblast came from Bartholomae (1894). He stigmatized all the serious testimonia (where diachronic problems of structure could not be shown) as loans, ultimately from Middle Indo-Aryan. He especially disliked (189-90) Fortunatov's attempt (1881:219-20) to assign a 'Sanskrit prototype' to those forms which even he admitted to be borrowings. The equation of *jaṭháram* and *kilṗei* (in view of Verner's law) ignores the difference of PIE accent position (194); and the relevant etyma reduce to seven at most, of which only *laṣ- really* supports Fortunatov (195). Bartholomae's rejection of the shift involves the supposition of a prior move (of the six forms which he *might* entertain) into a shape containing *-rC-*, from which *r* may then be lost. This is argued with the help of seven firmly proposed input words which have etymological /r/ (188-89); these include *kaṭu-* (Lith. *kartùs*) and *kaṭa-* (Gk. κάρταλ(λ)ος).

Wackernagel (1896:167ff.) and Brugmann (tentatively at 1886:211 n.1, decidedly at 1897:427 note.) were on Bartholomae's side: the law is 'unproved and unprovable'. Schmidt (1895: 1-2 and n.1) with characteristic trenchancy stiffens this verdict to 'positively false'. He objected to the phonetics of it all; indeed, a critical plank in the opposition platform was that Sanskrit /l/ is described (e.g., by Pāṇini) as dental, but /r/ as retroflex; so that, where the latter might naturally affect the stop as the law requires, the former does so only unnaturally. Fortunatov himself worried about the point, and did his best to deny the significance of retroflex pronunciation of /r/ (1900:6ff.). Still, when PIE /kʷ/ can give Greek /t/, or *sa-sd-* develop in Sanskrit to /sayd-/ (*sed-*), or PIE initial /w/ pass to Armenian /g/ (as in *gitem*, 'know'), incredulity over [ld] → [ḍ] seems rather naive and need not trouble the defence. But the law's credibility was shaken. The reply of Fortunatov in 1900 merely counter-etymologized, although it did establish *gáldayā* as a solitary undeniable exception. Lidén (e.g., 1906:335) was an unbeliever; and in his influential etymological dictionary (1956-1980) Mayrhofer repeatedly warns the reader of the law's non-existence: see his entries for *jaṭharam, paṭaḥ, bhāṣate, laṣati*, for instance. It is no doubt understandable that the alternative *histoires* are ad hoc, including some forays into Dravidian for the origins of various disputed words (see Burrow 1972:533; he still accepts that origin for *kaṭu-*, 545).

Yet help for Fortunatov has recently come from a vigorous quarter. In 1971 Burrow ventilated the likelihood of 'spontaneous cerebralization' in Sanskrit (an unmotivated shift, in apicals, from dental to retroflex co-articulation; or, if you will, a loss of the feature [anterior]). He relied on a series of articles by H.W. Bailey in the 1950s and 1960s (Burrow 1971:540n.4); and, in particular, decided that *ṇḍ-* [-ṇḍ-] is the result of an Old Indo-Aryan (whence MIA and Sanskrit) act of unmotivated retroflexion across a cluster. (One recalls that the *ruki* rule smacks of a retroflexion tendency.) This led in 1972 to the cleansing of the Fortunatov word-list. Those items which include *-ṇḍ-* were removed (the liquid and dental, in sequences like /plind/, are not contiguous, anyway); so were those based on syllabic /l/, as *paṭa-* if supposed to relate to Gk. πλατύς, "salty". These measures, in Burrow (1972), offset much of Lidén's objection. One could extend Burrow's remark on contiguity to exclude problematic items like *pūrṇá-* or *ū́rṇā*, where the PIE liquid was /l/ but separated from the dental by /H/. Possibly a time-limit on the law's validity is not unthinkable: if **maldh-* gives Gk. μαλθακός but Skt. *márdhati*, the distinction between Sanskrit /r/ and /l/ is progressively obscured, perhaps, by word-by-word compromises between the rhotacizing wave of immigrants to the North West (whence Vedic fusing) and the earlier /l/-preserving wave to more central areas and (ultimately) the North East. Then the complex relation of Sanskrit /r/ and /l/ distribution to the PIE state of affairs is matched, as one would expect, by complexity in the law's diffusion (see also Hock 1975). (But Brugmann's idea at *BDG* §254 of a *Rückverwandlung* of some /r/s to some /l/s − despite *lumpáti*, Lat. *rumpit* − is as unmotivated and unsettling as Fortunatov's doubling of PIE /l/ types.) The character of the liquid to be credited to the PIE form of a word is often a matter of etymological debate, too: does *kaṭa-* "mat" link with Greek κάρταλ(λ)ος (Bartholomae) or κάλαϑος (Burrow), which both refer to woven baskets?

Burrow's main cleansing contention is that Prakritic, or Pali, versions of liquid+stop clusters show gemination of the stop (or compensatory vowel length) and usually − but not always − retroflexion: so Skt. *vartate* but 'Middle Indian' *vaṭṭai, vattai*. On the other hand, Fortunatovian output is never geminated and never lacks retroflexion; and it can thus be diagnosed and defended. One may object that this is so by definition; but there are about twenty words of certain orthography to validate that definition. Besides, un-

changed */- ⌐C-/ is not really there in Sanskrit; as to *galda-*, this solitary literary
form is allowed by Burrow as an exception which dates the law to the early
Ṛgvedic period (542). That precise claim is, frankly, puzzling. If this word's
emergence postdates the law (so Fortunatov 1900:12), then Vedic *might* be
within the province of the law but have as it happens lost all the other *-lC-*
clusters as such, and so is vacuously 'affected' by the law, which then withers
away. But if the law is to be confined to North Central and East Indic — and no
positive evidence leads in any other direction — then North Western *galda-*,
for all its solitariness and mystery, is simply irrelevant. It cannot provide a
terminus in time. The whole affair is, in fact, bedevilled by the lack of parallel
Vedic and classical histories of the same lexemes.

Burrow's 1972 stance (which costs him a change of opinion on *laṣati*, returning to the traditional origin in reduplicated **le=ls+eti*; cf. λιλαίομαι, 543) rests
on a reasonable calculus of etymological likelihood, plus the strong point that
for instance **vắṭai* (< **wert-*) is a shape which does not turn up. But Hamp
(1981), from a rigorous comparative scrutiny of the evidence, deduces that the
law can be sustained only if the dental in the input cluster is /s/ or /t$^{(h)}$/, as the /l/
when assimilated to the voiceless dental would become too perceptually weak to
survive as a full segment. Possibly, however, /n/ is to be included (because of the
relation of *pāṇi-* to Greek παλάμη; OE *folm* etc.): so judges Hamp (1983),
comparing Scheftelowitz (1925). (The generalized type of phonetic effect may
even extend to /-Vrs+l-/ > /-V:ḷ-/; cf. Hamp 1982.)

The vicissitudes of the Indic liquids are still without a full history; for a
doubtful, but not incredible, part of it Fortunatov's law (I)* may still serve as
a useful label.

REFERENCES

Allen, W.S. 1973. Xϑών, *ruki*, and related matters. *TPS* 1973.98-126.
Bartholomae, C. 1894. Zur *l*-Frage. *IF* 3.157-97.
Bechtel, F. 1892. *Die Hauptprobleme der indogermanischen Lautlehre seit
    Schleicher*. Göttingen; Vandenhoeck & Ruprecht.
Bezzenberger, A. 1890. Die indogermanischen gutturalreihen. *BB* 16.234-60.
Bradke, P. von 1887. Etymologien. *KZ* 28.295-301.
─────. 1897. Etymologisch-grammatikalische bemerkungen und skizzen.

* For Fortunatov's law II (in Slavic), see Appendix IA.

KZ 34.152-59.

Burrow, T. 1971. Spontaneous cerebrals in Sanskrit. *BSOAS* 34.538-59.

――――. 1972. A reconsideration of Fortunatov's law. *BSOAS* 35.531-45.

Collinge, N.E. 1976. Global rules, active derivation, and Latin *mellis*. *Fs Palmer*, 57-62.

Fortunatov, F.F. 1881. *L + dental im Altindischen. BB* 6.215-20.

――――, 1900. Die indogermanischen liquiden im Altindischen. *KZ* 36.1-37.

Hamp, E.P. 1981. An amendment to Fortunatov's law. *Mem. Chatterji*, 106-12.

――――, 1982. *Kā́la-*, 'black'. *IIJ* 24.38-39.

――――, 1983. A revised amendment to Fortunatov's law. *IIJ* 25.275-76.

Hirt, H. 1927. *Indogermanische Grammatik*, vol 1. Heidelberg: Winter.

Hock, H.H. 1975. Substratum influence on Rig-vedic Sanskrit. *SLS* 6.76-125.

Hoffmann, O. 1892. Etymologien. *BB* 18.285-92.

Johansson, K.F. 1890. Etymologische Beiträge. *KZ* 30.428-52.

――――, 1893. Sanskritische Etymologien. *IF* 2.1-64.

Lidén, E. 1897. *Studien zur altindischen und vergleichenden Sprachgeschichte.* Uppsala.

――――, 1906. Zur germanischen Wortgeschichte. *IF 19.335-59.*

Mayrhofer, M. 1956-80. *Ein kurzgefasstes etymologisches Wörterbuch des Altindischen.* (I 1956, II 1963, III 1976, IV 1980). Heidelberg: Winter.

Persson, P. 1895. Etymologisches. *KZ* 33.284-94.

Petersson, H. 1911. *Studien zu Fortunatovs Regel.* Lund: Lindstedt.

Pokorny, J. 1948-69. *Indogermanisches etymologisches Wörterbuch.* Berne: Francke.

Scheftelowitz, J. 1925. Ein urindisches Liquidgesetz. *KZ* 53.248-69.

Schmidt, J. 1889. *Die Pluralbildungen der indogermanischen Neutra.* Weimar: Böhlau.

――――, 1895. *Kritik der Sonantentheorie.* Ibid.

Thumb, A.J. 1930. *Handbuch des Sanskrit.* 2nd ed. Heidelberg: Winter. (1st ed., 1905.)

Uhlenbeck, C.C. 1898. *Manual of Sanskrit phonetics.* London: Luzac (= Transl. of *Handboek der Indische Klankleer in vergelijking met die der Indo-germaansche stamtaal.* Leiden: Blankenberg, 1894.)

Wackernagel, J. 1896. *Altindische Grammatik I.* Göttingen: Vandenhoeck & Ruprecht. (Repr. 1957.)

Windisch, E. 1885. Etymologische miscellen. *KZ* 27.168-72.

Zwicky, A.M. 1965. *Topics in Sanskrit phonology.* Diss. Cambridge, Mass.:, Mass. Inst. of Technology.

GRASSMANN'S LAW

Hermann Grassmann (1809-1877), his career in banking interrupted by ill-health, thereafter achieved fame as a mathematician as well as turning an enviably deft hand to philological (and specifically Vedic) studies. For linguists, his attempt to assert such regularity as is possible in a corner of Indo-European phonological history is his titular memorial. It was in 1863 that, in a voluminous article typical of the period, he wrote on the aspirated consonants of IE. He legislated for their non-occurrence in succession at the onset and the release of the same syllable, within roots: on this topic von Raumer (1837:74) may actually have been the first to speculate, at least as to Sanskrit. To make diachronic sense of all the reflexes in the data, Grassmann propounded (1863: 110-11) not one but two laws − or, if you will, one law with two clauses − running thus:

(1)   'Given a root with a final aspirate and an initial consonant capable of aspiration, and given also that the final element loses aspiration (by some separate sound law), then that feature is retracted to the initial element.'

(2)   'Given two consonant-groups in a word, separated by a vowel and themselves aspirated, and provided that they are within the same root, then one (and normally the first) is deprived of its breath feature.'

The dual nature of Grassmann's own form of the ordinance, although clear enough in Lehmann's recent presentation (1967:112), is rarely noticed in subsequent discussion of the phenomena. Vennemann (1979) is an exception to the general blindness; but he links clause 2 to 'reduplicative' stems only. Yet the law's first clause is clearly identical with what is now fashionably called Aspirate Throw-Back (ATB); only clause (2) corresponds to 'Grassmann's law' in the stricter modern usage. The inventor's own reservations also deserve to be rescued from oblivion. For him, clause (1) applies in Indic only if, in a root C_1VC_2, (a) C_1 is voiced and not palatal, (b) C_2 is a voiced aspirate; and it applies in Greek only if C_1 is /t/ − a condition quickly shown to be if necessary yet not sufficient by τεύξομαι or τρύξω. As for clause (2), this ruling may operate

– but only sporadically (*vereinzelt*) – even where C_1 and C_2 are *not* part of the same radical string and/or are separated by more than a single vowel: hence ἐκε#χειρία, τηλε#θόωσα. Even the abnormal (and, because of laryngeal history probably mythical) direction of shift admitted in θυγάτηρ is called 'Regelmässig' (126).

The progress of reaction to these rulings has been curious. For a century there was none. At best, acceptance of the shift and its embodiment into the manuals was punctuated by occasional almost shamefaced resorts to ad hoc explanations of oddities – or a mere noting of them. So, for example, Hammerich (1947); or again Georgiev (1958; this latter differentiating the Aegean language 'Pelasgian' from Greek by allowing it to have undergone what one may call a cousin of Grimm's law *after* Grassmann's, instead of a devoicing of aspirates *before* Grassmann's: e.g., *bhurghos > *burghos > πύργος).

But in the mid 1960s began the probing and the doubting; and from 1964 to 1980 there broke forth a positive torrent of intricately argued polemic. The swiftest glance at the list of references below will confirm this phenomenon. The likeliest reason is that rules-grammarians, of whatever persuasion, had freshly encountered a body of well-attested and easily interpreted data which maddeningly resisted all attempts to express it by neat paths of derivation. Either the necessary rules were incredibly context-sensitive, or they were impossible to assign to a regular order, or (if unordered) they bled one another unmercifully, or they evinced a fearsome inconsistency of output from comparable input. (This last might be a matter of 'lexical diffusion'; but it is *not* to do with 'variable rules' applying to the same strings, unless variability refers to content rather than to mere implementation.) The struggles of generativists for survival in these waters have been heartrending to watch, where not comical.

Of the many interlocked questions which arise the following schedule is the roughest of guides; it pretends to no logic of order:

(1) Are we always dealing with one and the same shift?
(2) Is the shift natural, transparent, systematic?
(3) Is the shift simplex, or is it a linkage of distinct processes? If the latter, should we fuse any part of it with other 'laws' or their parts?
(4) What, in precise phonetic terms, are the segments which change and the changes which they undergo?
(5) What is the shift's domain in terms of morphology, and what are its favourable candidates in terms of phonology?
(6) Do nouns and verbs behave differently? If so, why?
(7) Do boundaries constrain the shift? Some (e.g., Stemberger 1980:

120) say no; but those who apply them should distinguish – or should they? – syllable frontier ($), minor morphological seam (=), major morphological seam (+), derivational boundary (#) and word boundary (# #), which give a hierarchy based on blocking strength.

(8)   Is relexicalization a major factor?

(9)   Why is there so much plain inconsistency? Or is this a mirage, for those who forget chronology?

Every one of these headings refers to a matter of public debate. Their defeating intersection has broken the faith of some scholars in the law's very existence (cf. Bubeník, Hastings, Sag); others merely chop it up and paste the fragments on to other laws, notably Bartholomae's. Magnusson (1969) relates it to other laws as a matter of plosive-opposition evolution, without special consideration of its own complexities.

The law and related phenomena in Indic (or 'Grassmann and Bartholomae')

Here 1965 saw the start of generativist interest, when Kiparsky put together (1) the loss of prior obstruent aspiration in clusters ('deaspiration' or DA), (2) Grassmann's second clause of 1863 (GL), and (3) the interfering process known in its own right as Bartholomae's law (BL). Given a root such as *dh(e)ugh, DA led for instance to dhug+dhve, GL to, e.g., doh+ay+ati, doh+āma (in Sanskrit gh> h is normal in the environment), while BL shifted -gh+t- to -gdh-. (For the moment BL is to be taken as a whole, and seen as insensitive to formation boundaries.) Now the nuisance is this: first, dhugdhve shows the shift order to be DA, GL; and secondly, labdha- (< labh+ta-) indicates the order BL, DA, in the new sense that Bartholomae's edict is best regarded as a two-stage affair, consisting of (1) 'BL proper', a progressive assimilation by which -bh+t- → -bh+dh-, and (2) DA, by which bhdh- becomes bdh- (so Anderson, S.R. 1970:388). Very well; the combined sequence should then be BL, DA, GL. Hence the output of, e.g., *dhu(g)+thas must be (→ *dhu(g)h+dhas →) *dhug+dhas, which would thereafter remain, because the /+/ means that the aspirates are now not root-mates and there is no legitimate input to GL. Yet the actual form is dugdhas – and cf. *dheugh+ti > dogdhi. So the path must really be

either *dhugh+thas → *dhugh+dhas (BL)   **or** → *dugh+thas (GL)

   → *dugh+dhas (GL)   → *dugh+dhas (BL)

   → dugdhas   (DA)   → dugdhas   (DA)

with the order **either** BL, GL, DA **or** GL, BL, DA. Thus there arises an ordering crisis, leading to special arguments which Stemberger (1980:113) fairly describes as 'very messy'.

Anderson (1970) bases his solution on his 1969 thesis in which (166) he introduces [Root] as a feature in the context of his own Grassmannian 'rule'. He accepts the difficulty which Kiparsky (and Zwicky, both 1965) noted in the ordering of related rules. He is suspicious of Zwicky's condition on context, namely that it be / −t(h)/; and quite sceptical of Kiparsky's appeal to cycles of diachronic rule application, as seeming 'labored and overly complex'. His own concept scarcely avoids the same reproach. It is an appeal to 'local ordering', where the order of shifts is based on an unmarked sequence of phonic events; their sequence varies according to morpheme-conjoining, but is thereafter adhered to for that particular derivation. Vennemann (1979) offers two better attempts at reordering than does Anderson, but would rather formalize Whitney's adequate description of the facts. Anyhow, Anderson still needs an anchoring constraint; and this baldly states that in Sanskrit GL always precedes BL. Of course, that ruling is the ordering counterpart of Whitney's idea (1879, §160(b)), that in forms where BL has already applied GL does not apply, at least not in its 'two-clause' Grassmannian form. The shifting rightwards of the aspirate in the consonant cluster at the end of the apparent domain of BL (i.e., -Ch+C- → -CC^h-, as with -(g)h+ta- → -gdha-) precludes the restoration of the aspirate feature in the onset consonant, Grassmann's *anlaut*. 'Restoration' is the critical term: where GL and DA apply, the final result of the latter is for Whitney a kind of compensation by an undoing of the GL effect (so §155(a)) − a view of the most orthodox and unadventurous sort, quite in accord with the spirit of the law's first century. Vennemann backs Whitney; he sees no use in GL and BL as bases for rules-grammar theorizing (1979:578).

Next come Phelps & Brame (1973), who pick up Anderson's [Root] feature but in effect corroborate its obvious 'non-feature'-ness. This they do by changing its physical shape in the BL rule. In fact they actually shift the position of /+/ in the formation: so *dhu(g)h+thas* becomes now *dhu(g)hdh+as*, whence (by DA) *dhugdh+as*, a form then susceptible to root-sensitive GL, which emerges from *that* shift as *dugdhas*. At all events, it gets there. Sag's approach (1974, 1976) is quite otherwise; in fact, it is reminiscent of the thinking of some GL theorists in Greek, in that it talks of ATB without apparent awareness that this effect was already envisaged by Grassmann himself, not to mention Pāṇini (8.2.38). Sag (like Schindler 1976) denies that diaspirate roots are available at all in Sanskrit; although the availability would not, as a merely contingent fact, create any confusion in Sanskrit; so Hoenigswald shows (1965). For this view

Sag can count Schindler, against Phelps and Hoard (both 1975). Each root-initial aspirate is triggered by the loss of a root-final aspirate, this view says, if it is before +s or +dhve or dhvam or a boundary of at least strength /#/. Now no such thing happens before the phonetically similar +dhi (imperative); this has to be recognized, as by the Hellenists, as a most idiosyncratic formant (cf. dugdhi). Even so, special treatment is twice required: (1) forms like bodhi show +dhi where -hi might be expected, and (since in that root bhū is certain) they show that +dhi is not inert in the diaspirate sequence it creates (− but what of dhehi?); (2) dhattha- (from dhā) lures Sag into tinkering with the morphological boundary, so that /da+dh+/ becomes /da=dh#/. Certainly, by using /+/ and BL one can establish a string in which the root has no aspirate at its Auslaut (dug+dha-): so Darden 1978, who sees BL as essentially a law which transfers features across /+/. That such an idea is unnecessarily positive is one thing; less important is its failure to produce the correct output for *da=dh+tha-, in that the result *daddha- is not even close to dhatta-. But the sequence dadh behaves very oddly (despite Gray's attempt to make it respectable: see on Bartholomae's law). Schindler (1976:628) remarks that in the present tense it acts as if it were dhad (but scarcely in order to distance itself from forms of the root dā, seeing that datta-, dhatta- form a less opposed pair than datta-, *daddha-). For Schindler āttha (2sg of pf. āha) is also a maverick (from ādh+ta, cf. Avest. ādarð, 3 pl.). Schindler regards GL, once extended to reduplicated forms (even to disyllabic reduplicates, as davi=dhvat, davi=dhāva), as thereafter tied to that domain, namely the pre-root syllable. (It is that environment which Ejerhed, 1981.143, reasonably uses to argue that what really happens is the left-ward copying of the leftmost segment of a cluster of which /h/ is the static rightmost segment; on the other hand, the segment /h/ itself moves in ATB (146).) To return to Schindler, such a form as budh (or, by 'reverse GL', bhut) must be a restructuring. This leaves budbhis, which he cannot then derive from *bhudh+bhis via *budh+bhis; so his answer is a special effect of compositional sandhi (following Kuiper IIJ 10,103ff. [1967]). This is a sort of intricate calculation of boundaries which differentiates Cl.Skt. viṭsu (nom.sg. viṭ) from Vedic vikṣu, deriving these respectively from viś#su but viś+su.

Stemberger (1980:117) restricts ATB to roots with suffixes in voiceless dentals. This solves the problems of +dhi, and echoes Zwicky's condition on BL (but dhā is still an unexplained non-participant in BL, which justifies dhatta- without piercing its mystery). Stemberger calls GL the 'opposite' of ATB (123). He requires the two aspirates to be 'in the same morpheme' and yet to begin their respective syllables: so dohmi ← *dho(g)hmi, but dhokṣyati ←

$dho(g)h$sya $ti. So what of (post-BL) *dhu(g)h+dha- → dugdha-? Well, GL
works because (g)h counts even so a syllable-initial item, being clustered with the
syllable-onset stop of the suffix (124). Sophistry, indeed. In fact, dhatta- and
dhattha (2pl.indic.) need their own histories: perhaps an inflexion can develop
a rule that looks rather like a morphologically conditioned, but different, law
(cf. Butler 1974)? If GL were an active rule for Sanskrit users, /s/ must be
treated as a pro-aspirate (so Stemberger 128, cf. Schindler 1976:630), to arrive
at Ved. bapsati from *bha=bs+ati (← *bha=bh's+ati); Schindler prefers to use an
aspirated sibilant: hence '/Dzh/ → /Ts/' is for him a pre-Vedic, post-GL, affair.

   The sceptical ruminations of Jacob Mey on all this (Mey 1972) are a by-
product of his offensive against Bartholomae's law and may be found under
that heading. Now let us rather catch our breath and turn our eyes to Greek.

The law and related phenomena in Greek

   First, the data and what is problematic in them:

(i) The domain
GL occurs across /=/ (πέ=φευγ+α) and is sometimes apparent across /+/
(ἐ=τέ+θην). Across /#/ it is spasmodic; yet the incidence is normally stable
in a given lexical item in a given dialect (so the curious ἐκε#χειρία alongside
ἐχέ#θυμος and ἐχέ#φρων). The precluding force of /+/ before -θη-˙ and -θι will,
as always, be debated separately. At least /=/ is always disregarded, and the
reduplicated root is, for GL, the root par excellence. Indeed, in Greek as in Indic
(as for Ejerhed's theory) the relevant perfect tense forms are the best domain of
all. Yet Miller (1974:219) looks back to a golden age when the law operated
across any boundary at all, short of sentence; which is an odd judgement,
considering the Homeric status of ἐχέθυμος and ἐχέφρων and the later emergence of ἐκεχειρία. (The 'long domain' credited to e.g. ἄλοχος (<*sm+ logʰ-,
*ἀλοχ-) is unsafe because of the unknown etymological details: the prefix may
be *n̥; so Winter 1952.)

   Another curiosity is the claimed long-distance operation of the law in Homeric
τηλεθόων, τηλεθάοντες (Od. 7.114, 22.423), as opposed to the 'normal'
τε=θηλ- forms (e.g. Od. 5.69), from present θαλέ(θ)ω. The sequences εθ and
ηλ seem to be transposed; and, in view of Plotinus' reputed ἀνα-μνη-μί-σκω
for ἀνα-μι-μνή-σκω (Schwyzer 1939:269), this ought not to be made into a
complexity of GL. Besides, if dissimilation is 'avoidance of repetition of an

articulatory action' (Allen 1968:25n.4), this constraint must fade after several segments.

(ii) *The consistency*

Three factors of interference destroy consistency of GL output: the dialectal, the chronological and the (so to say) local.

a) Dialectal interference

Initial psilosis must skew the reflexes; in dialects where /# #h-/ is not found, the ἔχω-ἕξω difference is obscured. Again, a sort of take-it-or-leave-it alternation, as in δέκομαι versus δέχομαι, may mislead the earnest Grassmannian, as will the *Hauchversetzung* of χιτών, κιθών (Ion.); βατραχός, βαθρακός (Ion.); χαλκός, καυχός (Cret.); φάτνη, πάθνη (later koine, <PIE *bhndh-*) and, even better, θεσμός, τεθμός (Dor.). And there is, in some areas, mere insensitivity to the whole thing: so West Ionic θυφλός, Cretan θιθέμενος. And the ordinary Greek probably had imperfect *h*-control anyway: more ostraka than not spell Themistocles as Θεμισθοκλῆς.

β) Chronological interference

This is really an extension of dialectal variety, as the Greek dialects tended to pursue similar paths of evolution but at different speeds and with different patterns of diffusion. Some incidence of GL has to be credited to each of the classical dialects; but it could be denied to Mycenaean (with no aspiration marking in the spelling). That GL is post-Mycenaean, or occurred only in a short period just before the palace destructions which are usually dated to the late fifteenth century BC, is argued, respectively. by Ruijgh (1967:44-46) and Janko (1977). Slings (1979:257-58n.52) is against Janko, and any firm dating; for him GL was merely preceded by loss of voice and aspiration − in labials only − before a consonant in all dialects. The Attic forms ἔχω, εἶχον indicate a GL effect later than either (*s >)h > ∅ / # # −, or e + e > [ε:] (η). Yet ἔχω rather stands alone: cf. e.g. ἀφή − but there is Acarnanian ὄφατα. For Miller (1977b) Grassmann's law is late in Greek as a whole and slow to spread, not showing up before the ninth century and (as urged in a private response from Cowgill in 1974) not getting established in Boeotian until even after 550. So GL is (for Miller) later than *ky* > *ss*, *p^hm* >*mm* (138; he anticipates Slings 1979), and of course than aspirate devoicing. From this argument, if Wyatt (1972) sees in *t^hit^hemi* > τίθημι a shift of virtual PIE date, he is implying willy-nilly two similar laws for Greek; cf. Davies (1976). (The liveliest exponent of a chronological view along those lines is Kiparsky; see below.)

γ) *Local interference*

Sometimes, seemingly wild reflexes offer themselves. Alongside ἐτρέφϑην is found ἐϑρέφϑην, which can be handled by ATB (→ ἐϑρέπ + ϑην) plus post-Grassmann *ptʰ → pʰtʰ* (cf. Miller 1974:222), although this last could be a mere spelling convention, anyhow. Is it, however, separable from things like ἐϑάλφϑην (root ϑαλπ) or ἐϑέλχϑην (root ϑελγ), which are not input to either clause of GL? Conversely, deaspiration sometimes comes to stay: so *bh(e)udh + s/ + t*, gives not *φεύσομαι, *φυστός but πεύσομαι, πυστός. But this touches on phonetic variety and on relexicalization, of which more presently.

(iii) *Phonetic variety*

Only dental obstruents tolerate the law's demands on a regular basis, even before /+/ and the curious +ϑη- formant: so ἐχύϑην but ἐτύϑην. The alternation ϑρίξ (n.sg.) — τριχός (g.sg.) also argues for a similar regularization of ATB (whatever its status within the formulation of the law). Yet, against ϑρέψω, τεύχω permits *ϑευξ- (cf. Hesychius' συνϑύξω) to pass to τεύξ(ομαι), (ἔ)τευξ(α); and ATB is blocked if the pre-syllabic obstruent is post-strident: ἔστρεψα (from στρέφω). If labials and velars are more recalcitrant, the types ἐχύϑην and κέχυμαι show that velars merely deny the non-aspirate to the non-reduplicated slot. But labials *never* show aspiration root-initially, once derivation has begun: πυνϑάνομαι, ἐπυϑόμην, ἄπυστος, or πάσσων (< *φαχ- cf. Skt. *bahu*). We must conclude that κέχυμαι and πέφευγα look alike only to deceive. The stability of the derived π- reflexes therefore leads some (such as Miller 1977:149-50) to explain them as 'relexicalization'. (On the effect of labials *following* the Grassmann domain, see Slings [1980:257-58]; and for ATB affecting labials in quite other contexts note φροίμιον, φρουρός [<*προ+h-]

(iv) *Diffusional variety*

It is fashionable to seek a solution for spotty reflex phenomena in a differential diffusion of shift. Lexical grouping or declensional classing holds the controls. But hard evidence is lacking — except for the idiosyncratic awkwardness of +ϑι (impv.) — cf. Indic *dhi* — and +ϑη- (aorist passive). The matter may be outlined as follows. The contrasting ἐχύϑην (from χέ(F)ω and ἐτύϑην (from ϑύω) show a no and yes response to Grassmann and accept and ignore /+/ as a blocking feature, respectively. One might explain ἐτέϑην (Root ϑη) — notwithstanding the fifth-century form ἀνεϑέϑη — by the influence of the / τεϑη / string in, e.g., perfect τε=ϑη+κα. But not so τυϑη by τεϑυ, and only reluctantly ἐτύϑην by ἐτέϑην. Then come (1) φάϑι, τέϑναϑι, where /+/ seems to block the law; and (2) λύθητι, where both suffixes occur, and where alone +θι is involved in a process of deaspiration in the string, and finally where the direction of dissimilation is inverted. (To deny the inversion is to tread a stony path. 2 sg. +θι might be the initial result and be pushed to +τι under paradigmatic pressure from 3 sg. +τω; but it never is so pushed except after +θη- not even in the stative-based rival formation in +η-, as στράφηθι shows — despite some Septuagint manuscript variants offering ἐπιστράφητι by late analogy.) Are these suffixes preceded rather by /#/? Why? And why only when used separately and not when conjoined (at least, as regards the second boundary in, e.g. χυ#θη+τι)?

Miller's answers (1974: 226-27) are these: (1) The stretch between the boundary before the affected aspirate and the inter-aspirate /+/ (a stretch which in /-θυ+ / and /-χυ+ / is the root, in /+θη +/ is the voice-aspect marker) is given special treatment because it is monosyllabic: so the general constraint on GL which is imposed by /+/ is waived. Then one correctly predicts ἐ=τύ+θην but ὠρθώ+θην, λύ+θη+τι but Κορινθό+θι. (2) The /+/ constraint is so waived only if the affected aspirate attaches to a dental segment: hence ἐχύθην, φάθι are unaffected. (3) When these conditions are met θη has an ambivalent status in *λυ+θη+θι, being flanked by /+/, and being half trigger and half target. This causes a mirror-image version of GL to operate, with its blocking formant boundary to the left of the leftmost aspirate. Later Greek speakers misinterpreted this as centrifugal radiation: whence Galen's τίθητι.

Sommerstein (1973:45) devised a control which, as he saw its obvious shortcomings, he later retracted (in 1975; see Miller 1977b:142n.3). Still, it deserves a mention, being an interesting prosodic approach in which some truth may lurk. An ad hoc leftward-operating assimilatory feature [A] is assigned, regardless of /$/ or /+/, to all prior obstruents in a cluster of which the last obstruent has [+A], a value characteristic of +θη- and +θι and also +(σ)θαι and +(σ)θε. A rule of leftwards de-Grassmannizing then gives

(* ἐ=χύ+θην →)   *ἐκύθην   (GL)   → ἐχύθην   (← κυθ [+A])
(* ἐ=θρέφ+θην →) *ἐτρέφθην (GL)   → ἐθρέφθην (← τρεφ [+A]θ[+A])

The leftward aspirate must not be of the same class as the [+A] consonant (cluster) — so GL stays valid in ἐτύθην. Clearly +θη+θι in imperatives is then a case where a doubled impetus to leftwards assimilation is nevertheless blocked by shared dentality (or something); that is doubtful, and the unmotivated inverted direction within the stretch itself is worse. But this discarded idea, however 'notational', at least healthily recognises that phonology is of the piece as well as of the segment.

Hellenic theorists in effect offer four strategies of solution:

(1) by splitting up the processes of the Grassmann-complex.

This means separating aspirate throwback from any dissimilatory (pure GL) activity, and from aspirate devoicing, deaspiration in clusters, and s-aspiration. Sommerstein (1973:45) allots part of the exceptional sort of GL process to his Manner Assimilation rule; Miller (1974) is a determined separatist (of GL and ATB in particular − cf. 1977b also, on $\vartheta\rho\acute{e}\mu\mu\alpha$); but, even more, he has 'old GL' and 'new GL'; and that despite a conviction that the whole thing is late in Greek (as $\vartheta\rho\acute{e}\mu\mu\alpha < *t^h rep^h+m$- again would show).

(2) by admitting relexicalization.

This is usually placed early enough to remove all diaspirate roots, leaving the reduplicated perfect as practically the only dynamic form. Here the champion is Kiparsky (1973b; cf. 1976, who relies on independent and systematic ATB − which is actually at odds with Kiparsky (1973a) where ATB is said to be only apparent (121) and, e.g., $\vartheta\rho\acute{e}\psi\omega$ is derived from cluster reduction and GL (clause 1?). Relexicalization (with free ATB) and the excision of diaspirates has the vote of Bubeník (1976, citing Langendoen 1966), as a prehistoric neutralization process. A natural outcome is then the plea for 'different verbs', a commonplace in generative grammar but here resting on actual history; so that $\tau\rho\acute{e}\varphi\omega$ is, plausibly, the homophonous Greek shape of both (1) $*dhreg^Wh$-, 'nurture' (Myc. *to-ro-qa*), and (2) $*dhrebh$-, 'thicken (liquid)'; cf. Miller 1977: 142n.2.

(3) by rule re-ordering.

Although Anderson's 'local re-ordering' in Indic has had a rough reception, Kiparsky's (1973a) ordering shift within the history of Greek may be salvaged; not, however by a parallelism to order-change in generative rules (against which there has long been a powerful lobby) so much as by the succession of two distinct, productive, shift-groups. Greek, it is suggested, first had the sequence of cluster reduction − GL − devoicing of aspirates (and s- aspiration), but later preferred CR − DA − GL. Miller rejects this idea (1977b − despite his own attitude earlier, 1974:219). Still, the '2 GLs' concept recurs − and perhaps only the second such shift was truly Hellenic; in general, loss or shift of aspiration is not uncommon in the world. But Schindler (1976) will not have it so; and the question of identity as between the Indic and the Greek processes remains (see below).

(5) by simple denial of the law.

This, in essence, is the stance of Sag (1974, 1976), Bubeník (1976), and Hastings (1978); also, on special phonetic grounds, of Gamkrelidze (1981) − see Appendix II. In passing one notes that Dressler (1975:63-64) offers a five stage history of GL in Greek, but as a single process merely differentiated by morphological domains. He rightly sees the lone nature of ἐκεχειρία and ἀμπέχω (but his own rule will not in fact generate both); but he wrongly includes an ῥ →ῥ shift (for ῥ is not really aspirated but voiceless).

Finally, the identity question. Kiparsky (1973a) — in what was not his last word on the subject — ventilated the possibility that the first version of GL in Greek, in the older sequence of phonological processes, is actually the same event as GL in Indic. Zipf (1936:82-86) had no doubt of that (he saw the shift as loss only, related to 'magnitude of complexity' and its toleration). Butler (1974) also saw an identity. The idea is diametrically opposed to Grassmann's own conception (and to, e.g. Janko 1977). It depends on the sphere of activity of the same relevant ripple within a wave-theory model (or else a late-IE cohabitation of Greeks and Indo-Iranians: cf. Birwé 1955). It also rests on the degree of confidence to be reposed in some Greek reflexes with odd voiced segments: notably βρεχμός, βοϑρός, βυϑός, δρύπτω, δεῖσα and ἀγαϑός. The counterblast in Miller (1977), however, includes more than fifteen equally unusual yet fundamental lexical items where the initial or prior stop is *not* voiced and where the processes are not the same (among them are παχύς, κεφαλή, πενϑερός and τεῖχος). If GL in Greek, at least in its heyday, postdates changes like φ > β/N- (στρομβός from στρεφ-), k(h)y > σσ (ϑάσσων) - both of which bleed ATB or GL of input — and nasal assimilation (ϑρέμμα), then a complete equation is impossible. But if there is an 'old GL' in Greek (as Wyatt and sometimes Miller thought), or even if a 'phonological affinity' is a likelihood (Allen 1977: 243-44), the chance of an Indic-Hellenic areal innovation just remains alive. Yet even then we must face the radical phonetic question which now hangs over the PIE (and IE) obstruents (see Appendix II).

Postscript

Does the law have cousins in other languages areas (where actual identity is not in question)? Well, outside IE there is always Dahl's law in Bantu, which it is fashionable to quote as some sort of parallel — but on that ordinance and its very varied statements a special excursus is useful (see Appendix IV). Even more arresting is de Reuse's observing (1981) of GL in an extinct Siouan language of the lower Mississippi. As for other IE languages, Grassmann himself noted (in 1863) that many of the exceptions to Grimm's law noted by Lottner in his work of the preceding year vanish if GL is applied to them. Prokosch reports (1939:203-204) the belief of Collitz and Brugmann in a Germanic domain for a combined operation of Bartholomae's and Grassmann's edicts to solve the problems over the forms of some class III preterites in Old English and Old Saxon. Closer to today is Allen's (1977:244-45) interesting recording of a 'latter-day GL' in Harauti (a dialect of Rajasthani), which amounts to (1) a reversed GL (*hātī*, against Hindi *hāthī*), (2) ATB (*khāmḍo*, against Hindi *kamḍhā*, and (3) medial DA of a voiced stop (*gaḍ*, against Hindi *gaṛh*). True GL is not really there; but it is curious that a preceding /s/ acts as if it were /h/ (*sātī*, against Hindi *sāthī*) – which reminds one of an idea of Stemberger's (1980: 128).

Perhaps GL is a widespread process, surfacing sporadically in time and space, but in freely equatable phenomena across languages, *mutatis mutandis*. But who will go to the stake to defend the status of such-and-such as the true *mutanda*?

REFERENCES*

Allen, W.S. 1968. *Vox Graeca*. Cambridge, Univ. Press. (2nd ed., 1974.)

–––––, 1977. The PIE aspirates: phonetic and typological factors in recon- struction. *Fs Greenberg* Vol.II, 237-47.

Anderson, L.B. 1970. *Grassmann's law for speaker and hearer: Formal vs. func- tional explanations of leveling*. Chapel Hill, N.C.: Univ. of North Carolina. Mimeo.

Anderson, S.R. 1970. On Grassmann's law in Sanskrit. *LI* 1.387-96. (Based on MIT thesis, 1969.)

Birwé, R. 1955. *Griechische-arische Sprachbeziehungen im Verbalsystem*. Wall- dorf-Hessen: Vorndran.

Bubeník, V. 1976. Review of Sommerstein 1973. *Lingua* 38.170-73.

Butler, J.L. 1974. A murmured proposal regarding Grassmann's law. *IF* 79.18- 30.

Christol, A. 1972. Phonologie des aspirées grecques et parfait à aspirée. *BSL* 67.69-83.

Davies, A.M. 1976. Review of Wyatt 1972. *CR* n.s.26.88-90.

Dressler, W. 1975. Zur Rekonstruktion phonologischer Prozesse im Altgriechi- schen: Grassmanns Gesetz. *Fs Hamm*, 53-67.

---

* Of no little relevance are the contributions listed in the excursus (Appendix II) on the recent revisions to the reconstructed PIE plosive system, which if valid could transform this and other laws beyond recognition.

Ejerhed, E.I. 1981. The analysis of aspiration in Sanskrit phonology. *NJL* 4.139-59.

Gamkrelidze, T.V. 1981. See bibliography of Appendix II.

Georgiev, V. 1958. Das Pelasgische – eine neuentdeckte indo-europäische Sprache. *P(8)ICL*, 406-13.

Grassmann, H. 1863. Über die aspiration und ihr gleichzeitiges vorhandensein im an- und auslaute der wurzeln. *KZ* 12.81-138. (Partial English translation in Lehmann 1967:109-31.)

Hammerich, L. L. 1947. La dissimilation d'aspiration. *REIE* 4. 1/2.

Hastings, A. 1978. Should Grassmann's law be repealed? Paper to LSA meeting, December 1978.

Hoard, J. 1975. On incorporating Grassmann's law into Sanskrit phonology. *Proc. 1st Annual Meeting of the Berkeley Ling. Socy.* 207-20. Berkeley.

Hoenigswald, H.M. 1965. A property of Grassmann's law in Indic. *JAOS* 85. 59-60.

Janko, R. 1977. A note on the date of Grassmann's law in Greek. *Glotta* 55. 1-2.

Kiparsky, P. 1965. *Phonological change.* Diss., Cambridge, Mass.: MIT. (Publ. Bloomington, Indiana Univ. Ling. Club, 1971.)

––––––, 1973a. On comparative linguistics: the case of Grassmann's law in Greek. *CTL* 11.115-34.

––––––, 1973b. Abstractness, opacity, and global rules. *Three Dimensions of Linguistic Theory*, ed. by O. Fujimura, 57-86. New York: Holt, Rinehart & Winston; Tokyo: TEC. (Also in *The application and ordering of grammatical rules*, ed. by A. Koutsoudas, 160-86. The Hague: Mouton, 1976.)

Langendoen, D.T. 1966. A restriction on Grassmann's law in Greek. *Lg* 42.7-9.

Lehmann, W.P. 1967. *A reader in nineteenth-century historical Indo-European Linguistics.* Bloomington: Indiana Univ. Press.

Levin, S.R. 1969. 'Grassmann's law' in the early Semitic loan words χιτών, κιϑών. *SEMA* 8.66-75.

Lightner, T.M. 1973. On the formulation of Grassmann's law in Greek. *Fs Halle*, 128-30.

Lottner, C. 1862. See under Grimm's law.

Lyche, C. 1976. On Grassmann's law in Greek. *Oslo Working Papers in Linguistics* 7.174-77.

Magnusson, W.L. 1969. Occludent orders in IE. *Linguistics* 54.86-112.

Mey, J.L. 1972. See under Bartholomae's law.

Miller, D.G. 1974. Some problems in formulating aspiration and deaspiration rules in Ancient Greek. *Glossa* 8.211-32.

——————, 1977a. Some theoretical and typological implications of an IE root structure constraint. *JIES* 5.31-40.

——————, 1977b. Was Grassmann's law reordered in Greek? *KZ* 91.131-58.

Nyman, M. 1981. Paradigms and transderivational constraints. *JL* 17.231-46.

Phelps, E. 1975. Sanskrit diaspirates. *LI* 6.447-64.

——————, & Brame, M. 1973. On local ordering of rules in Sanskrit. *LI* 4.387-400.

Prokosch, E. 1939. *A comparative Germanic grammar.* Philadelphia & Baltimore: Linguistic Socy. of America.

Raumer, R. von. 1837. *Die Aspiration und die Lautverschiebung: Eine sprachgeschichtliche Untersuchung.* Leipzig: F.A. Brockhaus. (Repr. Hildesheim: Gerstenberg, 1972.)

de Reuse, W.J. 1981. Grassmann's law in Ofo. *IJAL* 47.243-44.

Ruijgh, C.J. 1967. *Etudes sur la grammaire et le vocabulaire du grec mycénien.* Amsterdam: Hakkert.

Sag, I.A. 1974. The Grassmann's law ordering pseudoparadox. *LI* 5.591-607.

——————, 1975. Grassmann's law: Unsafe at any speed. Paper to Ling. Socy. of America meeting, December 1975. Mimeo.

——————, 1976. Pseudosolutions to the pseudoparadox: Sanskrit diaspirates revisited. *LI* 7.609-22.

Schindler, J. 1976. Diachronic and synchronic remarks on Bartholomae's and Grassmann's laws. *LI* 7.622-37.

Schwyzer, E. 1939. *Griechische Grammatik.* I:2. Munich: Beck.

Slings, S.R. 1979. ΑΠΑΙΠΠΕΝΑ ΓΕΝΗΩ: Some problems in Lesbian grammar. *Mn* 32.243-67.

Sommerstein, A.H. 1973. *The sound pattern of Ancient Greek.* (Philological Society, Public. 23.) Oxford: Blackwell.

Stemberger, J.P. 1980. Another look at Grassmann's law. *Glossa* 14.113-35.

Vennemann, T. 1979. Grassmann's law, Bartholomae's law, and linguistic methodology. *Fs Penzl,* 557-84.

Whitney, W.D. 1879. *A Sanskrit grammar.* Leipzig: Breitkopf & Härtel. (2nd rev. ed., Boston: Ginn, 1889.) (12th unchanged ed., Cambridge, Mass.: Harvard Univ. Press, 1972.)

Winter, W. 1952. An Indo-European prefix *ṇ 'together with'. *Lg* 28.186-91.

Wyatt, W.F., Jr. 1976. Early Greek /y/ and Grassmann's law. *Glotta* 54.1-11.

Zipf, G.K. 1936. *The psycho-biology of language: An introduction to dynamic philology.* London: Routledge; Cambridge, Mass.: MIT Press. (Repr. Bloomington: Indiana Univ. Press. 1965.)

Zwicky, A.M. 1965. *Topics in Sanskrit phonology*. Diss. Cambridge, Mass.: Mass.-Inst. of Technology.

GRIMM'S LAW

"If non-specialists know anything about historical linguistics, it is Grimm's law" (Lehmann 1967:46). Perhaps, then, nobody will consult this entry; yet again it may be the likeliest site for a test-probe. Sheer familiarity limits obligations: here, to providing a respectably sized bibliography, with no more than an introductory aid to its digestion.

In the simplest possible terms using only one (dental) positional set of consonantal segments, traditionally defined and referring to the First Sound Shift alone), a triple set of reflex equations as between PIE and Germanic demonstrates the law's provisions:

$$/C \left\{ \begin{array}{l} +\text{voi} \\ +\text{asp} \end{array} \right\} / \quad \text{e.g. Skt. } \textit{madhya-} \sim \text{Goth. } \textit{midjis} \quad \text{(aspiration goes)}$$

$$/C \left\{ \begin{array}{l} +\text{voi} \\ -\text{asp} \end{array} \right\} / \quad \text{e.g. Skt. } \textit{daśa-} \sim \text{Goth. } \textit{taíhun} \quad \text{(voicing goes)}$$

$$/C \left\{ \begin{array}{l} -\text{voi} \\ -\text{asp} \end{array} \right\} / \quad \text{e.g. Skt. } \textit{traya-} \sim \text{Goth. } \textit{þreis} \quad \text{(occlusion is diminished and release-period extended)}$$

Accept this triad, apply it also to labials, velars and 'labiovelars', and the Germanic non-strident consonants come neatly into line with your PIE inheritance. What a pity that all is not really so simple.

With reason Rasmus Kristian Rask (1787-1832) is credited with first controlling, certainly in North Germanic history, so many wild discrepancies (as they had seemed): cf. Collitz (1926:174ff.) and Piebenga (1971). Rask's prize essay of 1818 noted the crucial sound correspondences (even those affected by Verner's law) between 'Thracian' (meaning PIE) and 'Gothic' (meaning pre-Germanic). Rask thought that PIE /b/ remained inviolate, which is understandable; Jakob Bredsdorff (1790-1841) set that to rights (1821:21-22). Grammar is wisely seen as the key to genetic relations; and the absence of Indic evidence, despite Bopp's work on Sanskrit conjugations having appeared in 1816, did little damage.

But the role of Jacob Ludwig Karl Grimm (1785-1863) cannot be despised. He was at first a friendly correspondent of Rask's, later estranged; there is a wealth of biography on him and his brother, at least in German sources. He read Rask's study when most of his own German grammar was in the press (1819), realised its implications and was in time to say so in his own preface, and re-wrote relevant parts for a re-edition of 1822 (I 580-92). Pedersen (*PedS* 261) saw no progress there over Rask's results, and less insight. Collitz judged better, recognizing Grimm's wider demonstration (a) that whatever the articulatory position of the consonant, the feature-shift is identical, and (b) that the shifts are interrelated and system-preserving. 'Grimm's law' is a valid title. Thomsen did not doubt it in 1902; Benware did not in 1974. Grimm's own milder term (*Lautverschiebung*), and his reservations as to its incidence (". . . erfolgt in der masse, thut sich aber im einzelnen niemahls rein ab", 1822:590) no longer con-strain scholars, except perhaps in his own language. Graver doubts are cur-rently surfacing and the law's whole existence is under threat; but at least for the present one may accept the name.

For succinctness, let a series of questions and answers steer the commentary.

(1) *What are the special features of Grimm's own presentation?*

   (i)   Phonetic niceties are ignored (he speaks of 'letters') in favour of a systemic exploration. Three positional types of consonant are recognized. As to the distinguishing articulatory co-features, the 'aspirate' input is in fact of the Greek voiceless series, misinter-preted somewhat as spirants. Whence a cycle of shifts or *Kreislauf* suggested itself (so says Streitberg 1896:104, §114).

   (ii)   The nine rules are really statements of correpondences, but they are used as a 'touchstone' (*prüfstein*, 589) – which implies the testing of a law.

   (iii)   High German is marked by a secondary shift which is an exact match of the first.

   (iv)   Fuzziness is freely admitted. Its causes are given as (a) loaning, (b) analogical reshaping, (c) unpredictable segment variations in PIE roots, and (d) uneven diffusion of change (although on the two latter counts his examples are inapposite).

(2) *Can the Rask-Grimm data be digested raw?*

No. At least four gross modifications must precede progress on causation, on timing or on the actual course of events:

   (i)   Some false input be excised, where this comes from the working of Grassmann's law – so Grassmann himself (1863) saw, as did

Verner (1876). As it happens, Grimm's own 1822 data are clean.

(ii)   The High German forms must be handled separately. General explanations, covering both the First and Second Sound Shifts (hereafter, '1LV' and '2LV'), should not obscure the difference of nature and time; Fourquet and others sometimes disregard this point.

(iii) The process known as Verner's law must, conversely, be embodied as a coda into '1LV'.

(iv)   Some qualified input segments occur in sheltering environments and do not shift. They impose a greater delicacy on the formulation.

Bynon (1977:83) has a neat diagram which honours points (iii) and (iv). Evidential etyma abound in all the grammars; Priebsch & Collinson (1962:59-70) is perhaps still the handiest source in English (but ignores (ii) above). See also Keller (1978, chap.3); and Russ (1978:31-38).

'2LV'(*die zweite oder (hoch)deutsche Lautverschiebung*) moves in essence thus:

$$(a) \quad \text{Gmc. } p \; > \; \text{HG} \left\{ \begin{array}{l} f \; / \; \left\{ \begin{array}{l} V- \\ -\#\,(\#) \end{array} \right\} \\ pf \text{ elsewhere} \end{array} \right.$$

$$" \quad t \; > \; " \left\{ \begin{array}{l} s \; / \; \left\{ \begin{array}{l} V- \\ -\#\,(\#) \end{array} \right\} \\ ts \text{ elsewhere} \end{array} \right.$$

$$" \quad k \; > \; " \left\{ \begin{array}{l} [x,\varsigma] \; / \; \left\{ \begin{array}{l} V- \\ -\#\,(\#) \end{array} \right\} \\ [\widehat{kx}] > k \text{ elsewhere} \end{array} \right.$$

(Fourquet requires an interim stage (e.g., $p > p^h > (p)f$) – but so he also does for '1LV'. No doubt '$t>s$' obscures some intermediate value (cf. Goth. *itan*, OHG *ezzun*, NHG *essen*, when -*zz*- cannot with safety be phonetically described). And [$\widehat{kx}$] rests on early Upper German spellings like *khorn*. Graphic gemination and degemination disturb the picture: so $p > f > ff$ (*offen* etc.), but $pp > ppf > pf$ (hence medial *Apfel, schöpfen* etc.), with freshly realized oppositions.) The dentals move soonest and over the widest area, geographically and lexically; the labials come second in this, and the velars are the most sluggish. Many other complexities are possible: for instance, Simmler (1981:730ff.) has $p > p$ (Otfrid), f (Alemannic), pf or p^h elsewhere.

(b)   further dental shiftings:

Gmc. þ   > HG (đ >) d

 "   d   > " t

— with perhaps a like devoicing (or move to fortis) in labials in Old Bavarian *hapen*, in velars in Upper German *focal*. The High German main frontier (the Benrath Line) is clear enough; the incidence otherwise is very spotty and obscured by spelling (so Prokosch 1939:78ff.). Heller (1973) puts (a) and (b) in a different relation and decides that '2LV' is really two separate shifts.

A recent major issue has been the direction of spread. The obvious idea (Braune's for example) is that it moved from south to north, petering out. But South Germany and North Switzerland were scarcely centres of influences at the right time; and Prokosch (1939:79ff.) argued conversely for a partly southward shift, interrupted by the Roman *limes*. Becker (1967) and King (1969:92) trusted to the generative dictum that the generality of a linguistic rule increases as the rule spreads its domain: hence the more affected southern dialects are the final receivers of the HG consonantism, if it is seen as a set of revised generating rules. Simmler (1981:730-69) agrees; Vennemann (1972) and others defend the old view; Beade (1974:66) is agnostic. Moulton (1969) attempts the hard task of establishing the true OHG system.

(3) *Are the traditional components of '1LV' independent or interdependent? If the latter, do they move in series or in parallel?*

Independence seems never to have won serious adherents; this is the big difference between 1LV and 2LV. Given interdependence, scholars then divide:

(a) for serial movement:

   (i)   Many have employed a general principle of articulation, but not always the same one. The two relevant forces are pressures of airflow and degree of muscular tension. Prokosch, with Nordmeyer's approval (1936), evolved a complex theory between 1912 and 1938 (finally expressed at 1939:50ff.). It is argued that a constriction of the vocal cords, or buccal occlusion, prompts a reactive release of breath; but partial constriction in the mouth (spirant release) conversely produces checking, first in the glottis and then in the mouth. Two tendencies must then oppose each other, and the whole process of checking and releasing engenders its own succession to create a *Kreislauf*: so $t > þ > đ > d > t$ (one notes that the medial stop of NHG *Vater* already started life as /t/ in PIE). This concept of a cyclic shifting has constantly recurred in connection with Grimm's formulation; it is found as early as Bredsdorff (1821). Relevant texts are:

- Twaddell (1939): (see below).
- Kurath (1940): defends Prokosch against the physiological doubts of Strong and Willey.
- Zabrocki (1951): surmises that there is a 'double-peak' of air pressure, in initial syllable and at point of stress.
- Galton (1954): sees the shift as the *cause* of a surplus of expiration, which in turn leads to expiratory accent, compensated by a further reduction in muscular activity (see below).
- Weinstock (1968): offers a part-serial, part-parallel interpretation.

and the best general critique of the whole articulatory school of thought, to the 1940s, is in Abrahams, (1949:78ff.).

(ii) Or a phonological principle is invoked: that the equilibrium of the system — usually defined in terms of opposition of features — positively reasserts itself after every shift. This in turn entails that every readjustment is to some degree parochial, and causes inefficiency elsewhere. Such is in essence the approach of Voyles (1967), although his mechanism is of ordered rules (cf. Halle 1962); of Weinstock (1968), who distinguishes redundant features (unstable) from central features (conservative); of Lakoff (1968), who notes restructuring; and of Lass (1974), who works with a design strategy aimed at keeping an efficient system while removing one awkward type of segment. 'Chains' and 'rings' are the metaphors of system shifting: Fox (1976, quoting Martinet, 1955 ch.2) has much in general to say about them; and so (on Grimm's law) has Bynon (1977:83-86).

(b) for parallel shifting:

Here the big name is Jean Fourquet. For him the stop consonant system shifted by stages but as a whole, and its crucial oppositions were always undisturbed. (It is quite misleading to call this 'simultaneous' change; it is 'phonemic' and not coincidental.) Fourquet (1948) — probably the single most influential study of Grimm's law — contends that:

(i) IE plosive evolution differs as between two areas. The 'bharāmi' area, including Germanic, inherits /p,b,b^h/ etc.; the 'pherō' area (Hellenic and Italic) has /p,b,p^h/ etc. Of the first group Armenian and Germanic initially shift to /p^h,p,B/ etc. — where 'B' etc. is a notational device to avoid precise diagnosis as to voice or lenition.

(ii)   '1LV' is a second step. It represents a slackening of muscular effort (where Grimm believed in increasing effort), as the expression of Germanic 'muth und stoltz' — and for a review of the similar range of suggestions of ethnological or climatic causation, see Abrahams 1949 (78ff.)). The output of '1LV' is /f, p, b̵/ etc.; and Verner's law is its coda.

(iii)   '2LV' is a third step, and gives OHG. Its initial output is the new labial series /f,p^h,p/ — so that it partly echoes the change in (i). Secondary readjustments spirantize /p^h/, assibilate /t/, and sometimes diminish the occlusion of /k/.

(iv)   The core concept is that prehistorically an opposition of voice gives way to one of aspiration (/p,b/ > /p^h,p/) and vice-versa //b,b^h/ > /p,b/): so 1948, 1954. Verner's law further diminishes the distinctive role of voice (1963). (Against which Abrahams [1949:217] offers a mixed motivation: that the phonetic cause is a separation of the vocal cords by increased air-pressure (voiceless stops then being unstable, anyway, in Germanic); and the phonological motive is the enhancement of aspiration as a distinctive feature; Danish being the exemplar.) Cf. Boer (1924); Waterman (1963).

Systemzwang moved Kuryłowicz also (1973:68-69); '1LV' and Verner's law are for him not four phases of phonetic shift, however, but just two 'phonemic' mergers. Most recently, Vennemann (forthcoming) pleads the case for seeing '1LV' and '2LV' as parallel paths of evolution (the 'bifurcation' theory), with Verner's an early event.

(4) *Is word-accent responsible for '1LV'?*

Hirt thought so (e.g., 1931:79ff.), and deduced the accent itself from a substrate source. Twaddell (in a serialist shift-schedule) listed the fixation of stress on root syllable as an intervening stage, the third of six stages of 1LV, after Verner's law and before the de-aspiration of /b^h/etc. Forchhammer started the notion which converted Boer and (somewhat) Prokosch and finally Abrahams, namely that air pressure was the physical cause of it all; but for him this led to an 'accent of intensity' which then had the effect of lessening muscular tension — on which Galton has written, but subtly differently (1954; see above: Zabrocki 1951 also needs a position of accent). Again, '1LV' and '2LV' are differentiated by Van Coetsem, Hendricks & McCormick (1981) as having occurred, respectively, in a 'prominence-independent' (pitch) and a 'prominence-dependent' (stress) language (where segment and accent are closely linked).

(5) *Might it not all be an interplay of relative segment 'strengths'?*

This is the 'natural phonology' treatment; an explanation of it is given in Appendix I B, under 'Grammont's laws'. (Zabrocki 1951 is relevant but of a more phonetic cast.) The interpretation of '1LV' as a consistent, across-the-board, process of 'strengthening' is partly based on, and partly helps to base, one or other of the suggested hierarchies (or groups of interrelated hierarchies) of that theory.

(6) *Can sense be talked on chronology?*

'2LV' probably dates to AD 500-700. Absolute chronology for '1LV' has ranged from about 500 BC (Fourquet) to even the ninth century after Christ (Rosenfeld). An early date based on archaeology, in fact the Negau helmet, is denied by Pisani (1959, quoting his work of 1953) by recourse to onomastics. (Pisani holds that different dialectal forms of Germanic names in the text of Tacitus (*Annals* 2. 11,62) indicate incomplete reshifting of consonants by AD 16-19 — as if proper nouns were trustworthy in such matters.) Prokosch (1939: 56) is no doubt wise to use the larger bracket of the whole Germanic migration period ranging vaguely from 'several centuries BC' to about AD 500.

Subtler are the essays on relative timing. Twaddell and Prokosch set out the whole array of shifts in numbered stages; cf. Jung (1956). Verner's law is merely a comparatively late chapter, usually set inside '1LV' (cf.Voyles 1967.642ff.) Halle (1962) uses the theorems of generative (rules) phonology to set Verner's edict after Grimm's; but King (1969:186-87) challenges this conservative finding (as possibly secondary and derived by rules-reordering). Chen (1976:211ff.) hesitates between (a) regarding them as a single (composite) law, by which forms are affected whenever they satisfy input requirements (cf. Davidsen-Nielsen 1976 on '1LV' 'false input'); or (b) defining Grimm's law as a short-lived historical event which happened within the longer life-span of Verner's.

(7) *Can Grimm's law as we know it survive the recent radical revision of the PIE obstruent system?* (See Appendix II)

Briefly, no. From the first direct attack (by Emonds 1972) it has been in jeopardy. An ejective series /p'. t', k'$^{(w)}$ / is the widely agreed true source of each of the reflexes earlier cited as /*b,d,g$^{(w)}$/. If it is so, while other languages

replaced glottal ejection by vocal cord movement Germanic will have done much
less: merely sensibly reverted to a pulmonary air stream for this segment-type
when set in the context of an otherwise entirely subglottal source of breath.
(Emonds thought Germanic actually did nothing at all – that was to go too far,
as most revisionists now think.) The new version of b^h' etc. is less uniform;
but in the Gamkrelidze-Ivanov-Hopper theory Germanic /b/ etc. represent an
aspirate-free variant (or, in other words, a variant without concomitant inter-
ruption of voicing), assigned in an 'allophonic' situation, which has then been
generalized. There is no shift, nor anything but a loss of 'glottalic' nature in
Germanic /p/ etc.; only the spirants show change. Either way, Germanic is very
conservative (if not, as Emonds thought, partly reversive).

It is true, as noted above, that the PIE 'voiceless' series /p,t,k,k^w/ changes to
a spirant realization with context-sensitive voicing and subsequent spotty despirantizing. But this is to be handled by a more comprehensive form of Verner's
law, now an independent chapter of local IE realization, as '2LV' must also be.
(Whether voicing or lenition is really involved may be doubtful, as with Notker's
law.) But Grimm's law as such vanishes: so judges, for instance, Normier (1977).

Still, enough scholarship has been invested in it for Hopper's remark (1981:
137: see Appendix II) to be apt; that Grimm's law "will not be ceded without
a struggle". Davenport & Staun (1983:220-21), for instance, go no further
than questioning the nature of 'dh' etc. And the onus is fairly evenly on both
the traditionalists to show that there is something to defend and the radicals to
decide on the single 'true' form of PIE consonantism (and to demonstrate its
existence somewhere in the world). An ocean of ink takes time to evaporate;
and empirical typology is not the speediest of trades. Hence it has been worth
while writing even this brief sketch of a famous chapter of Indo-European
scholarship. It just may have been an obituary.

REFERENCES

This list does not pretend to be exhaustive, quite apart from the process by
which old theories change and new emerge. Appendix I B (under 'Grammont's
laws') contains material on 'phonological strength'; and Appendix II is devoted
to the new PIE consonantism which in effect destroys Grimm's law. What follow are simply major discussions and suggestive applications; for precursors to
Rask and Grimm consult Agrell (1955).

Abrahams, H. 1949. *Etudes phonétiques sur les tendances evolutives des occlusives germaniques.* Aarhus, Univ. Press.

Agrell, J. 1955. Studier i den äldre språkjämforelsens allmänna och svenska historia fram till 1827. Uppsala, Univ. Årsskrift, 13. Lundquist; Wiesbaden: Harrassowitz (German summary, 204-211).

Back, M. 1979. See on Appendix II.

Barrack, C.M. 1978. The High German consonant shift: Monogenetic or polygenetic? *Lingua* 44.1-48.

Beade, P. 1974. Diffusion, generalization, and the High German sound shift. In *HL(A&J)* 2.61-67.

Becker, D.A. 1967. *Generative phonology and dialect study.* Diss. Austin: Univ. of Texas.

Benware, W.A. 1974. *The study of Indo-European vocalism in the nineteenth century. SiHol* 3. (2nd corrected ed., 1984.)

Boer, R.C. 1924. *Oergermaansch Handboek.* 2nd ed., Haarlem: Tjeenk, Willink & Zoon. (1st ed., 1918.)

Braune, W. 1874. Zur Kenntnis des frankischen und hochdeutschen Lautverschiebung. *PBB* 1.1-56.

————, 1975. *Althochdeutsche Grammatik.* 13th ed., prepared by Walter Mitzka. Tübingen: Niemeyer. (1st ed. 1886.)

Bredsdorff, J.H. 1821. *Om Aarsagerne til Sprogenes Forandringer.* Roskilde. (New ed. by Vilhelm Thomsen, Copenhagen: Gyldendalske Boghandel, 1886; repr. Copenhagen: Levin & Munksgaard, 1933. English translation, with introd., by H. Andersen, *HL* 9.1-41 (1982).

Brinkmann, H. 1941. Der lautliche Vorgang der germanischen und der hochdeutschen Lautverschiebungen. *AVP* 5.10-20.

Bugge, E.S. 1887. Etymologische Studien über germanische Lautverschiebung. *PBB* 12.399-430.

————, 1888. (contin. of above) *PBB* 13.167-87.

Bynon, T. 1977. *Historical Linguistics.* Cambridge, Univ. Press.

Chen, M.Y. 1976. Relative chronology: Three methods of reconstruction. *JL* 12.209-58.

Collitz, H. 1926. A century of Grimm's law. *Lg* 2.174-83.

D'Alquen, R.J.E. 1973. The Germanic sound-shift and Verner's law: a synthesis. *GL* 13.79-89.

Davenport, M. & Staun, J. 1983. Dependency phonology and the First Germanic consonant shift. *FoLH* 4.219-45.

Davidsen-Nielsen, N. 1976. A theory of the exceptions to the Germanic and

High German sound shifts. *AL(Haf)* 16.45-56.

Davies, A.M. 1975. Language classification. *CTL* 13.605-716.

Delbrück, B. 1869. Die deutsche Lautverschiebung. *ZDP* 1.1-24; 136-56.

Douse, T. le M. 1876. *Grimm's law: a study, or hints towards an explanation of the so-called "Lautverschiebung"; to which are added some remarks on the primitive Indo-European k and several appendices.* London: Trübner.

Emonds, J. 1972. A re-formulation of Grimm's law. *Contributions to generative phonology*, ed. by Michael K. Brame. 108-22. Austin: Univ. of Texas Press.

Feist, S. 1910. Die germanische und die hochdeutsche Lautverschiebung sprachlich und ethnographisch betrachtet. *PBB* 36.307-54. (Also Noch einmal. . . , *PBB* 37.112-21[1911].)

Foley, J.A. 1970, 1977. See on Appendix I A (pp. 245-46). (But see also Assimilation of phonological strength in Germanic, *Fs Halle*, 51-58 [1973].)

Fourquet, J.P. 1948. *Les mutations consonantiques du germanique: Essai de position des problèmes.* Paris: Les Belles Lettres. (For curious nature of place and form of this publication, see Moulton 1950.)

——————, 1954. Die Nachwirkungen der ersten und der zweiten Lautverschiebungen. *ZMf* 22.1-32; 193-98. (Repr. in Fourquet 1979:399-437.)

——————, 1959. Genezis sistemy soglasnix v armjanskom jazyke. *VJa* 1959. 6.68-77 (Russian transl. by M.M. Makovskij; See under Fourquet 1979.)

——————, 1963. Einige unklare Punkte der deutschen Lautgeschichte in phonologischer Sicht. *Fs Maurer*, 84-90. (Repr. Fourquet 1979:540-46.)

——————, 1979. *Recueil d'études.* Ed. by D. Buschinger and J-P. Vernon. Paris: Champion. (Includes L'évolution du consonantisme en Armenien et en Germanique, 438-49 = enlarged version of 1959.)

Fox, A. 1976. Problems with phonological chains. *JL* 12.289-320.

Fullerton, G.L. 1974. The development of obstruents in four Germanic dialects. *Linguistics* 130.71-82.

——————, 1975. Grimm's law and the West Germanic 2 sing. verb ending -*s*. *Linguistics* 145.87-102.

Galton, H. 1954. Sound shifts and diphthongization in Germanic. *JEGP* 53.585-600.

Gamkrelidze, T.V. & Ivanov, V.V. 1972ff. See on Appendix II.

Gartner, T. 1910. Zu den zwei Lautverschiebungen. *PBB* 36.562-64.

Grassmann, H. 1863. Über die aspiration und ihr gleichzeitiges vorhandensein im an- und auslaute der wurzeln. *KZ* 12.81-138. (Partial English translation in Lehmann 1967.112-31.)

Grimm, J. 1822(-37). *Deutsche Grammatik* I-IV 2nd ed. Göttingen; Dieterich. (1st ed. 1819; repr. Hildesheim; Olms, 1967). See esp. I 584-92. (Transl. of relevant passages in Lehmann 1967.48-59.)

Güntert, H. 1927. Über die Ursache der germanischen Lautverschiebung. *WS* 10. 1-22.

Guxman, M.M. et al 1972. *Sravitel'naja grammatika germanskij jazykov.* Moscow; AN SSSR.

Halle, M. 1962. Phonology in generative grammar. *Word* 18.54-72.

Hammerich, L.L. 1955. Die Germanische und die hochdeutsche Lautverschiebung. *PBB(T)* 77.1-29; 165-203.

Heinertz, N.O. 1925. *Eine Lautverschiebungstheorie.* Lund: Blom.

Heller, L.G. 1973. The second Germanic consonant shifts: A typological parametric view. *FoL* 6.305-13.

Hirt, H. 1931. *Handbuch des Urgermanischen.* Heidelberg: Winter.

Hopper, P.J. 1973.ff. See on Appendix II.

Holtzmann, A. 1870. *Altdeutsche Grammatik.* Leipzig: Bockhaus.

Jellinek, M.H. 1891. Germanisch *g* und die Lautverschiebung. *PBB* 15.268-97.

Jung, E. 1956. Chronologie relative des faits phonétiques en germanique commun. *EG* 11.294-320.

Karsten, T.E. 1930. Der Gotenname und die germanische Lautverschiebung. *ZDAL* 67.253-56.

Keller, R.E. 1978. *The German Language.* London: Faber & Faber.

King, R.D. 1969. *Historical linguistics and generative grammar.* Englewood Cliffs, N.J.: Prentice-Hall.

Kiparsky, P. 1971. *Phonological change.* Bloomington; Indiana Univ. Ling. Club. (Diss., Mass. Inst. of Technology 1965.)

Kluge, F. 1884. Die germanische Consonantendehnung. *PBB* 9.149-86.

—————, 1913. *Urgermanisch.* 3rd ed. Strassburg; Trübner. (1st ed., 1909.) (= Paul's *Grundriss*, 2.)

Krahe, H. 1959. Eigennamen und germanische Lautverschiebung. *Mem. Mossé,* 225-30.

Kräuter, J.F. 1877. *Zur Lautverschiebung.* Strassburg; Trübner.

Kretschmer, P. 1931. Die Urgeschichte der Germanen und die germanische Lautverschiebung. *WPZ* 19.269-80.

Kuhn, H. 1961. Anlautend *p-* im Germanischen. *Zmf* 28.1-31.

—————, 1970. Fremdes *t-* Anlaut im Germanischen. *Mem. Foerste,* 34-52.

Kurath, H. 1940. Prokosch's theory of the Germanic and the High German consonant shift: A reply. *JEGP* 39.376-82. (See Strong & Willey 1940.)

Kuryłowicz, J. 1973. Internal Reconstruction. *CTL* 11.63-92.

Lakoff, G. 1968. Phonological restructuring and Grimm's law. *Fs Jakobson* (3). 168-79.

Lass, R. 1974. Strategic design as the motivation for a sound shift: The rationale of Grimm's law. *AL(Haf)* 15. 51-66.

Lehmann, W.P. 1963. Some phonological observations based on examination of the Germanic consonant shift. *MDU* 60.229-35.

——. 1967. *A reader in nineteenth century historical Indo-European linguistics.* Bloomington: Indiana Univ. Press.

Lottner, C. 1862. Ausnahmen der ersten Lautverschiebung. *KZ* 11.161-205. (Written 1860: partial transl. in Lehmann 1967.98-108.)

Magnusson, W.L. 1969. Occludent orders in IE. *Linguistics* 54.86-112.

Markey, T.L., Kyes, R.L., & Roberge, P.T. 1977,. *Germanic and its dialects: A grammar of Proto-Germanic.* Vol. III: Bibliography and indices. Amsterdam: Benjamins.

Martinet, A. 1955. *Économie des changements phonétiques.* Berne: Francke. (3nd. ed., 1970.)

Meyer-Benfey, H. 1901. Über den Ursprung der germanischen Lautverschiebung. *ZDA* 45.101-28.

Moser, H. 1954. Zu den beiden Lautverschiebungen und ihrer methodischen Behandlung. *DU* 6:4.56-81.

Moulton, W.G. 1950. Review of Fourquet 1948. *JEGP* 49.98-100.

——, 1954. The stops and spirants of early Germanic. *Lg* 30.1-42.

——, 1969. The consonant system of Old High German. *Fs Fourquet*, 247-59.

——, 1972. The proto-Germanic non-syllabics (consonants). In Van Coetsem & Kufner 1972.141-73 (Esp. 164-65.)

Nordmeyer, G. 1936. Lautverschiebungserklärungen. *JEGP* 35.482-95.

Noreen, A. 1894. *Abriss der urgermanischen Lautlehre.* Strassburg: Trübner.

Normier, M. 1977. See on Appendix II.

Paul, H. 1874. Zur Lautverschiebung. *PBB* 1.147-201.

——, 1900-9. *Grundriss der germanischen Philologie*, vols. 1-3. Strassburg; Trübner. (2nd ed., 1913.)

Piebenga, G.A. 1971. *Een studie over het werk van Rasmus Rask, in het bijzonder over zijn "Frisisk sproglaere".* Ljouwert (Leeuwarden); Frisian Acad.

Pisani, V. 1959. Nachträgliches zur Chronologie der germanischen Lautverschiebung. *Mem. Mossé* 379-86.

Pokorny, J. 1929. Keltische Lehnwörter und die germanische Lautverschiebung.

WS 12.303-15.

Priebsch, R. & Collinson, W.E. 1962. *The German language*. 5th ed. London: Faber and Faber/Paris: les Belles Lettres. (1st. ed., 1934.)

Prokosch, E. 1912. Forchhammers Akzenttheorie und die germanische Lautverschiebung. *JEGP* 11.1-9.

—————, 1917. Die deutsche Lautverschiebung und die Völkerwanderung. *JEGP* 16.1-26.

—————, 1922. Lautverschiebung und Lenierung. *JEGP* 21.119-26.

—————, 1933. *An outline of German historical grammar*. New York & Oxford: Oxford Univ. Press.

—————, 1918/9. Die indogermanischen "Media aspiraten". *MPh* 15.621-28; 16.99-112, 325-36, 543-52.

—————, 1939. *A comparative Germanic grammar*. Philadelphia & Baltimore: Ling. Socy. of America.

Rask, R.K. 1818. *Undersogelse om det gamle Nordiske eller Islandske Sprogs Oprindelse*. Copenhagen: Gyldendalske (Danske Videnskabers Selskab). Also in *Ausgewählte Abhandlungen*, ed. by L. Hjelmslev, I; Copenhagen: Levin & Munksgaard, 1932. (Selection in English transl. in Lehmann 1967:31-37.)

Russ, C.V.J. 1978. *Historical Germanic phonology and morphology*. Oxford: Clarendon Press.

Russer, W.S. 1931. *De germaansche klankverschuiving: Een hoofdstuk uit de geschiedenis der germaansche taalaeltenschap*. Haarlem: Tjeenk, Willink & Zoon.

Schrodt, R. 1973. *Die germanische Lautverschiebung und ihre Stelle im Kreise der indogermanischen Sprachen*. Vienna: Germanistisches Institut.

Simmler, F. 1981. *Graphematisch-phonematische Studien zum althochdeutschen Konsonantismus*. Heidelberg: Winter.

Sommerstein, A.H. 1977. See on Appendix II.

Steblin-Kamenskij, M.I. 1963. Some remarks on the mechanism of the Germanic consonant shifts. *SL* 17.77-86.

Stockwell, R.P. & Macaulay, R.K.S., ed. 1972. *Linguistic change and generative theory*. Essays from the UCLA Conference on historical linguistics in the perspective of transformational theory, 1969. Bloomington: Indiana Univ. Press.

Streitberg, W. 1896. *Urgermanische Grammatik*. Heidelberg: Winter. (Repr., 1934.)

Strong L.H. & Willey, N.L. 1940. Dynamic consonantal permutation. *JEGP* 39. 1-12. (See Kurath 1940).

Thomsen, V.L.P. 1902. *Sprogvidenskabernes Historie: En kortfaltet Fremstilling* Copenhagen: (German transl. by Hans Pollak, Halle/Saale: Niemeyer, 1927.)

Twaddell, W.F. 1939. The inner chronology of the Germanic consonant shifts. *JEGP* 38.337-59.

Van Coetsem, J. 1972. The Germanic consonant shift: Compensatory processes in language. *Lingua* 30.302-15.

—————, & Kufner, H.L., ed. 1972. *Toward a grammar of Proto-Germanic.* Tübingen; Niemeyer.

—————, Hendricks, R. & McCormick, S. 1981. Accent typology and sound change. *Lingua* 53.295-315.

Velten, H.W. 1932. A note on the sound shifts. *GR* 7.76-80.

—————, 1944. The order of the pre-Germanic consonant changes. *JEGP* 43.42-48.

Vennemann, T. 1968. *German phonology.* Diss. Los Angeles: UCLA.

—————, 1972. Sound change and markedness theory: On the history of the German consonant system. In Stockwell & Macaulay 1972: 230-74.

—————, forthcoming in *PBB(T)* 106. (1984). Hochgermanisch und Niedergermanisch.

Verner, K.A. 1876. Eine ausnahme der ersten lautverschiebung. *KZ* 23.97-130. (Partial English transl. in Lehmann 1967:134-63.)

Voyles, J.B. 1967. Simplicity, ordered rules, and the First Sound Shift. *Lg* 43.636-60.

—————, 1981. *Gothic, Germanic, and North-West Germanic.* (*ZDL Beiheft*, 39.) Wiesbaden: Steiner.

Waterman, J.T. 1963. The Germanic consonant shift and the theories of J. Fourquet: A critique. *GQ* 36.165-70.

Weinstock, J. 1968. Grimm's law in distinctive features. *Lg* 44.224-29.

Wilmanns, W. 1911. *Deutsche Grammatik* vol.I, 3rd ed., Strassburg: Trübner. (1st ed., 1893.)

Zabrocki, L. 1951. *Usilnienie i lenicja w językach indo-europjskich i w ugrofińskim.* [Strengthening and weakening in the IE languages and in Finno-Ugric.] Posnań: Poznańskie Towarzystwo Przyjaciół Nauk (Prace Komisji filologicznej, 13.3.)

Zipf, G.K. 1929ff. See in Appendix I B, under 'Zipf's principle(s)'.

HARTMANN'S LAW*

Writing of Russian word-accent, Morris Halle (1973:337) presents a succinct version of what "students of Slavic accentology. . . know as Hartmann's law". The law, reports Halle, makes the stress of a class of derived adjectives sensitive to the accentual category of the 'stem' (that is, of the source noun). First, if the nominal stem has stress, and is in Halle's terms 'acute', the accent remains so placed in the adjective: thus *goróxovyj, lúkovyj*. Secondly, if the original stem is stressless, but has undergone an oxytonizing rule (Halle 1973:317) – as *bobjór* – the adjective's accent is on the formative suffix: *bobróvyj*; cf. *dvoróvyj*. If, thirdly, an unstressed nominal stem is not made oxytone, then the accent is on the adjective's desinence: *gorodovój, beregovój*. The second and third types are (using Saussure's label) 'metatonic'; but 'intonation' as it is usually understood – see Appendix III – is not used by Halle.

These types do indeed figure in Hartmann's own treatise (1936), which establishes the triple relationship. Using his paragraph and sub-group notation, one may refer to them thus:

Hartmann's CI	=	Halle's third type
" CII	=	" first type
" CIII	=	" second type

Red'kin (1964:55) lists the Hartmannian reflexes in the order which Halle adopts.

These adjectives are, however, all derived from masculine nouns, and they relate respectively to nouns with 'falling intonation' (CI), 'rising intonation' (CII), and end-stress (CIII). Hartmann's own thesis is that Russian stress, in this instance at least, reflects proto-Slavic 'intonation' (cf. Saussure 1894:426). The relevant class of adjectives (*Beziehungsadjektiva*) is exemplified by *lesnýje (plody)*, "(fruits) of the forest"; that is, these are the lexically attributive epithets, semantically glossed as 'connected with X'. Some derive from feminine nouns; but there the division is into (DI) those whose source is barytone, and

* See Appendix III

(DII) those whose source is oxytone – this term having its traditional rather than Hallean sense. But the group DII has a double set of reflexes: so *zímnij* and *zimovój* (from *zimá*); or Russ. *nožnój* but S.Cr. *nòzni* (from, e.g., Russ. *nogá*; cf. Lith. *nagà*). The upshot is that Hartmann's findings are codified into a 'law' by later users only in respect of his 'masculine' C group. (Yet DI is regular enough, like CII: *gríva* → *grívnyj* is typical.) The law does not apply to Baltic.

Halle (1973:337) reveals that the law has many exceptions (and V. Kiparsky 1962, Red'kin 1964, Coats 1970, and Gimpelevič 1971 are cited as having all discovered their own counter-examples). To give one example in each group, we have for CI *sadóvyj*, for CII *formovój*, for CIII *jazykovój*. Valentin Kiparsky (1962:261ff.) believes, with Unbegaun, that end-stress was generalized when the adjective was (re)nominalized, and even that suffixal stress was characteristic of the names of kinds of wood. Garde accepts the law (at 1976:65-66, 78-79, 432-33) and sees in it a type, which remains even in (the different accent positions of) modern Russian. Thereafter (Garde 1978:389 and n.20) he concentrates on weak or 'non-dominant' adjectival suffixes, and restricts that sort to long-form adjectives, and to 'nouns of family' together with adjectives of 'belonging' in *-ev, -ov* (cf. Gimpelevič 1971). Red'kin (1964), on the other hand, believes the historical path of the law was via the short-form adjectives. Dybo refers to the law (1968:154) in the course of an essay which links accent with word-formation (cf. also Dybo 1981:60).

Hartmann's basic idea of a kind of stress-predetermination is sound enough (and V. Kiparsky [1962] approves). But a less simplicistic version must eventually prevail, if all the phenomena are to be adequately motivated.

REFERENCES[*]

Coats, H.S. 1970. Word stress assignment in a generative grammar of Russian. Diss., Univ. Illinois, Urbana, Ill.

Dybo, V.A. 1968. Akcentologija i slovo-obrazovanie v slavjanskom. In *VIth Int. Cong. of Slavists* (Prague): Russian contributions (fuller version), *Slavjanskoe Jazykoznanije*, 148-224. Moscow: AN SSSR. (Esp. 152-74.)

* Relevant or quoted also are:
Dybo 1981*; Garde 1976*; Saussure 1894*; Stang 1957*
– on which see Appendix III

Garde, P. 1978. Modèle de description de l'accent russe. *BSL* 73.367-98.

Gimpelevič, V.S. 1971. Akcentologičeskie nabljudenija nad prilagatel'nymi s suffiksom '-ov(-ev)'. *Russkij Jazyk v Škole* 1.13-19.

Halle, M. 1973. The accentuation of Russian words. *Lg* 49.312-48.

Hartmann, H. 1936. *Studien über die Betonung der Adjektiva im Russischen.* Veröffentlichungen des Slavistischen Instituts, Univ. Berlin, 16; ed. by Max Vasmer.) Leipzig: Harrassowitz.

Kiparsky, V. 1962. *Der Wortakzent der russischen Schriftsprache.* Heidelberg: Winter.

Red'kin, V.A. 1964. K akcentologičeskomu zakonu Xartmana. *Slavkanskaja i baltijskaja akcentologija (Kratkie soobščenija Instituta Slavjanovedenija),* 41.55-67. Moscow: AN SSSR.

––––––, 1971. *Akcentologija sovremennogo russkogo literaturnogo jazyka.* Moscow: Izdatel'stvo 'Prosveščenije'.

HIRT'S LAW I*

Of the discoveries affecting Balto-Slavic accentuation, this is generally agreed to be among the earliest in incidence. It states that a leftward syllabic shift of word accent occurred under conditions of phonological structure which argue of themselves for a date preceding the split of Baltic and Slavic. Herman Hirt (1865-1936) made his declaration first in 1895 (94, 165-66). It was not the only law about accent, or indeed about left-moving accent, which he offered around that time, but his essay on a similar shift in Greek tribrachic sequences failed to achieve a like respectability. This one, however, refined and revised by Lehr-Spławiński (1928), Dybo (1961), Mikkola (1913ff.:122), and others (for whom see Shevelov 1964:45-46), has come to stay. One may note also the acceptance by Garde (1976:333-34).

Where the accentual testimony of Indic (and sometimes of Greek) confirms a post-long-syllable accent in PIE in words containing the shape $/\# \ldots V{:}C_1V$ $\left\{ \begin{matrix} : \\ C \end{matrix} \right\} \#\#/$, Balto-Slavic evidence indicates accent movement to the left by one syllable: so Skt. *dhūmá-*, Gk. ϑυμός, but Russ. *dýma* (gen.sg.). As Ebeling (1967: 582) points out, the input includes recently established final accent ('oxytone-sis'). Illič-Svityč (1963:80-81, 156 = 1979:63, 138-39) perceived that the target syllable (of rising intonation for Shevelov [1964:45]) often had a presumable checking laryngeal: so **griHwáH* > SCr. *grȉva* (Skt. *grīvā́*), or **kaHwlós* (Gk. καυλός) Latv. *kaûls*. He saw also that, by contrast, the sequence *VRH* blocked the shift: **golHwáH* > Lith. *galvà*. It is not clear why acc.pl. *gálvas* or inst.sg. *gálva* (even in the proto-form **gólHwaH*) seem to have no such immunity from the law. Saussure (1896) saw here the influence in Lithuanian of the consonant-stems; even then *gálvas* has followed Greek πόδας rather than Indic *padás*. Cf. Pedersen (1907:213). Paul Kiparsky (1973:827) prefers to operate with a Lithuanian repositioning of accent governed by 'strength' of noun-case. Dybo (1961) links the shift with vowel-shortening in Italo-Celtic. Kortlandt (1974: 298; 1975:2ff.) handles the apparent exception (Russ.) *pilá* — versus SCr. *píla*

*See also Appendix III.

— as the result of a revised sequence of segments in that historical branch line. Using Beekes' (1969:173) rather doubtful reflex-conflation of H^i/u with $^i/uH$, he reconstructs *$pHiláH$. Kortlandt is quite given over to laryngeal causation (so on Dybo's, Ebeling's, and Meillet's laws, q.v.); here it results in the split between $/\bar{V}CV/$ and $/VHCV/$, which are susceptible to Hirt's law, and $/VRHV/$ or $/HVCV/$, which are not (cf. Dybo 1974:298, 300; 1975:22-23). Yet what other diagnostic sorts out PIE VH (so as to oppose HV) from $\bar{V}$ inside Balto-Slavic? Still, Kortlandt has a firm Hirtian explanation for the accent difference between Russ. *máteri* (gen.sg.) and *materjáx* (prep.pl.): of the inherited *$maHtrés$, *$maHtrsú$, only the first is really disyllabic and so input to the law (provided the BS1. generalization, from other cases, of *-ter-* in the second syllable is put later). But firmness is not enough. Kortlandt (1975) lists eight corroborating etymologies for his stance, including *$mātr$-; but the 'mother' word in Greek seems to resist retraction on the Balto-Slavic pattern. It allows the effect partially (only in nom-sg., voc.sg.) — and if this is actually the 'remnant of an old type of mobility' (so Kortlandt 1975:80), Hirt may have failed to separate close-set layers of causation. Anyhow, 'noms de parenté' are awkward; they are acknowledged exceptions to Vendryes' law (q.v.), for example.

Hirt's law at least suggests (if no more) why some word-forms fail in some cases to show the end-stress demanded by their paradigm (Stang's third or *c*-stressed type); cf. Kortlandt (1977:321). It also allows for apparent root accent in words which were not accented in PIE. Just why nominal *u*-stems do not permit observation of the law (see Ebeling 1967:582) is not obvious. The fabric of Hirt's case is not without holes (see especially Shevelov 1964:51); but leftward shift of word-accent is positively epidemic in Indo-European.

REFERENCES*

Beekes, R.S.P. 1969. *Development of the PIE laryngeals in Greek.* The Hague: Mouton.
Dybo, V.A. 1961. Sokraščenije dolgot v kelto-italijskix jazykax, i ego značenije dlja balto-slavjanskogo i indoevropejskoj akcentologii. *VSJa* 5.9-34.

*Also relevant or quoted are:
Ebeling 1967*; Garde 1976*; Illič-Svityč 1963* (= 1979*); Kiparsky 1973*; Kortlandt 1974*, 1975*, 1977*, 1978*; Lehr-Spławiński 1966*; Saussure 1894*, 1896*; Shevelov 1964*.
— on which see Appendix III.

Hirt, H. 1895. *Der indogermanische Akzent.: Ein Handbuch.* Strassburg: Trübner.

————, 1929. *Indogermanische Grammatik, vol. 5: Der Akzent.* Heidelberg: Winter.

Lehr-Spławiński, T. 1928. Najstarsze prasłowiańskie prawo cofania akcentu. *Symbolae Rozwadowski* (Kraków) 2.85-100.

Mikkola, J. J. 1913-50. *Urslavische Grammatik* I-III. Heidelberg: Winter.

Pedersen, H. 1907. Neues und nachträgliches. *KZ* 40.129-217.

HIRT'S LAW II

Herman Hirt claimed for himself several 'laws'. His pronouncement on Balto-Slavic accentology has at least been freely labelled with his name (see Hirt's law I). His most successful attempt at fathering another ordinance concerns the evolution of Greek pitch-placing; and the relevant texts are 1895 (esp. 36), 1902 (191), and especially 1904. Despite early and continued scepticism he maintained his position in the second edition of his Greek *Handbuch* (1912: 274).

The 'law' delineates a leftward shift of word accent within a three-mora matrix: so | xẋx | > | ẋxx |, as in *welú+trom* (Skt. *varútram*) > ἔλυτρον. The affinities with Bàrtoli's and Wheeler's laws are obvious; but there are important differences. Hirt (like Vendryes) dialectally limits his field to Attic-Ionic, and in effect to Attic alone. He also assigns a widespread penultimate syllable accent to PIE, which is not easy to accept. After all, if ἠίϑεος answers to Skt. *vidháva-*, the Indic accent may reflect a speculative native etymology (*vi+dhā*); and the Doric pattern as in ἐλῦσαν etc. may as well reflect not Hirt's earlier placing of accent but a rightward deviation from a basic verbal pattern which Attic in fact retains.

Hirt is ambivalent about the role (if any) of syllable structure. He seems to regard /xxx/ as the favourable field for his shift (1904:77), and even excuses the absence of shift in τιϑέντος (in the paradigm of ppl. τιϑείς) on the grounds that the central syllable has 2 moras. But his major testimonia include *ἑσταότος > ἑστῶτος and παιδῶν > παίδων. He is honest in noting exceptions, such as some adjectives in -ῖνος (e.g. not † ἴκτινος) and the infinitives in -ῆναι (e.g. not † λύθηναι), whence perfect ῖναι; and a notable plus mark for him is the obviously derived accent on the purely Greek 'prothetic vowel': so ἔρεβος Skt. *rájas*; or ὄνομα, *nómen-*.

The initial reaction was adverse: cf. Solmsen (1903). After Hirt's full and firm restatement (1904), Bally took over the offensive (1908). He regarded the penultimate syllable accent in Greek as a purely local innovation, disguising the really archaic nature of Greek in this respect (in that it reflected a PIE predilection for either a word-initial or a word-final accentuation — unlike Sanskrit). Five mechanisms explain penultimate placing, one being Wheeler's law; if one applies, the penultimate placing is then derivative and abiding. Hence the forms αἱματόεν, ἐτοιμάζον (ppl.), achieved by analogy and fatal to both stages of Hirt's scheme; Hirt's example θύγατρα is declared not to need *θυγάτρα, but to be linked to θυγατέρα as is ἄνδρα to ἀνέρα; and if the influence of monosyllabic stems (πόδα) is not the reason then the pervasiveness of word-extreme accent is: cf. ἀμαχεί, ἄμαχος. Hirt's reliance on encliticized stretches (ἄνθρωπός τις), to show the interim stage in his concept of movement from *φέρομενος (bháramāṇas) via *φέρομὲνος to φερόμενος founders in the absence of the end-result - † ἀνθρώποστις. On the other hand, γυναῖκες is *not* a case telling against Hirt (pace Bally 1908:14); rather, if this form could be proved to be output of his law (and Doric accent in γυναίκες to represent the original, rather than insensitivity to contour), then Hirt would give us a good explanation for an awkward exception to Vendryes' law.

The shift presumed in δοῦναι (< δοϜέναι?; Cypr. to-(w)e-na-(i), Vedic dāváne), and also in θεῖναι, εἶναι etc., has to be reconsidered in the light of Cowgill (1964: esp. 359). If the Ϝ is a mere glide and the form is really δο+εναι, from *+en or *+sen, then the accent *might* have been always predesinential, as in δό+μεναι (Vedic dā́mane). The perfect +εναι could be influenced by participial -ότ- (and it is a pity that Hirt fumbles about with an incredible form **εἰδοτός, supposed to be subject to Wheeler's law). There is, of course, a regularity of penultimate accent with the +ναι formant, as in present διδόναι etc.; but this does not help Hirt, because leftward movement is there conspicuously absent.

The 'law' is not sufficiently well-founded and is now mostly and rightly forgotten. True, there is something odd about Attic ἑστῶτος (ostensibly Hirt's best case). Yet (a) the feminine ἑστῶσα if from -ά+οντ+yᾰ (but note Hom. ἑσταῶσα) may have a part to play in the formation generally; and (b) τεθνεῶτος, presumably from *τε=θνη+ότος argues that the whole thing is a general provision for the circumflexing of a dimoric penultimate syllable if it precedes a final single mora — the rule which applies to νῆσος, etc. Not quite enough solidity remains.

REFERENCES

Bally, C. 1908. Accent grec, accent védique, accent indoeuropéen. *Fs Saussure*, 3-29.

Cowgill, W. 1964. The supposed Cypriote optatives duwánoi and dókoi. *Lg* 40.344-65.

Hirt, H. 1895. *Der indogermanische Akzent: Ein Handbuch.* Strassburg; Trübner.

—————, 1902. *Handbuch der griechischen Laut- und Formenlehre.* Heidelberg: Winter (2nd ed., 1912.).

—————, 1904. Zur Entstehung der griechischen Betonung. *IF* 16.71-92.

Solmsen, F. 1903. Review of Hirt 1902. *Berliner philologische Wochenschrift* 23. col.1004.

HJELMSLEV'S LAW*

Balto-Slavic accentology handles two phonological events. One is — or is on its way to becoming — a largely expiratory and energetic word accent, and involves the comparative enhancement of one syllable; the other is a pattern of pitch-transition, common between parts of a syllable and also (potentially) applicable to more than one syllable of the same word, but not actually marked unless coincident with accent. Appendix III contains a discussion of these things, and of the complex and inconsistent terminology attached to them. The separating out of 'intonation', as the pitch-patterning is called, is (at the *word* level) special to this branch of older Indo-European data; and it largely derives from Saussure 1894.

Saussure there identified, in particular, a curious and important change of pattern (for which he had no explanation) which is undergone by syllables with inherited long vowel nuclei; he called it 'metatony'. He ruled out 'superlong' vowels, and decided that in the preponderance of cases the movement was towards a rising ('douce') intonation: so Lith. *kója → pakõjui*; and some diminution of length may be entailed (note his phrase 'après coup' [1894:494]).

In his doctoral disquisition published in 1932 Louis Hjelmslev (1899-1965) offered an explanation of the phenomenon, which he restricted (at least in respect of his own causation) to common Baltic. What he said (1932:5 and 234) is often called his 'law'. He ruled simply that once a vocalic nucleus had received the accent it 'donned' the intonation of the next syllable to the right: "toute syllabe accentuée revêt l'intonation de la syllabe immédiatement suivante". Three points of novelty are worth noting: (1) length is no longer a prerequisite; (2) the result of the shift is basically as likely to be a falling tune as a rising one; and (3) it is not a primary but a consequent matter that morphological derivation often prompts metatony.

Pedersen (1933:10) disliked the width of applicability of the law and wanted to restrict it to words of more than two syllables. Stang (1966:163) was unhappy, no matter how many syllables were in the word (cf. Kortlandt 1977:327). Kortlandt (1974:304, 1977:327) also reports on the law, from a laryngealist

*See Appendix III.

standpoint. He quotes *êdesis* (Hjelmslev's leading example) and supposes a process of 'delaryngealization' of a vowel; that needs separate demonstration and goes well beyond Hjelmslev (see also what is said on Winter's law). The output is regarded as needing length, and so Kortlandt is led to state the result uniformly as /Ṽ:/ with a dimoric rising tune; but Hjemslev allowed a falling result (cf. *várna*), as did even Saussure as an abnormality. The shift is also, for Kortlandt, one of 'ictus', which should mean either incidence of point of high pitch (which is inadequate and misleading) or location of word-accent (which is erroneous). For Kortlandt, the law is simultaneous with Pedersen's law II.

Hjelmslev's basic example is *édu* ~ *êdesis* (1932:10); but see Winter's law (below). The metatony with falling result, as in *várna*, requires an earlier **vắrnā* with a long falling final vowel at the critical time of shift: therefore Hjelmslev's law must precede Leskien's law. After metatony has taken place the resultant forms evolve as do all words of their (new) shape: *vãlgis* is treated just as is *mẽdis* (which always had a rising, 'douce', intonation on its accented syllable). The big exception-class is the set of words of mobile paradigm: while *kõtenas* (acc.pl.) may derive from *kótenas*, the extreme-accented *puõlena* (voc.sg.) is not connected to *puolenà* by metatony. The equivalent of Sanskrit *udáram* can therefore, happily and irrelevantly, be permitted to be not †*vẽdaras* but *vẽdaras*.

More problematic is another supposed leftward shift of 'tune' which Hjelmslev offers (1932:48; 234). The target syllable this time bears no accent, but the specific context required is a non-low back vowel in the following syllable. This separate rule is not needed as part of Hjelmslev's main law and its validity is for others to judge.

REFERENCES

Hjelmslev, J. 1932. *Études baltiques.* Copenhagen: Levin & Munksgaard. (Esp. 1-99; 234.)

Pedersen, H. 1933. *Études lituaniennes.* Copenhagen: Levin & Munksgaard.

Stang, C.S. 1966. *Vergleichende Grammatik der baltischen Sprachen.* Oslo; Univ. Press.

* Also relevant or quoted are:-
Kortlandt 1974*, 1977*; Saussure 1894*
— on which see Appendix III.

HOLTZMANN'S LAW

A purely Germanic affair, this — except for odd citations of supposed like behaviour in Bantu. Yet there are attempts to base it on (or to base on it) general theories of accentual effects including the 'natural phonology' concept of 'strength' of elements (see under Grammont's laws in Appendix I A). For its originator it was just an observed evolutionary quirk which helped to define the geographical noding of the Germanic part of the IE genetic family tree. Adolf Holtzmann (1810-1870) first called attention in 1835 and 1836 (cf. also 1870: 29, 42-43, 109) to the emergence of geminated obstruents between etymologically contiguous vowels and glides in Gothic and Old Norse. Thus:

> *dwey-, "2": (Skt. *dvayoh*); Got. *twaddjē*, ON *tveggja*.
> *drew-, "true": (O.Pruss. *druwis*); Got. *triggws, triggwa*, ON *tryggr, tryggva*.

The descent appears to be: PIE -$V\underset{\smile}{R}$- > PGmc -$V\underset{\smile}{RR}$- > NGmc and EGmc $Vgg\underset{\smile}{R}$ (but *ddj* in Gothic), against WGmc -$\underset{\smile}{VR}$+$\underset{\smile}{R}$-. Usually the whole discussion rests on the history of a set of 16 (or perhaps 18) words, cognates for most of which are given by Kuryłowicz (1967:448-49). The process is commonly called 'Verschärfung'.

Prokosch (1939:92-93), after noting the facts in much the form (if not the actual notation) given above, and citing Braune (1884) as an early codifier, states two important reservations. First, that the pronunciation of Gothic *ddj* and *ggw* is debated; secondly, that there are a lot of pretty troublesome exceptions to Holtzmann's law. On the second point, it is not just that some reflexes fail to show the obstruents (so Got. *aiz*, where Skt. *ayas*, Lat. *ayes(-no-)* > *aes, aēn(e)us*, indicate PIE *ayes-) but that North and East Germanic sometimes part company (got. *frijōn* "love", but ON *Frigg*, where PIE has *priyó-*, Skt. *priyá-*; Got. *hawi* "hay", but ON *hoggua*, 'cut', where OCS has *kovati*). Bugge (1888) had long since annoyingly observed that the effect seemed to have spread sporadically to West Germanic, as in the "bridge" word: O.Fris. *brigge, bregge*, OHG *brucca*). As to the phonetic values: *ddj* is for Prokosch a mere graphic variant, identical in sound to Norse *ggj*, that is [jj] or the like: he compares Hungarian *Magyar*, as does Smith (1941:95). It is, curiously, only the most recent essayists on this law who have fretted over the *ddj* problem, some wishing it were not there and some conversely hostile to *ggj*. The question about *ggw* turns on the Gothic use of the spelling *gg* after the Greek fashion (where it normally, but not universally, represents [ŋg]). Did the prenasalized pronunciation spread to all words so spelt, including the Holtzmann phenomena? An affirmative answer is given by Marchand (1959:442) and Bennett (1964); but a firm no is recorded by Voyles (1968) and Brosman (1971) — the last-named using evidence from Romance borrowings (supplied by Corominas) to prove that some Gothic *ggw* words, at least, had no appreciable nasal in them.

The earliest explanations of the phenomena were scarcely more than refinements of observation. Brugmann (*BDG*.283) noted that the Germanic sequence /-VCCj/ (to use a later notation) succeeded to a sequence without obstruents but with syllable boundary /-Vj\$j-/ (or, perhaps, /-Vw\$k^W-/). Boer (1918) and Van Coetsem (1949) approve, though the latter imposes other conditions. Oddly, as will appear, it is to some notion of this sort, involving a rather vague reinforcement of the articulatory 'punch' of glide semivowels (in debated contexts), that fashion has in recent years reverted. Already in 1912 Prokosch had suggested that one cause was the greater expiratory pressure in Germanic consonants generally.

Yet there were already signs of an alternative approach of a more dynamic kind. Their motivation, if at first independent, was soon linked with Verner's success in pressing word-accent into service in connection with Grimm's law. But the concentration was initially on the first rather than the second stage of the shift that was Holtzmann's discovery: on the lengthening of inherited postvocalic glides. For Holtzmann himself the favourable context had been a long preceding vowel and a following accented syllable, for the effect which he called 'Verhärtung'. Kluge (1879, also 1913) voted for conditioning by accent, but by a preceding accent on a short vowel. Bechtel (1885) returned to the view that a following accent was responsible (purer Vernerism); and his adherents, with varying grounds for belief, number Trautmann (1906, 1925), Mikkola (1924), and Hirt (1931). Parallels in Hungarian-Slovenian, Irish and the Prakrits are adduced (see, inter alia, Lehmann (1952:38n.7). But the 'across-the-board' occurrence of the Holtzmann effect in (Gothic) strong verbs like *bliggwan*, *blaggw*, *bluggwum*, *bluggwans* is fatal to any explanation based strictly on accent position. Paul (1880:165) was already convinced that accent had nothing to do with it; and Hirt (1931) and Lehmann (1952:39) agreed later. Hirt (1931:114) pointed to two jokers in the pack: the anisomorphism of PIE and Germanic accent, and dialectal interference in Germanic itself. Streitberg (1927:323ff.)

rejected the relevance of the PIE accent at any rate, so that a Verner solution had gone by then. Yet as late as 1949 Van Coetsem (following Boer 1918) speculates on the influence of two flanking and counterbalancing stresses, one a Germanic novelty and the other a PIE inheritance; and (as we shall see) accent reappears as a factor sporadically, and even in 1970.

The next great impulse to seek a tailor-made solution came when PIE 'laryngeals', which had previously been adduced by Cuny (1912:112) but as a rather shadowy group of protosegments of uncertain number and unclear phonetic shape, were (for a time) transformed into an apparently factory-produced set of well-polished phonic elements supplied in America for all Indo-European diachronists to use. This was Sturtevant's triumph (*sit uenia uerbo*). Despite his own contribution on the issue (1942), one may preferably cite Smith (1941) as a paradigm of what this new school wanted to say about Holtzmann's law. This was that 'Indo-Hittite' y/w became 'hj/hw' – meaning 'long voiceless semivowels' – after a laryngeal (which disappears) and before an accented syllable. (This is scarcely an easy shift to put into generative phonology notation, to say the least.) Sturtevant himself was disinclined to insist on the accent-context. The most eager defender of this approach was Polomé. He faced directly, for instance, the difficulties of which the Americans were not unaware. Thus, the sequence -*wHw*- has every inducement to odd behaviour; and in Old Norse itself *bryggja* "bridge" stands against *rȳja* "to pluck (wool)". Smith thought that maybe the accent had shifted back to the root syllable on some words, or that maybe all roots containing H were susceptible to some pretty ad hoc syllabification. Polomé (1949) preferred to separate -*úH*- from -*u-Hw*-́, and to set up a pre-Germanic – but pan-Germanic – accent-sensitive rule:

$$* \text{-}uHw\text{-} \; > \; \left\{ \begin{array}{c} \text{-}úH\text{-}(w) \\ \text{-}u\text{-}gw\text{-}́ \end{array} \right\}$$

The problems attendant on the Smith-Sturtevant attitude are discussed by Lehmann (1952:39-46), but he remains a firm adherent of a laryngeal solution: for him the required context for affecting w is of a *following* laryngeal. As one might put it, Lehmann believes in detail

$$\text{PGmc } /w/ \rightarrow [\text{+long}] \; \Big/ \; \left[\begin{array}{c} V \\ \text{-long} \end{array} \right] \; - H \qquad (\rightarrow \; \text{-}\breve{V}ww\text{-})$$

$$\text{PGmc } /y/ \rightarrow [+\text{long}] \; / \left\{ \begin{array}{ll} \begin{bmatrix} V \\ +\text{high} \\ -\text{back} \end{bmatrix} H \, \underline{}^{1} & (\rightarrow \text{-}ijj\text{-}) \\[2ex] \begin{bmatrix} V \\ +\text{low} \end{bmatrix} <H \, \underline{}^{*}> & (\rightarrow \text{-}ajj\text{-}) \quad (\text{i.e. Hj or jH}) \end{array} \right.$$

- but H must be contiguous to the affected glide. (See Polomé 1970:180, for a fuller informal summary.) No explanation is offered for the further shift to obstruent value. Polomé (1959) at least sees the laryngeal as developing of itself to a uvular fricative, as a partial progress to obstruence; but then he, like other laryngealists, works with the sequence HR, not RH. Sniping between laryngealists, together with disquiet inside the movement over the excessive proliferation of H (and kinds of H) in diachronic speculations (cf. Cowgill and others in Winter 1960 & 1965; also Jonsson 1978), soon led to a disenchantment which ended the laryngealist heyday in Holtzmannian studies. Cowgill (1960) is in effect a denial of any need of H in respect of Gothic *iddja* (Skt. *ayāt*); but against his history (*$eiy\underset{\circ}{n}t$ > *$eyy\underset{\circ}{n}(t)$ > *$iyyun$ > *iddja*) Lindeman (1967) fires a splendid late laryngeal countersalvo: *$H_1eH_1yóH_2e$ > *$\bar{e}y\bar{a}$ > Gmc *$\bar{e}j\bar{o}$ > *$eej\bar{o}$ > *$eij\bar{o}$ > *$ejj\bar{o}$ > *iddja*.

The most direct anti-laryngeal statement came from Beekes (1972), himself a powerful demonstrator of how H-theory works in detail. Too many unproved etymologies bothered him (being a rather cautious and orthodox laryngealist). He even declares (327), of Holtzmann's law, 'there is no rule'; and he is especially virulent against Lindeman (1964), where gemination of /R/ is pushed back into PIE. He shows that (a) *Verschärfung* sometimes demonstrably does not occur when the inherited sequence contains a laryngeal, yet (b) it occurs, after all, when no H is acceptably established for the PIE reconstruction. He actually produces no clear case of (b), lamely claiming that one cannot prove the absence of H. Well, it is notoriously hard to prove you have not committed atrocities; but laryngeals are a different affair and the onus on proof is on those who seek to presume them and dispense with them anywhere. As to (a), one would be happier with a theorist who was less ready to pluralize and phonetically characterize these shadowy phonemes and more ready to see variant forms of roots

---

1) At least he *says* (1952:46 line 11) "when reflex of a laryngeal preceded -j-"; but his evidence is of the form, e.g., '/preyX/' (45).

(with and without *H;* or with *H* and some other segment in alternation, etc.). This kind of elasticity (whereby *go-bhih* and *gavā* against *gām* can represent *$g^{W}ow$* (cf. Latvian *guòvs*) alongside *$g^{W}oH$*, with *gauḥ* a purely Indic vṛddhi) would reduce the nuisance-value of, say, Got. *sniwan* beside ON *snǫggr* (the semantic equation is by Beekes). Laryngeal alternation may save North and East Germanic from inconsistency.

Still, the laryngeal tide is out at present, in this sector at least: it may flood in again soon from the Balto-Slavic shore. Some idea of glide-reinforcement is now most fashionable in *Verschärfung* theories. Hammerich (1955) talks merely of the articulatory 'stopping' of one semivowel of two in succession (to preserve a separate segmental value, it seems). Foley (1971 – his 1977 book, pp.90-93, offers on this no novelties) sees Holtzmann's law as essentially a consonantal process and:

(i) as the second (dentalizing) step in a six-step process of assibilation, a process characterised as the natural shift path for velar consonants before front vowels (e.g. *kera* → 1 *kyera* → 2 *ktyera* → 3 *ktsyera* → 4 *tsyera* → 5 *tsera* → 6 *sera*)

(ii) as a 'universal law' (though rather of predentalizing of /y/), surfacing also in Italian *Giove* from Lat. *Iouem* or Greek *ζυγόν* from PIE *yugóm* (so Cowgill also, in Winter 1965:163) – which is nicely diametric to Beekes's total denial of a law, and equally opposed to the prevailing belief that, pace Gothic, the *Verschärfung* basically produces velars even before *j*.

But the answer of Kuryłowicz (1967, 1968) – another anti-laryngeal laryngealist – makes more appeal to morphology (as he increasingly did) and is a sort of multilevel treatment. Indeed, it stands curiously aside from the determinably phonological thrust of all other recent speculators. Kuryłowicz will have a three-step process. Step one is a matter of apophonic misinterpretation: zero grade *CuwV* (a 'Sievers-Edgerton' reflex of zero grade where full grade is *CewV*) is falsely thought to correspond to a full grade *CewwV*, which is then restored – on which possibility, namely a return to guṇa in zero contexts, see Collinge (1953), Poultney (1976), and even Smith (1941) on Got. *triggws*. Step two is the only purely phonetic act: *eR̥R̥(V)* and *eR̥(#)* evolve as positional variants. In step three, *R̥R̥* is replaced by *R̥R̥R̥* as a purely morphological phenomenon (although Kuryłowicz calls it both morphological (1968:330) and morphophonological (ibid., 333)). The emergence of plosives remains to be explained.

The law that seems universal to some and non-existent to others appears to Voyles (1968) as a convenient label for groups of changes – phonological again

– which are related in different ways in different idioms. As between Old Norse and Gothic the law means two different paths of shift (p.743). In Old Norse itself it is a pantechnicon term for three separate sound changes. Likewise for Cathey (1970) – for whom it is all an affair of 'hiatus neutralization', if you please – the process takes a different course in North and East Germanic. In the former branch *gR* passes to *ggR* (much as in Bantu (Ganda); cf. Meussen [1955], who starts from /pR/); in Gothic, however, there is just no neat solution as to why the alveolar-velar difference arises. Which is strange, since articulatory effects and feature phonology would both point to ON *ggj* as the oddity (as is implicit in Foley and explicit in Tanaka).

Nor is accent yet defunct as a motivator. In 1965 and 1970 Tanaka sets out the resonant gemination as a purely Germanic event. The context is, he says, conditioned by stress, by a short nuclear syllable, and by an equal 'weighting' of syllables in sequence (1965); and sequences like -*yy*- etc. are just not already there (as Lindeman [1964] would claim) in late PIE. Tanaka's idea of the second aspect of Holtzmann, the consonantism, is that we have allophonic variants. A strong variant, with obstruent realization, interplays with a weak one, with retained glide. Why *allophones* have 'strength' (rather than contextual fitness) is not clear. But at least Tanaka sees *ggw* ([g:w]) and *ddj* ([d:y]) as the natural reflexes; to explain North Germanic *ggj* he imports supporting testimony, just to show it can happen, from Spanish.

Accent? Apophony? Allophones? Laryngeals? Or a confusion of conspiratorial (or accidental) shifts? A mirage, or a universal rule? It looks wide open.

REFERENCES

Austin, W.M. 1946. A corollary to the Verschärfung. *Lg* 22.109-111.

––––––, 1958. Germanic reflexes of Indo-European -*Hy*- and -*Hw*-. *Lg* 34. 203-211.

Bechtel, F. 1885. Ueber die urgermanische Verschärfung von *j* und *v*. *NAWG* 6.235-39.

Beekes, R.S.P. 1972. Germanic Verschärfung and no laryngeals. *Orbis* 21.327-36.

Bennett, W.H. 1946. The cause of West Germanic consonant lengthening. *Lg* 22.14-18.

––––––, 1964. Gothic spellings and phonemes: some current interpretations. *Fs Starck*, 19-27.

Boer, R.C. 1918. Syncope en consonantengeminatie. *Tijdschrift voor Ned. Taal- en Letterkunde* 37.161-222 (esp. 218-21).

Braune, W. 1884. Gotisches *ddj* und Altnordisches *ggj. PBB* 9.545-48.

––––––, 1944. *Althochdeutsche Grammatik.* (6th. ed.) Halle: Niemeyer.

Brosman, P.W. Jr. 1971. Romance evidence and Gothic ggw. *IF* 76.165-73.

Bugge, S. 1888. Zur altgermanischen Sprachgeschichte: germanisch *ug* aus *uw. PBB* 13.502-15.

Cathey, J.E. 1967. *A relative chronology of Old Icelandic phonology based on distinctive feature analysis.* Diss., Univ. of Washington, Seattle.

––––––, 1970. A reappraisal of "Holtzmann's Law". *SL* 24.56-63.

Coetsem, F. van. See Van Coetsem, F.

Collinge, N.E. 1953. Laryngeals in IE ablaut and problems of the zero grade. *ArchL* 5.75-87.

Cowgill, W. 1960. Gothic *iddja* and Old English *ēode. Lg* 36.483-501.

Cuny, A. 1912. Notes de phonétique historique, Indo-Européen et Sémitique. *RPh* 2.101-32.

Foley, J.A. 1971. Assibilation as a universal phonological rule. *FoL* 6.251-62.

––––––, 1977. *Foundations of theoretical phonology.* Cambridge, Univ. Press.

Hammerich, L.L. 1955. Die germanische und die hochdeutsche lautverschiebung. *PBB* 77.165-203.

Heusler, A. 1913. *Altisländisches Elementarbuch.* Heidelberg: Winter. (6th ed., 1964.)

Hirt, H. 1931. *Handbuch des Urgermanischen,* vol.I. Heidelberg: Winter.

Holtzmann, A. 1835. Review of H.F. Massmann, *Skeireins, Heidelberger Jahrbücher der Literatur* 28.854-63.

––––––, 1836. Ed. of Isidor, *Epistulae ad Florentinam sororem.* Karlsruhe: G. Holtzmann.

––––––, 1870. *Altdeutsche Grammatik.* I: *Die specielle Lautlehre.* Leipzig: Brockhaus.

Jellinek, M.H. 1926. *Geschichte der gotischen Sprache.* Berlin & Leipzig: W. de Gruyter.

Jonsson, H. 1978. *The laryngeal hypothesis: a critical survey.* Lund: Gleerup.

Kieckers, E. 1928. *Handbuch der vergleichenden gotischen Grammatik.* Munich: Hueber.

Kluge, F. 1879. Beiträge zur Geschichte der germanischen Conjugation (Excurs über Gotisch *dd* und *gg*). *Quellen und Forschungen* (Strassburg) 32.127-30.

––––––, 1913. *Urgermanisch.* 3rd rev. ed. Strassburg: Trübner. (1st ed., 1909.)

Kögel, R. 1884. Uber w und j im Westgermanischen. PBB 9.523-44.

Kuhn, H. 1944. Review of F. Maurer, Nordgermanen und Alemannen. ADA 63.5-13.

————, 1955. Zur Gliederung der germanischen Sprachen. ZDA 86.1-47.

Kuryłowicz, J. 1967. The Germanic Verschärfung. Lg 43.445-51.

————, 1968. Indogermanische Grammatik. II (esp. pp.329-33). Heidelberg: Winter.

Lehmann, W.P. 1952. Proto-Indo-European Phonology. Austin: Univ. of Texas Press. (Chapter 4.)

————, 1966. The grouping of the Germanic languages. Ancient IE dialects, ed. by H. Birnbaum and J. Puhvel. 13-27. Berkeley & Los Angeles: Univ. of California Press.

Lindeman, F.O. 1962. La Verschärfung germanique. SL 16.1-23.

————, 1964. Les origines indo-européennes de la 'Verschärfung' germanique. Oslo: Oslo Univ. Press.

————, 1967. Gotisch iddja und altenglisch ēode. IF 72.275-86.

————, 1969. Nochmals Verschärfung. NTS 23.25-36.

Marchand, J.W. 1959. Über ai, au im Gotischen. PBB (Halle) 81.436-55.

Meussen, A.E. 1955. Les phonèmes du Ganda et du Bantou commun. Africa 25.174-77.

Mikkola, J.J. 1924. Die Verschärfung des intervokalischen j und w im Gotischen und Nordischen. Fs Streitberg, 267-71.

Noreen, A. 1894. Abriss der urgermanischen Lautlehre. Strassburg: Trübner. (Esp. pp.160-62.)

Paul, H. 1880. Ausfall des j vor i und des w vor u im Westgermanischen. PBB 7.160-68.

Polomé, E. 1949. A West Germanic reflex of the Verschärfung. Lg 25.182-89.

————, 1950. Laryngeal-Theorie en Germaanse Verscherping. Handelingen der Zuidnederlandse Maatschappij voor Taal- en Letterkunde en Geschiedenis 4.61-75.

————, 1953, Review of Lehmann 1952. RBPhH 31.537-44.

————, 1959. Théorie 'laryngale' et germanique. Mem. Mossé, 357-402.

————, 1970. Remarks on the problem of the Germanic Verschärfung. Fs Buyssens, 177-90.

Poultney, J.W. 1976. A problem of zero-grade vocalism. Fs Palmer, 285-98 (esp.291).

Prokosch, E. 1912. Forchhammers Akzenttheorie und die germanische Lautverschiebung. JEGP 11.1-9.

––––––, 1939. *A comparative Germanic grammar.* Philadelphia & Baltimore: Ling. Society of America.

Roe, H.A. 1965. *Verschärfung in Faroese.* Diss, Harvard Univ.

Smith, H.L. Jr. 1941. The Verschärfung in Germanic. *Lg* 17.93-98.

Streitberg, W., Michels, V. & Jellinek, M.H. 1927-36. *Germanisch: Allgemeiner Theil und Lautlehre.* (= *Geschichte der idg. Sprachwissenschaft II*: (1-2.) Berlin & Leipzig: W. de Gruyter.

Sturtevant, E.H. 1942. *The Indo-Hittite laryngeals.* Baltimore: Linguistic Society of America.

Tanaka, Y. 1965. *The West German double-graph.* Diss., UCLA.

––––––, 1970. A proposed hypothesis for Holtzmann's Law. *La Linguistique* 6.65-80.

Trautmann, R. 1906. *Germanische Lautgesetze in ihrem sprachgeschichtlichen Verhältnis.* Diss., Königsberg.

––––––, 1925. *Suum cuique. KZ* 53.89-90.

Van Coetsem, F. 1949. Le renforcement des semivoyelles intervocaliques en germanique (j/jj > jj > Gotique *ddj* etc.). *Leuvense Bijdragen* 39.41-78.

Van Helten, W. 1905. Germanisches 67: zur entwickelung von altgerm. *jj* und *wu. PBB* 30.240-48.

Voyles, J.B. 1968. Gothic and Germanic. *Lg* 44.720-46.

––––––, 1981. *Gothic, Germanic and North-West Germanic,* (= *ZDL, Beiheft* 39). Wiesbaden: Steiner.

Wiget, W. 1922. Altgermanische Lautuntersuchungen. *Acta et Commentationes Univ. Dorpatensis* (Tartu) 2.1-54.

Winter, W., ed. 1960. *Evidence for Laryngeals.* Austin: Univ. of Texas Press.

––––––, 1965. *Evidence for Laryngeals.* 2nd rev. ed. The Hague: Mouton.

Zabrocki, L. 1974. Die Entwicklung des ungermanischen auu, aii im Altsächsischen. *Kwartalnik Neofilologiczny* (Warsaw) 21.5-14.

ILLIČ-SVITYČ'S LAW*

This dates from 1963. It is in no way the same as Dybo's law or Hirt's law I, although each of those has had Illič-Svityč's name attached to it in subsequent discussion, such being the reward of pertinent revision or comment by him. The Russian scholar Vladislav Markovič Illič-Svityč, who died tragically young (in his early thirties in 1966), has been honourably and deservedly credited, especially among Netherlands experts, with an ordinance purely his own. For the recognition and title, see Kortlandt (1975:28). The field is again Slavic accent movement. The law was enunciated by Illič-Svityč (1963:118-19 = 1979: 103-104), and provides for a change in the paradigmatic accentuation pattern of inherited masculine o-stem nouns. If these were of Stang's second or b-stressed type they became of his third or c-stressed type. In other words, instead of their stress being basically on the last stem-syllable, with occasional forms in the paradigm having stress on the first syllable of the ending, they became 'laterally mobile' and had the stress alternating between the initial stem-syllable and the final syllable of the ending. Neuter o-stems were unaffected, and their stem-stressed original form then passed to Stang's second type of accentuation as a result of Dybo's law followed by Stang's law. (That they subsequently became masculine is slightly confusing, of course.) One may conversely claim that, by shifting the accent of the masculine b-stressed stems, Illič-Svityč's law entirely bleeds Dybo's.

The law works by analogy, in that the laterally mobile stress pattern already existed and was simply extended to the masculine o-stem paradigm. Ebeling (1967:585) dates the extension to the period, before Dybo's law, when the paradigms differed accentually (in actual realisation) only in plural oblique cases. Some dialects (e.g. Susak or Istrian) were specifically excepted by the law's inventor.

* See Appendix III.

REFERENCES*

Johnson, D.J.L. 1980. Dybo's law and metatony in the present tense of the Slavonic verb. *SEER* 58.481-99.

Vermeer, W.R. forthcoming in *FoLH*. On clarifying some points of Slavonic accentology: the quantity of the thematic vowel in the present tense and related issues. (Opposes Johnson 1980.)

* Also relevant or quoted are:
Dybo 1981*; Ebeling 1967*; Illič-Svityč 1963* (1979*); Kortlandt 1975*, 1978*; Stang 1957*.
– on which see Appendix III.

LACHMANN'S LAW

The datum is a rather curious phenomenon of vowel-lengthening in Latin, which may have the audacity to impinge on our optimistic formulating of linguistic universals, in two connections: (a) the phonetic and phonotactic control of actual duration of segments, and (b) the strategy and economy of morphological marking. The law's traditional starting point is a section (9.6) of that encyclopaedic ragbag of information, called *Noctes Atticae*, published by Aulus Gellius in the mid-second century of our era. His argument is over the length of the root-syllable vowel in Latin frequentative verbs like *actitare*. Mistaken adherents of the short quantity persuasion rely on the simple present stem as base-form (*ăgere*) to which the frequentative quantity conforms. But Gellius points to the anomaly (for them) of *ēsitare* (their base: *ĕdere*) or conversely *dĭctitare* (their base: *dīcere*). He himself derives the vowel-length in the frequentatives from that in the past participle passive of the simple verb: so *āctus, ēsus* but *dĭctus, răptus*, we credibly learn. In another passage (12.3) Gellius counters a presumed objection to linking the noun *līctor* with the verb *lĭgare* by citing words like *lēctor, strūctor*, (from *lĕgere, strŭere*); an underlying further derivation is to be understood, from participial **-tó-* to *nomina agentis* in *-tor*. Interesting is what Gellius does *not* do: he does not either motivate the assignment of any given verb to the *āctus* or to the *răptus* group, or explain the lengthening process in the participle itself. Two problems — or one and the same?

Things lurched forward fractionally in 1850. Karl Lachmann (1793-1851), one of Blücher's warriors who became a renowed editor of classical texts, in discussing variant readings at Lucretius 1.806 (in his own commentary's second edition, ad v.805) ruled thus (my translation):

> 'Those passive participles which derive from roots generating a present stem *ending* in a consonant, where that consonant is a liquid or /s/, agree with the present-stem form in the length of the root-syllable vowel. But if the present-stem *ends* in a voiced stop, then the *root-syllable vowel* is lengthened in the participle.

At least, that *seems* to be his message. In fact, the actual wording is distressingly imprecise:

> Participia passiva, ea quorum in praesenti consonans est aut liquida aut *s* semivocalis, quantitatem praesentis secuntur . . . contra, ubi in praesenti media est, participia producuntur.

Hence the emphasized parts of the translated version.

Lachmann's law, therefore, makes no mention at all of any target but the (past) participle passive in -tó- (not, for instance, even the supine). It fails to be explicit as to *what* is lengthened. It omits the necessary restriction to stems actually ending in a consonant (the formula would equally predict, e.g., *rōgātus*). It actually ignores the case of verbs with a voiceless obstruent in root-final position, such as the apparently relevant *rumpere, facere* (as well as interesting things like *uĕhere → uĕctus* from *wĕgh-*). Not too auspicious a beginning; and scarcely improved by the implicit error of a predicted *strīctus* (although the length in *ēmptus* is correct for Lachmann's formula, despite his own quoted false quantity here, and only becomes wrong for later explicators), or by the absence of clear guidance on the apparently converse process in *dīcere → dĭctus*. Nor is it clear how to fit in Lachmann's actual lemma, the discussion of *ambusta* (With *ŭ* or *ū*?) ← *ambūrere*.

Still the quantitative facts are not in dispute. Apart from Gellius (and, e.g., Porphyrion on *lecto* at Horace, *Sermones* 1.6.122) there is other evidence:

(i)   transliterative: ρεδηνπτα (for *redēmpta*)

(ii)   epigraphic: *léctus* (with 'apex': so at *CIL* 11.1826)

(iii) evolutionary: *tēctus* > French *toit*; but *lĕctus* (the noun) > French *lit*.

(iv)   deducible from other processes: *făctus → *cónfăctus* whence stress-affected *confĕctus*; but *āctus → redāctus* (as *ā* is never raised), as in *depāstus*, from root *pā(s)*.

Occasionally historical repetitions or accidents cloud the testimony (like *obtrectare* alongside *retractare*, or Ital. *detto, ditto*); but mostly we know what vowel lengths we have in any verb, and the puzzle is simply to discover why we have it. Lachmann himself obscurely contributes only the derivational constraint to roots of the *ăg-, lĕg-* type.

Until very recently Pedersen's (1896) purely phonetic explanation was accepted and most critical thrust was sporadically directed towards separating the regular from the exceptional among input verbs (and guessing at the phonological waywardness of the latter). More centrally, it presumed an 'Uritalisch' reversion from late PIE *aktós* to *agtós* in order to present two Latin events, ([+voice] → [−voice]/[C] *and* [−long] → [+long]/[V], which may seem to be somehow connected. Saussure (1885:256), Sommer (1914:122-23; Sommer-Pfister 1977:101) and Leumann (1963) are names to cite in this context; but murmurs of a very different approach are now and again audible, as by Osthoff (1884) and Kent (1928). The nuisances are that we have:

(i)   dĭctus (where the present has dīc-);
(ii)   ēmptus (where voiced /m/ is unchanged in the derivation from ĕm+);
(iii)   fŏssus (← fŏd+) and like forms with short vowel but affected consonant;

and (iv) the group comprising strĭctus [← strĭ(n)g+) and similar verbs. Of these, (i) is (pace Lachmann, q.v.) irrelevant: the present-stem vocalism is first of all in an apophonic (ei:i), and later in a quantitative (ī:i), alternation with the radical vocalism, and it is the latter which directly generates the participial form. There is no Lachmannian input. Of the interesting special case (ii) more will be said in a moment. Case (iii) deserves this comment: that, in spite of the constant and accepted equating of the type cāsus (← căd+t-) with the type āctus (← ăg+t-) and its being opposed to the type fŏssus, it is more likely that a spasmodic but clear phonological equivalence in Latin is (at least) entirely obscuring the matter or (at most) corroborating the Lachmann-Sommer theory (so to call it). Many examples show how -V:C- forks into the -V̄C or -VC̄(VCC) alternates in Latin: hinnuleus/īnuleus, Iuppiter/Iūpiter, allec/ālec, olla/aula (=*ōla); although the alternation is not free (cf. iousit > iussit) and the choice elsewhere is exploited as a disambiguator of otherwise colliding items (as in ānus from ās 'sit' but ănnus from ās 'be hot' – cf. perennis). Vīsus but fĭssus, ēsus but -sĕssus, (-)ōsus but fŏssus may therefore reflect arbitrary choice; and in the case of uīsus the simplification of -d+t-, and not a devoicing of root final -d, looks like the cause of lengthened /i/, for -V̄sus need not presume -V̆ssus except as a brief spelling convention (so Quintilian IO.1.7.20; see Collinge 1975:231,247-48.). It is perilous to bring any of these -Vss- forms into debate on the intricacies of Lachmannian dynamics, at least as proof of anything more than surface preferences.

Problem (iv) –strĭctus etc. – leads us on to the offering of Maniet (1956), who links the lengthening to voice-loss in the following consonant, but only where the latter is /g/. If it is /d/ the vowel's quantity is dictated by the finite perfect-stem (ēsus by ēdī, uīsus by uīdī); and /b/ does not occur as root-final in relevant verbs. The nonconformity of /i/ Maniet recognises, but writes vaguely of 'un certain hesitation en ce qui concerne l'exclusion de la voyelle i'. These gaps in the input seem to some to make the Maniet statement implausible (so Watkins 1970:56): its form, shorn of the hedging remark above, is:

une voyelle brève, à l'exception de *i*, s'est allongée
à la suite de l'assourdissement d'un *g* précédant (sic).

Relevant at this point is the generally recognized inherent shortness of high (and
especially front) vowels, so marked that even a lengthened [i] "nicht bis zur
Länge führte" (Leumann et al. 1963:105) or "fails to break through the perceptual threshold" — sc. of 'long' — (Drachman 1968:19). This means that verbs
of this root-vocalism may be allowed to stand down as witnesses, because strong
marking based on etymological syllable 'tenue' (cf. *deīco* > *dīcō*, or *uīcī* <
?wi-wik-ai) is required to achieve vowel length in them. But one squirms uneasily
at this. Less awkward is the absence of /b/; the non-occurrence of, e.g., **scāptus*
is simply a matter of lacunae in the testimony. Besides, Jonathan Kaye's notion
(in Collinge 1975:246) that we really have an interim form **ĕmb+tos* (like
*-ĕmb+si, as after *co-*, *pro-*, *su-*) plus a movement to *ĕmptus* like that of *yŭ-n-*
gtos to *ūnctus*, fills the labial gap with underlying **ĕmb-ō*. (This is much as the
verb whose past forms are *pressī*, *pressus* needs underlying root-alternant **pred-*
(some say **pres-*, which seems less likely) to explain the consonantism which is
not predictable from the root **prem-* used in the present.) Pisani (whose basic
notion up to 1974 was always of **/agtos/* as the source) has recently suggested,
prompted by Strunk (1976), that the mere fact that the post-vocalic consonant
is in a devoicing situation is enough to cause lengthening: he cites (Pisani 1981)
Polish *bóg* # # versus *boga*, *wód+ka* versus *woda*.

The assumption, in all this, of 'pre-Latin' **agtos* (as by Saussure; see *MSL*
6.256) has some colour at least: the present-stem *ag-* must exert associative
control, on any mentalist analysis of morphology as part of grammar (so also
Meillet 1908/9:265-66; Sommer-Pfister 1977:101). This is the correctly stub-
born view of Maniet (1979:5), and now part of his computerised history of
Latin. Whereupon a 'recoverable' and re-created **agtos* would be speedily
re-subjected to a removal of the phonically unacceptable /gt/ sequence. Less
defensible — except purely as an abstract entity in a generativist's derivation — is
the **āgtos* which blooms briefly in the ordered (and re-ordered) rules of Kiparsky (1965) and King (1969:43ff.):

(1) $V \rightarrow$ [+long] $\diagup$ — $\begin{bmatrix} \text{+obstruent} \\ \text{+voice} \end{bmatrix}$ $\begin{bmatrix} \text{+obstruent} \\ \text{−voice} \end{bmatrix}$

(2)   [+obstruent] $\rightarrow$ [α voice] $\diagup$ — $\begin{bmatrix} \text{+obstruent} \\ \alpha \text{ voice} \end{bmatrix}$

in which by 1: *ăgtos* → *āgtos*; by 2: *āgtos* → *ăktos* (*āctus*). At least *both* forms
with 'Latin' *-gt-* are here equally abstract; but it is a pity that this path leads to
things like **scīssus* and **-sēssus*, and presumably **ĕmptus* – for *em+t-* is input
to neither rule. Rule ordering is not now fashionable. So for his part King,
faced with these and other posers, switches to a largely morphological conditioning. First (1970:5), he opines simply that 'if the perfect is formed by
lengthening the vowel of the present. . . . then the passive participle is too'. Later
(1973:575-76), he readmits phonological considerations but limits them to a
filtering role, to avoid **căptus* and the like.

Whence comes this urge to seek a solution within the strategy of tense-stem
(or aspect-stem) marking? Initially from Osthoff (1884:113), who saw a spread
of, for instance, the *ē* of *lēgī* into other declensional forms of this sort. Then
Kent (1928) agrees – although his own thrust here is towards explanation by
a battery of analogies, with the aim of avoiding colliding homonyms; and (188)
he regrets the appearance of Lachmann's law in the text-books – but cf. Kent
1932, § 184): and, two decades before Benveniste, he is ready to cite **āgī* as
the relevant perfect form of its verb. But above all stands Kuryłowicz, who
crystallizes this idea (that *lēgī* 'sponsors' *lēctus*) into an instructive *exemplum*
of his own complex notion of analogy and the 'founding' of forms (1968, a and
b) – on which see Appendix I B. For him, present *lĕgō* transforms into perfect
lēgī by (1) the special perfect endings and (2) the vowel-lengthening triggered by
those endings. Then the derivational movement *lĕgō* → *lĕgor* is balanced by that
of *lēgī* → *lēctus (sum)* – the *forme fondée*. Next, the effect is extended to verbs
(like *rĕgō*, *rēxī*) where vowel lengthening is not the sole perfectum marker. The
first verb-type has odd interfering factors: for example, Osthoff's law will shift
predicted **uēntus* to *uĕntus*. Otherwise the major constraints of Kuryłowicz's
theory operate only on verbs of the second type (*regere*): these constraints are –

(1)   The root-final consonant must, at the time of the law's effect, be
        g or *d* or *m*.
(2)   The participial root must not differ in form from the root seen in
        the present, except in the matter of root-final consonant voice.
Here,   (1) precludes **făctus* etc.;
        (2) precludes **fissus*, **strĭctus* (loss of *-n-*);
        (1) plus (2) precludes **uĭctus (uĭncō)*, **relĭctus*.

– and (1) is credited, curiously, with ruling out **fŏsus* (*fŏdere* < **bhŏdh-*)
despite the fact that this is a verb of the first or *legere* type. (*Pāctus* is said to be

an etymological archaism, and *tāctus, frāctus* to follow its analogical lead.)

On this base, really more solid than it looks, a cleaner edifice was erected by Watkins (1970a). His version of the process – sometimes called the 'Harvard', but better the Osthoff-Kent-Kuryłowicz-Watkins (or OKKW), formulation – admits no phonological conditioning whatever (Watkins 1970:61). In other words, Kuryłowicz' constraint (1) is discarded, and as to (2) effectively verbs like *regere* are not set apart from the *legere* group. To be sure, on the latter point some nudging of the evidence is needed. It has to be asserted that *-rēgī* and **tēgī* and **āgī* (cf. ON *ók*) are the real perfect forms to cite; that *pĕpĭgī* is a reduplicative surrogate for unachievable ***pāgī* (but *tĕtĭgī* is regarded merely a late variant for **tēgī*, while **āgī* is not seen as, possibly, < reduplicated **H₂e-H₂g-*). All other aberrant profiles (e.g., *fŭndō ~ fūdī ~ fūsus; tŭndō ~ tŭtŭdī ~ tūsus; fŏdiō ~ fōdī ~ fŏssus; sĕdeō ~ sēdī ~ -sĕssus*) are explained away as having arrived too late upon the scene, or having complex specific histories, in whole or part. Objections to judgements on particular verbs suggest themselves readily; for some such objections Collinge (1975:247n.15) is a handy source. Besides, the wider aspects of the $\bar{V}C/\breve{V}CC$ alternation, already ventilated, somewhat vitiate the OKKW solution. Even so, this solution does away with **agtos*, which is unsafe at any time; and the *conditions* of the law's operation become entirely morphological.

It is not easy now to find thorough disbelievers in the OKKW solution. Some accommodate their own generative thinking to a largely morphological conditioning: so King (1973:575-76), but with a lingering affection for phonological filters. Others, like Strunk (1976), embroider new patterns of paradigm relations on to the Harvard sampler – such as thematic formation in the present. Strunk (who seeks a general Latin rule linking perfect and past participial vocalism: but see the comments in Peters 1977) proposes that not more than two opposed features may differentiate the finite and participial perfect roots, and the vowel's length may have to be assimilated to conform to this constraint: so *īcī ~ ĭctus* at once conforms, but *lēgī ~ *lĕctus* needs attention.

Three notes appeared in succession in *Linguistic Inquiry*, volume 10, merely seeking to tidy the morphological solution. Joseph (1979) and Stephens (1979) offer corrections to Perini's (1978) device of deriving the participial form by simply omitting one contextual feature, [+ active], from a morphophonological rule, thus 'generalizing' it. The former believes that 'surface pressures', rather than a simplified underlying rule, are the cause; the latter suggests the need for a Kuryłowiczian sort of analogy-formalism here, because surface-oriented functional motivation is not expressible within 'a derivationally-oriented process-format'. Both take as crucial Watkins' insistence on vowel-length as the sole marker of perfectivity, where it really occurs. Klausenburger's (1979b) contribution there comes closer to the ideological frontier: for him, the law (if put as a rule) is morphophonological, its context being

$$\bigg/ \underline{\hspace{2cm}} \begin{bmatrix} C \\ <+ \text{voi}> \end{bmatrix} + \begin{bmatrix} + \text{ affix} \\ + \text{ perfect} \\ <- \text{ active}> \end{bmatrix}$$

— a point to recall later. (Cf. also Klausenburger 1979a, and at *Lingua* 40.318, [1979].)

Davies (1979, reviewing Strunk 1976) declares (260) that "of one thing I am persuaded — Lachmann's Law is a morphological and not a phonological process"; a remark which oddly follows her healthy antipathy to such tactics as those noted above, and as explaining *cāsus* by quantitatively equating *lēg* and *cĕcĭd-* (and anyway *fŏssus* is metrically equivalent to *cāsus*). Bynon (1977:120) abandons the phonological approach — yet she seems to identify that approach with the law itself. Drachman (1980) trims, but interestingly; he uses a 'strength hierarchy' (as Foley, below), but is led to reject it in favour of paradigm pressure on the past participle, the effect being quite morphologized in pre-classical Latin. So the pure phonologists seem to deserve their continued mention.

Collinge (1975), noting assailable details in Watkins' presentation (as do Strunk 1976 and Stephens 1979), polishes up Maniet's phonetic essay. But the trading of a vowel's duration against a consonant's glottal quality (which is not the same either as having the duration *conditioned* by the quality, or as *compensating* by added duration for segment loss) must be justified by some positive motivation. It is suggested that perhaps nine grades of inherited duration of vowels have to be (conventionally) reduced to two systemic values only, and that if the syllable structure is changed a vowel may find its grading altered. But this is highly speculative in the absence of native speakers whose output can be timed; and if Latin vowel contractions offer some support (Collinge 1975:241, 219), Osthoff's law and the selective shortening of vowels in closed final syllables pull the other way.

Foley (1977:136-42) adopts the 'natural phonology' standpoint — see Appendix I B under 'Grammont's laws'. The Latin vowel cline (weak to strong) is *i-e-o-a*, with *u* uncertainly placed. Then /a+g/ is seen as a most favourable Lachmann domain (of value 6), as a very strong vowel precedes a very weak consonant (see Foley 1977:28-52). A table of combined /V+C/ values is given for

Latin (140): /i+d/ is of value 2. The law is held to apply mechanically to all combined values $\geqslant 4$ (with *ēsus, uīsus* as exceptions, and even *passus* said to need explanation, but unnecessarily). The law joins Aitken's and Grimm's as a client of the 'strength' phonologists.

Drachman (1980) brought the consonant into the shift by 'global' operation. If the Latin derivation can 'squint' back even as far as PIE, a reinstated pre-Latin */agtos/ is not needed. So that much ingenuity has always been expended on Lachmann's edict, even to the extent of believing (as does Kortlandt 1978:117) that the 'new look' of PIE consonantism must redesign this law too — which seems to test credulity to the limit, and is discussed in Appendix II.*

REFERENCES

Allen, W.S. 1978. *Vox latina.* 2nd ed. Cambridge, Univ. Press. (1st ed., 1965.)

Bohnenkamp, K.E. 1977. Zur Lachmannschen Regel. *Glotta* 55.88-91.

Bynon, T. 1977. *Historical linguistics.* Cambridge, Univ. Press.

Campbell, L. 1971. Review of King 1969. *Lg* 47.191-209.

Collinge, N.E. 1975. Lachmann's Law revisited. *FoL* 8.223-53. (Cf. also ibid. 9.397 [1976].)

Davies, A.M. 1979. Review of Strunk 1976. *CR* n.s.29.259-60.

Drachman, G. 1980. Phonological asymmetry and phonological analogy: or, will the real Lachmann's law please stand up? *Lautgeschichte und Etymologie,* ed. by M. Mayrhofer, M. Peters, & O.E. Pfeiffer, 79-101. Wiesbaden: Reichert.

Flobert, P. 1977. Review of Strunk 1976. *BSL* 72.2.155-56.

Foley, J. 1969. An interpretation of Lachmann's Law. *P(10)ICL*, 133-37. (As paper, 1967.)

—————, 1977. *Foundations of theoretical phonology.* Cambridge, Univ. Press.

Gellius, Aulus. c.A.D.180. *Noctes Atticae* (9.6 and 12.3). (Ed., e.g., by P.K. Marshall, Oxf. Classical texts, Oxford, 1968.)

Joseph, B. 1979. Lachmann's Law once again. *LI* 10.363-65.

Kent, R.G. 1928. Lachmann's Law of vowel lengthening. *Lg* 4.181-90.

---

* Note. This law is, of course, quite other than Lachmann's provision for a 'bridge' (absence of word division) between successive iambic feet, as a general rule, in Latin quantitative verse. But that metrical constraint is sometimes called 'Lachmann's law', as by Bohnenkamp (1977).

—————, 1932. *The Sounds of Latin.* (Linguistic monographs, 12.) Baltimore: Ling. Socy. of America.

King, R.D. 1969. *Historical linguistics and generative grammar*, Englewood Cliffs, N.J.: Prentice-Hall.

—————, 1973. Rule insertion. *Lg* 49.551-78.

Kiparsky, P. 1965. *Phonological change*. Diss. Cambridge, Mass.: Mass. Inst. of Technology.

Klausenburger, J. 1979a. *Morphologization: studies in Latin and Romance morphophonology*. Tübingen: Niemeyer.

—————, 1979b. Is Lachmann's Law a rule? *LI* 10.362-63.

Kortlandt, F.H.H. 1978. Proto-Indo-European obstruents. *IF* 83.107-118.

Kuryłowicz, J. 1968a. A remark on Lachmann's law. *HSCP* 72.295-99.

—————, 1968b. Dehnstufige Perfekta und Lachmanns Gesetz im Lateinischen. *Indogermanische Grammatik* II.526-28. Heidelberg: Winter.

Lachmann, K. 1850. Lucretius: *De rerum natura.* (L's edition and commentary.) (Reprinted New York & London: Garland Publ. Inc., 1979.)

Leumann, M. 1963. *Lateinische Grammatik* (ed. by M. Leumann, J.B. Hofmann, & A. Szantyr.) vol. I. Munich: Beck.

Lisker, L. 1974. On 'explaining' vowel duration variation. *Haskins Lab. Status report on speech research* 37.8.225-32. New York.

Maniet, A. 1956. La 'loi de Lachmann' et les antinomies de l'allongement compensatoire. *Fs Niedermann*, 230-37.

—————, 1979. De l'indo-européen au latin ancien par ordinateur. *Rev. de l'organisation internat. pour l'étude des langues anciennes par ordinateur*, 1/2. 1-23 Liège.

Matthews, P.H. 1972. Some reflections on Latin morphophonology. *TPS* 1972. 59-78.

Meillet, A. 1908/9. Sur la quantité des voyelles fermées. *MSL* 15.265-72.

Miller, D.G. 1969. The role of derivational constraints in analogical restructuring. (Unpubl.)

Osthoff, H. 1884. *Zur Geschichte des Perfects im Indogermanischen.* Strassburg: Trübner.

Pedersen, H. 1896/97. Bartholomaes Aspirativlov og Lachmanns Tydning af Gellius ix 6 og xii 3. *NTF* 3.5.28-38 (esp. 32-38).

Perini, M.A. 1978. The latest note on Lachmann's law. *LI* 9.144-46.

Peters, M. 1977. Review of Strunk 1976. *Die Sprache* 23.67-68.

Pisani, V. 1981. A proposito della legge di Lachmann. *IF* 86.207-208.

Saussure, F. de 1885. Sur un point de la phonétique des consonnes en i.-e.

MSL 6.246-57.

Sommer, F. 1914. *Handbuch der lateinischen Laut- und Formenlehre* 2nd & 3rd ed. Heidelberg: Winter. (Now 4th ed. of vol.I, rev. by R. Pfister, 1977.)

Stephens, L. 1979. Once again Lachmann's law. *LI* 10.365-69.

Strunk, K. 1976. *Lachmann's Regel für das Lateinische: eine Revision.* (= *KZ, Beiheft* 26.) Göttingen: Vandenhoeck & Ruprecht. (See reviews noted in *BL/LB* 1980, entry 4632.)

Watkins, C. 1970. A further remark on Lachmann's law. *HCSP* 74.55-65. (Repr. in *Generative studies in historical linguistics*, ed. by M. Tsiapera, 73-87. Edmonton & Champaign: Ling. Research Inc., 1971.)

LESKIEN'S LAW*

August Leskien (1840-1916), a famous member of the central quartet of the *Junggrammatiker* and the chief proponent of *Ausnahmlosigkeit*, also propounded a law; this was in the area of Lithuanian phonological development. He provided (1881:188-90; cf. 1919:137-38) for the shortening of those final syllable vowels which carry a falling (*acute*) accent. So *rankàs* (acc.pl.), *rankà* (instr.sg.) — with single-mora syllables remaining under the accent — versus *rañkõs* (gen.sg. or nom.pl., with abiding long *o*). In each of these cases the inherited basic syllabic nucleus is *-ā*. The different accent type, and its position, pose questions which must be taken up.

First, it is well to note Leskien's own two preoccupations: — (1) He wanted to distinguish final position from medial position, which even when secondary is not susceptible to the correction. So adjectives protected by an enclitic (definite pronoun) keep the length: in the acc.pl. fem. *geràs#ias* is opposed to uncliticized *geràs*, in the instr.sg. or nom.-acc. dual masc. *gerúo#ju* is opposed to *gerù*. (2) He insisted that, of the originally long final vowels, those with a rising (*circumflex*) accent on that syllable kept their length. Thus gen.sg. *mergõs* or nom.pl. *dëvaĩ (dievaĩ)* show no shortening, just as if the accent position was on the stem, as it is in nom.pl. *mẽrgos, rañkos, põnai*. (On the meaning of the signs *acute* and *circumflex* in Lithuanian, see Appendix III.) In this form the law must precede the effect now called 'Hjelmslev's law'.

Kiparsky (1973:824) formalizes the law thus:

$$\begin{bmatrix} V_i \\ -acc \end{bmatrix} \rightarrow \emptyset \Big/ [V_i] \!-\! C_o \ \#\#$$

— that is, the second mora (unaccented in a falling contour) is lost in the final syllable of the realized word. Kiparsky nevertheless wonders (1973:824.n16) whether, at least as a productive rule, the process should be conversely stated as a preclitic lengthening of short lexeme-final vowels (citing Kuryłowicz 1968:

* See Appendix III.

134ff.). A *circumflex* accentuation would, however, then be expected, unless a special sub-rule were invoked; Kiparsky seems to lean even in that direction.

If Germanic also once had contour accents of like placement, then forms like Gothic *gibă* (nom.sg. < PIE *-ā́*) − versus *gibō* (gen.pl. < 'circumflexed' PIE (-) (-) *-a + o m)* − may themselves have been sensitive, as regards quantity shift, to final syllable accentuation and its direction. Shortening might link with acute 'accent'. Such was Hanssen's thesis (1885) − linking Baltic intonation types as described by Hirt with mono-, bi- and trimoric vowels in Germanic. It remains Kiparsky's suggestion (1973:844-45); but of course the sensitivity is then to 'intonation' rather than 'Hauptton'; and the affected segment responds to rising movement, the *converse* of Leskien's law.

What is unclear in Lithuanian itself is why the declensional types *kója* and *galvà* seem to conform, as pseudo-input. The original vowel length is as required for the law (*ā*), and the shortening duly occurs (acc,pl. *kójăs, gálvăs*, instr. sg. *kójă, gálvă*. But there is no accent on the final syllable in relevant cases (other than nom-sg. *galvà*, which is probably a special case as far as accent in concerned). As for *rankà* etc., the accent is commonly believed to have arrived on the ending from the non-acute stem by Saussure's law (on which see the various detailed interpretations). Finally, Kortlandt (e.g., 1977:328) opines that Leskien's law forces a loss of tonal opposition on final diphthongs, except in some dialects.

REFERENCES *

Hanssen, F. 1885. Der griechische circumflex stammt aus der ursprache. *KZ* 27.612-17. (Cf. A. Bezzenberger's comment at *BB* 7. 66-68 [1883].)

Kuryłowicz, J. 1968. *Indogermanische Grammatik* II. Heidelberg: Winter.

Leskien, A. 1881. Die Quantitätsverhältnisse im Auslaut des Litauischen. *ASlPh* 5.188-90.

−−−−−, 1919. *Litauisches Lesebuch.* Heidelberg: Winter.

* Also relevant are:
Ebeling 1967*; Garde 1976*; Kiparsky 1973*; Kortlandt 1974*, 1975*, 1977*, 1978*.
− on which see Appendix III.

MEILLET'S LAW*

This contribution to phonology is by a famous master of diachronic study, Antoine Meillet (1866-1936). The realm is the Slavic mobile paradigm and its accentuation, and the crux is an intonational difference (evidenced by later contour difference) as between. e.g., Serbo-Croat nom. *gláva* and acc. *glãvu* (with 'irregular' circumflex). Meillet (1902) represented the historical dynamic in Slavic to be a matter of change of contour on the root syllable, whereby Balto-Slavic acute > Slavic circumflex. But it may be a phenomenon of 'pretonic' position. Baltic allows original end-stress to move to the left (by Hirt's law I, although this particular word is problematic in that regard); but not in all forms, and not necessarily involving a major contour difference even so: Lith. nom. *galvà*, instr. *gálva*. For Slavic, the oblique cases allow a change whereby acute-root mobile types and circumflex-root mobile types fall together; so Stang (1957:9-10), who explains it by the analogical influence of words like *zīma̅*, *zîmǫ*. Essentially, the law caters for loss of acute intonation in early Slavic: there may be more than one relevant position in the word.

Appeal to laryngealism, initiated by Illič-Svityč and carried on by Kortlandt (1975:11-12, 27), evolves a complicated version of the law. Successive losses of *H* (for which, see on Hirt's law I) operate thus:

(1)   pretonic *H* goes: **golHváH* > **golváH* (but *gólHvaH+m*)
(2)   paradigm-levelling induces **golváH* (nom.), **gólvaH+m* (acc.)
(3)   postvocalic *H* goes: **golváH* > **golvá̇*, **gólvaHm* > **gólvą̄*.

But then the Baltic accent positions are still odd, however old; and why Serbo-Croat should not end up with (simply levelled) *gláva*, **glávu* remains obscure, despite Garde (1976:198). Kortlandt says (1975:2ff.) that originally end-stressed nouns with root laryngeal gain mobility by Meillet's law; but the gain appears to be really of contour or tonal distinction. That analogy is involved is reiterated by Kortlandt (1983:32).

* See Appendix III

REFERENCES

Bulaxovskij, L. 1960. Drevnejsaja slavkanskaja metatonija akutovyx dolgot (Zakon A. Meillet). *Ezikoredsko-etnografski izsledovanija v pamet na Stoyan Romanski.* Sofia: Bulgarsk AN.

Dybo, V.A. 1958. O drevnejšej metatonii v slavjanskom glagole. *VJa* 1958. 6.55-62.

Meillet, A. 1902. O nekotoryx anomalijax udarenija v slavjanskix imenax. *Russkii filologičeskii vestnik* 48.193-200.

* Also relevant are: —
Ebeling 1967*; Garde 1976*; Kortlandt 1975*, 1978*, 1983*; Stang 1957*.

— on which see Appendix III.

NIEMINEN'S LAW*

Eino Nieminen (1891-1962) published in 1922 his work on the Baltic ō-stem neuter plural nominative-accusative reflexes (in effect, the reflexes in PIE pronominals). A large section of the book (125-70) is devoted to "the riddle of Lithuanian accentuation" (as he calls it, 125), and more especially to the question as to why, alongside nominative plural ō-stem (masc.) forms like dēvaĩ (dievaĩ), the singular counterpart is not *dēvàs (*dievàs) but dẽvas (diẽvas) "God" (134). (See the account of Endzelin's law.) Nieminen in general supports the views on this of Endzelin and van Wijk, as against Meillet. This particular leftwards shift in words of this shape (as PIE deiwós suggests that it must be) belongs to proto-Baltic. Van Wijk (1918: 20 n.137) would even claim that the shift moved other cases in the direction already attained by some, notably the accusative plural or nominative-accusative dual; and he credited the consonant stems with imposing a pattern of accent mobility. Forms like gaidỹs "cock" represent the PIE oxytone inheritance, whereas dẽvas (diẽvas) etc. result from a special Baltic development (142). The shift as such is found, according to Nieminen himself, only in the nominative, accusative, genitive, and dative singular (146); and the accusative singular was the first form to be affected.

The paradigm type kélmas "stump" – also an inherited oxytone – is more puzzling. Its accent is falling (see Appendix III), whereas that of dẽvas is rising. That is, the retraction in the former is over two moras, not one. Again, in its case the accusative plural is now affected: kélmus versus dëvùs. Possibly secondary stress is at work, so that the sequence /x̄ x $ x/ becomes /x̄ x $ x/, as in pẽlenus (< *pęlenùs) and presumably kélmus (< *kelmùs): so Nieminen (1922: 165). But /x x̄ $ x) – in dëvùs – is not input to the law. This strategy handles the accusative plural difference, but at the expense of (1) van Wijk's view of that case form – which may be false – and (2) the shift-parallelism of dëvas and kélmas. No doubt this is why Kortlandt (1974:305) presents Nieminen's law as applying only where the (1) final syllable contains /ă/ and (2) the preceding syllable has a long nucleus (he seems not to include -el-, i.e., /-VR-/, although that sequence is for accent purposes the same as /-VV-/ or /-VY-/). Hirt speaks

* See Appendix III

more generally (1899:43); Endzelin puts the shortening, as in *gĕras*, first (Nieminen 1922:157-58 – also *IORJS* 21.296ff.).

Phenomena like the rare *anàs*, "that one", *katràs*, "which", are taken by Kortlandt as a sign of the lateness of the law. They are respectable as exceptions to the analogical pull of Nieminen's law on words whose target syllable has a *short* vowel, but only as long as their time as such is not excessive. For Nieminen himself (152) it is a matter of the analogical reshaping of these (among other) pronouns.

Hirt's law I, though similar, is of Balto-Slavic vintage. Leskien's law is akin and may be fed by Nieminen's; so, apparently, Kortlandt (1974) suggests. What *that* seems to mean is that vowel length in final syllables became otiose once the Nieminen retraction had occurred. Then even forms like **rankós* were ripe for loss of length in their last vowel, despite the acuteness; whence comes the shift to *rankãs*.

REFERENCES*

Hirt, H. 1879. Akzentstudien. *IF*10.20-59 (esp. 43-55).

Nieminen, E.V.K. 1922. *Der urindogermanische Ausgang -āi des Nominativ-Akkusativ Pluralis des Neutrums im Baltischen.* (=*Annales Academiae Scientiarum Fennicae*, Ser. B.16.5.) Helsinki.

Stang, C.S. 1966. *Vergleichende Grammatik der baltischen Sprachen.* Oslo, Univ. Press.

van Wijk, N. 1918. *Altpreussische Studien.* The Hague: Nijhoff.

* Also relevant are:-
Garde 1976*; Kortlandt 1974*, 1975*, 1977*, 1978*,
– on which see Appendix III

NOTKER'S LAW

Notker III, who was also called Labeo or Teutonicus and so set apart from other religious recluses of like name at St. Gall (St. Gallen) monastery, lived from about 950 to 1022. His life's work was the translation, into the High German of his time and place, of originals as diverse as treatises of Aristotle and of Martianus Capella and Boethius, classical poetic texts from Terence, Virgil and the Disticha Catonis, and a body of psalms. A wandering scholar he, in a special sense. The most convenient modern conspectus of the necessary biographical and bibliographical details is to be found in Sonderegger (1970:79-123).

Notker's writing is noteworthy for a spelling practice, in respect of obstruents in word-initial and syllable-initial position, which may reveal facts of pronunciation otherwise beyond recall. To put it as simply as possible, his convention was this: after a boundary of at least strength /$/ — but with a debatable upper limit of strength — he wrote *b, v, d, g* if the preceding segment was a vowel or a liquid or a nasal. Everywhere else he wrote *p, f, t, k(c)*, although the words (or syllables) containing these symbols were the same (in any other sense) as partners written with the other set of signs. Sibilants were not varied. Notker does not defend, or even discuss, the practice; but later scholars have titled it his 'rule' or 'canon' or 'law'. Its wider interest has won it the usual modern name of Notker's *Anlautgesetz* (or *Anlautsgesetz*, on which variation Mohr (1973) is at least informative if not normative). Yet *Anlaut(s)wechsel* might be a safer term.

The sort of questions which have exercised Germanists since Grimm (1822: 107) first noted the usage can be listed:

(1)   Was there regularity? If so, was it maintained across time and across types of segment?

(2)   Did the practice reflect distinct origins (that is, are the segments which are regularly affected of different PIE origin from those (if any) which are sporadically written in different ways)?

(3)   Did the sign difference reflect contemporary phonological distribution (of obstruents)?

(4)   Whatever it meant, what prompted Notker to do it?

Nobody regards it as free variation; nobody has seen morphological conditioning. Otherwise, very varied answers have been given.

Some dispose of question (1) by textual emendation; then the graphology becomes systematic in a very obvious way. This is the method of (above all) Sehrt & Starck (1933, 1934; cf. Sehrt & Legner 1955). Carr (1934:283) adds 'corrections' which Sehrt has missed. But the apparent inconsistencies offer the key to a subtler solution, and are anyway more fun. The text is usually accepted as more or less what Notker really intended. In his earlier work he took speech pauses (deduced from sentence boundaries, or clausal and phrasal antithesis) as inhibiting his graphic effect: *ih fáho, tu vahést*, where *f-* and *v-* obey the rule but colon-initial *t-* escapes it. So it looks like sandhi, and so phonic. Perhaps he later became less punctilious over the 'in pausa' cases (as Weinberg thought [1911:20ff.]; but Sehrt & Starck disagree); and the choice between *f* and *v* was always the least predictable. Weinberg decided on three stages in Notker's work; and Clausing (1979:367ff.) offers a revised allotment of them: first, only sentence boundary blocked the rule; then *f* and *v* became and remained confused; then even sentence boundary was disregarded.

Braune (1891, §103. n.2) decided that the 'voiced' variants were sporadic; Notker did not get the etymologies right. But *ter brûoder* and *unde des prûoder* are typical regularities, alternating in the same etymon; so that Hoefer (1893) believed that inherited voice difference had become blurred (see on question (3)). Jellinek (1897) tried to tidy it all up: *t* appears before *r* and is preferred after *-V/R##(#)*, but otherwise a basic Germanic /f/, /þ/, /h/ reflects in Notker's script as *b, d, g.* Yet after *-N #(#)* Germanic /d/ [đ] may turn up as *d* instead of *t* (cf. Jellinek 1935:109). (Proper names may be, as so often, phonologically wayward.)

Questions (3) and (4) are not easy to separate. Jellinek (1897: 86) pointed to the medial d of *hendi* (OHG, normally, *henti*), and proclaimed an Alemannic assimilation, honestly recorded by Notker as he kinetically accompanied with his speech organs what he was writing with his pen — not a scribal carelessness, as Sehrt & Starck would have it. On the one hand, internal and external and compositional sandhi need not agree (cf. Sanskrit); and progressive assimilation is always a little doubtful (cf. Bartholomae's law). On the side of honest awareness, Clausing (1979) finds seven previous St. Gall scribes, between 788 and 909, who wrote like Notker; only in the case of initial obstruents after a word-final nasal do they vary. Again, Penzl (1980) has evidence of Notkerism before Notker, while Steinmeyer (1873) spots the usage in pre-Notkerism before documents (cf. Schatz 1921: 154; Kranzmayer 1956:77) and speculates that it dates to the period 700-1100 which was marked by much unstable output of the 'second (HG) sound-shift' (*die zweite Lautverschiebung*). But it might go on to the 14th century; Boesch (1946: 152-53) offers post-Notkerian data.

The influence of other languages has been canvassed; but without much cogency. Insular Celtic mutates its initial consonants; and St. Gall was indeed founded in 613 by an Irishman who was known as Gallus. Heinertz (1925) is for this influence; Penzl (1955) doubts it, as do others. Lenition in Irish was dead as a productive rule by the tenth century; it was a syntagmatic and morphological device and pretty well fixed as such (cf. Clausing 1979:362). Penzl (1955) had the ingenious notion that Notker had bilingual competence in Latin and Alemannic, recognized the 'phonemic' distinction of voice in Latin, and was acute to the similar sound distinction in morph-initial position in his own native tongue. The phonetics were perhaps the same and perhaps not – in 1980 Penzl decides in favour of lenis and fortis allophones of lenis phonemes – but the function and distribution different. But only one language is affected, as Notker never spells Latin words in a non-Latin way; and the proximity of his Swiss pronunciation of Latin to what Virgil, or even Boethius, would recognize was not likely to be great (cf. Moulton 1979:243). So that there are grave doubts about it; and only a watertight theory would explain how Notker was highly sensitive to Alemannic allophones and not to its phonemes – quite a paradox.

Lehmann (1971:20ff.) summarily dismisses this solution from the standpoint of 'systematic phonology', and interprets Notker as reflecting pre-Alemannic systematic phonemes through a fortis-making rule (cf. also Lehmann's remarks in *Romance Philology* 29.47ff., [1975]). Morpholexical favouring of least marked forms is also suggested (Lehmann 1971:25). Moulton (1979) also rejects Penzl's idea (but more politely, in Penzl's own *Festschrift*). He reverts to a solution based on a lenis-fortis difference, in context. 'Reverts', because Penzl had considered the idea (1955:201 - cf. 1980), as had Priebsch & Collinson (1962: 121). Also, in the same year as Moulton, Clausing (1979) ventilates the whole question as to whether Alemannic speakers of the time used voice or lenition. He decides on the latter, without explaining how significant segment distinction was then regularly maintained; and he takes the fortis to be the basic value (*pace* Lehmann) with lenition spreading, but less than voicing would (cf. *erdpûwo*). If this means that voice is more assimilatory than lenition, or more functional and less purely graphic, he does not say or prove.

Moulton's own conclusion (1979:250) is not only that Notker's *b, d, g, v* stand for lenis obstruents and p, t, k(c) f for fortis, but also that there was considerable supersession of the difference, mostly after pause and in clusters. In which case the p, t etc. series was used as the unmarked variant. Thus he moves towards Lehmann; but, presumably, special considerations must handle the variety with dentals. So Notker's native speech had voice, but only in vowels, liquids and nasals (sonorants). Finally, Moulton would judge that Notker's disposition, so to speak, was towards surface taxonomic phonology (241-47).

Yet a deal of ingenuity has scarcely yet justified a decision as to whether the practice as St. Gall was important or unimportant.

REFERENCES

Baesecke, G. 1913. Zu Notkers anlautgesetz von dr. Israel Weinberg. *ADA* 36.237-40.

————— 1918. *Einführung in das Althochdeutsch*, Munich: Beck.

Boesch, B. 1946. *Untersuchungen zur alemannischen Urkundesprache des 13. Jahrhunderts.* Berne: Francke.

Braune, W. 1891. *Althochdeutsche Grammatik.* 2nd ed. Halle: Niemeyer.

(1st ed., 1886; 13th ed. by Walther Mitzka, Tübingen: Niemeyer, 1963.)

Carr, C.T. 1934. Review of Sehrt and Starck 1933. *JEGP* 33.282-84.

Clausing, S. 1979. Notker's Anlautgesetz. *JEGP* 78.358-73.

Coleman, E.S. 1968. Bibliographie zu Notker III von St. Gallen. *Fs. Sehrt*, 61-76.

Grimm, J. 1822-(-37). *Deutsche Grammatik* I-IV 2nd ed. Göttingen: Dieterich.

(1st ed. 1819).

Heinertz, N.O. 1915. *Eine Lautverschiebungstheorie.* Lund: Blom.

Hoefer, A. 1893. Das Notkersche Anlautgesetz. *Germania* 18.200-206.

Jellinek, M.H. 1897. Zu Notkers Anlautgesetz. *ZDA* 41.84-87.

—————. 1935. Bemerkungen zum Notkertext. *ZDA* 72.109-112.

Kranzmayer, E. 1956. *Historische Lautgeographie des gesamtbairischen Dialektraumes.* Vienna: Osterreichische Akademie der Wissenschaften.

Lehmann, W.P. 1971. Grammatischer Wechsel and current phonological discussion. In *Generative Studies in historical linguistics*, ed. by M. Tsiapera, 9-43. Edmonton & Champaign: Ling. Res. Inc.

Mohr, W. 1973. Is it Notker's Anlautgesetz or Anlautsgesetz? *MPh* 71.172-75.

Moulton, W.G. 1979. Notker's 'Anlautgesetz'. *Fs Penzl*, 241-52.

Ochs, E. 1913. Zweierlei Notker. *PBB* 38.354-58.

Penzl, H. 1955. Zur Erklärung von Notkers Anlautgesetz. *ZDA* 86.196-210.

——––. 1968. Die Phoneme in Notkers alemannischen Dialekt. *Fs Sehrt*, 133-50.

——––. 1971. *Lautsystem und Lautwandel in der althochdeutschen Dialekten.* Munich: Hueber.

——––. 1980. Notker's Anlautgesetz and generative phonology. *Fs Beeler*, 441-48.

Piper, P. 1882/3. *Schriften Notkers und seiner Schule*, 3 vols. (*Germanischer Bücherschatz*, 8-10.) Freiburg: Mohr.

Priebsch, R. & Collinson, W.E. 1962. *The German language*. 5th ed. London: Faber and Faber. (1st ed., 1934.)

Schatz, J. 1927. *Althochdeutsche Grammatik.* Göttingen: Vandenhoeck & Ruprecht.

Sehrt, E.H. & Legner, W.II. 1955. *Notkers Wortschatz: Das gesamte Material zusammengetragen von E.H. Sehrt and T. Starck.* Halle: Niemeyer.

Sehrt, E.H. & Starck, T. 1933. *Notkers des Deutschen Werke nach den Handschriften.* vol. I. Halle: Niemeyer.

——––. 1934. Zum text von Notkers Schriften. *ZDA* 71.259-64.

Sonderegger, S. 1970. *Althochdeutsch in St. Gallen: Ergebnisse und Probleme der althochdeutschen Sprachüberlieferung in St. Gallen von 8. bis 12. Jahrhundert.* (= *Bibliotheca Sangallensis*, 6) St. Gallen: Verlag Ostschweiz. (Esp. 79-123.)

Steinmeyer, E. von 1873. Zur althochdeutschen Litteraturgeschichte. *ZDA* 16. 131-41.

Wardale, E.E. 1893. *Darstellung des Lautstandes in den Psalmen Notkers nach der St. Gallen Handschrift.* Diss., Zurich.

Weinberg, I. 1911. *Zu Notkers Anlautgesetz.* (= *Sprache und Dichtung*, 5.) Tübingen: Mohr.

Wilkens, F. 1891. *Zum hochalemannischen Konsonantismus der althochdeutschen Zeit.* Leipzig: Fock.

OSTHOFF'S LAW

Hermann Osthoff (1847-1909) was radical, ebullient and industrious. His energy found its major outlet as a polemicist on the neogrammarian side (does not Brugmann [1909:218] call him "ein geborener πρόμαχος"?), and in many a brave essay on outstanding problems of IE history. His waspish part in the diffusion of the 'law of the palatals' repays study. From 1879, and in particular in 1881 and 1884, he commended a law of vowel quantity shift, apparent mostly in Greek, which now bears his name. One writes 'now' because at first, and for a long time in Germany, the law was debated (even accepted) without ascription to him. Thus Solmsen (1891) cites it as a law but does not mention Osthoff; Schmidt's posthumously published attack (1905) ignores him personally (indeed, so does Hirt's approving discussion [1912:152-54]); and even in 1939 Schwyzer cites him only as a discussant and in a footnote (279). But elsewhere it is 'Osthoff's law': so in the writings of (inter alios) Meillet (1905/6), Lejeune (1946[1955]), Ruipérez (1972), Sommerstein (1973), and Palmer (1980).

The ordinance sprang from observations in 1879 (56-58) on the identity, already stated by Pott, of Gk. *λύκωις with Lith. vilkaĩs, Skt. vŕkais. This was part of a larger argument in favour of deriving λύκοισι etc. as a quite independent formation, seeing analogy to consonant-stem declension therein. The necessary shortening in the former type -ωις > -οις was proclaimed as a law in 1881 and again in 1884 (84-85); and the actual phrasing is worth noting:

> jeder lange vocal ist in der stellung vor sonorlaut . . . und einem weiteren consonant innerhalb desselben wortes urgriechisch verkürzt worden.

The domain was widened to Latin (with no solid evidence — but see Sommer-Pfister 1977:102) and hopefully to Gothic (e.g., winds < *wend(a)-s) and even to Baltic (cf. Osthoff 1879:129ff.; so mergàs < mergăns < *mergāns — and contrast Leskien's law) — but the post-sonorant consonant, in Baltic, must be either a full consonant segment (i.e., not a feature of the preceding sonorant) or else voiceless — constraints which, as it happens, would allow the law to work.

Sommerstein's (1973:67) modern formulation is:

$$V \rightarrow [\text{-long}] \ \Big/ \ \underline{\quad} \begin{Bmatrix} \begin{bmatrix} \text{-cons} \\ \text{+high} \\ \text{<+back>} \end{bmatrix} < \begin{Bmatrix} C \\ \text{<[+WB]>} \end{Bmatrix} > \\ [\text{+nas}][\text{+cons}] \end{Bmatrix}$$

— but that the shift occurred before /Y # #/ (WB means word-boundary) is not Osthoffian orthodoxy, and Greek shortening there is later if it occurs at all. Also, unless there is restriction to Greek and within Greek, [+nas] is a less correct prescription than [-syll, +son, +cons]. Sommerstein also requires a morphological boundary *before* /NC/, to remove such false output as ἄγωντοι > *ἄγοντοι. Kiparsky's version is given below.

To begin with the converted, Lejeune and Schwyzer (for instance) concern themselves primarily with the relative chronology of processes in Greek prehistory. Schwyzer (1939:279) puts the law later than the shifts of *-ns-* to *-nn-* and of *-VsV-* to *-V(h)V-* (so * āusōs-* > *āuhōs* > *(h)ā(w)ōs* > ἠώς); Hirt (1912: 153) seems to fuse these shifts. So far Lejeune agrees (189); and so do all adherents, although Palmer (1980:301) notes that *s* is lost earlier after *r*. But Lejeune puts Osthoff's effect *before* the loss of word-final stops (*ἔγνωντ* > *ἔγνοντ* > ἔγνον; a form occurring at Pindar, *Pyth*.4.4.120) — while, because ἔγνων is conversely offered by all manuscripts (but not nervous editors) at Pindar, *Pyth*. 9.79 and *Isth*. 2.23 as the 3.pl. form, Hirt tentatively puts the loss of final stops *first*. Solmsen (1891:329) is more firmly of that opinion, and sees the *-ων/-ον* variety as an alternation of external sandhi forms (/−N # # V/C−) — a concept which is a major reformulation of Osthoff (1884; v. supra). Lejeune (1972, §225). is unmoved. As he inclines to see loss of final stops as a pre-Mycenean affair he has a possibly more precise terminus ante quem for the law. And Ruipérez (1972:149) exploits the identity in quality of original short vowels and those which derive from Osthoff's law in order to date the law at an epoch when long vowels were not 'open' and syllables were not subject to the removal of 'checking'. That same period saw Wheeler's law, too. Clearly, a final date for the law must precede (a) vowel contraction (hence τιμῶντες) and (b) paradigm levelling in subjunctives (so φέρωνται after φερώμεθα) These facts nullify Kiparsky's rival notion (1967:116ff.) that the law is 'waived' (as he quaintly puts it) in the subjunctive because the mood had developed a long vowel as its sign (as perhaps it had); also, that the temporal augment as in ᾤκουν is similarly immune. Still there is the archaism φής, and the alternative Aeolic preference for monophthongizing (as τίθη); so the law may be dialectal in incidence. Kiparsky also believes (to balance his theory that λέγεις, λέγει come from *λεγε+σι, *λεγε+τι with metathesis of +*Ci*) that Homeric τίθεις, τίθει or τιθεῖ (as at *Iliad* 13.732 — cf. Attic imperfect ἐτίθεις, ἐτίθει) are Osthoffian output of metathesized *τίθηις, *τίθηιτ. His version of the law is:

$$
\begin{bmatrix} +\text{voc} \\ -\text{cons} \end{bmatrix} \rightarrow \emptyset \Bigg/ \underline{} \begin{bmatrix} +\text{voc} \\ -\text{cons} \end{bmatrix} \begin{bmatrix} +\text{son} \end{bmatrix} \begin{bmatrix} +\text{cons} \end{bmatrix}
$$

whereby $VV(=V\colon) > V$. Of course, [+sonorant] is too imprecise and should be limited to /N/, /R/ or /Y/, if general belief and acceptance is sought.

But even so not everybody has been converted. The centrepoint of dissension has long been that component of the law which admits /Y/ (i̯, u̯, in Osthoff's formula) as the postvocalic conditioner. So we are involved with 'long diphthongs' and their history, and whether Ζεύς comes from Ζηύς (which most, like Thumb-Kieckers 1932:177-78, take for a novelty in Theran-Melian) or βοῦς from *βωύς (whereas the lone ναῦς (cf. νηύς, νηυσί) seems to derive from *neH₂w- (cf. OHG *nacho*)). Allen (1976:13) points out that the law's output, if /Y/ is admitted, 'tends to be modified', whereas with /R/ or /N/ it is stable. Schmidt's last attack on the law (1905, esp.52) denounces /V:iC/ as input as strongly as in 1899 he rejects /V:uC/; and Jacobsohn (1910) is with him, believing Ζηύς to be original and *γᾱυθ- retaining ᾱ (whence E.Gk. η), to be via γη ρ- the pre-Greek source of γηθέω (44). Bally's voice is on that side (1905/6:6-8), and declares inscriptional 'Αριστήιδης the correct Attic form, even in the fourth century. As for Schmidt, he even thought to rescue from the law's clutches the type γνοῖμεν where the long diphthong is most expected and most strikingly absent, by means of a revised inheritance such as *g̑ noi-y-?).

Schwyzer (1939:279), fighting back, dislikes Schmidt's over-heavy reliance on ablaut or loans; Meillet (1905/6) supposes a deliberate pre-Greek removal of 'superlongs' — as long diphthongs would be — and not only in Osthoff's contexts. (One is reminded of Seebold's like notion on Sievers' law, and the use of 'trimoric' vowels to explain absence of shortening in Germanic.) For Hirt (1912: 153) θνήισκω is not an old form but a post-law emergent. And Lejeune has /Y/ along with /R/ and /N/ in the postvocalic slot.

Even so, the facile conflation of all -Vυς words into one sort is discouraging, although it persists in Palmer (1980:277); but Streitberg's law at least acknowledges the difference. Whereas *nāus (possibly from *neH₂-u-) is a firm reconstruction for PIE, **dyēus, **g^wous are much more speculative. We have νηϝ-forms; but we do not have *ΖηϝF- or *βωϝF-. If oblique βοϝ- is generalized from an Osthoffian nominative in Attic (as $\beta\tilde{\omega}\varsigma$ is conversely achieved in West Greek), then the $Z\eta\nu$- (or $\Delta\iota$-) forms still stand out. We have only to discount the purely Indic nominative v$\underset{\circ}{r}$ddhi (cf. Szemerényi 1956) to reduce the explicanda there, for example, to go, gav(V-) and $g\bar{a}$(C-). Then a pattern $/C^e/o^W/H/$, with PIE alternation (not, pace Georgiev, combination) at position C_2, can serve for all reflexes other than late analogies. And the $g\bar{a}$- type could rest on a compensatory process, anyway: so suggests Szemerényi (1956:197), and – for a theory without /H/ – Schindler (1973), offering, e.g., $*g^W\acute{o}u+m > *g^W\acute{o}mm > *g^{W\acute{\epsilon}}\bar{o}m$. The Greek nouns in -$\epsilon\upsilon\varsigma$ may be considered as Osthoffian, with the reflexes -$\epsilon\upsilon\varsigma$ (nom.) and -ηF- (elsewhere) before one or other quantity is levelled through the paradigm – as $*g^W\bar{o}w$- seems to be levelled in Lettish – on a dialectal basis. But this nominal type seems to be a Greek innovation; and anyway it cuts out even more firmly the oblique forms of $Z\epsilon\acute{\upsilon}\varsigma$. Besides, alternants in -$\eta\varsigma$ are rife (see Perpillou 1973).

Ruipérez (1972:141) is very sensible to say "on est très mal renseigné sur la loi d'Osthoff". Furthermore, the non-process when a nasal is followed by a nasal (cf. $\lambda\tilde{\eta}\mu\mu\alpha$, $\sigma\kappa\tilde{\omega}\mu\mu\alpha$, $\kappa\rho\eta\mu\nu\acute{o}\varsigma$, Aeolic $\mu\tilde{\eta}\nu\nu o\varsigma$) is unexplained; perhaps some cross-paradigm analogy is at work (so Wackernagel 1890:294-95) – and perhaps not. For the variable shift /V:N/ > /VVN/ or /VNN/ can be a Latin choice (see on Lachmann's law) but is not a Greek choice inside a given dialect; and /V:N:/ might be a special exception-sequence for Osthoff's law. In fact, the morphological and phonological domains of this ordinance ought soon to be a dissertation subject; otherwise the law may lose all its utility.

REFERENCES

Allen, W.S. 1976. Long and short diphthongs. Fs Palmer, 9-16.

Bally, C. 1905/6. Les diphtongues Ω, $\bar{A}$, H de l'Attique. MSL 13.1-25.

Brugmann, K. 1890. Griechische Grammatik: Lautlehre, Flexionslehre und Syntax. 2nd ed. (Iwan von Müller's Handbuch der Klassischen Altertumswissenschaft, II:1.236). Munich; Beck. (4th ed., by Albert Thumb, 1913.)

—————, 1909. Obituary notice of Osthoff. IF Anzeiger 24.218-21.

Hirt, H. 1912. Handbuch der griechischen Laut- und Formenlehre. Heidelberg: Winter.

Jacobsohn, H. 1910. Zur Geschichte des Diphthonges $\eta\upsilon$ im Griechischen. KZ 43.42-54.

Kiparsky, P. 1967. A phonological rule of Greek. Glotta 44.109-34.

Lejeune, M. 1955. *Traité de phonétique grecque.* 2nd ed. Paris: Klincksieck. (1st ed., 1946.)

——————, 1972. *Phonétique historique du mycénien et du grec ancien.* Paris: Klincksieck.

Meillet, A. 1905/6. Hellenica. *MSL* 13.26-55 (esp. 29-32).

Osthoff, H. 1879. Kleine beiträge zur declinationslehre der indogermanischen Sprachen II. *MU* 2.1-47. Leipzig: Hirzel.

——————, 1881. Review of G. Mayer, *Griechische Grammatik. Philologische Rundschau* 1, cols.1593ff.

——————, 1884. *Zur Geschichte des Perfects im Indogermanischen.* Strassburg: Trübner.

——————, 1888. *Etymologica* I. *PBB* 13.395-463.

Palmer, L.R. 1980. *The Greek language.* London: Faber & Faber.

Perpillou, J-L. 1973. *Les substantifs grecs en -ευς.* Paris: Klincksieck.

Ruipérez, M.S. 1972. Le dialecte mycénien. *Acta Mycenaea* (*Proc. 5th Int. Colloq. Myc. Stud.*, 1970) ed. by M.S. Ruipérez; = *Minos* 11.136-69.

Thumb, A. (& Kieckers, E.) 1932. *Handbuch der griechischen Dialekte.* I, rev. ed. Heidelberg: Winter.

Schindler, J. 1973. Bemerkungen zur Herkunft der idg. Diphthongstamme und zu den Eigentümlichkeiten ihrer Kasusformen. *Die Sprache* 19.148-57.

Schmidt, J. 1905. Zur geschichte der langdiphthonge im Griechischen. *KZ* 38.1-52. (Seen into print, as posthumous work, by W. Schulze.) (See also *Sitzungsb. Kön. Preuss. Akad. Wissenschaften*, 1899, 307ff.)

Schwyzer, E. 1939. *Griechische Grammatik* I (Iwan von Müller's *Handbuch der Klassischen Altertumswissenschaft*). Munich: Beck. (2nd ed., 1953.)

Solmsen, F. 1891. Zum griechischen vocalkürzungsgesetz. *BB* 17.329-39.

Sommer, F. 1914. *Handbuch der lateinischen Laut- und Formenlehre.* Heidelberg; Winter. (Vol.1, rev. 4th ed. by R. Pfister, 1977.)

Sommerstein, A.H. 1973. *The sound pattern of Ancient Greek.* (*Philological Society. Publ.*, 23). Oxford: Blackwell.

Szemerényi, O. 1956. Latin *res* and the Indo-European long-diphthong stem nouns. *KZ* 73.167-202.

Wackernagel, J. 1890. Miscellen zur griechischen Grammatik. *KZ* 30.293-316.

THE LAW OF THE PALATALS

Das Palatalgesetz is a markedly untypical creature in Indo-European. Its important implications for PIE vowel and consonant inventories must be faced, however radical and intrepid one's phonology (see Appendix II). Yet obscurity clouds its initial formulation and the identity of its inventor. All that is tolerably clear is that its birth lay between 1874 and 1879, with 1875 as the earliest probable date.

Two problems were then seen to be two aspects of the same problem: so Collitz first judged in print in 1878 (305). Sir William Jones, prompted by Halhed and others, brought Sanskrit into the limelight in 1786, Schlegel confirmed its IE centrality in 1808, and Bopp underlined it in 1816. It remained the canonic data-source until the close of the nineteenth century. Possibly Hrozný's unveiling and Kuryłowicz's exploiting of Hittite in the early 20th century were needed to shift men's gaze from an Indic orientation which resulted in as many errors as insights – as Mayrhofer (1983) amply shows. Curtius, for one, lamented the demotion of Sanskrit (cf. Jespersen 1922:91); and its 'eldest sibling' status is noted in Benware (1974:70ff.); but its prestige occasioned exactly our double-headed puzzle, which is as follows.

Sanskrit offers a simple vowel triad (/i,a,u/), rather in the Semitic manner, and this satisfied scholars even as early as Grimm. Yet Hellenic, Italic, early Slavic, and Celtic (and Gothic when its spelling is understood) suggest a PIE array of /i, e, a, o, u/. It was gradually seen that if a Sanskrit /i/ answered to /a/ elsewhere, as it sometimes does, the 'sonant coefficient' concept held the key. That concept was an offshoot of a theory of syllabic apophony, which linked /i, u/ to /y, w/ and both (in their syllabic role) to nasals and liquids. Non-syllabic function of /N/ and /R/ induced an *a*-vocalism. Hence the *inherited* vowel /a/ could be recognised as a free-standing full non-high vowel. Then 'truer' /a/ in Indic was found to have *prime* comparative relations (with non-high segments elsewhere in IE generally) which extended its reputation, so to speak, for behaviour of a low sort *and* a mid-front sort *and* a mid-back sort. Very well. Then had a set of PIE non-high vowels collapsed into one in Indo-Iranian? If so, the event must be late in IE terms; yet once the Indo-Iranian group has left the IE line of true descent no direct evidence of the collapse remains. Or had a single PIE vowel been replaced elsewhere by a triad – the 'splitting' theory of Fick still accepted by Hübschmann in 1875 (citing, e.g., for "ten" PIE *dakan* at *KZ* 23, passim), but no longer in 1879? Then the timing looks better; but what is the motivation for the split, of environment or function? By hindsight we see the correctness of the former path. Yet, as early as 1837 (911), Theodor Benfey suggested that the Greek vowel system was the original one. That was, however, a guess without circumstantial support.

Sanskrit causes another nuisance in its reflexes of PIE dorsal stops. Cognates show a triplet of equations in respect of the central feature of articulation (the position of the tongue in relation to the upper member, from prepalatal to velar): *śatam,* ἑκατόν; *kravi-,* κρέας; *kim,* τί; whence three PIE segments /k´, k, kʷ/ are deduced. The ensuing 'centum-satem' distinction of languages is famous, if now rather blurred (see Gamkrelidze & Ivanov 1980; Shields 1981). As no single language has more than one reflex-pair, we have a dilemma. Has PIE a luxuriance of dorsals, trimmed in every IE language? Or was a pair of them the PIE legacy? If so, do we have an adding of /k´/, after a collapse of /k/ and /kʷ/, in part of the field (the 'Meillet solution')? Or an emergence, in another part of the field, of /kʷ/ after /k´/ and /k/ are merged (the 'Kuryłowicz solution')? For rival supporters and critical point of debate, one may consult Allen (1978: 96ff.). But − and this is the critical point − if Sanskrit has *pañca* and *roc(ati)* where Greek has πέντε and λευκ(ός) then it has palatalization to *c* where no /k´/ is reconstructable. And that this is a novelty shown by the voiceless result *c* [ɕ], as against *s* [ʃ] from original /k´/. Subsequent palatalizing in IE idioms is commonplace. Slavic suffered it up to five times, and Albanian has a complex experience of it (Allen 1978:91). But once grant it and you destroy the Indic claim to be the treasury of trustworthy vestiges of ancestral PIE. Which may be the reason why Ascoli in 1870 put even this reflex, as a fourth velar variant, into the *Ursprache*.

Two other factors encouraged this 'Sanskritic' ideology. First, the palatalizing effect of a following front vowel would be noticeable in Sanskrit (which has /i/), and especially so to Scandinavian scholars whose native tongues respect it so much − a point to recall later when inventors are considered − were it not that the obvious *cid* is offset by the equally obvious *kim*, which was only subsequently recognized as a loan from another line of phonological descent. Other comparanda giving such a sequence are surprisingly rare (e.g. Ved. *apa-citi-*). Secondly, to accept an Indic effect limited to a following *front* vowel in, say, *cakāra* (*kʷe-kʷo-*) is hard when affected *vacas* (*wekʷos*) or *pacanti* (*pekʷonti*) are in plain view. Of course, they arise by paradigmatic levelling. But that levelling, so easily acceptable as an explanation of the absence of (expected) anomaly in morphology once a phonic shift is known, is stifling in its effect on speculation beforehand: one cannot cope with exceptions if one cannot see them. Yet Ascoli's answer so complicated PIE that it seemed to prompt a rebellion; and Pedersen (*PedS* 281) actually called it a mistake (cf. also Pedersen 1983[1916]:67-70).

If only /e/ — and to balance it /o/ — were credited to PIE and (as an inheritance) to Indic, such an evolution as $*k^w e > *ke > *ce > ca$ (with paradigmatic spread in the latter stages) became available as a cure for Sanskrit ills. Or, if the palatalization were firmly put inside early Indic, /e/ must enter its inventory and apophonic theorizing would sponsor /o/; whereupon the paradigms would react as we have seen. This dual recognition — so brief and simple an answer, in contrast with the inspissated statement one is forced to make of the problems — might just as well have been called 'the law of the Proto-Indo-European vowels' — especially as an acrid debate on that score involving Schmidt, Brugmann, Collitz, and Saussure was going on at the time. But the emergence of the palatals was the more immediately cogent fact, whence the traditional title. Yet in 1874 Amelung independently re-floated Benfey's notion that PIE (and Greek) /e/ had fallen together with /a/ in Sanskrit. And so we come to the brink of 'discovery', while by 1879 Collitz and Hübschmann were writing as on a codified and registered law. The quinquennium is therefore known; can we know, within it, who first declared the essentially two-handed answer?

This law, alone among major IE ordinances, is not dignified with a proprietor's name. Jespersen (1922:90n.1) declared futile any attempt to find one. Two possible claimants (Thomsen and Verner) both deplored any search to establish the paternity; indeed Thomsen calls the resulting disputes 'unedifying' and Verner cited the *Code Napoléon* against such enquiry. He likens the law to an overripe fruit, and derides scholars' claims to the dubious credit of having shaken the tree hardest (see 'document 4'). Yet a noble itch to laud a hero, or a cruder curiosity, propels us after a century to set one researcher of the time against another. Some are fringe figures, easily put aside: such — despite their spadework — are Benfey, Ascoli, and Amelung. Others merely guided their followers or helped contemporaries to clear their thoughts: these were Fick, Bezzenberger and Bugge. Four of those who were certainly on the scene clearly have no claim to the *Prioritätsrecht* (as it was called): Osthoff admits to the role of chief informee ('document 3', below), when the law was first made known in a Leipzig restaurant in October 1876. (This restaurant was presumably in the striking building at Kleine Fleischergasse 4, still known as 'Haus Kaffeebaum'. It was built in the 16th century, its facade being redesigned in 1725; its decorative lintel displays 'Turkish' figures and a coffee-bush.; During the 1730s J.S. Bach was among the members of the 'Collegium Musicum', an off-duty performing club for professional musicians which met there on Friday evenings (in winter), knowing it as 'Zimmermann's coffee-house'. In 1741, after the first two years of Bach's final period of residence in Leipzig, Zimmermann died and the musical gatherings seem to have terminated.) Thwarted in his eagerness to organize a colloquium on the law, Osthoff published its substance in 1878 – and carefully gave the credit elsewhere. And of those to whom it came as news – and on *this* point there seems no reason to doubt Osthoff's later report – Brugmann and Leskien did not even publish on it, while Hübschmann wrote his paper (1879) as about accepted doctrine, and named Verner – as had Osthoff – as its source. Which means that the field is narrowed to six candidates: alphabetically; Collitz, Saussure, Schmidt, Tegnér, Thomsen, Verner. And it may be that we should go no further, but allow each equal and independent rights of ownership. That is the balanced conclusion of Mayrhofer's enquiry into the matter (1983), although he does essay an ordering according to the moment of enlightment (p. 142 and 82), thus: 1 Thomsen, 2 Verner, 3 Collitz, 4 Saussure, 5 (equal) Schmidt and Tegnér.

The reader must judge personally; and what follows is a brief review of the case for and against each claimant. Above all, five papers are prime evidence and may be called the 'documents in the case': no.1, Schmidt 1881; no.2, Collitz 1886 and 1887; no.3, Osthoff 1886; no.4, Verner 1886; no.5, Thomsen 1920. Each will be cited in its place. To revert to alphabetical listing:

Collitz, Hermann (1855-1935)
'Collitz 1878' appeared in May of that year and on its last page predicts the discovery. In 1879 the promise is made good. Collitz is critical of Osthoff's 1878 (July) paper as betraying failure to find a copy of his own submission of two months before. The 'law' was, he says, the subject of talk between himself, Fick, Bezzenberger (as they confirm) and Benfey in the summer of 1876 (the date chosen is noteworthy). Collitz's first paper calls for a courageous revision of the PIE vowel system. His second unerringly links the vowel problem to the palatal-problem (so does Hübschmann 1879:409-10). In 'document 2' Collitz concedes that Thomsen, Verner and Saussure have independent claims to the law; and he continues to commend Benfey to our notice; but in the 1887 defensive postcript he asserts his 'right'.

On Collitz's side are the claims made by others for him, starting with *Literarisches Centralblatt* for 1886 (he is named with Schmidt) and continued by such as Prokosch (1939:93) and Porzig (1954:27 – but with a false date of 1879); so more recently Allen (1973:123). There is no proof that Collitz was affected by Scandinavian thinking before 1878 (and his is the first *publication* of the essence of the law). Yet, at the crucial time of 1875/76, Collitz was 20.

Saussure, Ferdinand de (1857-1913)

Streitberg twice (1913 and 1915) named Saussure as, at the least, among the law's discoverers. Szemerényi (1967:68n.1) is only persuaded by the vividness of Osthoff's 'document 3' not to repeat his (1964:4n.6) ascription of credit to Saussure – who had, after all, begun this line of opinion by his own personal claim to the idea (Saussure 1879:369). Lately, another supporter has appeared (Koerner 1973:22-23; 1976:343; 1978:199). Saussure's famous *Mémoire* (1878) laid the foundations for laryngealist theorizing; and his 'delicacy' in his 1879 paper in splitting the monolithic /a/ of supposed inheritance – even if derived to some extent from Brugmann – seems to be a seminal innovation of equal fruitfulness. And 'document 2' names Saussure (but not alone) as discoverer of the *Palatalgesetz* (cf. Arens 1969:314-15).

But Saussure was rarely an independent thinker (cf. Collinge 1979:209, Koerner 1978:149, Scaglione 1981:54). Moreover, his *Mémoire* not only treats the PIE vowels as obscure objects of manipulation but fails to relate the quality range in $\varphi\epsilon\rho$-, $\pi o\delta$-, $\dot{\alpha}\gamma$- to the Sanskrit levelling in *bhar-, pad-, aj-*. His 1879 array of non-high vowels /A, A_2, a, a_2/ does not set the first two apart from the others as 'back' from 'front': indeed, most cases of apparent PIE /o/ underlie the /a2/ reflexes. Yet *arcāmi* is granted a palatalization before /a_2/, which argues for frontness (and in fact falsely so) against /A/ in *arka-* and /A_2/ in the second syllable of *cakāra* (*$k_2a=k_2A_2r+A$). There are other mysteries here, chiefly in the Greek etyma. But the major mystery is whether Saussure could have aired this thesis in a paper in Paris in July 1877, having worked on it in Leipzig (where he studied from 1876-78), without any knowledge of the fully-fledged palatal theory which at the time of his presentation had been common property in Leipzig for nine months. Yet so he later professed, in answer to a direct question from Streitberg 1915.206). No doubt (as Mayrhofer [1983:141 n.74] correctly deduces) the group of professors who heard Verner's remarks direct in the famous 'Kaffeebaum' episode would not have included the newly-arrived Swiss student (despite Osthoff's contrary report, concocted ten years later and inspired by his approval of Verner). But Saussure cannot have remained unenlightened, especially if he was working on a Brugmannian vocalism; Brugmann (who writes afterwards as if he knew Saussure well) would not have failed to make the relevant points, having very likely been among Verner's auditors and quite certainly close to Osthoff whose excitability guaranteed a continued buzz of excitement. Saussure's 1878 *Essai* promises a follow-up which perhaps the *Mémoire* was; but his 1877 and 1878 papers display different attitudes to IE vocalism (cf. Mayrhofer 1983:141n.78). Well, "inter uirtutes grammatici habetur aliqua nescire" (Quintilian, *IO* 1.8.21); yet hardly in this case.

Schmidt, Johannes (1843-1901)

'Document 1' was written (says Schmidt) in the spring of 1878, but submitted to *KZ* in June 1879. It certainly makes the right point about Indo-Iranian palatalization, and thus corrects his attitude of 1877 (*KZ* 23). It comes late in the day. It is a surprise that he declares May 1877 to be the date since which he had included the doctrine of the law in his lectures. He half-claims the credit of invention in his 1881 paper (62); he certainly believes that Collitz and Saussure did not publish their views until after his own contribution was at least composed. In 1884 he still imputes some credit to himself, but scarcely with his whole heart.

Yet Schmidt is ready to mention Thomsen (1881:63) as the earliest authority for the real history of things like Sanskrit *ca.* 'Document 2' (by Collitz) has much to say in praise of Schmidt; but it carefully gives others the limelight when discussing the law. Schmidt was great enough to accept a disturbing theory at once; perhaps that much alone is safe to say.

Tegnér, Esaias Henrik Vilhelm (1843-1928)

E.H.V. Tegnér, the grandson of the famous bishop-poet of Sweden, is the most shadowy of the contenders. He was a biblical and lexicographical expert and wrote only one paper on IE history (1878), which at the crucial time was an interrupted (printed) fragment with a gummed-in explanation of the author's sense of being *de trop* in the whole affair. (So we learn from 'document 4'.) From its references it dates Tegnér's own thinking. or writing up of his thoughts, to the spring of 1877 at the earliest. Yet Osthoff names him with honour in 'document 3'; and Thomsen states that Tegnér's conclusion agreed with his own in substance and in timing ('document 5'). But, with too late a data and no direct word on his deductions, we cannot be too free with our recognition.

Thomsen, Vilhelm Ludvig Peter (1842-1927)

Thomsen and Verner agreed that they discussed the substance of the law in the summer of 1875 in Copenhagen (just after the birth of Verner's law, q.v.).

Thomsen claims (in 'document 5') to have reached the correct answer by himself in late 1874 or early 1875 (he does *not* put it so early in 1902) – as early as he could have located it, in view of Amelung (1874). Verner ('document 4') admits to having revealed all in the 'Kaffeebaum' restaurant in Leipzig in October 1876 (and implies that for his auditors it was a startling revelation); but he mentioned Thomsen as one involved and about to publish on the law. Indeed, Verner had written in August 1875 to the editors of *KZ*, giving Thomsen's past (and likely future) part in it all. Thomsen is sure that neither in letters nor conversation did Verner speak of himself (Verner) as the discoverer. Thomsen believed himself to be the 'father'; and he declared in a way reminiscent of Schmidt, that his lectures since 1875 had contained his finding. Only the disinclination by Ernst Kuhn to publish what seemed an otiose repetition of what Schmidt and Hübschmann were about to write, and that on a notion which was 'floating in the air', prevented Thomsen's 1877 paper from appearing. It had in any case been delayed by his visiting appointment in Oxford in 1876. That paper (which appeared, half revised, in 1920) is in German; its highly emotional vernacular preface is essential reading for detectives in this case.

Verner, Karl Adolf (1846-1896)

Against this candidate four facts stand out: (1) He did not actually publish on the law; (2) he gave credit elsewhere in public and in correspondence; (3) he was contrite over his 'leak' of it in Leipzig, at least in part on another's behalf; (4) he deplores the whole *Prioritätsrecht* fuss ('document 4').

But for him one might marshal three considerations: (1) By 1875 his own work had led to his theorizing on ablaut and that in turn (via syllabic metaphony) must have underlined the need for the mid vowels /e, o/ in the PIE inventory; (2) the confrontation of seemingly separate historical clues (here between Indic consonantism and non-Indic vocalism) is a curiously Vernerian feature; (3) both Osthoff (1878:116n.) and Hübschmann (1879:409n.1.) name him as the 'father', and the former implies a discovery date of 1876. Together these points seem suggestive.

More will without doubt come to light one day. For the present it is safest to accept Mayrhofer's verdicts: (1) the law was found roughly simultaneously by six researchers in entire independence, and (2) it is still in essence a matter of considerable relevance to modern abstract phonology (as treated in, for example, Kiparsky 1982).

REFERENCES

Allen, W.S. 1973. Χϑών, 'ruki', and related matters. *TPS* 1973.98-126.

──────, 1978. The PIE velar series. *TPS* 1978.87-110.

Amelung, A. 1874. Erwiderung. *KZ* 22.361-71. (Reply to Leo Meyer, *KZ* 21. 241-49.)

Arens, H. 1969. *Sprachwissenschaft.* 2nd rev. ed. Freiburg and Munich: Alber. (1st ed., 1955.)

Ascoli, G.I. 1870. *Lezioni di fonologia comparata.* (= *Corsi di glottologia* 1.) Turin: Loeschner. (Cf. *Vorlesungen über die vergleichende Lautlehre des Sanskrit, des Griechischen und des Lateinischen,* transl. by J. Bazzigher & H. Schweizer-Sidler. Halle: Waisenhaus, 1972.) (Esp. 42-43.)

Benfey, T. 1837. Review of A.F. Pott, *Etymologische Forschungen auf dem Gebiete der indogermanischen Sprachen,* I. Lemgo: Meyer, 1833, in *Ergänzungsblätter zur Halleschen Allgemeinen Literaturzeitung,* Dec. 1837 (nos. 114-17), cols.905-33 and May 1838 (40-43), cols.313-41. (Cf. *Kleinere Schriften,* ed. by A. Bezzenberger. Berlin: Reuther. 1890, 1.2.1, esp.p.10.)

Benware, W.A. 1974. *The study of Indo-European vocalism in the nineteenth century. SiHoL* 3. (2nd corrected ed., 1984.)

Bopp, F. 1816. *Ueber das Conjugationssystem der Sanskritsprache in Vergleichung mit jenem der griechischen, lateinischen, persischen und germanischen Sprache.* Ed. by K.J. Windischmann. Frankfurt: Andreä.

Collinge, N.E. 1979. Review of T.A. Sebeok, ed., *Current Trends in Linguistics* 13. The Hague: Mouton, 1975. *Lg* 55.207-211.

Collitz, H. 1878. Uber die annahme mehrerer grundsprachlicher *a*-laute. *BB* 2.291-305.

──────, 1879. Die entstehung der indo-iranischer palatalreihe. *BB* 3.177-234.

──────, 1886. Die neueste Sprachforschung und die Erklärung des indogermanischen Ablautes. *BB* 11.203-42. (With the following, forms Document 2).

──────, 1887. Wahrung meines Rechtes. *BB* 12.243-48. Both above repr. in Wilbur 1977.

Gamkrelidze, T.V. & Ivanov, V.V. 1980. Problema jazykov 'centum' i 'satəm' i otraženije 'guttural'nyx' v istoričeskix indoevropejskix dialektax. *VJa* 1980.5.13-22 (cf. *ibid.* 4.21-35).

Hübschmann, J.H. 1879. Iranische Studien. *KZ* 24.323-415.

Jespersen, O. 1922. *Language, its nature, development and origin.* London: Allen & Unwin.

Kiparsky, P. 1982. *Explanation in phonology.* (= Publications in the Language

Sciences, 4). Dordrecht: Foris.

Koerner, E.F.K. 1973. *Ferdinand de Saussure* (= *Schriften zum Linguistik*, 7.) Brunswick: Vieweg. (Diss., Simon Fraser Univ., 1971.)

——, 1976. 1876 as a turning point in the history of linguistics. *JIES* 4.333-53. (= 1978:189-209.)

——, 1978. *Toward a historiography of linguistics: Selected essays.* = *SiHoL* 19.

Mayrhofer, M. 1983. *Sanskrit und die Sprachen Alteuropas. NAWG* 1983.5. 121-54.

Meillet, A. 1939. *Linguistique historique et linguistique générale II.* Paris: Klincksieck.

Osthoff, H. 1878. Formassociation bei zahlwörtern. *MU* 1.92-132. Leipzig: Hirzel.

——. 1886. *Die neueste Sprachforschung und die Erklärung des indogermanischen Ablautes.* Heidelberg; Petters. (Document 5; cf. Collitz 1886 and 1887; reprinted in Wilbur 1977.)

Porzig, W. 1954. *Die Gliederung des indogermanischen Sprachgebiets.* Heidelberg: Winter.

Prokosch, E. 1936. Hermann Collitz in memoriam. *JEGP* 35.454-57. (= Sebeok 1966: 2.74-77).

——, 1939. *A comparative Germanic grammar.* Baltimore and Philadelphia, Linguistic Society of America.

Rooth, E. 1974. *Das Vernersche Gesetz in Forschung und Lehre.* Lund: Gleerup.

Saussure, F. de 1878. *Mémoire sur le système primitif des voyelles dans les langues indo-européennes.* Leipzig: Teubner. (Dated 1879 but actually publ. Dec. 1878 = 1922:1-268).

——, 1879. Essai d'une distinction des différents *a* indo-européens. *MSL* 3.359-70 (as paper of 1877 = 1922:379-90).

——, 1922. *Recueil des publications scientifiques de Ferdinand de Saussure.* Geneva: Sonor; Lausanne & Paris: Payot.

Scaglione, A. 1981. *The theory of German word order from the Renaissance to the present.* Minneapolis; Univ. of Minnesota Press.

Schlegel, F. von 1808. *Ueber die sprache und weisheit der Indier.* Heidelberg: Mohr & Zimmer. (Repr., with an Introd. by K. Koerner, Amsterdam: Benjamins, 1977.)

Schmidt, J. 1877. Wa beweist das *e* der europäischen Sprachen für die Annahme einer einheitlichen europäischen Grundsprache? *KZ* 23.333-75.

——, 1881. Zwei arische *a*-laute und die palatalen. *KZ* 25.1-179. (Document 1.)

Schmidt, J. 1884. Address to Prussian Academy, recorded in *Sitzungsberichte der Königlichen Preussischen Akademie der Wissenschaften*, Berlin, (esp. 741).

Sebeok, T.A., ed. 1966. *Portraits of linguists.* 2 vols. Bloomington: Indiana Univ. Press.

Shields, K. Jr. 1981. A new look at the centum/satem isogloss. *KZ* 95.203-13.

Streitberg, W. 1913. Obituary of Saussure. *IF Anz.* 31.16.

——————, 1915. Ferdinand de Saussure. *IJb.* 2.203-13 (Repr. in Sebeok 1966: 2.100-10.)

Szemerényi, O. 1964. Structuralism and substratum. *Lingua* 13.1-29.

——————, 1967. The new look of Indo-European: Reconstruction and typology. *Phonetica* 17.65-99.

Tegnér, E.H.V. 1878. *De ariske språkens palataler.* Lund: Univ. Årsskrift, 14.

Thomsen, V.L.P. 1902. *Sprogvidenskabernes Historie.* Copenhagen: Gad.

——————, 1920[1877]. Der arische *a*-Laut und die palatale. In *Samlede Afhandlinger* 2.303-27. Copenhagen & Oslo: Nordisk Forlag. (Preface = Document 5.)

——————, 1927. *Geschichte der Sprachwissenschaft bis zum Ausgang des 19. Jahrhunderts.* (Transl. Hans Pollak, with permission and revisions by Thomsen.) Halle: Niemeyer. (1902 orig. repr. in *Samlede Afhandlinger* 1, 1919.)

Verner, K.A. 1886. Zur Frage der Entdeckung des Palatalgesetzes. *Literarische Centralblatt*, vol.49, cols. 1707-10. (= Rooth 1974:17-20; repr. in *Afhandlinger og Breve*, Copenhagen: Frimodt, 1903.) (Document 4.)

Wilbur, T.H. 1977. *The Lautgesetz controversy: A documentation.* Amsterdam: Benjamins.

PEDERSEN'S LAW I

Familiar indeed is the 'ruki' rule. Most obvious in Indo-Iranian, it allows an inherited dental /s/ to shift to some sort of 'shibilant' pronunciation when preceded in the same phonological word by a /k/ or /r/ (including vocalic /r̥/) or a high vowel (including the [-syllabic] offset of a falling diphthong – which in Sanskrit in turn entails the underlying offset of a monophthongized /e:/ or /o:/). In Sanskrit, rather specially, the strident sound is retroflexed; in Iranian /u/ seems reluctant to act as trigger. The constraints are set out in the grammars (not always as explicitly as could be wished); and exceptions are widely discussed (as by Burrow 1976) and prompt bold speculation.

That the rule is characteristic of the so-called 'satəm' languages was Meillet's proposal in 1922 (furthered by Martinet 1951 and 1955:237ff.). Yet it has commonly appeared to be impracticable to edit the phonology, within and across the relevant languages, so as to mould the four causing segments into a 'natural class'. Doubts were expressed by Entwistle (1944:33-34), Zwicky (1964 and 1970 – where he strangely chooses /k/, rather than /r/, as the odd man out – see the discussion by Allen, 1973:103ff.,) and Sommerstein (1973:53). The last-named is ready to follow Martinet in assigning [+high] to /r/; does this mean it was uvular? Then the class is of the subset of high segments which can immediately precede /s/ in PIE. Allen (1954 and 1973:105ff.) rejects that device, and prefers a variety of phonetic outputs to balance the variety of triggers. But he sees a common feature of 'lingual closeness'. Then in each affected language the result, of its choice, is generalized. This idea derives from Morgenstierne's (1929) work on Kafiri. But Sommerstein eyes it with scepticism (1973:53-54n.74), and opts for a unitary first result with special retroflexion, where found. But a smoothing of an awkward variety of 'high in the mouth' effects really seems credible enough. An appeal to acoustics (allophones similar at the auditory level) is made by Vennemann (1974:esp. 94).

Now this much general information has been required in order to place in its diachronic setting the particular evolutionary path of this 'indefinite fricative' (the phrase is Allen's [1973:106]) in Slavic. For there it is called 'Pedersen's law' (and is quite other than Pedersen's law II, q.v.). It was stated by Holger Pedersen (1867-1953). He claimed independence for his conclusions; but he granted credit for a similar revelation to Baudouin de Courtenay and to Zubatý. Pedersen's presentation (1895:74) assigns an input *s* [s] and an output *ch* [tʃ] to the law for Slavic. It limits the conditioning contexts by disallowing a plosive as the immediately following segment. (In Indic only a following /r/ or word-boundary in practice inhibits the rule. A non-contiguous /r/ sometimes seems to counter-condition, as in *sisarti* versus *viṣṭāra-*; cf. Whitney (1889, §181a). Data on non-coronal plosives is hard to assess, the words being of the etymologically opaque sort, like *puṣpa-*.)

An intermediate stage of [ʃ] was supposed by Pedersen, and Spanish invoked as having undergone that sort of sibilant history. The whole law is set out in modern dress (by features) by Kantor & Smith (1975:392), as the third historical process out of thirty-four such processes on the way from PIE to Contemporary Standard Russian. Their assurance that the form and the order of the processes has stood up to computer testing must give us all great confidence.

Pedersen (as can be gathered from 1895:87) exchanged ideas with Fortunatov. The latter had affirmed, at least in lectures, that the same shift was to be observed in Lithuanian. But there the input was to be split into:

$$/s/^1 > [\text{ʂ}] \Big/ \left\{ \begin{matrix} i \\ u \end{matrix} \right\} \underline{\quad\quad}$$

$$/s/^2 > [\text{ʃ}] \Big/ \left\{ \begin{matrix} r \\ k \end{matrix} \right\} \underline{\quad\quad}$$

Fraenkel (1950:113-14) is prepared to agree, despite Pedersen's own doubts. But [ʃ] can arise from /s/^{1}, and that was perhaps the basic result and only countered by morphological analogy: so argues Karaliunas (1966). On the other side, Andersen (1968:esp.183ff. and 190) questions *both* the [ʃ] output after *i, u* in Lithuanian *and* the constraint located in a following obstruent in Slavic.

The debates in this sector have subsided, certainly over the last decade. Possibly a flare-up is overdue.

REFERENCES

Allen, W.S. 1954. Retroflexion in Sanskrit. *BSOAS* 16.556-65.
———, 1973. Χθών, 'ruki', and related matters. *TPS* 1973.98-126.
Andersen, H. 1968. IE *s after *i, u, r, k* in Baltic and Slavic. *AL(Haf)* 11.171-90.

Burrow, T. 1976. Sanskrit words having dental -s- after *i, u,* and *r. Fs Palmer,* 33-41.

Entwistle, W.J. 1944. The chronology of Slavonic. *TPS* 1944.28-44.

Fraenkel, E.1950. *Die baltischen Sprachen.* Heidelberg: Winter.

Hamp, E.P. 1967. On IE **s* after *i, u,* im Baltic. *Baltistica* 3.7-11.

Kantor, M. & Smith, R.N. 1975. A Sketch of the major developments in Russian historical phonology. *FoL* 7.389-99.

Karaliunas, S. 1966. K voprosu ob i.e. **s* posle *i, u* v litovskom jazyke. *Baltistica* 1.113-26.

Martinet, A. 1951. Concerning some Slavic and Aryan reflexes of IE **s. Word* 7.91-95.

––––––, 1955. *Économie des changements phonétiques.* Berne: Francke. (3rd. ed., 1970.)

Meillet, A. 1922. *Les dialectes indo-européens.* Paris: Champion.

––––––, 1965. *Le slave commun.* 2nd ed. (1st ed. 1924.) Paris: Inst. d'Études slaves.

Pedersen, H. 1895. Das indogermanische *s* im Slavischen. *IF* 5.33-87 (esp.74-87).

Sommerstein, A.H. 1973. *The sound pattern of Ancient Greek.* (Philol. Society Publ., 23.) Oxford: Blackwell.

Vennemann, T. 1974. Sanskrit *ruki* and the concept of a Natural Class. *Linguistics* 130.91-97.

Whitney, W.D. 1889. *A Sanskrit Grammar.* 2nd rev. ed., Boston: Ginn. (1st ed., Leipzig: Breitkopf & Härtel, 1879.) (12th unchanged ed., Cambridge, Mass.: Harvard Univ. Press, 1972.)

Zwicky, A.M. 1964. Three traditional rules of Sanskrit. *Quarterly Progress Report*, MIT Research Lab. of Electronics, no.74.203-204.

––––––, 1970. Greek-letter variables and the Sanskrit *ruki* class. *LI* 1.549-55.

PEDERSEN'S LAW II*

One of the latest diachronic processes of the unified Balto-Slavic era, in the sector of word-accent, is described and assigned its conditions of occurrence by Holger Pedersen (1867-1953). This law (Pedersen 1933:25) concerns 'retraction', or leftward shift, of accent in words of more than two syllables within mobile paradigms of nominal lexemes. (The fronting of the accent in *verbal* *di*syllables has been covered, more recently, by the law of Ebeling, q.v.) Pedersen's limited concern was with the type (exemplified by numerous scholars, starting with Saussure − cf. Kuryłowicz 1958:201-202) seen in Lithuanian *dùkter-*, from **duktė̃r-* (cf. Greek acc. ϑυγατέρα). That is, in mora terms, . . . (x)x$x̃$x##> . . .(x)x̀xx##. The target syllable always gets a falling contour. Thus also **piemẽn- > piemeni*; but *piemuõ* (disyllabic). That the law is limited to mobiles is well shown by Kortlandt (1977:326-27).

Pedersen's (1933) achievement was not the recognition of the change (see already Saussure 1922[1896]:533), but his suggestion of a paradigmatic reason for it. If non-final accent contrasts with a final stress elsewhere in the paradigm, its essential non-finality induces polarity; that is, it becomes as far removed from final placing as possible. This was not (for Pedersen) the result of an urge towards maximal contrast (the motive which Ebeling saw for *his* law); rather, the over-careful production of an accent which must not be confounded with end-stress induced a semi-accidental 'antifinalizing' − and so fronting − process. It was 'exagéré et anticipé'. The effect is to enhance the mobility of accents in paradigms, and to assimilate vowel-stem declensions to the consonant-stem type. Of course, if proclitics induce the shift, then Pedersen's law is the mirror-image of Dolobko's: cf. **vedá > vĕda* (by Ebeling's law), whence **ne+vĕda > nèveda* by Pedersen's law (II).

The chronology, even the relative chronology, is not easy to establish, for several reasons. For Kortlandt (1975:9-10) it is possibly the earliest retractive law (even the earliest accentual law of any kind) in Balto-Slavic. He also sees it as operating twice, once in Balto-Slavic and again in Slavic after separation (1974:10; 1977:326-27). But there has been at many times a very pronounced leftward trend in Slavic accentuation, taking multifarious forms: stress even

* See Appendix III.

retracted to the proclitic itself when the postclitic syllable had a short or circumflex vowel. Traces exist; e.g. Russ. *ná-voda, vó-vremja*. The whole thing is a matter of drift.

Finally it is to be noted that Kuryłowicz (1958:193) prefers to convert this law into two similar shifts (cf. Stang 1957:11). So:

(1)   x ẋ x # # > ẋ x x # # *and*
(2)   x x ẋ # # > x ẋ x # #

(or, where the word has more than three syllables,

>.. ẋ x x x # #)

REFERENCES*

Pedersen, H. 1933. *Etudes lituaniennes*. Copenhagen: Levin & Munksgaard.
Saussure, F. de 1922. *Recueil des publications scientifiques de Ferdinand de Saussure*. Geneva: Sonor; Lausanne & Paris: Payot.

* Also relevant are:-
Garde 1976*; Kortlandt 1975*, 1977*, 1978*; Kuryłowicz 1958*; Illič-Svityč 1963* (= 1979*); Saussure 1896*; Stang 1957*
— on which see Appendix III.

SAUSSURE'S LAW*

Ferdinand de Saussure (1857-1913) needs no introduction. After careful consideration of his many contributions across the field of linguistic enquiry, it is strange but just to find his onomastic monument tucked away in an accentual corner of a single language, Lithuanian. Even there, his thinking in this particular sector owes much (as he acknowledged) to the pioneering work of Fortunatov and Bezzenberger. The law in question is often entitled that 'of Fortunatov and Saussure' (cf. Matyeeva-Isaeva 1930); but some, e.g. Shevelov (1964:55ff.) and Garde (1976:439-40), are fiercely determined to show that Fortunatov's idea was different and deserves separate consideration (hence, see Fortunatov's law II in Appendix I A).

First in 1894 (89), then again in 1896 (= 1922:526-38), Saussure proposed an explanation for such derived rightward shifting accent patterns in nouns as

> nom.sg. *rãtas*; acc.pl. *ratùs*
> nom.sg. *rankà* (? < *rañka*); acc.pl. *rankàs*.

That is, the stress passes from a short or *circumflex* (rising) syllabic nucleus to an *acute* (falling) one: so van Wijk 1922:1. Kortlandt (1975:26; 1978:68) exemplifies it by *blusà* (versus gen. *blùsos*) and interprets it thus: "the ictus is transferred from a non-falling to a following acute. . . vowel". This is similar to Halle and Kiparsky's version (1981:156): "the accent shifts from a non-acute syllable to the following acute syllable", which is more accurate in referring to syllables rather than vowels (cf. Garde 1976:191), despite their further description of it as an inter-phoneme transfer of 'tone' (cf. Saussure 1896:157). Kiparsky (1973:825) had already refined it further by the use of moras: the input is a 'second-mora' accent. Saussure's own contrastive examples are the affected *laikýti* > *laĩkyti*, as opposed to *ráižyti* where the original long vowel has given the initial syllable a marked acute — that is, in Lithuanian terms, a falling — contour or first-mora accent, which is unaffected. This applies even when the fall or rise operates over a vowel-plus-resonant sequence (see Appendix III).

* See Appendix III.

Intra-paradigm constraints clearly operate. Kiparsky's (rather unhelpful) formalization of the law (1973:825) is:

$$V \rightarrow \acute{V} \ / \ VC_0 + C_0 \text{ --- in strong cases.}$$

He puts it in informal terms eight years later (Halle & Kiparsky 1981:156), but with more clarity. His concept of strong and weak cases remains, but the specification as to which is which has been modified. In 1973 the critical discovery was of a move of accent from a stem-final (last stem mora) position to a case-suffixal (first suffixal mora) position. The morphological structure is, indeed, very relevant: non-acute *rãtas* has stem-final accent in Kiparsky's terms, whereas acute *púodas* has not, and *lángas* has a 'marginally alternating' stress. Original short vowels must obey the law. In 1981 the formula is contrastively instanced by (class 2) *rankà* and (class 4) *barzdà* – the noun classes deriving from Senn (see Kiparsky 1973:823). The former type has shifted the accent on to the ending from the strong non-acute stem, *both* in the strong acute nom. sing. *and* in the homomorphous weak acute instr. sing. The latter has had the same experience in the instr. sing., but its nominative singular marker (attached to a weak stem) is simply the first accentable element in the word. (One is reminded of the Dybo-Garde rule reported by Kortlandt [1978:275], whereby any word is stressed on its first strong morpheme.) It appears that we face a mere coincidence of outcome. The overall results of the law are a new generalized alternation and an increase in accent-types; in effect (for Garde 1976:192, § 267) a redoubling of the latter, as Saussure himself saw (1896:158=1922:527). The distinctive operation is discussed by Becker (1981 – citing Darden 1972), who believes in *two* Saussurian laws: a rightward shift from all short vowels in all noun types and cases, and a leftward retraction in class 2 and class 4 nouns. The latter shift causes the circumflex accent.

This all means that Saussure's law must be peculiar to Lithuanian – and may be restricted to disyllabic words. Its relation to Leskien's law is important (cf. acc.pl. *pirštùs, vardùs*). The older writers (Belić 1914; Lehr-Spławiński 1917, 1918) did not think so; nor, it seems, did Matthews (1960:42). But Stang (1957) and Kuryłowicz (1958 – really already in 1952 in *Rocznik slawistyczny*) had decided so (although Kuryłowicz's denial of intonation in unstressed syllables effectively rules out both this law and Fortunatov's law II). This was even before Illič-Svityč (1963), Darden (1970), and Kortlandt (1974:304-305; cf. 1975: 26; 1977:327) discovered that not even Latvian is in the law's domain: one may compare Latv. *bãrda* with Lith. *barzdà*. Whereas van Wijk (1922:1ff.) had boldly spoken of what happened in Slavic as an agreed analogue, it was only as such and no more ("ein ähnliches Gesetz"), and the supporters of Fortunatov's second law assert its difference. Equally, only tentatively can Halle and Kiparsky in 1981 (157) call Dybo's law "a process intriguingly similar to Saussure's law". The likeness is in the eye of the beholder; and it is not made clear whether Halle and Kiparsky, who declare (1981:171) Saussure's law to be a 'tone-flop' rule still productive in contemporary phonology, would say the same about Slavic.

As to chronology, Kortlandt (1974:304; 1975:10; 1977:327) puts Saussure's law after Pedersen's (II) — there is no effect in, e.g., *negãli* — but before Leskien's. The first decision is not entirely cogent; the second states the obvious.

REFERENCES*

Becker, L.A. 1981. De Saussure's Laws: the origin of distinctive intonations in Lithuanian. *IJSLP* 24.7-21.

Birnbaum, H. 1983. Review of Kortlandt 1978*. *IJSLP* 27.175-80.

Bonfante, G. 1931. Una nuova formulazione della legge di F. de Saussure. *SB* 1.73-91.

Darden, B.J. 1970. Accent in the Lithuanian noun declension. In Magner & Schmalstieg 1970:47-52.

—————, 1972. Rule ordering in Baltic and Slavic nominal accentuation. *SEEJ* 16.74-83.

Halle, M. & Kiparsky, P. 1981. Review of Garde 1976, *Lg* 57.150-81.

Kenstowicz, M. 1972. Lithuanian phonology. (Diss. Illinois 1971.) *Stud. Ling. Sci*. 2.2.1-85. Illinois.

Kortlandt, F.H.H. 1978b. Review article on Garde 1976, *Lingua* 44.67-91. (For Kortlandt 1978*, see App.III.)

Kurylowicz, J. 1958. *L'accentuation indo-européenne*. Wrocław: Polska AN.

Magner, T.F. & Schmalstieg, W.R. (eds.) 1970. *Baltic Linguistics*. University Park: Pennsylvania State Univ. Press.

Matthews, W.K. 1960. *Russian historical grammar*. London: Athlone Press.

* Also quoted or relevant are:-
Belić 1914*; Garde 1976*; Kiparsky 1973*; Kortlandt 1974*, 1975*, 1977*, 1978*; Lehr-Spławiński 1966*; Saussure 1894*, 1896*; Shevelov 1964*; Stang 1957*; van Wijk 1923*

— on which see Appendix III.

Matyeeva-Isaeva, L.V. 1930. Zakon Fortunatov-de Sossjura. *IORJS* 3.1.137-78.

Robinson, D.F. 1970. Stress placement and accent classes in the Lithuanian noun. In Magner & Schmalstieg 1970:119-26.

Saussure, F. de. 1922. *Recueil des publications scientifiques de Ferdinand de Saussure.* Geneva: Sonor; Lausanne & Paris: Payot.

Senn, A. 1966. *Handbuch der litauischen Sprache* I. Heidelberg: Winter.

van Wijk, N. 1922. Zur baltischen und slavischen Akzentverschiebungsgesetz. *IF* 40.1-40.

―――――, 1924. Das Gesetz de Saussures im Altpreussischen. *Tauta ir Židis* 2.29-34.

Zeps, V. & Halle, M. 1971. Outline of the accentuation in inflectional paradigms of literary Lithuanian. *Quarterly Progress Report*, MIT Research Lab. of Electronics, no.103.139-58.

ŠAXMATOV'S LAW*

It is useful to find a named shift of significant but small process, cross-linguistic but narrow domain, and citation and support which are markedly on the wane. Then one has a limiting case. Certainly, dimmer ordinances may justifiably be congregated into the communal and less individual world of an appendix; Šaxmatov's law perhaps just deserves a full mention.

In 1915 Aleksander A. Šaxmatov (1864-1920), a pupil of Fortunatov, proposed a regular, phonological, leftward shift of Slavic word accent. The retraction is from a short and circumflex syllable; and the language domain covers Serbo-Croat, Russian and (indirectly) Slovene. Examples are SC *ȕ grad, nȁ nokat* or Russian *próžil(o), nálil(o)* (versus *žȋlo, lȋlo*; wheras *bíla* with an acute first syllable does *not* prompt the effect when compounded: so *pobíla*). In Slovene, interim forms like *nâ goro* are offered.

Meillet objected (1934, §184; cf. 1916:67ff.) that no Slavic phonetic law was visible. Rather, Indo-European generally inherited, as a feature of morphological derivation, a tendency to assign early accentuation to a prepositional phrase or compound, as in Skt. *úpahita-*, Gk. ὑπόθετος (from the base *+d^hHtó-*, or equivalent). He said that Russian acted differently from Serbo-Croat, and he restricted the effect to 'semi-adverbials'. (Still, a PIE compound stress rule even with those limitations would be a find.)

Bulaxovskij (1947) defended the law by adducing eighteenth and nineteenth century Russian (and perhaps Ukrainian). But exceptions are rife and need special arguments; and the quantity of the vowel and the intonation of the syllable which receives the new accent are debatable. Ossowski (1965) finds the law unacceptable in its phonological implications; Dybo (1975:7) refers to it as if its name were unknown and Birnbaum's (1975:121) dismissive phrase of the same year "the controversial accent law attributed to Šaxmatov" perhaps gives the quietus.

* See Appendix III.

REFERENCES

Birnbaum, H. 1975. *Common Slavic.* Cambridge, Mass.; Slavica Publishers.

Bulaxovskij, L.A. 1947. Akcentologičeskij zakon A.A. Šaxmatova. In *A.A. Šaxmatov 1864-1920; sbornik statej i materialov*, ed. by S.P. Obnorskij. 399-434. Moscow and Leningrad: AN SSSR.

Dybo, V.A. 1975. Zakon Vasil'eva-Dolobko v drevne-russkom. *IJSLP* 18.7-81.

Meillet, A. 1916a. Review of Šaxmatov 1915. *BSL* 20.87-91.

––––––, 1916b. Notes sur l'accentuation des noms en indo-européen. *MSL* 19.67-84.

––––––, 1934. *Le slave commun.* 2nd ed., with A. Vaillant. Paris: Champion. (1st ed., 1924.)

Ossowski, L. 1965. Tzw. prawo A.A. Szachmatowa w słowiańskim. *Symbolae in honorem G. Kuryłowicz*, 220-22. Wrocław-Warsaw-Kraków.

––––––, 1968. Tzw. prawo Szachmatowa w świetle poglądow J. Kuryłowicza na bałto-słowiańska i słowiańska intonację. *Symbolae philologicae in honorem V. Taszycki*, 222.234. Wrocław.

Pirigova, N.K. 1959. K voprosu ob akcentologičeskom zakone A.A. Šaxmatova. *Voprosy istorii russkogo jazyka*, 158-82.

Šaxmatov, A.A. 1915. Očerk drevnekšego perioda istorii russkogo jazyka. *Encyklopedija slovjanskoj filologii*, ed. by V. Jagič. 2.7. Petrograd. (Repr. Mouton, 1967.)

SIEBS' LAW

In 1901 Theodor Siebs (1862-1941), renowned for his work on German pronunciation and on Frisian, wrote a long etymological paper which appeared in print three years later (Siebs 1904). Its nub was the claim that a systematic Proto-Indo-European word-initial alternation subsisted such that

#sk(h)- ~ #k(h)- ~ #g- etc.

The examples were cross-linguistic (MHG *schellen*, Kg. κέλαδος, OHG *gellan*) or intralinguistic (Swed. *dimba, stimba > stimma*) or both (Dutch *stoom, doom*, Eng. *steam*). The relation holds across the range of PIE plosives and their descendants. Only too obvious is the enrichment of etymological booty once the *voiced* series is included: Siebs presents an impressive if optimistic array of comparanda. He seems convinced (293) of the prefixal nature of the *s-*, but disavows Pott's earlier explanation of the phenomenon (reduced prefixes).

One start-point was the well-known but patchy instability of PIE /s/ in the context #–*C-*. Latin *speciō*, Skt. *paśyati*; Gk. στέγος, Lat. *tegō*; Lat. *tonō*, Eng. *stun* (and English *melt* and *smelt*, or even locutions like *harum-scarum*, *helter-skelter*) make the point. Hoenigswald (1952) is a paper devoted to the phenomenon and extends it to presumable cases where *C* is realized as not-yet-colouring H, subsequently lost. This means that *s-* appears sometimes – as it did already to Siebs (1904:293) – to be unstable before vowels also. But if some respectability is gained there, more questionable is Siebs' involvement of initial voiced stops.

Yet it is commonplace to hear of children, as language acquirers par excellence, who combine instability of initial sibilants with voicing (and occasionally aspiration) in nearby segments: so English *sky, sty, spy* are often heard in children's speech as [gaɪ], [daɪ], [baɪ]. For a report on just such a pronunciation stage, if perhaps an unusually regular one, a consultable source is Smith (1973). The evidence (on his pages 15, 21) is then formalized (p.25 rule 7, p.31 rule 25); and the effect is claimed as universal (15 n.1) but is admitted, on the basis of one word, to be also word-medial. Now the second segment in, e.g., Eng. *spy* is in sheer phonetic terms muscularly lax but accompanied neither by significant vocal cord activity nor by onset delay of subsequent voicing. In effect, it is practically identical to a typical voiceless initial /b/ in the language and unlike initial /p/ [pʰ]. Orthographic *sby could be defended. What is heard as [baɪ] is probably the natural result of a mere failure to produce the initial /s/ before a lax stop. An adult, however, interpreting in terms of his fixed system reinforced by spelling, will diagnose an alternation based on a lax/tense distinction in absolute initial position: #sp- ~ #b-, etc.

Of course, the facts of developmental phonology are actually far more complicated. What happens in children's speech to homorganic /st/, for example, is often idiosyncratic; and features like friction and aspiration can be confused and transposed. Still, at least a possible interpretive basis for the Siebsian effect can be found — provided that voice and aspiration *are* the features in play.

But are they? Ever since the roughly contemporaneous (1972ff.) speculations of Gamkrelidze & Ivanov, Hopper, Bomhard, and others (which are set out in Appendix II) a radical phonetic reappraisal of PIE stops has been available, especially of traditional 'mediae'. If Siebs' ordinance is dynamically valid at all it involves tension or voice, and Hopper and the others are wrong; but if the 'new look' school is correct, then the law implies a ready switch between phonation sources and is unlikely. So what Siebs discovered was only a random and perhaps an etymologically suspect phenomenon.

Support for Siebs in the traditional mould, but with revision of his pronouncements, has not been lacking. It really should not pass unnoticed that he himself speaks (1904, esp. 294, where he claims to restate his law but actually first codifies it) as if the #g(h)- form is basic and the presibilantized variant is secondary:

> Lautet die wurzel mit idg. media an, so beginnt die parallele s- form mit idg. s+ entsprechender tenuis; lautet die wurzel mit idg. media aspirata an, so beginnt die parallele s- form mit idg. s+ tenuis oder tenuis aspirata (1904:294).
> So g- is linked with sk, and gh- with skh- and sk-.

As the first notable reactor, Kuryłowicz (1935:53-54) approves Siebs' idea but somewhat misreports it, as simply #sgh- > #sk(h)- (ignoring basic #g(h)). He divides Indo-Iranian #(s)kh- etc. into (1) that arising from #sgh-, giving Gk. σχ-, sk- elsewhere, and (2) that arising from #(s)kH-, giving Gk. σκ-, sk- elsewhere. Later (1956:378) he adds to the testimonia of (1) some traces of non-sibilantized #gh- etc.: Lat. frāgor (< *bhrHg-) alongside Skt. sphūrja(ya)ti, Gk. σφαραγέομαι (< *sbhrHg-); and to the evidence for (2) traces of s-less #gH- etc. (Skt. bhuráti along with sphuráti and spūrdháti). But it is from Germanic, and really only thence, that he supports the central Siebsian position

(ON *demma, stemma*; MHG *briezen, spriezen* etc.). For, after all, the Indic, Greek and Latin results are only the normal ones, if we make play merely with the shifty character of PIE initial /s/.

Then came Illič-Svityč, who contributed so fruitfully to Slavic accentuation studies as well as PIE consonantism before his untimely death. He reformulates Siebs in order to accommodate some instances of Slavic initial *x*- (1961), which he parallels by the *s*-less MIA forms like *khaṇḍá*-. His citation of Siebs' law is also unhappily erroneous: the original publication is misleadingly dated 1901 (n.35); and the effect of prefixing /s/ to /gh/ in PIE is for Siebs not, as Illič-Svityč says, #*skh*- alone but rather #*skh*- or #*sk*-. Some of Siebs' etymologies are (perhaps deservedly) doubted; and Illič-Svityč, who dismisses /kh/ from IE, sees the reflexes as

1.   PIE #*sk*-   retained everywhere
2.   "   #*sg*   >   Ind. *sk*-, Gk. σκ-, Gmc. and Balt. *sk*-, Slav. *x*-
3.   "   #*sgh*   >   Ind. *skh*-, Gk. σχ-, Gmc. and Balt. *sk*-, Slav. *x*-

Szemerényi (*SEinf* 97-98) certainly and refreshingly reports correctly on Siebs; but in referring to the Illič-Svityč version of the law he omits the crucial anomalous reflexes there credited to Slavic (and Middle Indic). It is not really clear why the different behaviour of *medial* clusters of this type − or the odd Avestan imperative *zdī* (**s+dhi*) should induce him to doubt Siebs' law as fundamentally as he seems to do (Szemerényi 1970:136, cf. 1972:147). Presumably, one may add, quite late and secondary shifting is not to be included: so Armenian *skesur* < **sgesur*, already from **kʷwekʲur*- < PIE **swekʲur*- (cf. Skt. *śvaśura*-, *śvaśrū* for the like assimilation). Yet Cuny (1936:73) believes that the *sbh* > *sph* shift (as he sees it to be) is a relic of very old, because progressive, assimilation behaviour; whereas Armenian assimilation is here progressive long after it has been regressive.

On balance, there seem to be just enough sensible etymon-links to justify relating, e g., *sk(h)* and *g(h)* etc. in Siebs' way. After all, Skt. *sphuráti* and *bhuráti* clearly share a semantic core of "move jerkily", and *fragor* and σφαραγέομαι that of "noisy splitting". And a close relation of that kind is not good news for any 'voiceless *versus* murmured *versus* ejective' analysis of PIE plosive consonants. But in the end it must be the tally of generally agreed etymological equations which will judge the law's impact − and its credibility.

REFERENCES

Allen, W.S. 1977. The PIE aspirates: phonetic and typological factors in reconstruction. *Fs. Greenberg*, 2.237-47.

Cuny, A. 1936. Évolution préhistorique de l'indoeuropéen. (Review article on Kuryłowicz 1935.) *REA* 38.69-77.

Gamkrelidze, T. & Ivanov, V.V. 1972ff. See Appendix II.

Hoenigswald, H.M. 1952. Laryngeals and *s*-movable. *Lg*. 28.182-85.

Hopper, P.J. 1973ff. See Appendix II.

Illič-Svityč, V.M. 1961. Odin iz istočnikov načal'nogo *x*- v praslavjanskom. *VJa* 1961 4.93-98.

Kuryłowicz, J. 1935. *Études indo-européennes I.* (*Prace Językowej*, 21.) Kraków; Polska AN.

――――, 1956. *L'apophonie en indoeuropéen.* (*Prace Językoznawcze*, 9.) Wrocław; Polska AN.

Siebs, T. 1904. Anlautstudien. *KZ* 37.277-324.

Smith, N.V. 1973. *The acquisition of phonology: A case study.* Cambridge, Univ. Press.

Szemerényi, O. 1972. Comparative Linguistics. *CTL* 9.119-95.

SIEVERS' LAW I

The law's province is Indo-European phonology and phonotaxis; the battle-grounds are (a) Vedic metrics and (b) IE noun and verb morphology, especially in Greek, Latin, Germanic and Baltic. The inventor was Eduard Sievers (1850-1932), expert in phonetics and the history of English. He called it a 'law' at the outset, and he formulated it thus: (Sievers 1878:129):-

If, in Indic, /I/ or /U/ occurs before a vowel and itself carries no accent (not even the falling contonation of a post-acute syllable or of acute plus contraction), then − no matter what the accent position may be elsewhere in the word − this segment is realized as a consonant after a light syllable and as a vowel after a heavy syllable.

Im Indischen unbetontes (nicht svaritiertes) *i* oder *u* vor einen vocal ist consonant nach kurzer, vocal nach langer silbe ohne rücksicht auf die sonstige accentlage des wortes.

The accent conditions seem complex; they are in fact pellucid. The admirably clear expression of the segment realization compensates by turning out to be challengingly mysterious. The law seems to say:

$$
\begin{bmatrix} +\text{segm} \\ +\text{son} \\ -\text{cons} \\ +\text{high} \\ -\text{accent} \end{bmatrix} \rightarrow \begin{cases} [-\text{syll}] \\ \\ [+\text{syll}] \end{cases} \bigg/ \quad \begin{bmatrix} V \\ -\text{long} \end{bmatrix} \quad C_o^1 \;-\; V \;\; (i) \\ \begin{bmatrix} V \\ +\text{long} \end{bmatrix} \quad C_o \;-\; V \;\; (iia) \\ \begin{bmatrix} V \\ -\text{long} \end{bmatrix} \quad C_2 \;-\; V \;\; (iib)
$$

and should generate by (i) /aya, atya/; by (iia) /āia, ātia, āktia/; by (iib) /aktia/ etc.

These formulae of segment sequences are time-honoured in this setting. In them, *i, y* are self-explanatory as *V/C* realizates of a semivowel, with *u, w* symbolizing a second and different semivowel; *a* means any vowel other than the vocalic form of a semivowel; *t* stands for any consonant; and *k* for any second and different consonant. (But Edgerton's use of '/' is hereafter replaced by the more usual /#/ or /# #/.) Yet the formulae are not conducive to clear under-standing: there could scarcely be a warmer invitation to reinterpretation (and misinterpretation). At the very least, /āia/ must be amended to the /āya/ which really figures in the reflexes: e.g., *pāvaka-*, *sāya-* etc.

Edgerton's restatement of the law (1934, 1943) absorbed so much limelight that it would seem perverse to postpone its mention. It combined three additional elements, of which only the third was Edgerton's own; and it led to a temporary flowering (from 1934 to around 1970) of a pseudo-orthodoxy. Which is why so often 'Sievers-Edgerton' is the epithet of the law and of its related phenomena. Linguistic scholarship is no tideless sea: in current fashion this secondary creed has receded to become a virtual heresy. The novelties were:

(1)   – that in the second context of his formula Sievers really meant to account not for /ātia/ or /aktia/ but for /ātiya/, /aktiya/ (and /#tiya/). Hence, as Edgerton puts it, "after a heavy syllable Vedic post-consonantal *y, v* become *iy, uv* before a vowel" (1934:235; for supporting statistics, see Szemerényi, *SEinf* 101-102). This revision had been suggested by Osthoff (1881:399) and Wackernagel (1896:203) – and Benfey saw the alternation in these terms as early as 1871 (91ff.), although he interpreted it as a difference between classical Indic spelling and early or late practice. The consequence is that now *y, w* are assumed as starters; en passant, we are rid of **āia*. Yet Sievers cannot be thought tacitly to acquiesce. He saw a powerful generalization lurking in his vision of the law: namely, that a vowel in a subsequent syllable is, and remains, more substantially vocalic when the preceding syllable is heavy than when it is light (1878:130-31). Therefore /i, u/ must always be more to his mind than /iy, uw/ as realizates, and even than /y, w/ as primes. Well, well: recent scholarship is with Edgerton here; so Kuryłowicz (1964:566) and Seebold (1972:29); while Sihler (1971:64n.13) anachronistically but revealingly cites *[V̄tṃmo] as an expected output of 'Sievers' law' (as, in effect, does Nagy 1970). Interesting, too, is Grammont's view (1895) that *iV* becomes *i̯V* (9-10; cf. Szemerényi *SEinf* 100) – although this input *iV* is not too easy to reconcile with Grammont's idea (12) that *y(i̯)* only becomes *i̯* when not the onset of a syllable (i.e., /$X–, where X must not be null).

(2)   – that Sievers' observation turns out to be valid not just for /I, U/ but equally for /R/ (*r,l*) and /N/ (*n,m*) – and Edgerton even makes tentative overtures towards /H/, the PIE laryngeal (1943:108). The pairings *w, uw* (cf. Vedic *t(u)vām*) and *n, 'ṇṇ'* as in Greek δάκνω versus ἁμαρτάνω or the ἀνδάνω type) can then be subsumed under the second and third variants of the Kuryłowiczian reflex-triple /R̥, R, R̥R̥/. This extension had occurred, again, to the mind of Osthoff (1884:391-92 and 477) – at least for IE perfect verb stems and some

aorists — and to Wackernagel (1896:11,29) and Hirt (1921:198-99). On the whole it is accepted, at least as a basis for enquiry; but Kiparsky (1972) rejects it for Sanskrit.

(3) — that, if the restatement in (1) is accepted as the kernel of Sievers' law, it is really more fruitful to express the conditioned alternation thus:

— after a(n accentless) light syllable, that which is basically post-consonantal /iy, uw/ in Vedic before a vowel now becomes, secondarily, /y, w/ (*y,v*) (cf. Edgerton 1934:327).

(This direction of the process is etymologically supported by such cases as *su+varṇa-* > *svarṇa-*, *anu+vart-* > *anvart-*, where the derivation is actually obscured. This is the pronouncement known as 'the converse of Sievers' law' (which is presaged in Wackernagel 1896 I,59); it is toned down in 1943 to a statement of the mutual exclusiveness of *iy* and *y* — a more sensible attitude, considering the absence of, e.g., PIE **suweḱuros*. Once it is applied, to all semi-vowels and to as many IE languages as will stand it, it comprises the 'Sievers-Edgerton' theory as usually understood; its recent vicissitudes deserve the separate excursus below.

Point (1) may be seen as part of the shaping of the orthodoxy. Curiously enough, Edgren (1885) had confronted the Ṛgvedic phenomena at much the same time as had Sievers (i.e., in 1878). His solution blends economy and radicalism: /y, w/ are not in PIE at all, but arise in language-specific ways from various sandhi reflexes of /i, u/. Yet, one must ask, can it be denied that — unlike some clearly long-post-PIE segments such as /z/ or some briefly 'phonemicized' items like Brugmann's /ŋ/ — /y,w/ have always had a pretty strong claim to PIE status, especially as word initials? So it follows that the ordered shifts (1) /I/ → *y/i*, (2) *y* → *y/iy* (or else, in the more truly Edgertonian version: (1′) /I/ → *i/iy*, (2′) *iy* → *iy/y*) represent the 'minimal Sievers-Edgerton' formulation. As a formal rule it would be:

$$
\begin{bmatrix} +segm \\ +son \\ -cons \\ +high \\ -accent \end{bmatrix} \rightarrow
\begin{cases}
[-syll] & \begin{bmatrix} V \\ -long \end{bmatrix} & C_0^1 \text{——} V & (a) \\[2ex]
[+syll]_i\,[\,-syll\,]_i \Big/ \left\{ \begin{bmatrix} V \\ +long \end{bmatrix} \atop \begin{bmatrix} V \\ -long \end{bmatrix} \right\}
\begin{matrix} C_0 \\ \\ C_2 \\ C_1 \end{matrix} & & \text{——} V & (b) \\
& \# \# & & \\[2ex]
[+syll] \left\{ {C \atop \#\;\#} \right\}\text{——}C & & & (c)
\end{cases}
$$

It is a sensible, and could be a useful, presentation; but Edgerton would go too far.

This 'minimal S-E' is exploited by, for instance, Kuryłowicz (1935:90-91) who offers this triplet:

(a)　　$T\underset{\wedge}{i}o\text{-}$　　< primary　　　　　　　$Te\underset{\wedge}{i}o\text{-}$
(b)　　$T\underset{\wedge}{i}io\text{-}$　< secondary　　　　　　$Te\underset{\wedge}{i}o\text{-}$ (via $T_e\underset{\wedge}{i}o\text{-}$)
(c)　　$T\underset{\wedge}{i}o\text{-}$　　< $Tei\eth o$　　(via $T_e i\eth o\text{-}$, $T i\eth o\text{-}$)

But Kuryłowicz (1935:256ff.) opines that there are two basic ways of inheriting a sequence $C^y/wV\text{-}$ from PIE, and that these are evidenced by (1) Skt. *svapna-* (where, as Schindler says (1977:57), there is no form **suopno*-) on the one hand (*-CRV-*), and (2) *s(i)yam* (cf. Lat. *siem*) on the other (*-C(R)RV-*). This is much the same point as was made above on e.g. *swekuros*. Which means that *Anlaut* phenomena are predictably arbitrary, and suggests that Sievers-Edgerton is not a universal law in IE.

The 1970s produced two partial revisions of Sievers' position, in which Edgerton is either directly opposed or tacitly used but overtly ignored. The slighter and more slighting treatment is that of Horowitz (1974), in which (somewhat obscurely) Sievers' pronouncement is trimmed in its application so as to cover only the cases after certain 'short' syllables ending in a consonant. In that context, *-iy-* etc. are said to become *-y-* etc. The whole matter of the incidence of /R/ after heavy syllables is declared to be quite another story, which is not revealed in this brief thesis, mostly an anti-Edgerton polemic. Of greater weight is Seebold's (1972) book-length discussion. It surveys a whole

world of Sievers' phenomena and work on them (esp. pp.25-175). Then he
concentrates on Vedic, only to unveil at last (343-48) a revised model of the
PIE semivowel reflex system (which has not pleased everybody: see Hoenigswald [1980:84]). Seebold offers, apparently, these simple and unsullied
bloomings of PIE semivowel seeds in different beds:

(1)   – for /I/ etc. /aya, ayt, ay#: tya, tit, ti#; #ya, #it, #i#/
(2)   – for /IU/ etc. /aywa, auyt, ayu#; tiwa, tyut, tyu#; #iwa, #yut,
         #yu#/
(3)   – for /II/ etc. /tiya, #iya; tīt, #īt; tī#, #ī#/

– with odd tidying rules: e.g., #iwa may have #yuwa as 'Ausgleichprodukt'.
(In fact, Seebold's own notation uses O for *a*, k for *t*. He also offers an alternative model which allows *i, u* as primes and caters for e.g. /tīya/ > t-ĭ-ĭ-a. Edgerton's formulae are listed below.) Once notices that no dynamic relation (as
between (1) and (3) for example) is formulated. So /tya/ and /tiya/ are just
two available shapes, with different bases and no motivation for the apparent
gemination of a single semivowel in one etymology – the other pole from
Edgerton's over-powerful rationale for /atya/ versus /#tiya, ktiya, ātiya/.

Seebold does, however, have a shot at pushing Gothic back on to the stage.
This opposes Kluge (1891, 1911, 1913) who saw no Sieversian role at all for
Gothic. The big scene, as always, is the alternation *ei/ji* (for Szemerényi *SEinf*
100, **iji/ji* – but the question of **ii* versus **iji* is open) in the verbal and nominal paradigms. Among first class weak verbs, 2 sg. *rōdeis, sōkeis* seem to reflect
simply /CV:Ci+VC/, while under *lagjis, nasjis* there lies /CVCy+VC/. In masculine nouns the nominative and genitive singular *haírdeis* and *harjis* can equally
be seen as pure Sieversian products within the unrevised version of the law (cf.
Sievers 1878:125-26); they are as good testimony as anything in Vedic (where
the Edgertonian version has seemed to be motivated). It can be argued that *ei*
and *ji* are beginning to split into independent markers (at least in respect of
morphological conditioning): the latter wins out in neuters – cf. Murray &
Vennemann 1983:525 – (both *kunjis* and *kunþjis* have it despite the difference
of stem 'weight'), the former may become restricted to feminines and make a
paradigm type. Early Germanic evidence for the law is increased by Springer's
(1975) offering of early runic variants like *Holtijar, Harja*.

But if Seebold's ideas satisfy Lehmann (1955) they do not suit Marchand
(1955). Besides, when Seebold accepts Sieversian phenomena outside Indic
(against Ickler 1976), he is largely prompted by his own inventory of semivowel

reflexes. Much is made (1972:132) of the concept that PIE (or pre-PIE) offers three types of syllabic weight, thereafter reduced to two. So light syllables $/V_1^1C_0^1/$, and heavy syllables $/V_1^1C_2^2/$ or $/V_2^2C_0^1/$ survive, but super-heavy syllables, $/V^1C_3/$ or $/V_2C_2/$, are rejected (though this notation is not Seebold's). Of course, later morphology may engender super-heavy syllables: cf. Latin *yu-n-g+s-, *sa-n-k+to- > iūnxit, sānctus; and there is the Sanskrit *ta3* type. One must be pardoned for reading into this argument a movement from super-heavy *rōdjis* ($/CVVCy+Vs/$) to heavy *rōdeis* — or why have the weight theory? So Seebold's process really is a new element in the theorizing. So is Vennemann's (1971) notion of a generally enhancing feature F (of vocalic nuclei), of which duration is just one possible realization. If a nucleus which is +F can be equated with a syllable weighted by checking, then Sievers' law (in Gothic) can be re-written as Vennemann 1971:105):

$$\begin{bmatrix} -\text{cons} \\ +\text{high} \\ -\text{back} \end{bmatrix} \rightarrow [+\text{voc}] \Bigg/ +C_0 \begin{Bmatrix} VC_1 \\ \begin{bmatrix} V \\ +F \end{bmatrix} \end{Bmatrix} C - \begin{bmatrix} V \\ +\text{high} \\ -\text{back} \end{bmatrix}$$

— or (if $\bar{V} \equiv VV$, as $\bar{C} \equiv CC$) as (1971:107):

$$\begin{bmatrix} -\text{cons} \\ +\text{high} \\ -\text{back} \end{bmatrix} \rightarrow [+\text{voc}] \Bigg/ +C_0 \, V[+\text{segment}]_1 \quad C - \begin{bmatrix} V \\ +\text{high} \\ -\text{back} \end{bmatrix}$$

And if syllabic plurality in stems can be equated with syllabic weight, then the -eis form on disyllabic masculines (as *bōkareis, láisareis*, despite the light stem-final syllable) can be explained as conditioned by an 'enhanced' stem, a state to which a vowel +F would be one contributor; but this goes beyond Vennemann. Lahiri (1981) — starting from unpublished ideas of Schmieren — has other mechanisms for handling the uneven diffusion (across genders) of the noun reflexes of *ei, ji*; but while the conditioning factors are recognized and Vennemann is quoted there is no word about Sievers.

Beade's intervention (1972: esp.453) salvages something for Gothic also, at the same time as Seebold, but independently. His grounds are partly a greater sensitivity to the law's input (the vowels, taken as primes, must be both high and front); and partly a morphological determining of the environments. To preserve some power of prediction inside Germanic he proposes (455) this

Gothic modification of Sievers:—

$$i \rightarrow [+\text{long}] \quad\Big/\quad <\text{long root}> — i< \left\{\begin{matrix} s \\ \text{þ} \end{matrix}\right\} > \#$$

— although a subsequent truncation rule is, presumably, held up the sleeve.

Morphological boundaries, as such, seem not to play their common handy, joker-in-the-pack role in most speculations on Sievers' pronouncement (although the 'Anlaut' variation, as *s(i)yam* or *d(i)yaus*, is absent in plurisyllables, and that argues a constraining force for /##/; cf. Lindeman 1965). Some appeal to grammatical derivation does, however, enter the field with Seebold. He sees the forming of adjectives from nouns (by the IE affixal device, +/Y/) as at once formally and semantically differentiated into

(1)   X+*iya*- (accentless)   = 'having the qualities of X' (e.g. *náriya-*)
(2)   X+*yá*   = 'pertaining to X' (e.g. *gavyá-*)

Only after light syllables is the distinction visible even in Vedic, because of the 'revised Sievers' process by which the incidence of -*iya*- is enforced after heavy syllables. As Theodora Bynon (1974:242) points out, though, the variation *divyá-/divíya-* is just not solved by this idea.

On the phonological side Seebold (1972:130) is at one with Marchand (1958:18) in protesting that syllable features alone are the controlling factors in all this business. Apposite then is Grammont's suggestion (1895:12-13) that -*iy*- replaced -*y*- after a heavy syllable in order to avoid a consonant cluster at the start of a syllable. That is, one avoids *\$CC:, and so *mor\$tyos > *mor\$tiyos, etc. In a sense, this reflex with its cause is a centre-point of Seebold's essay. But it is not totally clear why, if the first consonant of the cluster has become a syllable-coda, the sequence \$ty- is then any less acceptable than word-initial ##ty-; and Indic *tvam* is generalized after Vedic into all contextual positions, in a way similar to the existing /##CY-/ generalization in plurisyllables.

Seebold (1972) will not have any motivation which is not sensitive to syllable structure. Hypotheses of other sorts, one has to admit, do tend to stand in splendid isolation, each with a lone proponent. For Hirt (1921:197ff.) the affair resolved itself as an inventory of realizations of PIE syllables in zero, or reduced, grade of ablaut — which is undeniable, of course, as the title of Edgerton (1934) rightly testifies. But nothing is uniquely predicted as to reflex-shapes in specific environments; and even Edgerton's delicacies are inadequate and predict far too little (see Collinge 1956:122-26). For some, like Boer (1924:§§147,170), metrical features and dialect peculiarities are crucial. For Lindeman (1965) the explicandum is the varied fashioning of the first syllable of the PIE word (cf. Hamp 1980), a variety which is lost as the word lengthens (in favour of a consonantal value of /R/). Kuryłowicz (1960:193-210 — despite the 1926 treatment) locates the solution within certain notions about contractions, derived from Wackernagel. Finally, Hoenigswald (1978:14) warns that the law may well be sensitive to 'cluster permissibility'.

The application of Sievers' law has been pushed, energetically and indeed as far as it will go, in numerous areas. With various degrees of reservation or disbelief, the thorough-going testers include: Lehmann (1955), Springer (1975), Schmieren (1977), Fullerton (1977), and Voyles (1981) for Germanic; Hamp (1965) for Celtic; Lindeman (after Kuryłowicz) (1965:84ff.) for Slavic — this in face of the negative findings in that sector by Schmalstieg (1959) and Seebold (1972:109). In Greek, Hill (1967), Nagy (1970:88-100), Yamashita (1971), and Dunkel (1982) must be counted; but the first three note the severe awkwardnesses of the full Sievers-Edgerton schemata (forms like βαίνω are obviously incongruent; the pair ἅζομαι, ἅγιος presents an instant exception even to Sievers' original statute as both are from *yagI+V-; and similar problems are rife — πότνια but (δέο)ποινα; τίν(F)ω but τανύω, etc.). Nagy tests out 'Sievers' rule' and 'Edgerton's converse' in other areas, especially Celtic and Baltic, and finds a common experience of breakdown and reshaping (although Perpillou [1974] defends Sievers against him). The Iranian metrical aspects figure in Schlerath (1951); yet in Old Persian Kuryłowicz (1964) allows Sievers' law for primary stems but not for productive suffixes. Schindler (1977:58) notes Old Iranian evidence for the law's losing its productivity. And Lindeman (1965:97) believes the law — as a phonetic affair — not to have lasted long after the loss of H. On the Sanskrit evidence Kiparsky (1973b:818) conducts a special debate against Szemerényi as to the relative chronology of (a) Sievers' law and (b) the reduction to zero grade of stem-ablaut. The less support Sievers gets outside Vedic the better the case, on Kiparsky's side, for having it as a later process than basic PIE apophony distribution. Schindler (1977:63) restricts the law (which he seems to see as a morphological option) so as to filter out Sanskrit vṛddized exceptions and forms like 'absolutives' in -tvī̄, to operations in closed single syllabic sequences. His rule (64) is:

$$\begin{bmatrix} +son \\ -syll \end{bmatrix} \rightarrow [+syll] \quad \Big/ \quad \left\{ \begin{bmatrix} +syll \\ +long \\ [+syll] \end{bmatrix} \begin{bmatrix} +son \\ -syll \end{bmatrix} \right\} \quad [-syll]_1 \quad \text{---} \quad [+syll][-syll]\#\#.$$

Finally, (a) the law has seemed useful in the handling of a notoriously tricky sector of Latin verb morphology (cf. Pariente 1946); this has deserved separate consideration in Appendix V; and (b) a Finnish analogue has been perceived (Ritter 1977).

Excursus: 'Sievers-Edgerton' phenomena (and law?).

Of Edgerton's reshapings of Sievers' law, the first has been assessed as a mere correction, conforming to what it is piously assumed the originator's intention must have been. Others had already understood it so, perhaps mistakenly. The extension of the statute to all resonants characterized as

$$\begin{bmatrix} +sonorant \\ \alpha syllabic \\ \alpha consonant \\ -low \end{bmatrix}$$

also derived from earlier scholars, together with the preference for the converse form of Sievers' pronouncement — these linked hypotheses were propounded by Edgerton with much vigour over thirty years. They gained all the attractiveness which notational clarity can command, especially when it is mistaken for a dynamic formalism. One devotee was Keiler (1970, esp. 80). The permitted 'Sievers-Edgerton' formulae as listed in 1943 (and ignoring the uncertain reflexes of three or more successive resonants) were as follows:

(i)   – for *-R-*:   (1) /tit, #it, ti#/
                           (2) /aya, #ya, ay#; ayt; atya/
                           (3) /ktiya, ātiya, #tiya/

(ii)   – for *-R₁R₂-*:   (1) /atyut, atyu#; ayut, ayu#; #yut/
                           (2) /ktiyut/ ātiyut, #tiyut; ktiyu#, ātiyu#,
                                #tiyu#/.
                           (3) /ktiwa, ātiwa, #tiwa/
                           (4) /atyuwa/
                           (5) /#ywa *or* #yuwa *or* #iwa/

(sic, Edgerton 1943:98ff.)

In more recent style the notation becomes:

(i)　　$R \rightarrow [+syll]$　　　／ $\left\{ \begin{array}{l} C \underline{\quad} \left\{ \begin{array}{l} C \\ \# \end{array} \right\} \\ \# \underline{\quad} C \end{array} \right\}$　(1)

　　　　$\rightarrow [-syll]$　　　／ $\left| \begin{array}{l} V \left\{ \begin{array}{l} ((C)) \underline{\quad} V \\ \underline{\quad} \left\{ \begin{array}{l} C \\ \# \end{array} \right\} \end{array} \right\} \\ \# \underline{\quad} V \end{array} \right|$　(2)

　　　　$\rightarrow [+syll][-syll]$　　／ $\left\{ \begin{array}{l} C \\ +long \\ \# \end{array} \right\} C \underline{\quad} V$　(3)

(ii)　$R_1 R_2 \rightarrow [-syll]_1 [+syll]_2$　／ $\left\{ \begin{array}{l} V(C) \underline{\quad} \left\{ \begin{array}{l} C \\ \# \end{array} \right\} \\ \# \underline{\quad} C \end{array} \right\}$　(1)

　　　　$\rightarrow [+syll]_1 [-syll]_1 [+syll]_2$　／ $\left\{ \begin{array}{l} C \\ +long \\ \# \end{array} \right\} C - (\left\{ \begin{array}{l} \# \\ C \end{array} \right\})$　(2)

　　　　$\rightarrow [+syll]_1 [-syll]_2$　　　／ $\left\{ \begin{array}{l} C \\ +long \\ \# \end{array} \right\} C \underline{\quad} V$　(3)

　　　　$\rightarrow [-syll]_1 [+syll]_2 [-syll]_2$　　／ $VC \underline{\quad} V$　(4)

$\left(\rightarrow \left\{ \begin{array}{l} [-syll]_1 [-syll]_2 \\ [-syll]_1 [+syll]_2 [-syll]_2 \\ [+syll]_1 [-syll]_2 \end{array} \right\} \right.$　／ $\# \underline{\quad} V$　(5)

Edgerton's base was Vedic and his diagnostics were the metrical variants of the Ṛgveda in their phonological contexts. To be kind (or merciful), one may see his generalizing of the formulae to all IE languages as simply programmatic and thought-provoking. Lehmann (1955) accepted the relevance to Germanic; and Seebold (1972) in effect offers a further delineation of the same IE phonotactic patterns. Others have been seen to be doubtful. Edgerton himself agreed (1962: 353) that not everything fits, even in Vedic; but he stoutly contests some merely apparent misfits challenged by Cowgill (1960). Lindeman (1965:101), for all that he regards the 'converse' formula as neither common IE nor fitting 'Anlaut' phenomena, nevertheless accepts it in general terms.

But more recent, and head-on, onslaughts on Edgerton's base position have been mounted by Sihler (1967, 1969, 1971) and Horowitz (1974). Horowitz's path of attack is much the same as the apparently earlier one of Sihler; he explicitly lists those metrically-controlled variations in R̥gvedic word-forms which alternate in Edgertonian fashion whether they are made up of 'Sievers-Edgerton' segment sequences or not. Despite Horowitz's claim of priority (1974:39), it is reasonable to produce Sihler's contentions as the big guns in this battle. He accepts /R̥R̥/ as a valid potential R̥gvedic alternant for /R/; he agrees that word-internal semivowels in the etymology therefore introduce indeterminacy not merely in syllable-boundaries but also in syllable-tally. But he is firm that what starts as a potential variant (of a phonetic nature) becomes a realized morphological alternant purely by sensitivity to metrical exigencies. The factors governing the alternations are the constraints of scansion and a consequent understandable demand for the availability of different shapes of the 'same word' — with syllable-count and syllable-weight as the variables.

These metrical and prosodic 'governing mechanisms' produce phenomena which

(a)   are not always rigidly Sieversian;

(b)   are as likely to contain sequences irrelevant to 'Sievers-Edgerton' as those which are relevant (cf. Horowitz);

(c)   are not necessarily to be taken to be the sole acceptable phonological shape of that lexical item in that context in a presumed parallel spoken idiom;

(d)   are entirely peculiar to Vedic (indeed, to R̥gvedic).

Sihler wins strong support from Ickler (1976), who thinks Seebold has strayed from the true path. Listed as an involuntary adherent also (by Sihler 1971:65) is Atkins (1968). To all this mixture, Klein (1977:429) stirs in (a) paradigmatic analogy — admitted by Edgerton, certainly — thus explaining things like *āpnumas*, and (b) an Indic tendency to change by syncope (so *t(u)vām* — because in absolute terms the /-uw/ variant is the one much preferred in the R̥gveda itself). After all of which, if Sievers' law remains an old orthodoxy of limited field and spasmodic usefulness, 'Sievers-Edgerton' looks like a heresy on its way to oblivion even among Vedic prosodists. But the habit of the nomenclature may persist; so in Hamp (1980); and even more in Voyles (1981:36-39) where a very complex set of inflectional rules justifies the shifts (1) /i/ → /ii/ − likened to Edgerton by the author − (2) /ii/ → /i:/. (Voyles [1981:1] justifiably believes that this law and Thurneysen's have regularly been misrepresented since their discovery.)

The contemporary relevance of Sievers' law must be, one supposes, above all to markedness theory (and its 'conventions'), which is a sad thought for those to whom chapter 9 of *The Sound Pattern of English* is a monstrosity. But if [u syll] → x, where x represents different outputs in different contexts, as Chomsky & Halle markedness theory permits, then it is difficult that

(1)   the input class is unnatural, in the sense that it is hard to define the set /i,u,y,w,m,n,r,l/ by features with the needed economy;

(2)   the output may have more segments than the input; and

(3)   individual languages have such different outputs that the only (P)IE generalization safe to make would presumably be the Chomsky & Halle basic negative featuring: [u syll] → [-syll]
− and then only if there were really a firm base in the belief that e.g. /y/ is prime; on that there is scarcely dogmatic agreement.

Maybe Sievers' law still offers suggestions as to what may happen, and in what contexts, to segments which are in PIE unequivocally [+sonorant] and equivocally [+/-syllabic]. Maybe (as Lindeman [1965:99,104] suggests) it is restricted to monosyllables, or at least it points to a tendency to lengthen some short words. It does little more.

Note: Prokosch, in *A comparative Germanic grammar* (1939:135), refers to Sievers' 'law of syncopation', quoting Sievers (1878, and also *PBB* 5. 23-61; 7.141-42). The compared phenomena are, e.g., Got. *nǎsida* > OHG *nerita* versus Got. *sōkida* > OHG *suohta*. But general acceptance of this loss of /i/ after heavy syllables (e.g., as what might be named 'Sievers' law III') seems not to have eventuated.

REFERENCES

Allen, W.S. 1966. Prosody and prosodies in Greek. *TPS* 1966.107-48.
————, 1973. *Accent and rhythm.* Cambridge, Univ. Press.
Arnold, E.V. 1905. *Vedic metre in its historical development.* Cambridge, Univ. Press.
Atkins, S.D. 1968. The RV *dyáus-* paradigm and the Sievers-Edgerton law. *JAOS* 88.679-709.
Beade, P. 1972. Sievers' law in Gothic and other related matters. *Lingua* 30. 449-59.
Benfey, T. 1871. Ist in der idg. Grundsprache ein nominales Suffix ia, oder statt dessen ya, anzusetzen? *NAWG* 16.91-133. (1872; paper issued separately 1871.)
————, 1881. Behandlung des auslautenden *a* in *ná* 'wie' und *ná* 'nicht' im Rigveda. *NAWG* 27.1
Boer, R.C. 1924. *Oergermaansch Handboek.* 2nd ed. Haarlem: Tjeenk, Willink & Zoon. (1st ed. 1918.)
Borgström, C.H. 1949. Thoughts about IE vowel gradation. *NTS* 15.137-87.
Bynon, T. 1974. Review of Seebold 1972. *BSOAS* 37.241-242.
Collinge, N.E. 1956. The limitations of historical phonology. *ArchL.* 8.111-28.
Debrunner, A. 1935. *Dyāvāpṛthivī* or *diyāvāpṛthvī?* *Lg* 11.117-19. (On which see Edgerton 1935.)
Dunkel, G.E. 1982. ῞Υπτιος. *Glotta* 60.53-55.
Edgerton, F. 1934. Sievers' law and Indo-European weak grade vocalism. *Lg* 10.235-65.
————, 1935. Review of Debrunner 1935. *Lg* 11.120-21.
————, 1943. The Indo-European semivowels. *Lg* 19.83-124.
————, 1962. The semivowel phonemes of Indo-European: A reconsideration. *Lg* 38.352-59.
Edgren, A.H. 1885. On the relation in the Rig-veda between the palatal and labial vowels (*i,ī,u,û*) and their corresponding semivowels (*y,v*). *JAOS* 11. 67-88. (Based on a lecture to the American Oriental Society, October 1878.)
Fullerton, G.L. 1977. *Historical Germanic verb morphology.* Berlin: W. de Gruyter.
Grammont, M. 1895. *De liquidis sonantibus indagationes aliquot.* Divione;

Davantière.

Hamp, E.P. 1965. Evidence in Keltic. In. *Evidence for laryngeals* (*EFL*[2]), ed. by W. Winter. 224-35. The Hague: Mouton.

––––––, 1980. IE *( )kúon- IF* 85.35-42.

Hermann, E. 1923. *Silbenbildung im Griechischen und in den anderen indogermanischen Sprachen,* (*KZ Ergänzungsheft,* 2.), Göttingen: Vandenhoeck & Ruprecht.

Hill, A. 1967. *Sievers-Edgerton's law and the Indo-European semi-vowels in Greek.* Diss. Univ. of North Carolina: Chapel Hill.

Hirt, H. 1921. *Indogermanische Grammatik.* II. Heidelberg: Winter.

Hoenigswald, H.M. 1978. Semivowel asymmetry in Indo-European. *Bull. Dept. Comp. Phil. and Linguistics,* Univ. of Calcutta, 3.14-18.

––––––, 1980. Initial semivowel clusters. *Fs Thieme,* 83-86.

Horowitz, F.E. 1974. *Sievers' law and the evidence of the Rigveda.* The Hague; Mouton. (Diss., Colombia Univ., 1971.)

Hübschmann, H. 1879. Iranische Studien. *KZ* 24.323-415 (esp.362).

Ickler, I. 1976. Bemerkungen zum 'Sieversschen Gesetz' unter besonderer Berücksichtigung des Rigveda. *OLZ* 71. cols.117-28. (= Review article on Seebold 1972.)

Keiler, A.R. 1970. *A phonological study of the Indo-European laryngeals.* The Hague: Mouton.

Kiparsky, P. 1972. Metrics and morphophonemics in the Rigveda. *New ideas in generative phonology* ed. by Michael K. Brame. 171-200 Austin: Univ. of Texas Press.

––––––, 1973a. Elsewhere in phonology. *Fs Halle,* 93-106.

––––––, 1973b. The inflectional accent in Indo-European. *Lg* 49.794-849.

Klein, J.S. 1977. Review of Horowitz 1974, *Lg* 53.428-30.

Kluge, F. 1891. Geschichte der gotischen Sprache. *Grundriss der germanischen Philologie* ed. by H. Paul. 497-517 Strassburg: Trübner. (2nd ed., 1901.)

––––––, 1911. *Die Elemente des Gotischen* (= Beiheft in Paul's *Grundriss,* 3rd ed.). Ibid.

––––––, 1913. *Urgermanisch* (= Beiheft in Paul's *Grundriss,* 3rd ed.), Ibid.

Kuryłowicz, J. 1926. Quelques problèmes métriques du Rigveda. *Rocznik Orientalistyczny* (Kraków) 4.210-20.

––––––, 1935. *Etudes Indo-européennes* I. Kraków: Polska AN.

––––––, 1960. *Esquisses linguistiques.* Wrocław & Kraków. Zaklad. Narod. im Ossolińskich. Polska AN. (Reprinted, Munich: W. Fink, 1973.)

––––––, 1964. Zur altpersischen Keilschrift. *ZPhon* 17.563-69.

Lahiri, A. 1981. Vowel-glide alternation in Gothic: a case of partial rule loss. *CLS* 17.172-84.

Lehmann, W.P. 1955. The Proto-Indo-European resonants in Germanic. *Lg* 31.355-66.

——, 1968. On the reading of some *ya-* suffixes in the Rigveda. *Pratidānam* (*Indian, Iranian and Indo-European Studies*), ed. by J.C. Heesterman, G.H. Schokker & V.I. Subramoniam, 39-45. The Hague: Mouton.

Lindeman, F.O. 1965. La loi de Sievers et le début du mot en indo-européen. *NTS* 20.38-108.

Marchand, J.W. 1955. *The sounds and phonemes of Wulfila's Gothic.* Diss., Univ. of Michigan, Ann Arbor.

——, 1956. The converse of Sievers' law and the Germanic first class weak verbs. *Lg* 32.285-87.

——, 1958. Sievers' law and a rule of IE syllable formation. *GL* 3.73-84.

Murray, R.W. & Vennemann, T. 1983. Sound change and syllable structure in Germanic phonology. *Lg* 59.514-28.

Nagy, G. 1970. *Greek dialects and the transformation of an IE process.* Cambridge, Mass.: Harvard Univ. Press.

Oldenberg, H. 1916. Zur Behandlung des auslautenden -*i* und -*u* im Ṛgveda. (Excursus.) *NAWG* 1915 (publ. 1916).529-43.

Osthoff, H. 1881. Die Tiefstufe im indogermanischen Vocalismus. *MU* 4.1-406.

——, 1884 *Zur Geschichte des Perfects in Indogermanischen, mit besonderer Rücksicht auf Griechisch und Lateinisch.* Strassburg: Trübner.

Pariente, A. 1946. see Appendix V.

Perpillou, J-L. 1974. Comparatifs primaires et loi de Sievers. *BSL* 69.99-107.

Ritter, R-P. 1977. Zur Frage der finnischen Evidenz für die Sieverssche Regel im Germanischen. *Die Sprache* 23.171-79.

Schindler, J. 1977. Notizen zum Sieversschen Gesetz. (= Rev. of Seebold 1972.) *Die Sprache* 23.56-65.

Schlerath, B. 1951. *Die Behandlung von y und w nach Konsonant in den metrischen Texten des Awesta.* Diss., Univ. Frankfurt.

Schmalstieg, W.R. 1959. The IE semivowels in Balto-Slavic. *Lg* 35.16-17.

——, 1980. *Indo-European linguistics.* University Park, Pa.; Penn. State Univ. Press.

Schmieren, R.J. 1977. *Theoretical implications of Gothic and Old English phonology.* Diss., Univ. of Massachusetts, Amherst.

Seebold, E. 1972. *Das System der idg. Halbvokale: Untersuchungen zum sogenannten 'Sieversschen Gesetz' und zu den halbvokalhaltigen Suffixen in den idg. Sprachen, besonders im Vedischen.* Heidelberg: Winter.

Sievers, E. 1878. Zur accent- und lautlehre der germanischen sprachen; II & III (esp. III: zum vokalischen auslautgesetz). *PBB* 5.63-163.

―――――, 1893. Zum Vedischen sandhi. *Fs Roth*, 203-207.

Sihler, A.L. 1967. *PIE post-consonantal resonants in word-initial sequences.* Diss., Yale Univ., New Haven; Conn.

―――――, 1969. Sievers-Edgerton phenomena and Rigvedic meter. *Lg* 45.248-73.

―――――, 1971. Word-initial semivowel alternation in the Rigveda. *Lg* 47.53-78.

Springer, O. 1975. Early Runic evidence for Sievers' law. *Arbeiten zur Germanischen Philologie und zur Literatur des Mittelalters.* 164-77. Munich: Fink.

Streitberg, W. 1909. Gotica. *IF* 24.174-81.

Thurneysen, R. 1879. *Über Herkunft und Bildung der lateinischen Verba auf -io der dritten und vierten Konjugation.* Diss., Univ. Leipzig.

Vennemann, T. 1971. The phonology of Gothic vowels. *Lg* 47.90-132.

Voyles, J.B. 1981. *Gothic, Germanic and North-West Germanic.* (= *ZDL Beiheft*, 39.) Wiesbaden; Steiner.

Wackernagel, J. 1896. *Altindische Grammatik*, Part I: *Lautlehre*. Göttingen: Vanderhoeck & Ruprecht. (New ed., with additions by L. Renou & A. Debrunner, ibid. 1957.)

Yamashita, K. 1971. *Sievers-Edgerton phenomena and Greek semivowel sequences.* Unpubl. diss., Univ. of Pennsylvania.

SIEVERS' LAW II

Another pronouncement of Eduard Sievers has been elevated to the status of 'law'. In 1878 (149) he listed a few examples of the loss, in proto-Germanic, of the obstruent component of the cluster *gw. This cluster /gw/ was the presumed first reflex of one or two labiovelar segments of PIE; but see Wood (1926). Indeed, Moulton (1972:143) denies that any such reflex of PIE /g^{W}h/ is present in any of the older Germanic languages, although later (171) he is oddly ready to discuss its different segmental make-up at the pre-Germanic and proto-Germanic stage, respectively. The *gw is not only that which had an onset element traditionally called *media aspirata* (on which see Appendix II) but also that with a PIE voiceless onset which gained voice by Verner's law. (If the labialization of the stop is itself secondary, the reflex probably remains obstruent: so Kluge 1886.) The resultant /w/ may become a diphthongal offset, if medial: Gothic *náus* (< *nagwis*), and 'Germanic' *hweulá-* from earlier *hwegwlá-*, are among the original cited forms. That the accent followed the affected cluster seems crucial, or at least that the preceding syllable was unstressed. Sievers promised to elaborate the rule and to give it a firmer basis. The promise was not redeemed; but Osthoff (1882:256) soon made it clear that the following vowel must not be [+back]. It is this law which Trautmann (1906:57-59) discusses, with a bibliographical list.

Kluge (1913:63, despite his earlier views on labial loss) accepted the loss of the stop element as a regularity, but not the accent condition; the reflex was, it seems, arbitrary. Likewise Fourquet (1948:24-25) recorded it as an unremarkable evolution, while Seebold (again a continuator of Sievers) in 1967 lists the other adherents of this position. But some people were sensitive to the fact that there appeared an alternative simplification, loss of the *w*. Zupitza (1896: 49ff.) accepted *that* solution for initials and was attacked by Hirt (1898:312ff.): see Lane (1936:17). Medially the result varied and the accent was crucial. Lehmann (1952:63) sketched a 'natural' explanation by a contextual constraint which sharpened Osthoff's notion: the velar disappeared when a front vowel followed the cluster, but before a back vowel the labial item dropped (although the etymology of OHG *warm*, NE *warm*, is then awkward [see Lane 1936:24]). Then 'regularization' was said to set in, apparently in either direction. Unhappily, the only really clear context for delabialization is /-u, at least in Gothic. Thus the root *mak^W* gives masculine *magus*, feminine *mawi* (whereas before low back *a* (*o*) Gothic has *hneiwan* (ON *hniga*), *snaiws* (< *$snaigwas$, *$snoig^Whos$). What then appears reasonable to assume before *u*(/w/) is a special degemination from /g^Ww/ to /gw/ or /gu/.

In 1967 two treatments of the matter appeared. Voyles reformulated the whole law, which he had no hesitation in naming 'Sievers' law' (not even deterred by the existence of Sievers' law I). He set up (651) three contexts for the shift, using early Jakobson-Fant-Halle distinctive features. (These permitted a readier subsuming of the segment types than do the Chomsky & Halle (or later) versions of feature-phonology.) In effect, the shift of *gw > w/u occurs:

(a)   between # # and /o/ (cf. *warms* < *$g^Whormos$);
(b)   between /l,r,e,i/ and /o, a, 'ə'/;
(c)   between /a,o,e,'ə'/ and /l,n,r,i/

— not the simplest of pictures. Twenty-eight etyma are adduced, from Gothic, Old Icelandic. Old Saxon, Old English and Old and Middle High German (Voyles 1967:656-57); these are the spoils of raids on the dictionaries of Feist (Gothic, 1939), Holthausen (Old English, 1934), Johannesson (Icelandic, 1956), Kluge (German, 17th ed., 1957) and Pokorny (1959, for IE as a whole).

But in the same year Seebold concentrated on the outcome of PIE '/g^Wh/', noting its divergent behaviour from PIE /k^W/ (Gmc. *χw, Goth. *hr*) and from /g^W/ (Gmc. *kw, Goth. *g*). Unlike Moulton, Seebold has no trouble in observing it and plotting its paths: in essence, only after a nasal does it retain velarity and labiality. The whole reflex-table (in our notation) is as follows (1967:132):

'*/g^Wh/'   1(a) b ╱## —
             1(b) g ╱## —u
             2(a) h ╱ — t

$$2(b) \quad g \diagup t - \left\{ \begin{array}{c} \breve{u} \\ \bar{o} \\ j \\ R,N \end{array} \right\}$$

             (c) gw ╱ N —

$$(d) \quad w(u) \quad \Big/ - \begin{Bmatrix} N \\ R \\ Y \end{Bmatrix}$$

$$(e) \quad g \quad \Big/ V - \begin{Bmatrix} \breve{u} \\ \bar{o} \end{Bmatrix} \quad or \quad \Big/ \begin{Bmatrix} \breve{u} \\ \bar{o} \end{Bmatrix} - V$$

$$(f) \quad w \quad \Big/ \begin{Bmatrix} i \\ e \end{Bmatrix} - V$$

– a list which does not exhaust the logical, and actual, PIE possibilities. The clusters /g´hw/ and /ghw/ are then in Sieversian fashion handled like the aspirated labiovelars: see further Seebold (1980).

With accent pretty well discounted, and with a complicated array of results (and battles over many of the comparanda), the matter is essentially a subject for further detailed debate. Markey (1980), calling the fate of '*gh^W' in Germanic "one of the thorniest problems" in this whole sector, sees a split between East and North-West Germanic, the latter characterized by labialization of back spirants before resonants. There may be a 'law' here somewhere. But Sievers' statement is in a field where extensive re-digging is in operation (see Speirs 1978), and it is scarcely in the shape to deserve such a title.

REFERENCES

Bezzenberger, A. 1880. "Zusätze" [to article by A. Fick]. *BB* 5.170-76.

Fourquet, J. 1948. See on Grimm's law.

Hirt, H. 1898. Grammatisches und etymologisches. *PBB* 23.288-357 (esp. 312-15).

Kluge, F. 1886. Labialisierung der idg. velaren tenuis im germ[anischen]. *PBB* 11.560-62.

—————, 1913. *Urgermanisch.* 3rd rev. ed. Strassburg: Trübner. (1st ed., 1909.)

Lane, G.S. 1936. The labiovelars before ō in Germanic. *JEGP* 35.17-26.

Lehmann, W.P. 1952. *Proto-Indo-European phonology*. Austin; Univ. of Texas Press.

Markey, T.L. 1980. Delabialization in Germanic. *FoLH* 1.285-93. (A revised and superseding version of the paper at *JIES* 8.199-211, (1980).)

Moulton, W.G. 1972. The Proto-Germanic non-syllabics (consonants). *Toward a grammar of Proto-Germanic*, ed. by F. van Coetsem & H.L. Kufner, 141-73. Tübingen: Niemeyer.

Osthoff, H. 1882. Zum grammatischen Wechsel der velaren *k*-Reihe. *PBB* 8. 256-87.

Polomé, E.C. (forthcoming) Initial PIE *g^Wh*- in Germanic.

Seebold, E. 1967. Die Vertretung idg. *g^Wh*- in Germanischen. *KZ* 81.104-133.

————, 1980. Etymologie und Lautgesetz. In *Lautgeschichte und Etymologie* ed. by M. Mayrhofer et al., 440-84. *Akten der VI Fachtagung der Idg. Gesellschaft*, Vienna, 24-29 Sept. 1978. Wiesbaden: Reichert.

Sievers, E. 1878. Zur Akzent- und Lautlehre der germanischen Sprachen. *PBB* 5.63-164.

Speirs, A.G.E. 1978. *The Proto-Indo-European labiovelars*. Amsterdam: Hakkert.

Trautmann, R. 1906. *Germanische Lautgesetze*. Kirchhain: Schmersow.

Voyles, J.B. 1967. Simplicity, ordered rules, and the First Sound Shift. *Lg* 43.636-60 (esp.649-52, 656-58).

Wood, F.A. 1926. *Postconsonantal w in Indo-European*. Philadelphia: Linguistic Socy. of America.

Zupitza, E. 1896. *Die germanischen gutturale*. Berlin: Weidmann. (Note data in Bezzenberger 1880:174-75.)

STANG'S LAW*

The name of Christian Stang (1900-1977) is illustrious in the field of Slavic accent.* An ordinance bearing his name is to be looked for; and it exists in the form of a sequel to Dybo's law. By *that* law an accent will, under the appropriate conditions in the Slavic period, have shifted within a word by one syllable to the right. If thereafter it finds itself on a final syllable of which the vowel is long and the intonation is falling (non-acute), then the affected accent will return to the preceding syllable. This leftward *Rückverwandlung* is of Stang's perceiving (1957:168-69). Of course, he saw it as affecting a final syllable accent which was given (hence, for him, there was no 'return'). Dybo's solution of the input came five years later.

Stang's law is an explanation — or, more properly, one of a series of changes which combine to form an explanation — of the so-called 'neo-acute' intonation. Not all Slavists are happy with that aspect of it. Yet Ebeling (1967:591) — with some modification— and Kortlandt (1975) canonize the law. Ebeling (593) even notes a special morphological (transitivity) opposition in stokavian which derives directly from Stang's law, when enclisis has varied the input condition.

The final syllable which is affected by the law sommonly suffered a shortening of its vowel (Kortlandt 1975:18). It remains *sub iudice* whether the correption stands as cause or as effect of the leftward stress shift.

Quoted or relevant are:
Ebeling 1967*; Garde 1976*; Kortlandt 1975*, 1978*; Stang 1957*.

* See Appendix III (as also for the asterisked references above).

STREITBERG'S LAW

The 'lengthened' grade in Indo-European ablaut, and even simply long vowels in positions where etymology does not suggest them, have exercised diachronists in many sectors: moreover, they have led to Brugmann's law. One generalized solution of a number of problem cases was offered by Wilhelm Streitberg (1864-1925). The relevant papers appeared in 1893 (addressed essentially to a classical readership) and 1894 (in a more 'Indo-European' forum). The priority of the one version over the other is probably beyond our deciding, The 1893 formulation is: (p.30)

> Schwindet eine akzentlose Silbe, so wird ein vorausgehnde Silbe zirkumflexiert, wenn sie lang, gedehnt, wenn sie kurz ist.

> If a syllable not bearing the accent disappears, a preceding syllable becomes circumflex if already 'long' and 'long' if previously 'short'.

This differs from the 1894 (313) version in that (1) a whole syllable is required to be lost, and (2) the syllable succession is not stated to be immediate. But the omission of the latter prerequisite is a mere oversight, at once corrected; and, as the law is said to be some sort of offspring of Fick's concept of mora-replacement, it can be understood to include quantity change (i.e., change in syllable part) as well as total syncope of the stressless syllable. But no debate follows about any such effect of a lightened syllable, which the term 'Morenverlust' (1894) should imply.

More important is that in 1894 it is made clear that the absence of word-stress on the lost syllable is less crucial than its presence on the target syllable, which is then affected either as to its accent type (→ falling contour) or as to its vowel quantity (short → long). Lehmann (1952:113) speaks of the first syllable of the two as having 'maximum', the other 'minimum' stress; and he dates the shift to the era before phonemic vowels existed in PIE. It is certainly a shift of the proto-language, and so a part of ablaut theory and of prehistoric morphological architecture.

Not an undue deal of attention has been accorded to the law in recent years. Streitberg did not see /+s/ as an essential nominative marker and so did not deduce vowel length in, e.g., πατήρ or ποιμήν direct from his own shift (wisely, no doubt, considering the accent of μήτηρ or δαίμων). It has been argued that nominative *Dehnstufe* arises from a cluster reduction *-VR/Ns > -VR/N (see Szemerényi's law) rather than by mere 'polarization' (as Kuryłowicz 1956:145). Now, loss of cluster-final /s/ and loss of a whole syllabic nucleus are very different; and yet Streitberg quoted τόνς > τούς as prop for his case (quasi < /ton + Vs/? — an incredible formation). On the other hand ναῦς is *not* like βοῦς (βῶς) or Ζεύς in structure (a fact which has misled too many people over Osthoff's law, q.v.); and Streitberg's supposed pre-Indic and pre-Greek paired shifts of (1) *gŏwos to *gŏus but (2) *nāwos to *nāus (ναῦς) at least nicely capture the essential difference (however doubtful the gunated suffix may be). But this is faint praise. Besides, what happens after the PIE period is either irrelevant (as when ἔλθω is derived from *ἔλυθω, as originally by Saussure) or even contradictory to the law (as when a presumed inheritance like *pŏtnī is seen as the outcome of syncopated *pŏti-nī): on this, see Szemerényi 1964 (3 and 395).

A modification of the law is offered by Purczinsky (1970). This adds the condition that the output must be long syllable (sic) standing before 'plus juncture'. This latter, rather dated, term means in effect a boundary of any value from '+' upwards. It excludes intra-root 'seams' like that before the third consonant in a Benvenistian construction; and so 'type I' comes out as *pĕr-k and not *pĕr-k (presumably from a potential **perek, also underlying 'type II' *pr-ek). But that a syllabic nucleus has really been 'lost' in such metaphysical speculations is scarcely verifiable in any sense; and 'plus juncture' can be arbitrarily suppressed, as when dual πόδε is derived from something like *pod(V)+HV.

Not surprisingly, Streitberg's law is well out of the limelight these days.

REFERENCES

Kuryłowicz, J. 1956. *L'apophonie en indo-européen.* Wrocław; Polska AN.

Lehmann, W.P. 1952. *Proto-Indo-European phonology.* Austin; Univ. of Texas Press.

Purczinsky, J. 1970. A modification of Streitberg's law. *Word* 26.386-94.

Streitberg, W. 1893. Ein Ablautproblem der Ursprache. *TAPA* 14.29-49.

—————, 1894. Die Entstehung der Dehnstufe. *IF* 3.305-416.

Szemerényi, O. 1964. *Syncope in Greek and Indo-European and the nature of the Indo-European accent.* Naples: Istituto Universitario Orientale di Napoli.

THURNEYSEN'S LAW

Gothic is maddening in the variability in respect of voicing shown by its spirant consonants. In Old Norse or Old English the spelling alternants *þ* and *d* do not systematically reflect, respectively, the voiceless and voiced forms [θ, ð] . But the Gothic symbols (in apico-dentals, labials and sibilants) do correspond to the glottal difference. It is true that *b*, for instance, may mean [b] initially or after a nasal or liquid, but [v] after a vowel; nevertheless *b* and *f* (or *d* and *þ*) are not confounded as to voice. But while such morphological paradigm alternations as *hláif* +s, *hláib-V-* are phonologically explicable and regular, it is an embarrassment when unexpected confrontations of voicing occur, as between *swáif* (past of *sweiban*) and *swarb* (past of *swáirban*), or *gōþs* and *gōds*, or *agisis* and *hatizis* (the genitives of *agis* and *hatis*). At the end of last century several scholars laboured away at these nuisances. Streitberg (1897, drawing on Sievers), Hench (1896, 1897), Kock (1900 − but this is a doglike return to an old thesis), and Van Helten (1903) all essayed solutions. These relied on sandhi phenomena, or syllable weight, or transitory spelling conventions (as when g̅þ̅s̅ is interpreted as denoting /gudis/), or analogical orthography − or simply the idiosyncrasy of East (Italian) Gothic. On these rather desperate remedies one may consult the references, or Jellinek (1926:57-58).

But (quite apart from apparent laxities before final -s or word boundary) some medial syllables − made medial by inflexional or derivational suffixes, and commonly central to trisyllabic words − particularly caught the eye. Streitberg noted the relations of *agisis* and *hatizis* (1897:67, §145n.5); and Schmidt (1895) attempted an accentual account of the varieties of the abstract formant which began as *tumni*, in

fastubni, "fasting"			
fráistubni, "temptation"	} versus {	waldufni, "might"	
witubni, "knowledge"		wundufni, "wound(ing)"	

It was in this sector that Rudolf Thurneysen (1857-1940), whose major field of endeavour was within Celtic, opposed the prevailing ideas (including those of Wrede 1891) and succinctly adumbrated a law in 1896. It was published two

years later, and Thurneysen's name adhered to this edict on Gothic. His notions
were these (1898:209):

(a)   that a spirant is realized as voiced when (1) it immediately follows a
      vocalic nucleus which does not bear the main word stress, and (2)
      that vocalic item is itself preceded by a voiceless consonant (so -*tub*-,
      [tuβ]);

(b)   that if in the same context the preceding consonant is voiced then
      the spirant realization is voiceless (so -*duf*-);

(c)   that if the preceding consonantal element is a cluster, a post-obstru-
      ent liquid ensures a voiced syllable-onset and voiceless spirant at
      syllable-end (so in *brōþrahans, niuklahs*), but a post-obstruent glide
      has no such effect (so *aúhjōdus, weitwōd*-); it is noteworthy that
      (voiced) liquid is thus credited with an overriding voicing effect in
      its own cluster ("hebt . . . die wirkung des vorhergehenden lautes
      auf").

The rightwards, or 'progressive', direction of the shift is not usual. Some say that
the natural impulse to self-monitored carefulness over a segment's sound after an
anticipatory 'error' at a previous segment may result in a misleading notion that
apparent leftward assimilation is a normal psychological process. Still, historians
must go by events, and the progressive effect does occur in some ramifications of
Grassmann's law and clearly enough in Bartholomae's law; and it must underlie
relations like that of Greek λείριον to Latin *lilium*. It may gain respectability
in the Gothic case inasmuch as the alternation provides allomorphy in a suffix.
But there are other awkward questions as to the law's rigour; and Thurneysen
himself countenanced four classes of exceptions, more or less controlled. They
are:

(1)   Where the affected spirant is word-final, because all final consonants are
      liable to devoicing in Germanic. (But this takes the sequence of -C_1VC_2-,
      C_1 being the trigger and C_2 the target, away from the medial placing. It is
      also chronologically doubtful; and Zadorožnyj (1959:140) claims that
      Gothic spirants actually led the way in this devoicing.)

(2)   Where the sequence is in the second member of a compound word (as in
      gastigōdei or *fidwōrtaíhun*), where the simplex form bears stress and
      decides the surface morphology even of the compound. But a compound
      form then needs to be carefully, but unusually, set apart from a derived

form. Even so, oddities remain: *unfrōþans* (Gal. 3.3) is sometimes said to be correct output, and *unfrōdans* (Gal. 3.1) a scribal error (cf. Jacobsohn 1920); might the reverse then be the truth?

(3) Where paradigmatic analogy has had its effect, or where such evolution has proceeded at different speeds in different lexemes (in inverse proportion to a word's isolation) – which is an interesting contribution to 'diffusion theory'.

(4) Where seven words need their own history. This Thurneysen supplies, at least for *arbaid-, barizeins, filigri, frumadei* and *ubizwa*; he leaves *háubid-* and *þiwadw* as sheer exceptions. Here one notes the suggestion of Voyles (1968:729n.9) that the law may apply only to certain classes of word, an idea refined later in Voyles (1981).

Now Chomsky & Halle, in their big phonological rules-book (1968:352), cite Thurneysen's diachronic law, as something well-known and fully recognized, to serve as an instance of 'polarity dissimilation' of features in a descriptive phonology (of a 'flip' rule, in fact). Their version is:

$$\begin{bmatrix} -son \\ +cont \end{bmatrix} \rightarrow [\alpha voice] \Big/ \begin{bmatrix} +cons \\ -\alpha voice \end{bmatrix} \begin{bmatrix} +voc \\ -cons \\ -stress \end{bmatrix} \underline{\qquad}$$

Here is no sensitivity to /TR/ and /TY/ cluster at the 'trigger' position 'C$_1$' (only to 'obstruents'); and although the [+voice] value of /R/ could be accommodated without revising the rule, the impotence of /Y/ to affect the voice shift seems to need a condition-linked segment X to the left of the unaccented vowel (or diphthong).

Thurneysen's suggestion did not sway the 'Hench group'; Kock (1900) ignored it. Yet in 1898 Hirt had already devoted eight pages (323-30) to an unusually enthusiastic reception of the law. He takes it to be substantially correct, early in Germanic history, and peculiar to East Germanic. To the exceptions he adds (326) in effect two more: the pair of forms *silubr* and *silubreins*, and the successive numerals *ainlibim* and *twalibim* (but Thurneysen could not recognize the former pair, as only /TR/ or /T/ can for him occupy the trigger position). Adventurously, Hirt explained most of the exceptions by a precluding effect of (supposed) word-final stress at the relevant time (as well as Thurneysen's constraint on stress between trigger and target). The resultant limitation to first syllable accent was subsequently disavowed by Hirt (1931:95-96 §62; "das

Gesetz ist also noch zu finden"!); and he never liked either the supposed effect of post-obstruent /R/ or the voicing part of Thurneysen's conception. Above all, there arose at once, for Hirt and other interested parties, a knotty problem of inter-law relation – on which more must be said in a moment: Thurneysen himself faced it, but hurriedly.

Over the next eighty years the law's reception was oddly sporadic. Streitberg (despite his 1903 article, discussed below) noted in his 1906 re-edition of his *Elementarbuch* (§117) both the law's effects and its trigger-conditions: but he refers there to nobody but himself. The post-Thurneysen editions of Braune's grammar all cite the basic article by Thurneysen (1898); but whereas Wrede, Streitberg and Hirt – and even Brugmann – are named (at least in respect of general theses or of 'follow -up' treatments), Thurneysen is not. Sievers, in Paul's *Grundriss*, fails to notice the law at all. Jacobsohn's long paper, on spirant alternations as evidence of sentence sandhi, only touches briefly and indirectly on Thurneysen's concerns (1920:160-61); his name does not figure in the suggestion which Jacobsohn makes as to scribal errors in things like *unfroþans.* In 1939 Prokosch ignores the Thurneysen data (and believes the other alternations in spirants to show simply that Gothic was incompletely susceptible to Verner's law (1939:89, §31)). Finally, in 1959 Zadorožnyj lists the Thurneysen effects as the third of three sets of spirant behaviour patterns. The sets are disparate (although phonetically similar) but specific to Gothic. (The other two are word-final spirant devoicing, and an earlier despirantizing of voiced segments after liquids.) Thurneysen's name is kept dark.

Nevertheless, Jellinek (1926:66-67, §63) attributes the finding, as a law of dissimilation, to Thurneysen, with sidelong credit to Streitberg. Wrede and Hirt are mentioned; and Leo Meyer (1869:68, 122) is said to have first noticed the relevant alternations. And it is as "Thurneysen's law" that Mossé (1942:60, §52 handles it, if with some unhappiness over the opposed exceptions *háubida* and *gabaurþs* (which must be protected by simplex *baurþei,* as Jacobsohn [1920:191] says if the intervening *-r-* does not invalidate it).

Hirt (1898:324) was concerned about the interaction of laws: how does Thurneysen's law stand in relation to Verner's? The inventor had declared (in opposition to, e.g., Wood 1895) that here was a separate process with its own dynamic. Hirt allows that it operates correctively on the output of Verner's law; but his agreement is lukewarm, and his notion of a varying domain of expiratory accent is unconvincing. The crucial issue is whether Thurneysen generates voiceless spirants after originally unstressed nuclei (the *-duf-* type), which Verner precludes; or indeed whether he produces the converse (the *-tub-*

type) if the vowel was stressed at the PIE or pre-Germanic stage, for that is equally non-Vernerian. Hirt first mentions only irrelevancies like *fri(j)ápwa* and *fi(j)ápwa*, and by 1931 has given up almost all resistance to the pressing claims of Verner's law (which seems indeed to be the source of the voice-values in *þiwadw*, if formed with PIE *+tvám*). But in 1903 Streitberg had moved up, in support of Thurneysen, a three-gun battery: *weitwōds, jukuzi* and *agizi.* On the first the PIE accent was undeniably on the suffixal syllable: Skt. *vidvā́n, vidúṣā*, Gk. *ἐιδότ* - As to *jukuzi*, if Noreen is correct in deriving it not from whatever sired *ζεῦγος* and Got. *(ga)juk* but again from the feminine perfect active participle, then the precursor **juk+ús-i* must, like **weitwōþ-*, receive by Verner's law a form which is reshaped by Thurneysen's (after a pre-Germanic leftward shift of stress) (494). The case of *aqizi* is less transparent, as it is not that same participle; but possibly **ak+wés-i* (cf. *ἀξύη*) underlies it. Clearly this battery's weapons are open to counter-attack, one being wayward, one of debatable origin and one scarcely knowable. It remains the case that the law needs a solid body of abidingly agreed evidence on its side if it is to be recognized as (at least) a separate and post-Verner process. Still, later developments do obscure Vernerian differentiae: cf. English *mother, brother*; and note what Sturtevant (1932) has to say on Old Norse and Old Saxon.

For convenience, the initial causation of alternant medial -CVC- sequences may be diagrammed thus:

A C_1 [αvoice], C_2 ($\rightarrow$) [αvoice]

B (i) C_1 [–voice], C_2 $\rightarrow$ [+voice] / -V- [–PIE accent] (*-tub-*):
          by Verner's.

(ii)   ",   "   / -V- [+PIE accent] (*-túb-* $>$ *-'tub-*):
          by Thurneysen's.

(iii) C_1 [+voice], C_2 $\rightarrow$ [–voice] / -V- [–PIE accent] (*-duf-*):
          by Thurneysen's.

(iv)   ",   "   / -V- [+PIE accent] (*-dúf-*):
          by Verner's.

Of these, cases B(ii) and B(iii) are the crucial ones: and to remove credible examples is to remove the need for Thurneysen's law.

The most recent attempt to do just that — to 'repeal' the law — is by Flickinger (1981), who argues for Verner's to stand alone. He starts and ends with the (in fact inadequate) rule of Chomsky & Halle discussed above; and he is no doubt justified in disliking such 'flip' rules as unnatural in generative phonology, and in doubting the efficacy of a debatable diachronic law as a proof of the utility of such descriptive rules. But that Thurneysen's law simply does not exist is not so easy to prove; and Flickinger's arguments are of unequal cogency. But they deserve consideration.

For one thing, the devoicing subcomponent of the law (= B(iii) and B(iv) above) is sliced away, but on the shaky ground that the C_2 input is nowhere originally voiced (67). This judgement rests on two equations: (1) of the $+asn^o/\frac{-}{a}$ formant (*hláiwasnōs*, "tombs") with the rare PIE and Sanskrit $+sn^{(\bar{a})}$, which is usually accented (cf. Whitney 1879:§1195); and (2) of $+uFni$ (in abstracts) with PIE $+men$, $+mn$, Skt. $+man$, which is really not accented on the purely Germanic intrusive vowel (*u*). But it is scarcely plausible to have Germanic $+umni$ lose nasality and voice (as if it were a buccal obstruent subject to Grimm's law) in passing to *underlying* status $*+ufni$ in Proto-Germanic (70); and in any case PIE $ste/_o+mn(-)$, Gk. στόμα, gives *stibna* in Gothic.

Thereafter, the voicing sub-rule (B(i) and B(ii) above) is allowed only five suffixes as clients: $+ufni$, $+\bar{o}pus$, $+isa$, $+ipa$ and $+asn(os/\bar{a})$. Of these, only $+ipa$ provides more than a handful of lexemes. Still, paucity of relevant formants is a factor encountered elsewhere (as in Lachmann's law). It needs to be positively demonstrated that other suffixes actually reject Thurneysen. But Flickinger quotes only -*ba*- and -*iza* (68); and these are irrelevant by his own preclusion of (claimed) Thurneysen devoicing. He extends the list of exceptions by adding *diupiþa*, *þwastiþa* and *weitwōdida* – but *weitwōdiþa* occurs, and this lexeme and its family are a puzzle for any version of the diachrony. It is then announced that C_2 voicing is purely Vernerian, the essential unstressed value of the preceding vowel being guaranteed by 'varied stress placement' (70), after the Sanskrit model as reported by Whitney (1879:§1151, §1161, §1168). It is admitted that the comparanda are ill-fitting (as in the relation of accent-placing to gender in the two languages, 71), and it is a pity that the Sanskrit marker $+t\bar{a}$ always has a preceding accent (except for the Ŗgvedic nonce-form *avíratā*). But Flickinger predicts (a) the unexpected and rare nature of -*ida* forms – and *auþida* and *wairþida* do really stand alone – and (b) the appearance of $+iz$- in the comparative (which inherits root accent) and $+þro$ in the adverbial which comes from $+tra$ (which always follows a presuffixal accent). Flickinger's case is good (and linked by Ohala [1981:194] to a Gothic strategy of alternating syllable weight). Yet Streitberg's (1903) battery is not noticed at all; and Thurneysen's law may still deserve to remain in more than 'some minor version' as a resolver of irregularities in voice distribution – whatever this magnanimous suggestion may mean (Flickinger 1981:73).

Indeed, also in 1981 Voyles compiled a very complex set of 'inflectional morphology' rules (50-52). By these, Thurneysen's law, so named, is (1) rescued from the misstatements which have dogged its career since discovery (1981:1 — the same is understandably said of Sievers' law), and (2) given a new formulation, and formalism, to replace the faulty original (1981:52). It becomes purely a voicing rule:

$$
\begin{bmatrix} -\text{sonorant} \\ +\text{continuant} \\ -\text{voiced} \end{bmatrix} \rightarrow \begin{bmatrix} +\text{consonantal} \\ -\text{low} \\ +\text{voiced} \end{bmatrix} \Big/ \#\#X \begin{bmatrix} +\text{vocalic} \\ +\text{stress} \end{bmatrix} Y \begin{bmatrix} -\text{voiced} \end{bmatrix}
$$

$$
\begin{bmatrix} +\text{sonorant} \\ +\text{high} \\ -\text{stress} \end{bmatrix}_o^1 \begin{bmatrix} +\text{vocalic} \\ -\text{stress} \end{bmatrix} \begin{bmatrix} A, N \\ \underline{\quad\quad} \end{bmatrix}
$$

where [-stress] means 'of less than third level of stress', and A, N means 'in substantival classes but excluding the suffix /-iþ-/' — so *diupiþa* etc. (This formant is seen in *armhairtiþa, garaihtiþa* and *weihiþa* also; but e.g. *auþida* remains.) If one looks closely one sees that this is, at the core, Thurneysen's edict in the dress of Hirt's early reformulation. The input and output of Voyles' rule (but not the context) are identical with those in his version of Verner's law (54-55). This fact makes for speculation as to the extent to which for him Thurneysen's law, like Sievers' is a useful historical but intrinsically meaningless label, not unlike the 'Order of the Bath'. Yet the application is restricted to adjectives, nouns and (vacuously) verbs; so the omission of adverbs tidies up the law by allowing *-þro* always to appear so. The *twalibim* type becomes regular (and comparative *-iz-* is properly excluded); and the law, as a law, is said to have failed to survive into Germanic outside Gothic (53-54).

The dispassionate observer must see Thurneysen's creation as long-embattled, often dishonoured and much transformed — but still just alive and doggedly clinging to its identity.

REFERENCES

Braune, W. 1880. *Gotische Grammatik*. Halle /S.: Niemeyer. 5th ed., 1900. (19th ed. by E.A. Ebbinghaus, Tübingen; Niemeyer, 1981.)

Brugmann, K. 1909. *Das Wesen der lautlichen Dissimilationen*. Abhandl. der

Sächs. Gesellschaften 27.5(141-75). Leipzig: Teubner.

Chomsky, N. & Halle, M. 1968. *The sound pattern of English.* New York; Harper & Row.

Flickinger, D.P. 1981. Dissimilation in Gothic without Thurneysen's law. *CLS* 17.67-75.

Guxman, M.M. 1958. *Gotskij Jazyk.* Moscow: Izd. literary na inostrannyx jazykax.

Hench, G.A. 1896. Gotisch *guþ. PBB* 21.562-68.

––––––, 1897. The voiced spirants in Gothic. *JGP* 1.45-58.

Hirt, H. 1898. Grammatisches und etymologisches. *PBB* 23.288-357 (esp. "V. Zum spirantenwechsel im gotischen", 323-30).

––––––, 1931. *Handbuch des Urgermanischen.* I. Heidelberg: Winter.

Jacobsohn, H. 1920. Zwei probleme der gotischen Lautgeschichte II. Zum gotischen Satzsandhi. *KZ* 49.129-96.

Jellinek, M.H. 1926. *Geschichte der gotischen Sprache.* Berlin: W. de Gruyter.

Kock, A. 1900. Zur gotischen Lautlehre. *KZ* 36.571-83 (esp. 571-79).

Meyer, L. 1869. *Die gotische Sprache.* Berlin: Weidmann.

Mossé, F. 1942. *Manuel de la langue gotique.* Paris: Aubier.

Ohala, J.T. 1981. The listener as a source of sound change. *Papers from the parasession on language and behavior. CLS.* 178-203.

Paul, H., ed. 1891. *Grundriss der germanischen Philologie.* I. Strassburg; Trübner. (2nd ed., 1901.)

Prokosch, E. 1939. *A comparative Germanic grammar.* Philadelphia & Baltimore; Linguistic Socy. of America.

Schmidt, J. 1895. *Kritik der Sonantentheorie: Eine sprachwissenschaftliche Untersuchung.* Weimar; Böhlau. (See review by Saussure, *IFAnz.* 7.216-18 (1897), *Recueil* 539-41.)

Streitberg, W. 1897. *Gotisches Elementarbuch.* Heidelberg; Winter. (2nd ed., 1906).

––––––, 1903. Germanisches. *IF* 14.490-98 (esp. "Zur Thurneysens Gesetz", 493-95).

Sturtevant, A.M. 1932. Germanic notes. *GR* 7.372-73.

Thurneysen, R. 1898. Spirantenwechsel im Gotischen. *IF* 8.208-14.

Van Helten, W.L. 1903. Zur gotischen Grammatik. *IF* 14.60-98.

Voyles, J.B. 1968. Gothic and Germanic. *Lg* 44.720-46.

––––––, 1981. *Gothic, Germanic, and North West Germanic.* (= *ZDL Beiheft,* 39.) Wiesbaden; Steiner.

Whitney, W.D. 1879. *Sanskrit Grammar.* Boston; Ginn. (Revised ed. 1889;

12th ed. Cambridge, Mass.: Harvard Univ. Press, 1981.)

Wood, F.A. 1895. *Verner's law in Gothic.* (=*Germ. Stud.,* 2.) Chicago; Univ. of Chicago Press.

Wrede, F. 1891. *Die Sprache der Ostgoten in Italien.* Strassburg: Trübner. (Cf. also *Deutsche Literaturzeitung* 6. cols. 172-73 [Feb. 1897].)

Zadorožnyj, B.M. 1959. K voprosu o čeredovanii spirantov v gotskom jazyke. *Trudy Instituta Jazykoznanija* (AN SSSR) 9.137-48.

THE LAW OF THURNEYSEN AND HAVET

It was Thurneysen (whose individual claim to legislative fame rests on his Gothic law) who first clearly expressed an evolutionary fact of Latin which his predecessors had occasionally noticed (as had Saussure, for instance, at 1879: 104) but had not regularized. In 1884 (in an article not published until 1887) Thurneysen wrote that PIE /o/ reflected in Latin as /a/ before /w/, regardless of quantity. So *"*fovejô*' gave *faueō*, '*octôvos*' issued as *octāuus*. Ennius' *co(h)us* (*Annales* 545 Vahlen; cf. Varro *de ling. Lat.* 5.135) does not conform, but it suffered an unusual loss of /w/ for that word; the loss is paralleled elsewhere between like vowels (*sīs, lātrina*). Again, *lōtus*, as against expected *lautus* or *·lūtus*, was affected by the Roman *au/ō* alternation, which was largely a matter of social register. The common exceptions *bouis, ouis, ouum* receive varied ad hoc explanations, or excuses; but even sequences like /-olw-/ are cautiously (or even incautiously) admitted as input (→ e.g., *ualuae, saluus*). Thurneysen allowed himself even some exploration of the inverted effect in /wo/ (if such it is) which gives *uac-* beside *uoc-* in the etymon meaning "free", "empty", "idle", as in *uacuus* alongside the comedians' *uocūus* (e.g., at Plautus, *Casina* 596).

Havet's contribution is similar but seems really quite independent; he refers to Thurneysen only in postscript fashion. His treatment (1885) derives Latin *ou* exclusively from either PIE /ew/ (as in *nouem*) or from borrowing (so *bouis* and *ouis* are said to come from Greek βοϜ-, ὀϜ-); therefore inherited /ow/ must appear as *au*. This applies whether the reflex is contextually diphthongized or not: *auris* but *caueō*. So *feu* and *fou* respectively must underlie *fou* and *fau* in *Fōmes* (< *Fou+m-*) and *Fauōnius*.

A decade later began the corrections and the disbelief. In *fóueō - fauílla* (cf. *Fauŏnius*) and *óuis - auíllus* the accent placing is critically different. Kretschmer (1895) noticed that, and thought *cáuus, láuō* must be analogical levellings and *fáueō* an analogically produced new lexeme. But the *cáuus* type troubled him, as it did Solmsen, whose 1904 essay (without acknowledging Kretschmer) establishes the same accent condition but more precisely: that is, only in a pretonic syllable was the shift *ow > au* validated (as also /ew/ > *o/u*) (13-14). Horton-Smith (1895, 1896) reviewed all the forms so far offered in evidence. He contracted the comparanda here (notably rejecting the relevance seen by

Saussure in *gnāuus, papāuer* and *flāuus*), and expanded them there (adding *raudus* from Lindsay, and, e.g., *Aufidus, haud,* and *Faunus* from his own surmising). For him, the law dates to the third century B.C. and its input is /ŏw/, whether as two-segment string or as diphthong, and whether the second element derives from PIE /w/ or g^W/ or /g^Wh/. His list of previous commentators (Horton-Smith 1895:444-46) is useful and excuses detailed listing here.

While Hirt (1900:17 §35a), Kretschmer (1895, 1904) and Solmsen (1904) have no difficulty in accepting the shift as basically regular and fuss only over the details of conditioning, yet one quaintly polemical figure of the time was more sceptical. Fay (1902) opposes the law absolutely. But his arguments rest on what Szemerényi (1952:66) fairly describes as "halsbrecherischsten Etymologien" and need not detain one.

The upshot is that the law is usually accepted, at least as applying to the string /ŏwV-/ with following stress. Subsequent paradigmatic and derivational analogy is freely adduced; and there is in the handbooks a discernible sense of reservation as to the extent of the regularity. Szemerényi (who conceded that there must be something correct about it, if only some etymologies were cleansed) essayed a morphophonemic control (1952:68): namely, that the major condition is that the affected syllable stand in some sort of morphological relation to an alternant which has a long-vowel nucleus. So it is *cāuī* and *fāuī*, for example, which shift first, by an exceptionless law, and ensure the shift to *caueō* and *faueō*, perhaps around 200 BC. The inflexional and derivational isolation of /o/ in *cloāca, nouem, nouus, ouō* is the factor which precludes the lowering. True, *moueō* is somewhat awkward, because it has an unaffected perfect *mōuī*. But perhaps there were unguessed complications in this lexeme in PIE (cf. Sanskrit *mīvati, -mūta-*); and *mōuī* may well be a reshaping, after *fōuī* or *uōuī*. For Szemerényi the long-vowel shift is the dominant one. So while some forms, such as *strāuī* (*sternō*), need special consideration, *flāuus* and *gnāuus* (also *prāuus* and *rāuus*) are rehabilitated. Yet *octāuus* remains the theory's main support (63). Even so, it is possibly easier to mould the etymologies of other words than to force this numeral into the Thurneysen-Havet pattern. After all, *octō* (like ὀκτώ, Vedic *aṣṭā́*) does not show /w/, despite alternative Vedic *aṣṭau*), while Greek ὄγδο(F)ος does not show vowel-length. It is therefore worth closing with the sobering thought that this very pair (*octō* ~ *octāuus*) propelled Martinet (in *Word* 9,253ff. [1953]) to another speculative solution of quite another set of data. This was, that Latin *ō*/*āu* stand as contextual variants before -C/-V respectively, as do Sanskrit *go-, gav-*; and that the source of their low quality and their quantity and rounding (or labial offset) is a laryngeal with the requisite features (A^w). And in *that* theory, too, this word-pair remained the only satisfying testimonium.

REFERENCES

Fay, E.W. 1902. An erroneous phonetic sequence. In *Studies in honor of Basil L. Gildersleeve*, 189-203. Baltimore: Johns Hopkins Univ. Press.

Havet, L. 1885. Mélanges latins, *MSL* 6.11-39 (esp. 17-20).

Hirt, H. 1900. *Der indogermanische Ablaut.* Strassburg: Trübner.

Horton-Smith, L. 1895. The establishment and extension of the law of Thurneysen and Havet. *AJP* 16.444-67.

————, 1896. [Idem (cont.)]. *AJP* 17.172-96.

Kretschmer, P. 1895. Review of W.M. Lindsay, *The Latin language*, Oxford: Clarendon Press, 1894. *Wochenschrift für klassische Philologie* (1895), cols. 923-24.

————, 1904. Zum lateinischen wandel von *ov* in *av. KZ* 37.274-76.

Saussure, F. de 1879. *Mémoire sur le système primitif des voyelles dans les langues indoeuropéennes.* Leipzig: Teubner. (Publ. December 1878.) (= *Receuil des publications scientifiques de Ferdinand de Saussure*, ed. by C. Bally & L. Gautier, 1-268. Geneva: Sonor; Lausanne & Paris: Payot, 1922.)

Solmsen, F. 1904. Beiträge zur geschichte der lateinischen Sprache. *KZ* 37.1-26.

Szemerényi, O. 1952. Ein lateinischer Lautwandel: $\bar{o}w > \bar{a}w$? *KZ* 70.51-76.

Thurneysen, R. 1887. Lateinischer lautwandel. *KZ* 28.154-62. (Written 1884.)

VAN WIJK'S LAW*

The Dutch scholar Nicolaas van Wijk (1880-1941) suggested in 1916 that, during the period in which proto-Slavic phonotactics were forming and the open syllable was achieving dominance, a rightwards 'knock-on' effect occurred. The trigger was the necessary simplification of consonant clusters; the effect was to modify the vocalism of adjacent syllables. Van Wijk's notion was that the tone or melody was affected — a prosodic matter. Ebeling has more recently reformulated the development (1967:587, 589). He prefers to represent the effect as being the lengthening of the vowel in the syllable immediately following the relevant cluster — or, rather, a 'breaking' of the vowel which then falls together with original diphthongs. Ebeling also temporally locates the law's operation as not much earlier than Dybo's.

The clusters are of /CR/, that is, consonant plus resonant (semivowel) — a fact which Ebeling fails to note. Where R is realized as Y (that is, by glides), the exemplary forms include *plàcjĕte > *plàcēte, or *vòljă > *vòlǎ (which is then shifted by Dybo's law to *volâ and then by Stang's to e.g. Slov. vǫ́lja, SCr. völja). Where R is realized as N (nasals), one may cite *gūbněsĭ > *gūněsĭ.

The law combines with other processes, such as stress retraction from final ъ or ь (jers), to increase the declensional types in the present tense of the Slavic verb. For this reason it is worthy of inclusion in the canon of laws indirectly or directly shaping Slavic paradigm accent patterns.

In some dialects its effect is apparently extended analogically to forms which are morphologically similar if phonologically different (so Vermeer, forthcoming).

Ebeling's operational dating (on which see Kortlandt 1975:29-32) seems doubtful to Johnson (1980:491); but then the latter's mistrust extends to the law in general. Vermeer counter-attacks Johnson. Hence the law's existence at least as a subject of debate seems at present assured.

* See Appendix III

REFERENCES

Johnson, D.J.L. 1980. Dybo's law and metatony in the present tense of the Slavonic verb. *SEER* 58.481-99.

van Wijk, N. 1916. Zur sekundären steigenden Intonation im Slavischen, vornehmlich in ursprünglich kurzen Silben. *ASlPh* 36.346-48, 368-74.

––––––, 1922. Zum baltischen und slavischen Akzentverschiebungsgesetz. *IF* 40.1-40.

Vermeer, W.R. (forthcoming in *FoLH*) See on Dybo's law.

* Relevant or quoted also are:

Ebeling 1967*; Garde 1976*; Kortlandt 1975*, 1978*; van Wijk 1923*

– on which see Appendix III

VENDRYES' LAW

Indo-European word-accent has commonly suffered sideways movement: to this the laws of Balto-Slavic accentuation bear witness (cf. Appendix III). In Ancient Greek the accent reflex was (basically) of a higher pitch on a short vowel, or on part of a long vowel or diphthong, a pattern of occurrence best handled by the 'mora' concept. An accentual matrix was established, partly by syllable count (from the word end) and partly by mora count; for three successive 'laws' achieving this result, see Hermann (1923:88). There, too, a tendency to leftward shift in given word types existed. This was weakest in the Doric dialects; but it was very strong in the Aeolic group, for there πόταμος, λεῦκος, φρόνην were the well-attested pronunciations against Attic ποταμός, λευκός, φρονεῖν – where the first two show as much as a 2-mora difference in placing. The limiting, and environmental conditioning, of retraction in Greek therefore offer scope for local laws: and those of Wheeler (1885) and Vendryes (though enunciated 44 years apart) make an interesting pair, alike and yet subtly different. Wheeler's law applies to all dialects, and is discussed in its place; and an attempt by Hirt to legislate equally widely is mentioned in Appendix I, as is Bàrtoli's similar law.

Joseph Vendryes (1875-1960) produced in 1929 a distinguished monograph on the Greek accent. Therein (263) he noted a special propensity of Attic from the mid-fifth century BC. on: "tout perispomène à antépenultime brève devient en attique proparoxytone". That is, the high pitch is moved (in this matrix) leftwards by one mora across a syllable boundary. If we mark each mora as x, the formula is:

$$\ldots x \$ \dot{x} x \$ x \# \# \longrightarrow \ldots \dot{x} \$ x x \$ x \# \#$$

Hirt had already made the observation in 1904 (88-89, 92); but Vendryes spelt it out. What is especially interesting is that the antepenultimate syllable must have an unchecked short vocalic nucleus: it must be 'light'. Or, to put it otherwise, it must contain just one mora. This rule works well, provided that a sequence /V̆C/ before C is counted as having two moras. And why not? Homeric manuscript evidence offers εἶτά τε and ἔνθά τε, which in effect equates /VY/ and /VC/ before /C/ as of two moras. (The 'acute' versus 'circumflex' diacritics are merely notationally different, and it is the consonantal offset of the syllable which bears, in effect, the lowering of the pitch.) Again, if the accent position in γέλασμα is seen as contextually identical not to that in πόλεμος but to that in ἄνϑρωπος (cf. Lucidi 1950:82-83), then the apparent oddity of the latter type is reduced. The positional rule must still juggle with moras and syllables, or 'contonation' and syllables — but that is another matter. (Allen's theory of stress in Greek [1966b:123; 1973:293] allows, in any case, for ancient Greek sensitivity to syllabic weight.) Once all this is recognized, Vendryes' law will not be expected to affect αἰδοῖος or ἀνδρεῖος (although ὄργυια causes Szemerényi [1964:237] to have doubts; cf. Hirt [1929:52ff]). But ἀχρεῖος has a light first syllable and *is* input, giving shifted ἄχρειος; so also Attic γέλοιος, ἔρημος, ἕτοιμος, ὅμοιος and τρόπαιον (the last is an adjectival noun; adjectives are the favourite haunt of the Vendryes effect). Now Atticisms like ἔγωγε (< *ἐγῶγε) and ἔπειτα (< *ἐπεῖτα) fall into place.

Some non-conformities are clearly special:

(1) that ὀδόντος does not comply does not argue for a non-equation of (?) 2-mora VC(VN) with 2-mora VV or VV̄ in the source syllable; it just shows the contrary influence of declensional paradigms where the location of accent is 'categorially' determined. This is usually effected by derivation from the nominative singular; so δοτῆρα, as is reasserted by Miller (1976:19). Bàrtoli's law is relevant (Appendix I).

(2) the type γυναῖκ-α/ες/ας is one of the sheer irregularities so endemic in 'noms de parenté' (so Vendryes, 221, 262).

(3) contract verbs receive accent according to their underlying form and after contraction move no further: hence φιλοῦμεν < *φιλέομεν.

(4) ἐκεῖνος may be felt as disyllabic, having a purely anacrustic e- (cf. Ion. κεῖνος, Dor. κῆνος); but anyway it is also contracted from κε + ενος (cf. Lith. anàs).

(5) the verbal augment is always a left barrier to accent shift: hence παρεῖχε (not *πάρειχε).

Beyond these morphological demands nothing really seems to disturb the Vendryes dogma. Just possibly we can be sure, as textual scholars, that τροπαῖον *was* the (non-Attic) usage of Thucydides; but then it is a stylistic anachronism (like his ξύν for σύν), or an anti-provincialism (like his -σσ- for -ττ-). The handbooks seem justified in asserting the validity of the law for unmarked Attic after 450 BC.

Still, Kiparsky (1967:80) regards the law as part of a leftward conspiracy which includes Bàrtoli's law; then it is an 'early' affair. Another dissentient voice is that of Miller (1976). He thinks that Vendryes' law was not an Attic innovation (19), and that its real, earlier, pan-Greek (but minor) effect was to produce the type ἄνϑρωπος, κέλευϑος, δίδωμι, etc. leaving the ἕτοιμος shift to be a late conformity enforced in Attic alone on a special group of conservative adjectives (so also Voyles 1974:73). The argument rests on questionable enclitic and non-enclitic parallelisms, such as the partial accent-identity of λόγων τι(νῶν) with ἄνϑρωπος; but several rival interpretations of enclitic accentuation are available, after all. Besides, the absence of any historical trace of *ἀνϑρῶπος or *κελεῦϑος is rather a difficulty for Miller. Mouraviev's similar concept (1972: 117-18), of a rule-governed transfer by one mora leftwards of an accent position generated by an antepenultimate 'moric vowel' (his 'Rule III'), would give a basis for the ἕτοιμος effect; but (unlike the ἄνϑρωπος case) it is acceptable only if a complex underlying general process can be supposed to permit a quite late surface shift special to one small dialect area. Hence Vendryes' ordinance had better, for the present, be assigned simply as an ad hoc event-report, special to Attic adjectives and true from 450 BC onwards.

REFERENCES

Allen, W.S. 1966a. A problem of Greek accentuation. *Mem. Firth*, 8-14.
—————, 1966b. Prosody and prosodies in Greek. *TPS* 1966.107-48.
—————, 1967. Correlations of tone and stress in Ancient Greek. *Fs Jakobson* (2), 46-62.
—————, 1973. *Accent and rhythm*. Cambridge, Univ. Press.
Bubeník, V. 1979. Historical development of the Ancient Greek accent system. *IF* 84.90-106.
Hermann, E. 1923. *Silbenbildung im griechischen und in den anderen idg. Sprachen*. (=KZ Ergänzungsheft, 2.) Göttingen: Vandenhoeck & Ruprecht.
Hirt, H. 1929. *Indogermanische Grammatik*. V. Heidelberg: Winter.
Kiparsky, P. 1967. See on Bàrtoli's law (p.230).
Lucidi, M. 1950. L'origine del trisillabismo in greco. *Ricerche Linguistiche* I. 69-92. (Repr. in *Saggi Linguistici*, 77-102. Naples: Istituto Universitario Orientale di Napoli, 1966.)
Miller, D.G. 1976. The transformation of a natural accent system: the case of the Ancient Greek enclitics. *Glotta* 54.11-24.
Mouraviev, S.N. 1972. The position of the accent in Greek words: a new statement. *CQ* n.s. 22. 113-20.

Szemerényi, O. 1964. *Syncope in Greek and Indo-European*. Naples: Istituto Universitario Orientale di Napoli.

Vendryes, J. 1929. *Traité d'accentuation grecque*. Paris; Klincksieck.

Voyles, J.B. 1974. Ancient Greek accentuation. *Glotta* 52. 65-91.

Wheeler, B.I. 1885. See on Wheelers' law.

VERNER'S LAW

All that has to do with this law is a well-told tale. It forms one stage in a series of diachronic readjustments of Germanic consonants. The speculations on its physiological or functional or systemic causation must apply to that whole chunk of evolution which comprises the First and Second Sound Shifts, with Verner's edict slung between. Much on this was said under 'Grimm's law'. What follows concerns only Verner's discovery and the reactions of others to it. Historical grammars of Germanic all set it forth; Jespersen (1933:13-14=1966: 539-40) has given us Verner's own vivid description of that sudden moment of his enlightenment; Rooth (1974) has amply evaluated practically a century of scholarship on the issue (with further help in Seebold 1975). One has therefore really only to publicize some discussions which postdate Rooth's collection, and ventilate somewhat four areas of particular complexity and uncertainty in the law's implications.

When the PIE voiceless plosives passed through Grimm's law they should have emerged as voiceless spirants; and sometimes they did. Rather more often they were voiced, and later despirantized. Thus two parts of the First Sound Shift seem sometimes to combine into a rather repulsive 'flip' rule: e.g. $b > p$ but $p > b$. Besides, if $p > f$ etc. was of 'natural' direction, $f (> v) > b$ etc. was not. These awkwardnesses were known long before Verner wrote. By then the voicing alternation in certain verb paradigms had been set out by Braune (1874: 573ff.) and, after Holtzmann (1870:346), these were regularly called 'grammatischer Wechsel'. In 1862 Carl Lottner had sorted the Grimm excipienda into three sets, of which one represented the deviation of output of PIE /p,t,k,k^W/; but he had no explanation of it. (On Lottner, Verner, and the interrelation of their papers, see Lehmann 1967:97-108 and 132-63.)

What Verner realized, when his convalescent eye chanced to light on the accent markings on some relevant Sanskrit words in Bopp's grammar (and it is a pity we cannot consult the letter he claimed to have written at once to Julius Hoffory), was that the Germanic reflexes of PIE /p,t,k,k^W/ and /s/ did not remain voiceless − or maintain their fortis articulation − unless protected by an *inherited* preceding accent. Even then they, in effect, masqueraded as the true succession; really, voicing or lenition was the expected coda to the transformation charted by Rask and Grimm. Such is the correct interpretation of Verner's presentation (1876a:114). But his title suggests otherwise, and has misled various scholars into chiding him for getting it wrong; Rooth parades them: notably Saussure, Vendryes, and to a less degree Prokosch.

The solution was hinted at in 1874 by Sievers, in a letter to Braune of 24th March. Osthoff (1886:13n.2) saw as much, and suggested that only a fool would have betted against Sievers' prior publication of it. Streitberg (quoted as 1936: 287; in fact written long before, as he died in 1925) gives the same credit. But Sievers noted only that the PIE accent-placing in verbs was somehow connected with consonantal features; whence he was led to deplore contemporary ignorance about accent-evolution. Later (1878:149) he exemplified Verner's effect in labiovelars, as part of a wider ruling on segment-loss: see on Sievers' law II. And Verner's own first adumbration was also in a letter (to Vilhelm Thomsen, in Danish, dated 1 May 1875; cf. Rooth 1974:12, and Thomsen 1896/7).

Karl Adolf Verner (1846-1896) was of uncertain health and undeveloped ambition; retiring and non-polemical, he wrote few public articles but many personal letters. His fame rests on the pair of papers, published at Thomsen's instigation, which appeared in 1876 in volume 23 of *Kuhns Zeitschrift* (1876a, b). In them he not only diagnosed the conditions (and regularity) governing the final Germanic reflexes of PIE voiceless obstruents, including /s/, but also established the importance of accent-control in diachrony. Indeed, Jespersen (1933:229-48) was moved to insist that the IE accent had always been of energetic and phonologically dynamic stress. Verner also made tentative moves towards a fuller understanding of IE vowel (or syllable) apophony. His finding of 1876a) is correct about the law's throughput and contexts; it is true that a consonantal alternation in one language group is unmistakeably geared to a pattern of word-accent evidenced only in an earlier and distant tongue (Vedic; Greek merely assists) — on which indirectness of proof this law chimes with, and only with, the 'law of the palatals'. Less defensible is the claim that Verner has never been seriously challenged; in fact, the law's phonetic mechanics, and the relative Germanic chronology of consonant shift and accent shift (of place and of type), have been hotly debated ever since. Nor is the law free from obscurity or inconsistency, as will soon appear. Still, a recent examination of Verner's presentational strategy (by Kindt & Wirrer 1978) gives it a high mark on most aspects, including adequacy of data-base and logicality of argument.

The solution may have been glimpsed in an intuitive flash; but the major paper argues the case for it in a notably systematic and rational manner. Setting himself the neogrammarian task of finding a regulation for the irregularity (1876a:101), Verner starts within the rigorous framework of the verbal paradigm, noting OE *lîđe* [liːθe], *lidan*, and adducing twenty-nine evidential verbs across Germanic. He rejects, as cause of the consonant variety, three of the four accepted conjugational mechanisms, namely the opposition of endings, of root-vowel, or of syllable-count: hence, by sober elimination ("nüchternes argumentiren" [111]), only change of accent position remains. The Indic paradigm accentuation is displayed (though *bhid* is a curious choice); and the strongly expiratory nature of the Germanic accent is more or less equated with the more rigid muscularity of the voiceless, or fortis, obstruent. And only then is lexical accent brought in (as in the famous kinship words), or the behaviour of suffixes or of verbal endings (as opposed to roots). Analogy is permitted (128); and five possibly amenable exceptions are listed (119). Once we grant that the Grimm ouput was regularly voiced in the end, and only kept from that *Nachleben* by a preceding but still free accent, then the First Sound Shift has no large group of exceptions outside certain sheltering clusters. But to believe that word-*initial* consonants are properly catered for in this ruling is (pace Rooth 1974: 159) anachronistic; and the supposing of an interim stage of lenition (on the way to regular voicing) is only speculative, if defensible.

A check-list of exempla would be handy. But most are spotty and need annotation, because there is no thorough Germanic-Indic concordance for all the phonetic relationships. Also, later shifts and further derivations spoil shapes. But one might offer:

PIE	C-;	-´C-;	-C– (´)
/p/	OE *fœder*	OE *hēafod*	Goth.(etc.) *sibun* [sɪvun]
		Lat. *caput*	Skt. *saptá-*
/t/	Goth. *þreis*	Goth. *brōþar*	OE *fæder*
		Ved. *bhrãtar-*	Ved. *pitár-*
/k/	Goth. *haiha-*	OHG *svehur*	OE *sveger*
	Lat. *caecus*	Skt. *śvásura-*	Skt. *svaśrū́*
		(or Goth. *taíhun*	Goth. *tiguś*
		Greek δέκα	Greek δεκάς)
/kʷ/	OE *hvaet*	Goth. *leihwan*	Goth. *magus* (**makʷó-*)
	Lat. *quod*	Lat. *lingere*	
		(or ON *ulfr*	ON *ylgr*
		Skt. *vŕ̥ka-*	Skt. *vr̥kī́*)
/s/	Goth. (etc.) *sibun*	OE(etc.) *wesan*	OE *ēare* (< **auz-* ´)
			Lat. *auris*

— and for nouns and adjectives as affected by the law, one may consult Barber (1932).

The lucubrations, on all this, of some fifty-six scholars are amply chronicled by Rooth (1974). Where their observations reveal areas of serious concern — namely as to the law's precise formulation and scope, its physiological base (if any), its chronology, and its geographical domain — a brief excursus follows here. In general it may suffice to hear, among the almost uniformly approving receptions, the dissentient voice of Boer-den Hoed (1948), for whom the voicing process and its checks are controlled by wider and more complex factors of Germanic speech-habits than a simple but theoretical stress-influence, and the unhappy complaint of Lerchner (1971:105) that Verner did not make clear the real role of the accent nor justify the peculiar sensitivity of the spirants to shifting features. Fourquet (1963:90 = 1979:546) separates 'grammatischer Wechsel' from Verner's law proper (as referring to a later collapsing of distinctively voiced and non-distinctively voiced Vernerian spirants). Otherwise, adulation is the norm and has even led to some injudicious extensions of Verner's idea into unfavourable fields (as by Conway 1887, afterwards quietly rescinded); Malkiel (1966) is in point.

As to the four troublesome areas:-

The problem of formulation and scope

Verner believed that the voicing of medial spirants in voiced environments was not only a Germanic but a natural process. Therefore the retention of voicelessness must be the equally natural concomitant of an intensified phonation, preceding but overlapping the consonantal occlusion (a view which Lotspeich [1915] directly opposes). Therefore the voicing is positive and so is its rejection; and either way the process is essentially a coda to Grimm's law. Prokosch (1939: 61) is entirely right to observe that to Grimm's effect Verner's law provides "not an exception. . . but an acceleration". But Verner also viewed the voiced result as somehow exceptional (as his paper's title suggests and as is implicit in D'Alquen's corrective treatment of 1973), and the voiceless forms somehow seem to be 'true' or 'original' reflexes. Hence his motivation and his labelling are incompatible. It might serve as a reconciliation of his notions to offer (as did, among others, but with different conditioning, Bennett [1968a:219]) a split result inside the First Sound Shift:

$$\text{PIE} \begin{bmatrix} +\text{cons} \\ -\text{voice} \end{bmatrix} \rightarrow \text{Gmc.} \begin{bmatrix} +\text{cont} \\ -\alpha\text{voice} \end{bmatrix} \Big/ \begin{bmatrix} +\text{segm} \\ \alpha\text{stress} \end{bmatrix} -$$

— but Verner's own first footnote rules this out; the split in inside Germanic. Still, Saussure typically goes wrong in claiming (1916:194-95 = 1922ff:200-201) that Verner assigned a positive role to a following stress and failed to recognize spontaneous voicing blocked only by preceding stress. To judge so is to show that one has not read beyond Verner's opening pages; so Collinder (1968: 187), Minissi (1970:4-5) and Rooth (1974:61) rightly admonish Saussure (but Brinkmann [1965] follows him).

Yet unless one adopts a non-Vernerian formulation — that is, unless *either* a split Grimm output is allowed *or* the voiceless reflex is taken as basic and voicing as a deviation — the problem of initial spirants becomes acute (see Bugge's rule, Appendix I A). More than one commentator over the years (for example, Williams [1906-7:243], or Lotspeich [1915:348-49] or Lerschner [1971:105]) has pointed out that Verner's own formula must predict things like Gothic *bader [*vađar] and *dreis [*đri:s] for actual *fadar, þreis.* The conditions which permit the prefix *ga-*, commonly linked with Latin *co-*, still puzzle people (see Bennett 1968b, and Rooth [1974:46]). To add sandhi effects (as Wilmanns [1893:14]) is to worsen matters. While a dynamic role for following stress is rejected, a unique constraint by preceding accent is inadequate. (Williams' [1906/7:244] idea of a leftward blocking by a first-syllable stress clashes with all the other events within the law.) At the least, one needs either a restatement of the syllable domain of strong expiration, to include not only /−VC$−/ and /−$CVC$−/ but also /##CVC$−/, or to accept, e.g., Lerchner (1971:108) who credits word-initial position uniquely with a special intensity to match its greater 'information' rating. Bennett (1972:101) regards an initial consonant as affected 'under the fixed word-initial stress' which antedates even Grimm's law; but why, or how, is this so? It does not tally in direction with the rest of his phonetic ideas, and he has to explain Gothic *hund* versus *gamáins* by separate shifts of accent. Which leads into the fuss over chronology.

The problem of chronology

Bennett combines a belief in very early (pre-)Germanic accent-shift with a reliance on a folk-memory that certain syllables 'had already borne primary accent' (cf. Prokosch 1933:37). Such sophistries are rare among those who link the shift of obstruent features to the stress placing (not all do). If stress is the factor, then it is inescapable that Verner's law must precede the Germanic re-positioning of accent. The output (if we allow for some paradigmatic levelling) is too regular to suggest that the accent-shift had a long diffusion period which merely overlapped the law. So the likeliest start-time is the first century before Christ, the First Sound Shift ('1LV') being complete at least by the second century (but see what is said on Grimm's law) and the new accent-placing possibly achieved before Rome's imperial period (Rooth 1974:135). Absolute timing is impossible. Relative placing of events needs agreement on their nature and on the relation of Verner's law to Grimm's (an alternative mode, or a subsequent coda — as the inclusion of /s/ suggests). And there is always King's (1969:187) disturbing cyclic hint, that the sibilant shift represents an operation of Verner's law *before* Grimm's, the shifting of stops its second application, *after* Grimm's — a complication of Halle's simpler deduction of 1962. (See on Grimm's law.)

The problem of phonetics

Verner appealed to a muscular and expiratory accent (1876a:115-16); to this he added a syllable division which gave a consonantal offset (*fad$ar* etc.), so that the incidence of preceding stress is really upon a tautosyllabic segment (Wells [1903/5:526] misses this point). Yet some complainants defend the retained musical nature of Germanic accent: so Gauthiot (1900) and Pedersen (1906) — with the apparent approbation of Meillet (Rooth 1974:69). They link higher pitch with vocal cord movement; yet they think that it blocks, in some dissimilatory way, the voicing of a following obstruent. Boer (1916, 1924) more cleverly assumes that the leftward accent-shift precedes the law but a trace of musical accent remains on the source syllable. That trace then prompts the lenition of its preceding obstruent (Boer 1924:124). This is a subtler and more Chomskyan notion than Bennett's (1972). Besides, co-existing pitch and stress patterns are commonplace, and it might be argued (as by Naert 1955) that it is their combined force which causes the Vernerian effect(s). Yet most people have been readier to acknowledge (with an eye to later Germanic languages) the single physical influence of stress, a more obvious and widespread phenomenon. This influence, set within a context of unusual fullness, and made to operate much as in Thurneysen's law, is acknowledged by Voyles (1981:54-55).

But how did it operate? More agree in being convinced by the Vernerian coincidence and seeking to relate it to physiology (see Enkvist 1979:7) than are in accord over the physical details. A greater 'intensity' is widely assumed; but one has to face the tricky timing (by Verner) of the process, which puts it after the word-accent has become expiratory but before it has ceased to be free. This is so awkward that Jespersen (1933:229ff.) is at pains to deny that the accent was ever *not* expiratory and forceful; then, for him, the voiceless spirant was kept precisely in order to contrast maximally with the energy of the preceding vocalic nucleus (a view which he calls 'more complete' than Verner's when it is really the opposite). Some would agree (see Rooth [1974:95], on Luick); but more usually muscles are believed to relax progressively. Bàrtoli (1929) concentrates on the accentual causation. Rooth cites, in detail and fairly, such idiosyncratic suggestions as that the voicing is conditioned by level ('gleichbe-tonte') stress on the flanking syllables (Kip 1905); or that the glottis closes on the consonant which precedes a stressed vowel, hence assimilatory voicing (Lotspeich 1915); or that after a stressed vowel the glottis is instantly relaxed by an instinctive contrast-reaction, hence voicelessness (idem); or that the accent involved is not a word-accent at all but a 'syllable-accent' — or else there is some interplay of the two — (Lerchner 1971, based on subtleties by Kacnel'son 1966). Bennett (1972:102) sees a fortis-lenis distinction in the affected consonants; and D'Alquen (1973) works in terms of a 'strength' value-system (cf. Appendix I B, under Grammont's Law(s)) and thinks Verner's law encodes a strengthening of fortis, weakening of lenis segments. More recently, Normier (1977: 198ff.) restricts the incidence of this lenition to segments belonging to (that is, beginning) syllables which have *neither* the early Germanic initial stress *nor* — and this is the novelty — an abiding previous secondary svarita-type stress ('Nebenakzent') later in the word. But the phonotactic deduction that the early Germanic syllable division was /(C)VC$V. . ./ and not /(C)V$CV. . ./ was the opinion of Abrahams in 1949, and may still be true. And finally,

The problem of Gothic

For its inventor the law was pan-Germanic. The various languages offered evidence of differing quantity and quality, but the conditioning was pre-Germanic and the effects perceptible across the entire region; so it must have applied to Gothic. And so it largely does, not only in voicing (*sibun, bairanda*) but also in incidence of voicelessness (*filhan, þarf*). The constraining influence of preceding stress works as it seems it should. Besides, the alternation *þarf, þaúrbum* shows Vernerian behaviour in an inflexional paradigm; and 'grammatischer Wechsel' was wisely chosen by Verner as a sector which worried Germanists and so was a source of cogent pairing of forms which neatly display spirants differentiated according to his recipe. But conjugations of strong verbs belong there; indeed, they form the morphological backbone of his rule-governed phenomena. Yet in Gothic the strong verb is almost an entire stranger to Verner's law: there in the root-final position the voiceless variant is regular. Even in the reduplicating type the root-initial /s/ is voiced in only one verb, and patchily (Sturtevant 1957). On this setback one may consult Rooth (1974: 127-31); and for the Gothic facts, see Wood (1895), Jellinek (1926) or Krause (1963). It has prompted several solutions – or excuses.

In time Gothic interposes between proto-Germanic and the languages of the North and West groups. So the prima facie likelihood is that it underwent the law but, in isolation, thereafter lost traces of the regular output in strong verbs. This is Verner's own idea (1876a:109): that analogical levelling, from the present, spreads the voiceless spirants across the paradigm. Special pleading is at hand for other Gothic awkwardnesses (ibid. 119): *huaþara-* has Greek πότερος on its side for accent position, despite Sanskrit *katará-*. and *fadi-* (Skt. *páti-*) has no precluding accent when it is, as invariably, the final item of a compound. (Other Germanic languages have these, and like, oddities.) Analogical restoration was less close to Leskien's contemporary notions than was analogical 'sheltering' (which has not been used in this matter); still, it was close enough. Kluge (1879) accepted Verner's solution; and more recent rules-operators (King 1969, or Vennemann 1978) have gone along that path, applying the mechanics of 'rule-loss'. Hogg (1979:59-62) has the generative viewpoint but refutes that version of what happened. He supposes not so much rule-loss as (one might say) rule-demise. Once the Vernerian effect becomes synchronically opaque the conditions are favourable for analogy to step in and restore the paradigm to a sensible shape. Still, among pronouns *þis*, *þize* remain opaquely different, and the presumed recue operation does not turn up where expected in other Germanic idioms.

Hirt (e.g. 1931:148, 155) preferred to believe that the physical isolation of Gothic, which others (notably Schwarz [1951:68-69]) have seen as explaining its spreading of voiceless spirants, rather resulted in a staggered implementation of the common Germanic shift of word-stress to root-syllables. Given at least two stages, one before and one after Verner's law, the Gothic strong verbs perhaps suffered the accent repositioning at the earlier time whereas other morphological and lexical sectors received it at the later. This idea, which interestingly anticipates recent diffusion-theorizing, effectively removes all ground for the voicing of root-final spirants in these verbs in Gothic: *warþ*, *waúrþum* etc. (although then *gróf*, *gróbum* or *gaf*, *gébum* is awkward). Adherents are not lacking, but are heterogeneous: so the devoted but unclear Prokosch (1939: 63) alongside the heterodox Bennett (1968:222-23).

Another answer comes from Milroy (1982) and is just the converse of Hirt's.

Leftward accent movement, and its gradual diffusion, are accepted; but the strong verbs are supposed to remain immune to it until *after* Verner's law has had its effect. The law is taken to be one of voicing; but the (general) set of forms to which these verbs might have conformed (Milroy's 'type B') is of those where, essentially, the stress has by then shifted (e.g., *fulgins*) so that the following syllable becomes unstressed. This means that what for Verner was a simple constraint on voicing by inherited preceding accent is elaborated by adding, as an alternative blocking feature, the *absence* of *new* (shifted) preceding accent. Therefore (if one understands aright) *kusún* escapes voicing because it has *not* yet become *kúsun*, and so is unlike *fúlgins* (or *fádar*). This ingenious but startling complication makes the law an entailment of accent shift, when the converse seems more obviously true (namely that the fact of the shift's having occurred − and so the freedom of the PIE accent − is entailed by the presence of a voiced consonant − cf. Kuryłowicz 1968:19-20). It also ignores the intuitively satisfying simple parallelism to Verner's effect afforded by phonetic alternants such as English as [-(g)z-] versus [-(k)s-], *exért* but *éxit*, *posséss* but *póssible*, and so forth (despite *assíst*, *precíse* etc.) like Schröder's German pair (1918) *Hannóver* and *Hannoveráner* ([-f-] versus [-v-]); and Bloch (1925) finds an Asian analogue.

Other avenues beckon. Kuryłowicz, for example (1968:24), links the Gothic loss of verbal paradigm alternation with its devoicing of final spirants. Connolly (1980) uses the uneven morphological incidence of the law (even outside Gothic the strong verbs accept 'grammatischer Wechsel' only spottily and for classes I-III) to argue for interference by laryngeals, at least as late as Proto-Germanic. Clearly the heart of this matter is yet to be reached and we may confidently await the penning of many further essays upon it.

REFERENCES

Note: Rooth (1974:169-77) supplies a most useful bibliography of a century of work on Verner's law. The really basic items are repeated here; others, less central, may be sought in Rooth. Even so, one or two items of importance are not in Rooth's list; and (of course) valuable papers have appeared more recently. This inventory, itself interim in nature, presents a 'state-of play' conspectus and includes all the works discussed above.

Abrahams, H. 1949. *Etudes phonétiques sur les tendances évolutives des occlusives germaniques.* Aarhus: Universitetsforlaget.
Baldi, P & Werth, R.H. 1978. *Readings in historical phonology.* University Park,

Pa.: Pennsylvania State Univ. Press.

Barber, C.C. 1932. *Die vorgeschichtliche Betonung der germanischen Substantiva und Adjektiva.* Heidelberg: Winter.

Bàrtoli, M. 1929. Le sonore aspirate e le sonore assordite dell'ario-europeo e l'accordo loro col ritmo. *AGI* 22/23.63-130.

––––––, 1942. Zum Lex Verner. *KZ* 67.102-111.

Bennett, W.H. 1968a. The operation and relative chronology of Verner's law. *Lg* 44.219-23.

––––––, 1968b. The accentuation of Gothic *ga-. Fs Sehrt*, 53-60.

––––––, 1972. Prosodic features in proto-Germanic. In Van Coetsem & Kufner 1972.99-116.

Bloch, J. 1925. L'intonation en Penjabi: Une variante asiatique de la loi de Verner. *Mélanges Vendryes* 57-67. Paris: Champion.

Boer, R.C. 1916. Over den samenhang der klankverschuivingen in de germaansche dialecten. *Neophilologus* 1.103-111.

––––––, 1924. *Oergermaansch handboek* 2nd ed. Haarlem: Tjeenk, Willink & Zoon (1st ed., 1918.)

Boer-den Hoed, P.M. 1948. Is de wet van Verner een wet? *Handelingen van het twintigste Nederlands Philologen-Kongress gehouden te Leiden,* 71-71. Groningen.

Braune, W. 1874. Ueber den grammatischen Wechsel in der deutschen Verbalflexion. *PBB* 1.513-27.

Brinkmann, H. 1965. *Studien zur Geschichte der deutschen Sprache und Literatur.* I: *Sprache.* Düsseldorf: Schwann.

Bugge, S. 1887/8. Etymologische studien über die germanische lautverschiebung. *PBB* 12.399-430, and 13.167-87.

Collinder, B. 1968. *Kritische Bemerkungen zum Saussureschen Cours.* Acta Soc. Ling. Uppsaliensis 1:5.181-210, Uppsala.

Collinge, N.E. 1978. Exceptions, their nature and place – and the neogrammarians. *TPS* 1978.61-86.

Connolly, L.A. 1980. 'Grammatischer Wechsel' and the laryngeal theory. *IF* 85. 96-123.

Conway, R.S. 1887. *Verner's law in Italy.* London: Trübner.

D'Alquen, R.J.E. 1973. The Germanic sound shift and Verner's law; a synthesis. *GL* 13.79-89.

Enkvist, N.E. 1979. 'What' and 'why'; causal explanations in linguistics. *FoL* 13.1-21.

Essen, O. von 1934. Das Kompensationsprinzip beim Sprachvorgang. *Vox*

20.67-107.

————, 1940. Sprechphysische Gesetzmässigkeiten und ihre Bedeutung für den Lautwandel. *IF* 57.161-77.

Fourquet, J. 1948. *Les mutations consonantiques du germanique: Essai de position des problèmes*. Paris: Les Belles Lettres. (See references under Grimm's law.)

————, 1963. Einige unklare Punkte der deutschen Lautgeschichte in phonologischer Sicht. *Fs Maurer*, 84-90 (Repr. in 1979:540-46).

————, 1979. *Recueil d'études*. Ed. by D. Buschinger & J-P. Vernon. Paris: Champion.

Gauthiot, R. 1900. A propos de la loi de Verner et des effets du ton indoeuropéen. *MSL* 11.193-97.

Halle, M. 1962. Phonology in generative grammar. *Word* 18.54-72.

Helm, K. 1949. Zur vorgeschichtlichen Betonung der germanischen Substantiva. *PBB* 71.250-65.

Hentrich, K. 1920. Das Vernersche Gesetz in der heutigen Mundart. *PBB* 44. 184-85.

————, 1921. Zum Vernerschen Gesetz. *PBB* 45.300-302.

Hirt, H. 1931. *Handbuch des Urgermanischen*. I. Heidelberg: Winter.

Hogg, R.M. 1979. Analogy and phonology. *JL* 15.55-85. (Esp.59-63.)

Holtzmann, A. 1870. *Altdeutsche Grammatik*. I. Leipzig: Brockhaus.

Jankowsky, K.J. 1972. *The Neogrammarians*. The Hague: Mouton.

Jellinek, M.H. 1926. *Geschichte der gotischen Sprache*. Berlin: W. de Gruyter.

Jespersen, O. 1933 [1897]. Karl Verner: Some personal recollections. *Linguistica: Selected Papers*. Copenhagen: Levin & Munksgaard; London: Allen and Unwin. 12.23; 229-48. (In undated repr., 805-816. Repr. further in *Portraits of linguists I*, ed. by T.A. Sebeok, 538-48. Bloomington: Indiana Univ. Press, 1966.)

Kacnel'son, D.A. 1966. *Sravitel'naja akcentologija germanskič jazykov*. Leningrad: Izdatel'stvo 'Nauka'.

Kindt, W. & Wirrer, J. 1978. Argumentation and Theoriebildung in der historischen Linguistik. *IF* 83.1-39.

King, R.D. 1969. *Historical linguistics and generative grammar*. Englewood Cliffs, N.J.: Prentice-Hall.

Kip, H.Z. 1905. Noch ein Wort über germ. *f, þ, h, s* > ƀ, ð, ʒ, *z. MLN* 20.16-18.

Kluge, F. 1879. *Beiträge zur Geschichte der germanischen Conjugation*. Strassburg: Trübner.

Krause, W. 1963. *Handbuch des Gotischen*. 2nd ed., Munich: Beck. (1st ed.,

1953.)

Kuryłowicz, J. 1952. *L'accentuation des langues indo-européennes*. Wrocław and Kraków: Polska AN.

——, 1968. *Indogermanische Grammatik II*. Heidelberg: Winter.

Lehmann, W.P. 1967. *A reader in nineteenth century historical Indo-European linguistics*. Bloomington: Indiana Univ. Press.

Lerchner, G. 1967. Nachträgliches zu Verners Gesetz. *PBB* 89.431-39.

——, 1971. *Zur II. Lautverschiebung im Rheinisch-Westmitteldeutschen: Diachronische und diatopische Untersuchungen*. (Mitteldeutsche Studien, 30.) Halle; Niemeyer. (Esp. 103-19.)

Lotspeich, C.M. 1915. The physiological aspects of Verner's law. *JEGP* 14.348-50.

——, 1918. Accent-mixture and sound changes. *JEGP* 17.157-74.

Malkiel, Y. 1966. Quelques fausses applications de la 'loi de Verner' aux faits romans. *Cahiers Ferdinand de Saussure* 23.75-87.

Milroy, J. 1982. On the problem of historical interpretation: Verner's law in Gothic. *P(5)ICHL*, 223-29.

Minissi, N. 1970. La formulazione della legge di Verner. *Euroasiatica: Folia philologica*, Suppl. 8.3-18. Pisa: Giardini.

Moulton, W.G. 1954. The stops and spirants of early Germanic. *Lg* 30.1-42.

——, 1972. The proto-Germanic non-syllabics (consonants). In Van Coetsem & Kufner, 1972:141-73.

Naert, P. 1955. La loi de Verner. *SL* 9.73-75.

Noreen, A. 1880. Weiteres zum Vernerschen Gesetz. *PBB* 7.431-44.

Normier, R. 1977. Indogermanischer Konsonantismus, germanische 'Lautverschiebung' und Vernersches Gesetz. *KZ* 91.171-218.

Osthoff, H. 1886. *Die neueste Sprachforschung und die Erklärung des indogermanischen Ablautes*. Leipzig: Petter. (See on 'the law of the palatals'.)

Prokosch, E. 1933. *An outline of German historical grammar*. New York: Oxford Univ. Press.

——, 1939. *A comparative Germanic grammar*. Philadelphia and Baltimore; Linguistic Socy. of America.

Ramat, P. 1981. *Einführung in das Germanische*. Tübingen: Niemeyer. (*Linguistische Arbeiten*, 95.)

Rooth, E. 1974. *Das Vernersche Gesetz in Forschung und Lehre*. Lund; Gleerup.

Saussure, F. de 1916. *Cours de linguistique générale*. Publ. by C. Bally and A. Sechehaye. Lausanne & Paris: Payot. (Pagination differs in 2nd ed. [1922] and subsequent editions.)

Schröder, H. 1918. Das Vernersche Gesetz im heutigen Deutsch. *PBB* 43.352-53.

Schultheiss, T. 1938. Das Fortleben der indogermanischen 'freien Betonung' im germanischen Norden. *KZ* 65.249-55.

Schwarz, E. 1951. *Goten, Nordgermanen, Angelsachsen.* Berne: Francke; Munich: Lehnen.

Seebold, E. 1975. Review of Rooth (1974). *Kratylos* 19.112-18.

Sievers, E. 1876. *Grundzüge der Lautphysiologie.* Leipzig: Breitkopf & Härtel.

–––––, 1877. Zur Akzent- und Lautlehre der germanischen Sprachen, I. *PBB* 4.522-39.

–––––, 1878. Idem, III. *PBB* 5.101-63.

–––––, 1901. *Grundzüge der Phonetik.* 5th rev. ed. Leipzig: Breitkopf & Härtel. (1st ed., 1876.)

Stang, C.S. 1969. La loi de Verner et la question des caractères de l'accentuation mobile en germanique. *NTS* 23.7-12 (Repr. in *Opuscula linguistica,* 258-64. Oslo, Univ. Press, 1970.)

Streitberg, W., Michels, V. & Jellinek, M.H. 1936. *Germanisch.* vol. I. Berlin & Leipzig: W. de Gruyter.

Sturtevant, A.M. 1957. Verner's law in the preterit tense of the Gothic reduplicating verb *slepan. MLN* 72.561-63.

Thomsen, V. 1896/7. Karl Verner (1846-1896). *NTF* 3.5.187-202. (Repr. in *Samlede Afhandlinger* I.183-202, Copenhagen & Oslo: Nordisk Forlag, 1919.)

Van Coetsem, F. 1972. Proto-Germanic morphophonemics. In Van Coetsem & Kufner 1972:175-209.

Van Coetsem, F. & Kufner, H.L., eds. 1972. *Toward a grammar of Proto-Germanic.* Tübingen: Niemeyer.

Vennemann, T. 1978. Phonetic analogy and conceptual analogy. In Baldi & Werth 1978:258-74.

Verner, K. 1876a. Eine ausnahme der ersten lautverschiebung. *KZ* 23.97-130. (Transl. by R. Stanley in Baldi & Werth II, 1978:32-63.)

–––––, 1876b. Zur ablautsfrage. *KZ* 23.131-38.

–––––, 1903 *Afhandlinger og breve.* Copenhagen & Leipzig; Selskab for Germansk Filologi.

Voyles, J.B. 1981. *Gothic, Germanic, and North West Germanic.* (= *ZDL Beiheft,* 39.) Wiesbaden: Steiner.

Wells, F.L. 1903/5. Experimental phonetics and Verner's law. *JEGP* 5.522-27.

Williams, R.A. 1906/7. The phonetical explanations of Verner's law. *MLR* 2.233-52.

Wilmanns, W. 1893. *Deutsche Grammatik.* I. Strassburg: Trübner.

Wood, F.A. 1895. *Verner's law in Gothic*. (*Univ. of Chicago Germanic Studies* 2:1.). Chicago, Univ. Press. (See 2:2: *The reduplicating verbs in Germanic* ibid.)

WACKERNAGEL'S LAW I

In 1964 Watkins (1036) affirmed: "One of the few generally accepted syntactic statements about Indo-European is Wackernagel's law, that enclitics originally occupied the second position in the sentence".

It was in 1892 that the Swiss Jacob Wackernagel (1853-1938) set out, in ample fashion, what began as a refutation of Thumb's facile syntactic and etymological equation of Homeric μή μιν. . . . and R̥gvedic mā sma . . . and developed into a wide-ranging demonstration of the typical IE position of sententially important enclitics. Although μιν (like οἱ) may be enclitic to the sentence-initial item in Homer as a basic rule, by the sort of placing which produces univerbals like ὅταν or ἐάν, yet it is often moved to third place; but that shift is prompted by another preceding enclitic like γάρ. Indo-Iranian, Latin, and even Germanic and Celtic show traces of the same structure, a kind of scramble among these clitic items for the envied second spot. (Even PIE accentless main finite verbs may slip into a post-subject position and so perhaps induce the SVO ordering towards which so many have recognized a regular drift.) Greek, rather awkwardly, possesses semi-clitics like δέ or ἄν; that the latter drifts to sentence-second place (even being repeated later in the sentence, for syntactic clarity) is shown by Howorth (1955) – but see also Kravar (Živa Antika, Skopje, 1955: 247). It had long been known (after Jacobsohn 1920:196) that (1) the precise nature of the sentence-initial item and (2) the dialect were conditioning factors.

Nilsson (1904) added evidence from Old Bulgarian and some modern Polish idioms. Ivanov (1958:613) brought in Anatolian (and, less directly, Lithuanian and Tocharian). Barrett (1964:346-47) demonstrates the law's effect in 'interlacing' word-order in Greek. In Germanic the sentence-initial item sometimes rejects enclisis and even loses its own stress, unless rebuilt; yet the basic sequence is really there (at least, so opines Hopper 1969). Renou (1936:61ff) and later Gonda (1971:146-47) note the Indic results, which include tmesis of regular compounds and perhaps the attraction of vocatives to sentence-second position. Comrie (1981:20-21) gives a good example of the phenomenon from modern Serbo-Croat. It is true that *Petar čita knjigu danas* ("Peter reads the book today") has twenty-four possible orderings of its words, all grammatical and all propositionally identical. It is, however, also true that if *mi* ('to me') is inserted it must follow the first word of the sentence, whatever that may be: thus *danas mi Petar čita knjigu*, or *knjigu mi čita danas Petar*, and so forth (with some choice as to whether a deictic-plus-nominal counts as one word or two). Kuryłowicz (1958:613) went so far as to deduce, from the emergence of the feature in Spanish (where it was not an inheritance from Latin), that the Wackernagel effect is a quasi-universal; but Watkins (1964:1036) disagrees.

Interest — not to say optimism — has recently flared up over the chances of effectively reconstructing PIE syntax. In Steever et al. (1976) some thirty-two essays start as many hares. But there has been a corresponding scepticism (as expressed by Lightfoot 1979:155-56); and Watkins (1976:205-306) fulminates against the deadening *ostinato* (in word-order speculations in PIE) of the 'typological' preoccupation with SOV versus SVO etc., the line of thought so characteristic of the 1970s. More fruitful seem the hypotheses, in this sector, which consider more precise matters such as Wackernagel's thesis. Watkins (1964) proposes a distinction between connecting particle (*N*), which *may* be enclitic, and a certainly enclitic pronoun (*E*). Then the typical PIE sentence onset is /## *N(E)*. . ./. PIE *so* (and *to*) is the 'fossilized connective' (1038), although Hittite commonly offers *nu*; and the combining of *N so(to)* with *E es* (Hitt. *-aš*) was claimed to be the origin of the heteroclite third person pronoun of IE (IH) by Sturtevant (1939, 1962). Watkins (1964:1042) would incline to see *NE* in the structure of <augment + finite verb> More recently the same writer (1976:319) records an idiosyncrasy of Insular Celtic, where the sentence-second (or clause-second) position was made regular for the *WH-* relative marker; but this is not PIE usage. Some mileage can clearly be made here, and the going is reasonably good.

When people can and do speak simply of 'the Wackernagel position', it smacks of temerity to fuss over the law's title. But Wackernagel himself (1926: 46) gives credit to Delbrück for discovering the rule, valid for early Indic prose, which assigned the position immediately following the opening word of the sentence preferably (and sometimes regularly) to enclitics. The reference is to the third volume (1878) of Delbrück & Windisch. Moreover, the problem of how to order two successive enclitics, when Watkins' *N* and *E* are both of that prosodic class, was already resolved by Delbrück (*BDG* V.51). The other central neogrammarians have each their eponymous law; and dual ownership is accepted elsewhere (as in the law of Fortunatov and Bechtel, or that of Vasil'ev and Dolobko). It thus appeals to one's sense of justice on two counts that this present ordinance should rather be known as 'the law of Delbrück and Wackernagel'.*

---

* On a possible second law by Wackernagel, see Appendix I A.

REFERENCES

Barrett, W.S. 1964. Ed. of Euripides, *Hippolytus.* Oxford, Univ. Press.

Comrie, B. 1981. *Language universals and language typology.* Oxford: Blackwell.

Delbrück, B. [& Windisch, E.] 1878. *Syntaktische Forschungen.* III. Halle/S: Niemeyer.

Gonda, J. 1971. *Die Indischen Sprachen: Erster Abschnitt: Old Indian.* (= vol.1.1. of *Handbuch der Orientalistik,* ed. by B. Spuler et al.; Zweite Abteilung, ed. by J. Gonda.) Leyden & Cologne: Brill.

Hopper, P.J. 1969. An Indo-European 'syntagm' in Germanic. *Linguistics* 54.39-43.

Howorth, R.H. 1955. The origin of the use of ἄν and κε in indefinite clauses. *CQ* n.s. 5.72-93.

Ivanov, Vjač. V. 1958. The importance of new data concerning Hittite and Tocharian languages for the comparative historical grammar of IE languages. In *P(8)ICL,* 611-13.

Jacobsohn, H. 1920. Zwei Probleme der gotischen Satzsandhi. *KZ* 49.129-218.

Kuryłowicz, J. 1958. Remarks on Ivanov 1958. *P(8)ICL,* 613.

Lightfoot, D.W. 1979. *Principles of diachronic syntax.* Cambridge; Univ. Press.

Nilsson, E. 1904. Wackernagel's gesetz im Slavischen. *KZ* 37.261-63.

Renou, L. 1936. *Etudes de grammaire sanscrite.* Paris: Maisonneuve.

Steever, S.B. et al. 1976. *Papers from the parasession on diachronic syntax.* Ed. by S.B. Steever, C.A. Walker & S.F. Mufwene. Chicago: Chicago Linguistic Socy.

Sturtevant, E.H. 1939. The pronoun **so *sā *tod* and the Indo-Hittite hypothesis. *Lg* 15.11-19.

——————, 1962. The Indo-Hittite hypothesis. *Lg* 38.105-10.

Wackernagel, J. 1892. Über ein Gesetz der indo-germanischen Wortstellung. *IF* 1.333-436. (See also *Kleine Schriften* III (1979), pp. 1865-69; a conference report.)

——————, 1926. *Vorlesungen über Syntax.* Basel: Birkhäuser. (2nd ed., 1950.)

Watkins, C. 1964. Preliminaries to the reconstruction of Indo-European sentence structure. *P(9)ICL,* 1035-42.

——————, 1976. Towards Proto-Indo-European syntax: Problems and pseudo-problems. In Steever et al. 1976:305-326.

WHEELER'S LAW

Like the law of Vendryes, and parallel to several of those which handle Balto-Slavic accentuation, this ordinance concerns a leftward shift of place of word accent. The domain is Ancient Greek (and not just one dialect) and the relevant accent reflex is of a contrastive high point of pitch. The diachronic movement is of one 'mora', across a syllable boundary. The system within which it occurs is discussed under Vendryes' law (above).

Benjamin Ide Wheeler (1854-1927), though an American, published his dissertation in German in Strassburg in 1885. In treating the evolution of nominal and adjectival accenting in Greek, he enunciated his 'rule IV' thus: "daktylisch ausgehende oxytona werden zu paroxytona". If x may stand for each mora, then:

$$\dots \left\{ \begin{array}{c} VV \\ VY \\ (V)VC \end{array} \right\} \; \$ \, x \, \$ \, \dot{x} \, \# \# \; > \dots \left\{ \begin{array}{c} VV \\ VY \\ (V)VC \end{array} \right\} \; \$ \, \dot{x} \, \$ \, x \, \# \#$$

In Vendryes' case the (light) syllable weight of the target syllable was crucial: the type ἄνθρωπος is *not* output of his law because a checked syllable agrees with a more obviously '2-mora' syllable in resisting the accent: cf. αἰδοῖος, etc. For Wheeler syllabic weight is equally important (a fact which allows Ruipérez (1972:149] to put the law in the same epoch as Osthoff's), but it need not be equated with a 2-mora value. The heavy syllable in the dactylic stretch, which may be checked or not, is neither source nor target for the high pitch; therefore the *metrical* value /– ◠ ◠ # #/ is the simple, and separate, requirement. So ποικίλος (< *ποικιλός, Ved. *peśaláh*), ἀγκύλος (<*ἀγκυλός, Ved. *aṅkuráh*); so equally γεωρύχος, ναυστόλος, παρθένος (but see Hamp 1972:178). One remembers, notably, Αἰσχύλος. Non-dactylic sequences are not input: ῥιγηλός (–– ◠), ἐρυθρός (◠ – ◠), ποταμός (◠◠ ◠). The generalization which suggests itself is that, within the word accent matrix, a stretch /–◠/ attracts the accent to its own light syllable.

The law explains several anomalies of morphology: πλησίος against σκολιός; ὀστέον (whence later ὄστεον) against κολεόν; τρισί as the norm but ἀνδράσι as derived (although τριήρεσι is awkward). Even so, there are many exceptions:

ὀμφαλός, ὀρφανός, μυελός, οὐρανός, ἀδελφεός, to name a few.

Maurice Bloomfield (1897:55n.2) believed that Brugmann was the father of the notion: certainly Brugmann accepted it into the *Grundriss* (*BDG* 1897: 545-46). But adverse reaction was not lacking. Bloomfield himself (1888) first objected to Wheeler's general thesis about Greek (a scenario of an inherited accent fighting it out, word by word, against a usurping secondary accent). Allinson (1891) offers seven classes of exceptions, including the special case of possible homophones accentually differentiated in order to mark active versus passive derivation: but he does not convince Hirt (even as late as 1912). Bloomfield, however, is with Allinson; and in particular he denounces (1897) what Hirt (1912:273) still accepts as the major dividend of Wheeler's law, namely an origin for the paroxytone accent of perfect middle participles (in –μένος). Wheeler permits the shift *πεφυγμενός > πεφυγμένος, and so equally εἰρημένος, whence by analogy λελυμένος etc. But for Bloomfield, –μένος (not *–μενός), is the natural PIE word shape. Other formants perhaps affected by the law are the adverbials –ίκα (αὐτίκα), –άκις (πολλάκις, etc.), and the adjectival –ηλίκος (ὀμηλίκος, etc.).

Kuryłowicz (1958:147ff.) rejects Wheeler's law as a general explanation for the type πατροκτόνος (at least in respect of its required long antepenultimate nucleus). Vendryes (1929:193-94, §249) discusses the law in relation to such compounds, preferring to set up a regular rule of penultimate placement of stress for 'active' meaning, after Herodian. Yet on the whole Wheeler appears to have more regularities on his side than exceptions: but it is a close thing. The law remains in the text books. Its affinity with Bàrtoli's and Vendryes' laws helps – though it didn't help Hirt's similar attempt (see Hirt's law II) – and so perhaps does its linkage with a general IE zero-grade retraction rule (so Miller 1976:15). For Kiparsky (1967:74) it is simply first cousin to Bàrtoli's law (see Appendix I A).

REFERENCES

Allinson, F.G. 1891. On paroxytone accent in tribrach and dactylic endings. *AJP* 12.49-58.

Bloomfield, M. 1888. The recessive accent in Greek. *AJP* 9.1-41.

—————, 1897. IE notes. *TAPA* 28.55-57.

Hamp, E.P. 1972. Παρθένος and its congeners. *Homenaje a Antonio Tovar*, 177-80. Madrid: Gredos.

Hirt, H. 1912. *Handbuch der griechischen Laut- und Formenlehre.* 2nd ed. Heidelberg: Winter.

Kiparsky, P. 1967. A propos de l'histoire de l'accentuation grecque. *Langages* 2.73-93.

Kuryłowicz, J. 1958. *L'accentuation des langues indo-européennes.* Wrocław-Kraków: Polska AN.

Miller, D.G. 1976. See on Vendryes' law.

Ruipérez, M.S. 1972. Le dialecte mycénien. *Acta Mycenaea (=Proc. 5th Int. Coll. Myc. Stud. 1970) = Minos* 11.136-69.

Vendryes, J. 1929. *Traité d'accentuation grecque.* Paris: Klincksieck.

Wheeler, B.I. 1885. *Der griechische Nominalaccent.* Diss., Univ. of Strassburg.

WINTER'S LAW

In 1976 Werner Winter proposed a law of vowel lengthening in Balto-Salvic; the article did not appear in print until 1978. Winter accepted the maintenance of inherited short vowels as such if the syllabic intonation were other than acute, and if the following consonant were other than traditional simple 'media' at the PIE stage. (The Balto-Slavic 'intonations' and the Lithuanian diacritics are discussed in Appendix III; the possibly quite different phonetic values of PIE 'mediae' and 'mediae aspiratae' are the concern of Appendix II.) Where, however, in an acute syllable the vowel preceded a consonant of the sort usually written *d* (etc.), Winter (439) declared the outcome to be a long acute vowel. Whereas we find Lithuanian *vèsti* alongside Sanskrit *vádhūḥ*, Irish *fedim* (from PIE *wĕdh-*), or OCS *vesti* with Skt. *vahati* (**wĕgh-*), the reflexes of PIE *(H)ĕd-* are Skt. *ádmi, átti*, Greek ἔδ-ομαι, but Lith. *ěsti*. Comparable is *sěsti*, "sit" (Greek ἕς-ομαι); cf. Hopper (1982:131-32). Winter offered a reason as to why this effect is restricted to 'mediae': this was their having voice as a distinctive feature (where the 'mediae aspiratae' had it as a mere phonetic concomitant).

One's immediate reaction is to suspect that more factors are at work, differently in different etyma, than can be conflated so simply: the possible presence, if no more than that, of a laryngeal in the affected syllable sorts out Winter's exempla. Kortlandt (1978c:279) brings in Latvian *uôst, nuôgs, uôga* (Lith. *úosti, núogas, úoga*); but as soon as Baltic *o* enters so do at least five different sets of comparative phonological relationships, conveniently set out by Watkins (1965:120-21); and these three words belong to separate generic sets. But there are worse worries.

For Kortlandt, who named the law and espoused it at once (1978a:447 — see also 1977 passim and 1981:30-37), the attraction is that the conditioning consonant can be considered — if one accepts the ideas of Hopper, Gamkrelidze and Ivanov, or Bomhard; see Appendix II — as 'glottalic' and 'ejective'. Hopper's Collitz lecture of 1983 included just such an explanation. Then Latvian *pêds, sêst, bêgt* (and the forms with other vowels) are declared to have a glottalic articulation which they share with the following plosive (1978c:280). Further, the glottalic feature is held to fall together with (traces of) an original laryngeal, and a syllable which has had either of these is to be marked thereafter as possessing acute intonation – so rehabilitating the theory of Vaillant (1936:114-15; cf. Kortlandt 1983b:170). Nevertheless:

(1) The Lithuanian result, given the normal diacritic usage, is *not* acute, although Latvian has 'Stosston'. (Kortlandt 1977:322-23 cites *dúodu* alongside Skt. *dadā́mi.*)

(2) A glottalized vowel is of itself *not* long; indeed, in contemporary English a glottal offset to a vowel is increasingly being imposed precisely to ensure recognition of the vowel as *short*; this is in order to have the following consonant thereby phonotactically recognized as voiceless or tense if it is final (a position where *actual* voicelessness or fortis value is disappearing).

(3) Laryngeals are notoriously hard to equate with precise glottal or pharyngeal activity, and a lengthening which is presumed to arise from the *loss* of a following *H* – whatever its precise cause, and it may only be durational 'compensation' after all – cannot without a stronger case be equated with a phonation which is ejective, has a reversed air-stream, and is applied to a retained consonant; anyhow, *dadā́mi* would then have a laryngeal item at positions C_1 (arguably), C_2 and C_3.

(4) If Kortlandt is correct, all the short vowel reflexes in the rest of Indo-European become a puzzle and need some quick-thinking explanation.

For all this the comparative arguments at present rest weakly on occasional lengthenings. Lachmann's law in Latin, which Kortlandt cites, apparently shifts the presumed glottalic effect entirely from consonant to vowel ($ăg(ŏ) → āc(tus)$). As for Bartholomae's law in Indic, that is relevant only in a negative and converse way: /-Vgt-/ must be presumed not to assimilate in the same way as /-Vght-/ precisely because the overall glottalic nature of /Vg/ must prevent a rightward spread of voice (thus *budhta- > buddha- but *vasudti > vasutti-), which is subtly different from the solution of Miller (1977). Despite some acceptance of the Winter-Kortlandt thesis (e.g. by Vermeer), much more work on the precise mechanics is needed. Hopper (1982:131-32, 139) offers positive and negative hints.

Even so, Winter's observation as to the context of derived vowel length in Balto-Slavic remains a valid startpoint; at least it separates the prehistory of inherited /dh/ and /d/ – or /d^{ɦ}/ and /t'/ (if such they are) – in a group which seems otherwise to merge them. Kortlandt (1977:319) locates the law at the very end of the Balto-Slavic period.

REFERENCES

Hopper, P.J. 1982. Areal typology and the early Indo-European consonant system. *The Indo-Europeans in the Fourth and Third Millennia,* ed. by E.C. Polomé, 121-39. Ann Arbor, Michigan: Karoma.

——, 1983. Some issues in PIE phonological structure. Collitz Memorial Lecture, Ling. Socy. of America (July 1983); unpublished.

Kortlandt, F.H.H. 1977. See Appendix III.

——, 1978a. Comments on Winter 1978. Ibid., 447.

——, 1978b. PIE obstruents. *IF* 83.107-120.

——, 1978c. See Appendix III (= 1978*)

——, 1981. Glottalic consonants in Sindhi and PIE. *IIJ* 23.15-19.

——, 1983a. On final syllables in Slavic. *JIES* 11.167-85.

——, 1983b. Linguistic theory, universals and Slavic accentuation. *FoLH* 4.27-43 (=1983*, cf Appendix III).

Miller, D.G. 1977. Some theoretical and typological implications of an Indo-European root structure constraint. *JIES* 5.31-45.

Vaillant, A. 1936. Le problème des intonations balto-slaves. *BSL* 37.109-15.

Vermeer, W.R. (forthcoming in *FoLH*) See on Dybo's law.

Watkins, C. 1965. Evidence in Balto-Slavic. *Evidence for laryngeals.* (2nd ed.), ed. by W. Winter, 116-22. The Hague: Mouton.

Winter, W. 1978. The distribution of short and long vowels in stems of the type Lith. *ėsti* : *vèsti* : *mèsti* and OCS *jasti* : *vesti* : *mesti* in Baltic and Slavic languages. *Recent developments in historical phonology,* ed. by J. Fisiak, 431-46. The Hague: Mouton (= *Trends in Linguistics: studies and monographs,* 4.)

APPENDIX I

Minor Laws and Major Tendencies

Various 'laws' of Indo-European evolution have been accorded less than star quality, but they have deserved some notice. Other edicts have a wider domain and are acknowledged to enshrine historical principles of methodological importance; these are distinguishable as a set because (as Malkiel has said) laws of language do not repeat themselves but tendencies must. The two sections which follow here attempt to do justice to them all, in their respective classes.

A: Minor Laws

Ascriptions have always proliferated, and still do. It seems inevitable that a mere naming will at present have to serve, if this discussion is to be kept within readable limits, for those potential ordinances which clearly still fall short of the threshold of public recognition. Such are the 'laws' of Ascoli and Darmesteter (concerning initial and pretonic syllables in Romance); of Hooper (see under Grammont's law(s) in section B); of Lehr-Spławiński (on a species of accent retraction in Slavic); of Lorentz (which applies Baltic accent conditions to Germanic final vowel shortening); of Nyman (handling the assimilation of dental+liquid clusters in Latin); of Petersson (in the sphere of heteroclisis); and of Vennemann (on the equivalent status of word and syllable initial placing). Credit of such a sort has been given on the odd occasion also to Ascoli, Collitz, Havlik, Lindeman, Torbiörnsson and Johannes Schmidt. Notably Hamp (*CLS* 11.275-79[1975]) offers the useful category of 'mini-laws'.

But a number of discoveries seem to call for rather more than a naming and a nod, if less exposure than has been given to the 'mainline' edicts. This set will comprise:

BÀRTOLI'S LAW

This concerns retraction (leftward shift) of ancient Greek word-accent. Some generally similar laws are listed in Appendix III; Greek has the edicts of

Vendryes and Wheeler as examples of this common change. To these in 1930 Matteo Bàrtoli (1873-1946) added the case where Sanskrit has oxytone words in *-tvanám* and Greek matches that formant as *-σύνη*, a suffix which has been shifted to paroxytone. Kiparsky (1967:77ff.) regards it as the functioning of a law of iambic retraction, from underlying ∪ ‒ to ∪́ -, before word boundary. So it becomes especially like his version of Wheeler's law (74). It explains, e.g., *θυγάτηρ* (Skt. *duhitā́*; note also *θυγατέρα*) and perhaps *πατέρων* (?<*πατερῶν*); but obvious exceptions include *ἡγεμών*, *γενεά*, and all cases of adjectives in *-ικός* (which ignore Wheeler, anyway). Again, given an iambic domain, why have we *πατήρ* but *μήτηρ*? Miller (1976:16) wisely restricts the application to anapaestic (∪∪ -) and cretic (-∪-) sequences, as *νεφέλη*, *ἐργάτης* versus *θηλή*, *βουλευτής*; then analogy, between roots and cases, could explain the regularity of the *-ικός* group. Miller (1976), however, also brings in the intrasyllabic (moric) change of /xx̀/ > /x̀x/, as *δοτήρ+α* > *δοτῆρα*, which seems to be quite another matter. (For another possible law by Bàrtoli, see G. Devoto at *Word* 3. 214[1947].)

REFERENCES

Bàrtoli, M.G. 1930. Ancora una deviazione del greco all'ossitonia asio-europea. *RFIC* 58.24-29.

Kiparsky, P. 1967. A propos de l'histore de l'accentuation grecque. *Langages* 2.73-93.

Miller, D.G. 1976. The transformation of a natural accent system. *Glotta* 54.11-24.

BERGIN'S LAW

The order of sentence elements in Old Irish texts is debatable, but VSO is the apparent surface norm, as commonly in Celtic. A marked order is available, with the verb at the sentence end. Osborn Joseph Bergin noticed (1938:197) that such an apparently extraposed verb, if it were not part of a splittable compound ('tmesis') or a pronoun-inclusive form, had to take a 'dependent', that is 'construct' or 'conjunct', shape. Kuryłowicz (1964:133) makes the 'old secondary' verb-form an added marker for the word order. Meid (1963) is relevant on the verbal form; and a useful note is contributed by Ahlqvist (1980) on various scholars' exploitations of the law. The latter also mentions the law's implications — on the understanding that the 'construct' form is archaic — for the debate on the origin of verb-fronting at some presumed earlier stage in Irish history (whereby VSO < SOV). This particular argument on order, started by Watkins in 1963, is carefully separated from Bergin's law by Friedrich (1975:61). The 'Bergin verb' can, in any case, be medial. Wagner (1967; 1977:209-12) believes rather that all sentence-final verbs in Irish are artificial and poetic locutions; and he has long been hostile to Berginism. Binchy (1979) offers a counterblast to Wagner's typological and cross-linguistic objections. On the whole, most reaction has been kindly.

REFERENCES

Ahlqvist, A. 1980. On word order in Irish. *P(4)ICHL* 107-13.

Bergin, O.J. 1938. On the syntax of the verb in Old Irish. *Ériu* 12.197-214.

Binchy, D.A. 1979. "Bergin's Law". *Studia Celtica* 14/15. 34-53.

Friedrich, P. 1975. *Proto-Indo-European syntax* (*JIES* monograph 1). Butte, Montana.

Kuryłowicz, J. 1964. *The inflectional categories of Indo-European.* Heidelberg: Winter.

Meid, W. 1963. *Die idg. Grundlagen der altirischen absoluten und konjunkten Verbalflexion.* Wiesbaden: Harrassowitz. (Cf. Calvert Watkins in *Celtica* 6. 1-49, [1963].)

Wagner, H. 1967. Zur unregelmässigen Wortstellung in der altirischen Alliterationsdichtung. In W. Meid (ed.), *Beiträge Pokorny*, 289-314. Innsbruck: Inst. für Sprachwissenschaft.

—————, 1977. Wortstellung im Keltischen und Indogermanischen. *Indogermanisch und Keltisch*, ed. by K.H. Schmidt, 204-235. Wiesbaden: Reichert.

BUGGE'S CANON AND BUGGE'S RULE

Sophus Bugge (1833-1907) sired two ordinances of note. One is commonly called his 'canon' (1874:400ff.) and sets out the expected reflexes of the third person singular active verb endings in Latin and the Italic languages. Normally, the PIE primary sequence *+t+i* becomes *-t,* and the secondary *+t* reflects as *-d* or $\emptyset$. Latin, however, allows the primary result to be levelled throughout the paradigm. This is still the accepted ruling; and so *esed* on the Forum Cippus (*CIL* 1².1) is held to equate with later *esset* rather than *erit.*

Later, in 1887, Bugge enunciated a 'rule' which catered for the secondary voicing of Germanic spirant reflexes of PIE voiceless stops in word-initial position — the great gap in the provisions of Verner's law. He accepted voiceless equations like Gk. κάνναβις with OE *hænep*, and Skt. *tr̥tīya-* with Goth. *þridja*; but he judged the voicing to [v, ð, γ] to be regular, instead, if the inherited word-accent fell not less than three syllables along from the word's onset (1887: 408). That *þiwadw* is then irregular (for the accent position cf. Skt. formations in *-tvám*, like *pitr̥tvám*) is explained by the effect of *þius*. The digesting grammarians Noreen (1894:125) and Streitberg (1896:125) were not convinced by Bugge's examples, and the 'rule' is still unproved. But Rooth (1974:42) gives it a fresh encouraging notice.

REFERENCES

Bugge, E.S. 1874. Altitalische studien. *KZ* 22.388-466.
—————, 1887. Etymologische Studien uber germanische Lautverschiebung. *PBB* 12.399-430.
Noreen, A. 1894. *Abriss der urgermanischen Lautlehre.* Strassburg: Trübner.
Rooth, E. 1974. *Das Vernersche Gesetz in Forschung und Lehre.* Lund: Gleerup.
Streitberg, W. 1896. *Urgermanische Grammatik.* Heidelberg: Winter.

FORTUNATOV'S LAW II

Saussure's law (q.v.) handles a rightward shift of stress from a syllable of one intonation to the next which has a different tune. It was a major finding of Stang (1957 passim) that the shift as described was purely a Lithuanian affair. But F.F. Fortunatov had helped in the thinking toward Saussure's pronouncement, and in his version the law might be assigned to the history of Slavic. The apparent counter-cases are numerous and the law has not really won general acclaim. But some Slavicists are prepared to establish it as a working hypothesis.

Fortunatov's chief domain (1880) was Russian, Serbo-Croat and Slovene, and the stress shift was conditioned by brevity and falling intonation of the source syllable and rising intonation on the target syllable: so SC *nová* (← *nõvŧ*), Russ. *nová*; or SC *gòra* → (dat.pl.) *gorán.* Garde (1976:439-40) rejects the intonation condition; certainly it is ineffective in the old dual SC *öba,* Russ. *óba.* Other criticisms point to exceptions like Russ. *gotóva,* SC *gòtova,* or to shift of stress by more than one syllable under like phonetic conditions, as in Russ. *veselá* (but *véselo*) — for which Pedersen (1905;307; cf.1906) proposed that Fortunatov's law applied by means of 'skipping' sub-rule (for Slavic only). Shevelov (1964:55-69) has a full critique of the law and its challengers to that date; he comes out, on the whole, in favour of its existence. For him, it operates analogously to Saussure's, but with respect to final syllables only; and it is (with Hirt's law I) a major source of the mobile stress paradigm of Slavic.

REFERENCES *1)

Fortunatov, F.F. 1880. Zur vergleichenden Betonungslehre des lituslavischen Sprachen. *ASlPh* 4.575-89.
Pedersen, H. 1905. Die nasalpräscntia und der slavische Akzent. *KZ* 38.297-421.
—————, 1906. Zur akzentlehre. *KZ* 39.232-55.

GARDE'S RULE

(This is *not* the same as 'Garde's principle', which is included in section B, below.)
The relevant pronouncement is at Garde (1976:209), and concerns the retraction of accent in Slovincian; the data-base is given in Lorentz 1903. A final syllable accent, if on a short vocalic nucleus, is shifted leftwards to the penultimate syllable in a plurisyllabic word. Kortlandt (1978:76) declares the formula inadequate: oblique plural cases of nouns have the shift but show long final nucleus. Besides, he claims that final stress in Slovincian is not otherwise retained (as Garde might suggest), but is invariably new.

REFERENCES *2)

Lorentz, F. 1903. *Slovinzische Grammatik.* St. Petersburg: Acad. Sci.

1) Also cited or relevant are: Garde 1976; Shevelov 1964*.
2) Also cited or relevant are: Garde 1976; Kortlandt 1978*.
(For these items, see Appendix III)

GEORGIEV'S LAW

This edict, concerning Slavic vowel length, was worked out in various papers between 1963 and 1965 (references are given at Ebeling [1967:578n.13]). By Vladimir Georgiev himself (1965:14-15) it is conveniently, but not adequately, set out thus: "la voyelle brève initiale accentuée sous intonation rude, et dans certains dialects aussi sous intonation douce, est allongée". A metathesis of initial syllable vowel and consonant segments is also part of the deal. Examples include

$$*\acute{a}km\bar{o}(n) > *\acute{a}kmu > *k\acute{a}my \text{ (O Bulg. } kamy; \text{ cf. SC } k\check{a}men);$$
$$*\acute{o}rbhos > *\acute{a}rbu > *r\acute{a}bu \text{ (OBulg. } rab\breve{u}; \text{ ORuss. } roba).$$

Ebeling (1967:578, 586) accepts the law, but notes that the affected syllable is originally closed. He thinks, nevertheless that the whole affair is one of dialectal conditioning, and dismisses the intonational constraint (for the terms of which, see Appendix III) in favour of 'special conditions'. So his notation includes the equivalent of $\overset{\smallsmile}{V}$ as input, and that goes beyond Georgiev. On the other hand, he goes less far in that he doubts that the effect occurs when the consonant is not a liquid. The metathesis is essential, but Georgiev (like Ebeling) does not make it the cause of the change, as did Horálek (1962:114-15).

REFERENCES

Ebeling, C.L. 1967*. See Appendix III.

Georgiev, V.I. 1963. Praslavjanskata phonemna sistema i likvidnata metateza. *Slavističen Sbornik* (Sofia), 19-31.

—————, 1964. *Vokalnata sistema v razvoja na slavjanskite ezici* (Sofia), esp. 14-18.

—————, 1965. Problèmes phonématiques du slave commun. *RES* 44.7-17.

Horálek, K. 1962. *Úvod do studia slovanských jazyků*. 2nd ed. Prague: Československe Akademie Věd. (1st ed. 1955.)

KORTLANDT'S LAW

In the course of accounting for accent position in Old Prussian, Frederik

Kortlandt judges that "a stressed short vowel lost the ictus to the following syllable" (1974:302). Possibly the syllable has to be open; but the shift is independent of the paradigm. There are affinities with Dybo's law. Kortlandt's suggestion awaits its accolade.

REFERENCE

Kortlandt, F.H.H. 1974. Old Prussian accentuation. *KZ* 88.299-306.

MAC NEILL'S LAW

There is a difference between such derived forms in Irish as *Erenn* and *Mumen*, or *Conall* and *Bresal.* The first of each pair possesses a 'strong' or 'delenited' version of the final consonant. The preceding vowel must be short and unstressed, or lost by syncope (*cornn, fernn*); and the consonant to the vowel's left must be a sonant, as must the affected consonant itself (in practice, only *l* or *n*). The double spelling is not invariable. All this was pointed out in 1908/9 (347) by John (Eoin) Mac Neill. His observation was too late for inclusion in the original (1909) version of Thurneysen's influential grammar; but it is to be found in the revised and translated version of 1946 onwards (89. §140).

Hamp (1974) remarks, not entirely justly, on the counter-intuitive nature of such final strengthening (and, in effect, 'deleniting' here for him means voicing). He proposes (178) to re-phrase the process as an assimilatory voicing of sonants across a weak, indistinct and feature-receptive vowel, this latter being itself the outcome of the concentrating of stress on an early syllable in the word. That the final segment is heard as 'strong' is a mere consequence. Hamp bravely sweeps in even some cases, noted by O'Brien (1956:175), where final -*rt##* derives from -*rd##* after an unstressed vowel; this contrary result, he believes, is made possible because the expected (assimilated) voicing is entirely 'absorbed' by the -*r*- (1979). And on that basis he renames it 'the Mac Neill-O'Brien law', and subsumes it within a generalized voicing rule of final spirants and sonants in Old Irish.

REFERENCES

Hamp E.P. 1974. The Mac Neill-O'Brien law. *Ériu* 25.172-80.

Mac Neill, J.(E.) 1908/9. Notes on the distribution, history, grammar, and import of the Irish Ogham inscriptions. *Proceedings of the Royal Irish Academy* 27, sec. C, 329-70.

O'Brien, M.A. 1956. Etymologies and notes. *Celtica* 3.166-84.

Thurneysen, R. 1946. *A grammar of Old Irish*. Dublin, Irish Acad. (= Transl. and revised ed. by D.A. Binchy & O.J. Bergin of *Handbuch des Altirischen: Grammatik, Texte und Wörterbuch*. 2 vols. Heidelberg: Winter, 1909.) Repr. 1975.

RIX'S LAW

Within PIE phonology the presumed laryngeals pose many problems. One problematic case in lexeme structure is where a laryngeal opens the word and is followed immediately (in apparent zero grade of ablaut) by a sonant, itself preconsonantal. Here Helmut Rix proposes (1970), specifically for Greek, that a vocalic element was inserted and coloured by the *H*. The process is of anaptyxis with normal laryngeal behaviour, including disappearance of that segment as such. An instance of the sequence will be ἀργός (< *H_2rg-). The coloration works in what some think to be an unusual direction.

The law's title is bestowed by Brian Joseph (1975:321 and passim). But Joseph widens the possibilities at the post-laryngeal position to include glides: that is, /Y/ is brought in as well as the consonantal sonorants /R/ and /N/ – or, if you like, /R/ is given its full Kuryłowiczian values. This explains αἰνός (Skt. *iná-*), for example. Joseph's input includes a vocalic value for /R̥/, and his revised and formalized ruling (1975:323) is perhaps best expressed, in our fashion and with an eye on final output, thus:

$$H_x \begin{bmatrix} +son \\ +syll \end{bmatrix} \rightarrow x^\partial \begin{bmatrix} +son \\ -syll \end{bmatrix} \Big/ \#\# \underline{\quad\quad} [-syll]$$

Here, (1) subscript x ranges over the colours of /H/; (2) the following vocalic insert is rightly seen as an intermediate process but unfortunately (if fashionably) equated with the old 'schwa' (328 n.3); (3) /R/ loses its syllabicity in the process (but difficulties are unnecessarily created by specifying vocalism at that abstract stage of morpheme structure: see Collinge 1956:122-27). Whether Rix's law leads quickly to opacity or not is a further interesting question.

REFERENCES

Collinge, N.E. 1956. The limitations of historical phonology. *ArchL* 8.111-28.

Joseph, B. 1975. Laryngeal before i/u in Greek: The role of morphology in diachronic change. *CLS* 11.319-28.

Rix, H. 1970. Anlautender Laryngal vor Liquida oder Nasalis Sonans im griechischen. *MSS* 27.79-110.

SZEMERÉNYI'S LAW

This appellation is sometimes used to dignify a simple morphological explanation of the nominative singular form of some PIE nouns. That a vṛddhi type in $*/-C^{\tilde{e}}/_{\bar{o}}$ R/N/s/ seems there to occur, as in *mātēr, *k(u)wōn, *megyōs, has worried people. Some see an apophonic polarization of quantity, producing, e.g., -tēr out of -těr to balance -tr- elsewhere in the paradigm. This, according to Kuryłowicz (1956:144-45), may be a disambiguating device. Others have a notion that the vṛddhi somehow symbolizes the informational importance of the nominative (the references are given by Szemerényi [1962:21n.9]). Streitberg and others believed in compensation for the loss of a following stem-vowel (see Szemerényi 1972:142).

Oswald Szemerényi has preferred a down-to-earth phonetic process (offered first at Oxford in 1957, then in 1962:13; 1970 (= *SEinf*) 109; 1972:142). That is:

$$*mātěr+s(\text{nom.}) > *matěrr \text{ [ma:ter:]} > mātēr \text{ [ma:te:r)}$$

and so forth. Here the syllable which has absorbed the final sibilant subsequently shifts the focus of its duration from the non-syllabic to the syllabic item in its domain. (A similar shift may account for some Latin alternants: see on Lachmann's law.) An immediate adverse testimony is the non-conforming accusative plural in +*Vns*, which commonly loses its *n*; but, even if this is not simply a different process at a different chronological stage, /ns/ is phonetically rather distinct from the other clusters and may have had to be levelled by analogy in the nominative singular.

Schleicher, interestingly enough, is credited with having already reconstructed *mātars, and was derided for it (cf. Delbrück [1880:49=1882:49] and Pedersen, *PedS* 270). Schindler (1973:153-54), in accepting the law, calls it an old one.

Szemerényi's idea, of course, explains the long vowel in forms like πῶς (ποῦς) and things like Latin *nepōs* (with paradigm levelling). That μῦς, *mūs*, is of that origin (and does not reflect a laryngeal) is the view of Polomé (1980: 28-29).

REFERENCES

Delbrück, B. 1880. *Einleitung in das Sprachstudium.* Leipzig: Breitkopf & Härtel.

—————, 1882. *Introduction to the Study of Language: A critical survey of the history and methods of comparative philology of Indo-European languages.* Transl. of 1880 by Eva Channing. Ibid. (Repr., with an introduction by E.F.K. Koerner, Amsterdam: Benjamins, 1979; 2nd corrected ed., 1984.)

Kuryłowicz, J. 1956. *L'apophonie en indo-européen.* Wrocław: Polska AN.

Polomé, E. 1980. Armenian and the PIE laryngeals. *Proc. 1st Internat. Conf. on Armenian Linguistics*, ed. by J.A.C. Greppin, 17-33. New York: Caravan.

Schindler, J. 1973. Bemerkungen zur Herkunft der idg. Diphthongstämme und zu den Eigentümlichkeiten ihrer Kasusformen. *Die Sprache* 19.148-57.

Szemerényi, O. 1962. *Trends and tasks in comparative philology.* (Inaugural address, 1961.) London: University College. (Cf. Szemerényi 1956; See on Osthoff's law.)

—————, 1972. Comparative linguistics. *CTL* 9.119-95.

WACKERNAGEL'S LAW II

Greek compound lexemes often display an etymologically unexpected long vowel at the point of junction. Any compositional vowel is lost and what was originally an initial vowel is lengthened: so στρατ+ηγός, στρατ+ᾱγός (root ἄγ) or, more awkwardly in negative lexemes, ν+ηνεμία (root ἄνεμ-). In 1889 Jacob Wackernagel (1853-1938) discoursed expansively on the matter and is sometimes credited with a lengthening law. He linked the Greek phenomena to others in Indo-Iranian; in Indic he saw the process as a spread of external sandhi into compositional environments. In Greek, compositional hiatus is avoided by elision of morpheme-final vowel plus lengthening of morpheme-initial vowel. The operation, when it occurs between words, is known as 'crasis': sc ἀνήρ < ὁ ἀνήρ, or μᾱναχαιτίσειε <μὴ ἀνα- (Euripides, *Bacchae* 1072; or, for crasis with initial long nucleus, notice ἢ οὐκ as a monosyllable at, e.g., *Bacchae* 649). The second vowel controls the 'quality' of the end-product (Wackernagel 1889: 28 = 1955:924).

Between words the process is optional and rare; in compounds the elision is normal but the lengthening optional – at least in late formations: e.g., ὕψ+ερεφής). Metrical convenience may be a factor. The effect is then obviously extended, into forms where the first vowel is kept (πολυ+ήρατος) or is diphthongal (εὐ+ώδης) or was never there (δυσ+ηχής, ἀν+ώμαλος); or into purely analogical forms (νή+ποινος); or even where there is no compounding at all: ἠνεκής, ἤλυσις. So-called 'Attic reduplication' (actually found in other dialects) and the temporal augment are somehow relevant. On the process and its systemization Kuryłowicz (1956:264-69) has much of interest to offer. Poetic exploitation, and widening, of the device is part of the subject-matter of Wyatt (1969).

REFERENCES

Kuryłowicz, J. 1956. *L'apophonie en indoeuropéen.* Wrocław: Polska AN.
Wackernagel, J. 1889. Das Dehnungsgesetz der griechischen Komposita. *Programm zur Rektoratsfeier der Universität Basel* (1889), 1-65. (Repr. in *Kleine Schriften* II, 897-961. Göttingen: Vandenhoeck & Ruprecht, 1955.
Wyatt, W.F. Jr. 1969. *Metrical lengthening in Homer.* (=*Incunabula Graeca* 35.) Rome; Ed. dell'Ateneo.

WATKINS' LAW

The third person in verbal paradigms, especially the third person singular, represents a participant outside the speaker-hearer axis of interaction. Its marking is commonly economical; its use with a quite unmarked person-value (or as the sign of 'non-person') is clear from 'impersonal verb' forms. That it is a 'non-person' or 'zero-person' was argued by Benveniste (1946, 1956): cf. Kuryłowicz (1964:28). It is therefore only a step to diagnosing it as the 'basic person'; it is a larger step further – taken by Calvert Watkins (1962:90ff.; cf. 1969:18 [and 49, on the nominal value of the 3sg.])– to declaring that it must have a pivotal role in paradigm evolution (at least for Indo-European). This is Watkins' law, expressed at (1962:93-96); and so greeted by, e.g., Arlotto (1972: 156). It may be taken (as by Arlotto) as the ground-rule in a process leading even to the incorporation of the 3sg ending, if any, as a stem-final element. It certainly seems to stand as a counsel of guidance to historians of morphology.

Belief has been otherwise; but Ross & Crossland (1954, esp. 118) had already swung in favour of accepting the mastery of the third rather than the second person. Kuryłowicz (1964:28, 148ff.) agrees: but he is ready to see the 3rd plural form in its turn shaping the singular (ibid. 44). Joseph (1980) explains, by Watkins' law, the absence of /a/ in the 'alpha-less' second person singular of the Modern Greek preterite: its capacity for reshaping is constrained by the power of the third person form. Thus what was for Watkins a positive influence is recast as a strong blocking control.

REFERENCES

Arlotto, A. 1972. *Introduction to historical linguistics.* Boston: Houghton Mifflin.

Benveniste, E. 1946. Structure des relations de personne dans le verbe. *BSL* 43.1-12.

——————, 1956. La nature des pronoms. *Fs Jakobson* (1) 34-37. (Cf. also *Journal of Psychology* (1958), 257-65.)

Joseph, B. 1980. Watkins' law and the modern Greek preterite. *Die Sprache* 26.179-85.

Kuryłowicz, J. 1964. *Inflectional categories of Indo-European.* Heidelberg: Winter.

Ross, A.S.C. & Crossland, R.A. 1954. The supposed use of the 2sg. for 3 sg. in 'Tocharian A', Anglo-Saxon, Norse and Hittite. *ArchL* 6.112-21.

Watkins, C. 1962. *Indo-European origins of the Celtic Verb.* Vol.I *The sigmatic aorist.* Dublin: Institute of Advanced Studies.

——————, 1969. *Indogermanische Grammatik.* Vol.III. Heidelberg: Winter.

B: Major Tendencies

These promote general principles of diachrony and its study, in Indo-European as much as elsewhere. They are:

BEHAGHEL'S LAWS I-V

In 1932 Otto Behaghel (1854-1936) opened the fourth volume of his German syntax with a series of five laws (1932:4-7). The last three of these provided that:

III	What belongs together, in a mentalist sense, is placed together;
IV	Of two linked elements, the more important comes second. *Or,* more fully, an element which picks up preceding information stands before one which does not: so the 'given' precedes the 'new', on the understanding that those terms refer to presentation rather than to raw fact;
V	A differentiating element precedes the element which it differentiates.

On these pronouncements one may observe that V is given exemplification by the sequences Adjective-Noun (or Genitive-Noun) or Adverb-Adjective, but that an article standing to the left of its NP is held to instantiate IV. Behaghel allows for clashes: the positioning of reflexives in German is claimed, not too cogently, to make III and IV somewhat incompatible.

To these new edicts Behaghel adds, as older conclusions of his own:

I	Where units of equal status are conjoined (or contrasted) the longest comes last in the sequence. This is often called 'Behaghel's law' par excellence, and is usually titled 'das Gesetz der wachsenden Glieder' (1909:139). It was based on copious and adroit quotations from Greek, Latin and different stages of German.
II	The differing degrees of sentence stress (full-weak-nil) explain different patterns of element order as between paraphrase sentences or clauses in German.

Vennemann (1974:339) uses III-V as a springboard for his own evolutionary essay on element order as based on a categorical principle, known as 'natural serialization'. III seems similar to notions of natural constituent structure, and IV to the theories which assign theme or topic or subject to a leftmost position. But V, which is believed to originate with Adelung (1782:459-60), is roundly denounced (by Vennemann) as a falsehood if it is meant as a universal, and as unsafe even for German itself, let alone English or French.

Rule I   was presumed for Latin by Lindholm in 1931. It was already to be found in Demetrius and Cicero, anyway, as a principle; and even the Iliad shows it in practice. Noteworthy is Wilkinson 1963:175ff.; he has some amusing and cogent examples of it (and its inversion) from various languages and registers: 'Friends, Romans, countrymen' is typical, as is *do dono dedico* as noted by Wackernagel in 1892 (*Kleine Schriften* III: 186-8[1979]). For a curious parallel *phonological* excursion (into 'vowel size' and sequential preference) see Löfstedt 1978:1001.

REFERENCES

Adelung, J.C. 1782. *Deutsche Sprachlehre*. Vienna: Edler.

Behaghel, O. 1909. Beziehungen zwischen Umfang und Reihenfolge von Satzgliedern. *IF* 25.110-42.

————, 1932. *Deutsche Syntax IV*. Heidelberg: Winter.

Lindholm, E. 1931. *Stilistische Studien zur Erweiterung der Satzglieder im lateinischen*. Lund: Ohlson.

Löfstedt, B. 1978. Review note of Bertil Malmberg, *Signes et symboles* (Paris: Picard, 1977). *Lg* 54.1001-1002.

Vennemann, T. 1974. Topics, subjects and word order: from SXV to SVX via TVX. In *HL(A8J)*, 1.339-76.

Wilkinson, L.P. 1963. *Golden Latin artistry*. Cambridge, Univ. Press.

GARDE'S PRINCIPLE*

In seeking a dynamic principle for a sensible genetic separation of the Slavic languages, Paul Garde eventually decided, in his essay of 1961, that 'resistance to

---

* For 'Garde's rule', see section A.

homonymy' will serve as such (62). This conclusion, however, rested on his earlier ideas that homonymy is produced – and not destroyed – by innovations (which links with his insistence on the irreversibility of mergers (38-39), and that loss of distinction, once so produced, will spread). That is, unless there is specific resistance, a speech area which possesses an essential distinction will lose it under the influence of a speech area which has already lost it (38-39). A critical instance is the Ukrainian loss, and so the possible future Russian loss, of the inherited difference between /i/ and /ɨ/ (*i* and *y*, ᴎ and ы): the homonymy in relevant words spreads on an orientation from South to North. Another example may be the loss of the infinitive in the Balkan area languages.

Such orientation of spreading homonymy is now called 'Garde's principle'. Hoenigswald (1977:192) uses it; but he offers a credible countercase, which is more than a mere fading away of a potential influence. Modern High German is a 'spreading' and influencing speech area, and among its effects is the carrying over of its maintained /d/ versus /t/ distinction; yet the general West Germanic system has long confounded original /þ/ and /d/, and the restructuring caused by NHG and towards distinctiveness is going against Garde.

REFERENCES

Garde, P. 1961. Reflexions sur les différences phonétiques entre les langes slaves. *Word* 17.34-62.
Hoenigswald, H.M. 1977. Intentions, assumptions, and contradictions in historical linguistics. *Current Issues in Linguistic Theory*, ed. by R.W. Cole, 168-94. Bloomington: Indiana Univ. Press.

GRAMMONT'S LAWS (AND 'NATURAL PHONOLOGY')

In 1895 Maurice Grammont (1866-1946) wrote on consonantal dissimilation in Indo-European, and especially in Romance. His unifying principle was that segments have degrees of relative strength; and that, of two pronounced in close context, the weaker will somehow suffer. The inherent principle – 'la loi du plus fort' – is codified in his *Traité* (1933:269-71). Strength may derive from 'mechanical' factors (accent, position) or 'psychological' factors (prominence, recognition of the complications attendant on change, membership of a well-recognized morpheme). The weaker segment is accorded less attention to its crucial features. This suggests that those distinctive features which identify it will be diminished; and so (in this admittedly intuitive method) *assimilation* might be a regular expected outcome. And Grammont does, to a lesser extent, study it similarly (1923:2 and 109).

An instructive study closely based on Grammont's law is that of Posner (1961); it is indeed the best place to see the law given a bench test. Posner ventilates Grammont's arguments in detail (8-17), quoting some continuators. She counters simple objections (like that of Meyer-Lübke [1921:598] that a universal cline of strength should predict identical cross-linguistic processes in the 'same' word) by revealing the real complexity of the law, which has fifteen sub-laws for particular cases. Moreover, a wider exemplification helps her to off-set charges of a priorism. But corrections to Grammont appear in Posner (e.g., 207-208); and Grammont's own actual calculus of relative strength is rejected (48).

In 1933 Grammont (176) announced another law, his 'loi du moindre effort' (and, as a counterforce, 'la loi du plus grand effort'). Thus he handled the tendency, scarcely beyond doubt, that all speech would become a flow of obscure and undifferentiated vocalism were the process not reversed by the interactive need to communicate via a system of recognized oppositions. Grammont merely made a remark; progress towards a formalism here belongs to Zipf (q.v.).

Schneider (1973:247ff.) discusses the status of these laws. Grammont saw them as exceptionless (in their time and place), but yet as only secondary formulae for noting the realization(s) of a universal tendency (1933:183, but see 167). Of the two, the first has had the more notable after-life (and some precursors: see Householder 1974:556-57). The school of 'natural phonologists' of the 1970s developed the concept of relative strength into a device for explaining various laws (e.g., Aitken's, Grimm's, Lachmann's) and deserve some coverage. They include Foley (1970, 1977), Hankamer & Aissen (1974), Hyman (1975), Vennemann (1972), and Zwicky (1972) — the latter two first presented in 1969 — and, on English, Lass & Anderson (1975, chap. V). One thing is clear: while Grammont's degrees of strength were relativized to speech-context and use, those of the new school are abstracted and to a large extent absolute (though Foley's claim [1977:144] that they are purely 'abstract relations' really means that they are not experimentally demonstrable).

These essays have two shortcomings (apart from objections to the whole concept of naturalism, as by Anderson 1981). First, they propose scales which offer overlap and differ (or the same scales differ even in respect of the same language). The divergences on (a) the place of labial versus dental spirants in

Germanic and (b) the relative strength of labial and dental stops in the world, are noted by Mitchell (1979:16-18). Secondly, attempted definitions are not altogether helpful. Vennemann (cited by Hyman 1975:165) indirectly defines 'weakening' thus: "a segment X is said to be weaker than a segment Y if Y goes through an X stage on its way to zero". This statement is applauded by Sommerstein (1977:229n.30) and Mitchell (1979:17): it gives grounds for relative placement. Yet it presumes in any given case an undeviating progress of Y towards zero, as well as the likelihood of any X's standing between. Besides, for some an essential element of the theory is that the 'strong' tend to strengthen and the 'weak' to weaken; so that *bi*directionality imposes reform on the scales. What is not usually noted is the consequent implication of a median group of segments which would be characterized by either stability or readiness to shift *either* way.

Now one may grant that frequency of shift across an obvious interim stage does establish weakness. But must the shift /p/ $>$ $\emptyset$ / ## – in Celtic necessitate an interim stage /##b–/ (weakening by voicing); or might that stage be /# #k(x)–/ (weaking by velarization)? If weakening is to be seen, this time across languages, in Latin *f-* $>$ Spanish *h*/$\emptyset$-, as in *fabulāre* $>$ *hablar*, do we start further back (in a progress of shifting over centuries) with the PIE /# #b^{h}ā-/? Do we then declare the Latin voiceless spirant /f/ surprisingly 'weaker' that the PIE voiced aspirate plosive [b^h] (or the murmured [b̤], if that is what it is)? Consequential defining of 'strengthening' (Hyman 1975:166) is handled by the ruling that 'stronger segments or segment types are more resistant to weakening processes' (which seems to mean that some Ys infrequently move towards zero); this gives a calculus of strength, but scarcely of added strength. There is an interesting critique of Foley and Zwicky, to 1974, in Householder (1974:556ff.).

Foley's later and fuller thesis (1977) is still the most ambitious project in this sector. It offers a clear improvement on the alternative 'sequences of change' (with weakening or strengthening a matter of direction of process) given by Lass & Anderson (1975:150); in their sequences it is not clear whether the shifting is serial or parallel. Foley works with four independent 'parameters'. These (given in the direction: weak $\rightarrow$ strong) are:

a = velar/dental/labial

β = voiced spirant/voiced stop/voiceless stop/voiceless spirant *or* affricate *or* aspirate *or* geminate

γ = sequences (kw, ph, bh)/'diphthongs' (k^w, p^h, b^h)/ unit segments (p,f,β)

ρ = stops/spirants/nasals/liquids/glides/vowels (cf. Murray 1982: 171).

– so that a voiceless spirant is β 4 but ρ 2, and /b^h/ is β 4 but γ 2. Hence a shift may be allowed to combine opposite movements: to go from PIE *g^w($\bar{i}$-) via Latin $v\bar{i}$- [wi:] to Italian $v\bar{i}$- [vi:], as in *vivere*, is to strengthen by one step in γ, first to strengthen by four steps and then weaken by three steps in ρ, to weaken (indirectly and overall) by one step in β, but to lose a weak component in α. The Germanic shifts which take /p/ via /f/ – a strengthening for Foley (1977:145) but the reverse for Lass & Anderson (1975:155) – and /ƀ/to /b/ (as in *sieben*) reflect vacillation of movement in β and ρ. This delicacy makes 'strength' harder to use as a cause of change; and a further awkwardness is the concept of 'modular depotentiation' (Foley 1977:123) which allows a strengthening of the already strong to result in a value of 'weakest'. In any case, adherents of the theory have not made it clear (1) whether the strong or the weak has presumption of influence, or (2) whether consonants and vowels counterbalance one another within a datum of strength, or conspire to promote unidirectional shifts (see on Aitken's law, in particular). Thus, Foley's ρ-scale and Hankamer & Aissen's 'sonority scale' (1974:136) agree *except* as to the inclusion of vowels (and as to whether /l/ and /r/ are alike – a common source of disagreement).

(i)　　　REFERENCES TO GRAMMONT'S LAWS

Grammont, M. 1895. *La dissimilation consonantique dans les langues indo-européennes et les langues romanes.* Dijon: Davantière.

––––––, 1923. L'assimilation (Notes de phonétique générale). *BSL* 24.1-109. (The studies of Indic and Armenian in *MSL* 19 & 20 are of less relevance)

––––––. 1933. *Traté de phonétique.* Paris: Delagrave. (4th ed., 1950.)

Meyer-Lübke, W. 1921. Review of E. Schopf, *Die konsonantischen Fernwirkungen.* Göttingen: Vandenhoeck & Ruprecht, 1919. *ZRPh* 41.597-603.

Posner, R. 1961. *Consonantal dissimilation in the Romance languages.* (= *Phil. Socy. Publ.* 19.) Oxford: Blackwell.

Schneider, G. 1973. *Zum Begriff des Lautgesetzes in der Sprachwissenschaft seit den Junggrammatikern.* (= *Tübinger Beiträge zur Linguistik*, 46.) Tübingen: Narr.

Zipf, G.K. See Zipf's law (below).

(ii)   REFERENCES TO RECENT 'STRENGTH' THEORIES

Anderson, S.R. 1981. Why phonology isn't 'natural'. *LI* 12.493-539.

Bruck, A. et al., eds. 1974. *Papers from the parasession on natural phonology.* Chicago: *CLS* (1974).

Escure, G. 1977. Hierarchies and phonological weakening. *Lingua* 43.55-64.

Foley, J. 1970. Phonological distinctive features. *FoL* 4.87-92.

———, 1977. *Foundations of theoretical phonology.* Cambridge, Univ. Press.

Hankamer, J. & Aissen, J. 1974. The sonority hierarchy. In Bruck 1974:131-45.

Householder, F.W., Jr. 1974. Review of Stockwell & Macaulay 1972; *Lg* 50.555-565.

Hyman, L.M. 1975. *Phonology: theory and analysis.* New York: Holt, Rinehart & Winston.

Johnson, L. 1973. Dissimilation as a natural process in phonology. *Stanford Occ. Papers in Ling.* 3.45-56.

Lass, R. & Anderson, J.M. 1975. *Old English phonology.* Cambridge, Univ. Press. (See chap.V.)

Mitchell, J.L. 1979. 'Sliding' in English dialects. *CJL/RCL* 25.7-24.

Murray, R.W. 1982. Consonant cluster developments in Pali. *FoLH* 3.163-84.

Parker, F. 1977. Perceptual cues and phonological change. *JPhon.* 5.97-103.

———, 1981. Resyllabification and phonological change. [Ibid] 9.29-34.

Sommerstein, A.H. 1977. *Modern phonology.* London: Arnold.

Stockwell, R.P. & Macaulay R.K.S., eds. 1972. *Linguistic change and generative theory.* Bloomington: Indiana Univ. Press.

Vennemann, T. 1972. Sound change and markedness theory. In Stockwell & Macaulay 1972:230-74.

Zwicky, A. 1972. Note on a phonological hierarchy in English. In Stockwell & Macaulay 1972:275-301.

HUMBOLDT'S 'UNIVERSAL'

This is apparently so established by Vennemann (1972:184). Wilhelm von Humboldt's (1767-1835) ideas on surface lexical and grammatical representation are summarized thus:

> suppletion is undesirable, uniformity of linguistic symbolization is desirable: both roots and grammatical markers should be unique and constant.

If what is desired can be demonstrated to be often attained, then diachrony will have gained a really major principle of causation. One remains sceptical.

REFERENCES

Vennemann, T. 1972. Phonetic analogy and conceptual analogy. *Schuchardt, the Neogrammarians, and the transformational theory of language change,* ed. by T. Vennemann & T.H. Wilbur, 181-204. Frankfurt: Athenäum-Verlag.
Vincent, N.B. 1974. Analogy reconsidered. *HL(A8J)* 2.427-45.

KRONASSER'S LAW

This law, on semantic evolution, might be known as the law of Kronasser and Kovács. Heinz Kronasser (1913-1968), prompted by judgements of the material-minded Meringer, proposed in 1952 (116-17) that word meaning naturally moves from the concrete to the abstract. Kovács (1961) elevated the proposal to a law. Examples easily suggest themselves. Sanskrit *dandayati* begins by meaning actually hitting somebody with a club, but soon conveys any sort of punishment or application of sanctions. Latin and English *tribulation(n)* quickly loses sight of its basic meaning, wherein what is suffered is being scraped under a heavy studded threshing board. But, equally, nomina actionis like Lat. *oratio* or Eng. *building* — and they are rife — show a ready movement the other way.

Kronasser is alive to the complexities. He allows for 'secondary concretising' (127ff.). But it is rather surprising to find the 'law' reasserted, at least as a 'definite trend', by Makkai (1972:202 and passim) as part of his control of idiom-formation. Despite statistical paraphernalia, his argument looks like a begging of the question. To say (as he does in this connection) that lexemes move from varied literal applications to a more uniform use is a different matter entirely; it may also be an equally questionable universal.

REFERENCES

Kovács, F. 1961. A propos d'une loi sémantique. *AL(Hun)* 11.405-411.
Kronasser, H. 1952. *Handbuch der Semasiologie.* Heidelberg: Winter. (2nd

ed. 1965.)
Makkai, A. 1972. *Idiom structure in English.* The Hague: Mouton.

KURYŁOWICZ AND MAŃCZAK, THE LAWS OF ANALOGY OF

In 1947 (publishing in *Acta Linguistica (Hungarica)* 5) Jerzy Kuryłowicz (1895-1978) offered a schedule of six guidelines for the understanding of analogical effects, analogy being one of the Neogrammarians' great diachronic engines. The six 'laws' appear to translate as:

1. A bipartite morpheme tends to take over from a simple isofunctional morpheme; that is, the composite form prevails.
2. The direction of effect is from 'foundation forms' to 'founded forms'.
3. A structure consisting of a 'constitutive' plus a 'subordinated' item is the foundation of an isolated constitutive form of the same function.
4. Given a morphological derivation resulting in two differentiated forms, the derived form takes over the primary function and the old form is reserved for secondary function.
5. A difference which is central may be re-established at the expense of one which is more marginal.
6. In a proportion formula, the first item belongs to the copied speech, the second term to the copying speech.

The relation of data to theorems is neither entirely clear nor entirely objective; nor can these laws easily be used on an equal basis or in concert. Law 2 is a tautology, and law 6 is a trite statement about an accepted notation. Law 5, a useful safety clause, may disguise a circularity: if in West Romance the Latin *pānis, pānĕm; pānēs, pānēs* has become *panes, pane; panęs, panęs* and so first has lost a number distinction in the nominative and has then regained it by a further shift to *pane, pane; panęs, panęs* (Kuryłowicz 1945-49:169), then it follows that number is arguably more central than case − that is, the obviously more 'syntactic' property is the more marginal. But there is no separate proof of this axiom, and the modern trend towards taking number to be a lexical category is relevant: cf. Beard (1982). Kuryłowicz's discussion (162) of εὐγενεῖς (nom → acc) in fact reaches an opposite conclusion, namely that the implication of the *nominative* as the major case here prevails (whereas it is the accusative *pane* and *panes* which are the 'foundation' in the other example) despite the axiomatic centrality of *plural* function. Laws 1 and 2 seem out of accord with 3 (as so expressed; even Kuryłowicz faces the problem [166]); and this is a pity, because law 1 seems to link analogy with redundancy, if the doubly marked *Bäume* is typical. Yet this insight is scarcely transparent; Bynon (1977:37-38) cites *Wälder* as a proof that analogy *increases* redundant alternation, while Vincent (1974:430) had been sure that it *eliminates* redundancy and reduces allomorphy, according to Mańczak's second (early) hypothesis.

Law 4 is the most famous. It seems to explain why English secondary *brothers* and primary *brethren* are used as they are (cf. also, as an example of wide application, Robertson [1975] on Mayan). Yet *height* and *Highness* do not fit; nor does the incidence of German *dessen* (so Lehmann 1962:169). Kiparsky (1974:266ff.) singles out law 4 for adverse comment and requires special conditions for its truth — such as that only gross reclassification of an item may enforce it: so *stretched* is needed as (primary) participle, but only because *straight* has become an adjective.

Kuryłowicz was a theoretical pioneer, groping his way. Witold Mańczak took up the enterprise and for over twenty years has refined the principles, seeking the empirical and inductive in place of the a priori. His nine 'hypotheses' of 1958 are accessibly set down in the original (French) form alongside Kuryłowicz's laws by Vincent (1974:439-40); they may be summarized thus:

I	Long words (in a paradigm) are remodelled on short words more commonly than the converse.
II	Root alternation is lost more often than created.
III	Flexional forms which have endings are remodelled on endingless forms more commonly than the converse.
IV	Zero endings are replaced by full endings more commonly than the converse.
V	Monosyllabic endings are more commonly replaced by polysyllabic endings than the converse.
VI	Indicative forms prompt the reshaping of other modal forms more commonly than the converse.
VII	Present tense forms prompt the reshaping of other tense forms more commonly than the converse.
VIII	Given the distinction between geographical names and other nouns, local cases retain an archaic form and non-local cases tend to innovate, but
IX	If a geographical name undergoes analogical reshaping, the source of the shift is usually in the local cases.

Too much ink has been spilled, without clear consensus, in relating these hypotheses to Kuryłowicz's laws. Vincent (1974) takes the whole array as a single and partly collapsible set of theorems (although Mańczak's slant is to performance), and equates 'K1' with 'M2', which is strange. He works with three principles as underlying the rules of both these analogists: (1) that unmarked forms have the control; (2) that exponents tend to lengthen and categories to be fully exponenced (though Mańczak's hypotheses I and III do *not* say so); (3) that redundancy decreases. The third principle, in particular, is linked by Vincent to 'Humboldt's universal:. on which something is said above. The possibility of verifying or falsifying these rules is ventilated in Best (1973).

Even so, it is fairest to work with Mańczak's own most recent and much clearer version, consisting of *five* laws based on *four* evolutionary movements. The latter four may be set down formally as:

(i)	AB > A (loss of B)
(ii)	AB > AB ′(analogical change in B)
(iii)	AB > AB ″(change in B directly caused by A)
(iv)	B > A (replacement of B)

The five laws are (again in a suggested notation):

1. The number of morphemes having the same meaning more often diminishes than increases (cf. hypothesis II)
2. Where A is a unit and B an extended form of that unit, A > B is more common than B > A (cf. hypotheses I, III, V)
3. Given A and B as in 2, AB > A is more common than AB > B; AB > AB′ is more common than AB > A′B or AB > A′B′; AB > AB″ is more common than AB > A″ B.
4. Given systemic terms (as indicative versus other moods, third versus other persons) where P is the more and Q the less frequent, PQ > P is more common than PQ > Q; PQ > PQ′ is more common than PQ > P′Q or PQ > P′Q′; PQ > PQ″ is more common than PQ > P″ Q; Q > P is more common than P > Q. (Note that frequency, not load, is in point.)
   (This replaces hypotheses VI and VII.)
5. Archaism (X, not X′) is more commonly retained in
   (*a*) local cases of geographical names (than of common nouns);
   (*b*) non-local cases of common nouns (than of geographical names);
   (*c*) common nouns than personal names.
   (For hypotheses VIII and IX.)

It is not clear where hypothesis IV now stands; hardly inside new law 2, unless (for instance) a form with case ending is regarded as an extension of one with zero. And new law 5 seems to belong to a different world.

In view of all this, Vincent's (1974:437) plea not to formalize all aspects of analogical change is a wise one. The absence of appeal to these laws in many relevant studies on analogy generally is noteworthy. But Best (1973:61-110) has a full discussion; and although Anttila (1977:76-80) begins by declaring that "the whole issue provokes ennui" he closes his analysis — in which the qualitative and formal nature of Kuryłowicz is contrasted with the quantitative and probabilistic approach of Mańczak — by allowing that even flawed 'laws' of this kind have led to definite progress in diachronic research. And, as Kuryłowicz said, analogy itself is like rain: that we know which way it will go will not ensure its coming.

REFERENCES

Anttila, R. 1977. *Analogy*. The Hague: Mouton.

——— & Bewes, W.A. 1977. *Analogy: A basic bibliography*. Amsterdam: Benjamins.

Beard, R. 1982. The plural as a lexical derivation. *Glossa* 16.133-48.

Best, K-H. 1973. *Probleme der Analogieforschung*. Munich: Hueber.

Bynon, T. 1977. *Historical linguistics*. Cambridge, Univ. Press.

Fisiak, J., ed. 1980. *Historical morphology* (= *Trends in Linguistics*, 17.) The Hague: Mouton.

Hooper, J.B. 1980. Child morphology and morphophonemic change. In Fisiak 1980:157-87.

Kiparsky, P. 1974. Remarks on analogic change. *HL(A&J)* 2.257-75.

Kuryłowicz, J. 1945-9. La nature des procès dits 'analogiques'. *AL(Hun)* 5.15-37 (= *Readings in Linguistics* II, ed. by E.P. Hamp, F.W. Householder, Jr., & R. Austerlitz. 158-75. Chicago, Univ. Press [1966]).

———, 1956. *L'apophonie en indoeuropéen*. Wrocław: Polska AN.

———, 1958. Ogólne tendencje zmian analogicznych. *BPTJ* 17.207-219.

———. 1960. Odpowiedź językoznawstra. *BPTJ* 19.203-210.

Lehmann, W.P. 1962. *Historical linguistics: An introduction* (2nd rev. ed., 1973.) New York: Holt, Rinehart & Winston.

Mańczak, W. 1958. Tendances générales des changements analogiques. *Lingua* 7.298-325, 387-420.

———, 1960. Odpowiedź Prof. J. Kuryłowiczowi. *BPTJ* 19.191-201.

—————, 1978. Les lois du développement analogique. *Linguistics* 205.53-60.

—————, 1980. Laws of analogy. In Fisiak 1980: 283-88.

Robertson, J.S. 1975. A syntactic example of Kuryłowicz's Fourth Law of Analogy in Mayan. *IJAL* 41:2.140-47.

Vincent, N.B. 1974. Analogy reconsidered. *HL(A&J)* 2.427-45.

POLIVANOV'S LAW

(on the prime role of diachronic convergence)

No doubt it is still acceptable doctrine that, to reconcile the array of significant sound segments at two different stages of a language's history, recourse will be had to processes of 'merging' and of 'splitting' available items. Those who are concerned with justifying the method and its postulates speak of movements as obeying (or disobeying) 'Polivanov's law'. That law said, in effect, that splits need mergers as their motivation, but not vice versa.

Evgenij Dmitrievič Polivanov (1891-1938) was a victim of internecine warfare between linguists in the Soviet Union and his opposition to Marrist doctrine led to his arrest in 1938, soon after which he died. He had gained fame by (amongst other things) pronouncing on the mechanics of language change in several publications in Tashkent in 1923 (see Leont'ev 1974:35); and an article in 1928 brought his thinking to Moscow. For him, with Latin as a major source of evidence, convergence was the predominant direction in linguistic evolution (although he did not distinguish between surface fusing and systemic simplification). The converse, divergence, was recognised in terms similar to the American concept of phonemic split; but this was not to be seen as an independent process. Rather, every divergence is the consequence of a prior convergence, which 'dictates' it. Presumably the motivation, if not obvious, should be sought.

Jakobson (1931:261) supported the idea and helped to publicize it although he preferred the Term '(de)-phonologization'. Marchand (1956:248) limited its scope to cases where the merger underlying the split is recoverable; that is, incomplete. Hoenigswald decided in 1960 (99), possibly by coincidence, that "merger is the central type of sound change"; but recognised the law as such later (1974:190 and 1977:186). In the latter place, it is defined so as to cover those splits which are conditioned by a merged *environment*, the phonetic variants thus losing all justification for being regarded as allophones.

Convergence is from time to time elevated to the status of the major – or the only true – diachronic event. Trubetzkoy's *Sprachbund* concept is an example of such thinking; so is the recent 'lingua franca' theory of Chew (1976, 1981), which is based on the internal and external relations of Japanese, but asserts 'extensive diversity' as the starting point of all 'genetic' groups.

REFERENCES

Chew, J.J. 1976. Standard Japanese and the Hirara dialect: A case of linguistic convergence. *Journal of the Assoc. of Teachers of Japanese* 11. nos. 2&3.

————, 1981. The relationship between Japanese, Korean, and the Altaic languages: in what sense genetic? (Paper to Int. Symp. on Genetic Relationships of the Japanese language, Kyoto, 1980.) *Bulletin Inst. Ling. Sciences*, Kyoto Sangyo Univ. 2:4.7-38.

Hoenigswald, H.M. 1960. *Language change and linguistic reconstruction.* Chicago: Chicago Univ. Press.

————, 1974. Internal reconstruction and context. *HL(A&J)* 2,189-201.

————, 1977. Intentions, assumptions, and contradictions in historical linguistics. *Current Issues in Linguistic Theory* ed. by R.W. Cole, 168-94. Bloomington: Indiana Univ. Press.

Jakobson, R. 1931. Prinzipien der historischen Phonologie. *TCLP* 4.247-67. (= *Selected Writings* I, 202-20. The Hague: Mouton [1962].)

Leont'ev, A.A. 1974. *Selected works of E.D. Polivanov*, ed. with an introd. The Hague: Mouton.

Marchand, J.W. 1956. Internal reconstruction of phonemic split. *Lg* 32.245-53.

Polivanov, E.D. 1923. *Fonetičeskie Konvergencii.* Tashkent.

————, 1928. Faktory fonetičeskoj evoljucii jazyka kak trudovogo processa. Moscow: *Inst. Jaz. i Lit. Ross. Assoc. naučno-issledovatel'skix institutov obščestvennyx nauk* 3.20-42. Transl. into English and reprinted as "The phonetic evolution of language as a work process", in Leont'ev 1974:66-80.

PROKOSCH'S LAW

A title proposed by Beade (1974:68) for a maxim concerning the 'ratio of change' of speech sounds which was put forward by Eduard Prokosch (1876-1938) in the posthumous publication of 1939 (54). Prokosch is discussing the speed, and more especially the geographical diffusion, of specific consonant shifts in Germanic. Devoicing of velars is confined, in the later Germanic Sound

Shifts, to High German and remains incomplete there; at the other extreme, the dentals are thus affected fully in HG and also patchily over a wider area (and perhaps sooner). Prokosch links the different speed and reach of shift to the "relative agility of the articulating organs"; and, undeniably, the tongue-tip is more agile than the dorsum or the velum. *Experientia docebit.*

REFERENCES

Beade, P. 1974. Diffusion, generalization and the High German shift. *HL(A&J)* 2.61-70.
Prokosch, E. 1939. *A comparative Germanic grammar.* Baltimore & Philadelphia: Linguistic Socy. of America.

TARDE'S LAW

As languages change they must reflect blurrings of frontiers of a social sort. Whether in phonology or in grammar or in style (in the sense of motivated choice between isofunctional forms), the incidence of items will shift in relation to layers of society. In 1890, in the sixth chapter of a famous work which saw many re-editions, the sociologist Gabriel de Tarde (1843-1904) propounded − as one of his 'laws of imitation' − that the predominant direction of such movements is from the higher prestige group to the lower. His analogy was from physics: the second law of thermodynamics lets heat move only from the hotter to the colder body.

Labov, who since 1973 has developed a large, varied and fully described database, demurs somewhat (and does so, in effect, on behalf of contemporary sociolinguistics). Certainly, innovation in the use of linguistic items may well mean its origination in *any* group, and undergo a move outwards which may as well be up as down the social scale (Labov 1973:216 and n.10). Imitability does not necessarily, or even frequently, entail higher social status. Much of contemporary British English reflects the prizing of choices originating in popular speech; and the empirical studies of the Philadelphia Project (1972-1978) − see Labov et al. 1980, and cf. Labov 1982:77-78 − locate the regular source of linguistic change in an *intermediate* social group. Yet the imitated must still be (in some sense) the desired; or, as Tarde more succinctly said, "l'aimant copie l'aimé". Labov's research also demonstrates the influence of speakers with the highest *local* status; hence, as long as prestige is relativized to the power group, Tarde's law must be valid. Correctly stated, it is negated by parody (including the deliberate style-shifting of politicians), but by nothing else.

REFERENCES

Labov, W. 1973. The social setting of linguistic change. *CTL* 11.195-251.

––––––, 1982. Building on empirical foundations. *Perspectives on historical linguistics*, ed. by W.P. Lehmann & Y. Malkiel, 17-92. Amsterdam & Philadelphia: Benjamins.

––––––, et al. 1980. *The social determinants of sound change in Philadelphia.* Philadelphia: US Regional Survey.

Tarde, G. de 1890. *Les lois de l'imitation: Étude sociologique.* Paris: Baillière. (7th ed., 1921.)

ZIPF'S PRINCIPLE(S)

In 1929 George Kingsley Zipf (1902-1950) established a phonological principle of relative frequency. This was that a sound segment will be stable as long as it remains within its range of acceptable frequency of incidence. If it becomes either too frequent or too rare it is susceptible to change. The Germanic *Lautverschiebungen* were thought to originate from this instability; but no quantitative basis, independent of the shifts themselves, was available. Zipf conceived that added features such as aspirate offset or assibilation – or even voicing – increased a segment's conspicuousness; and that these will be lost where a sound becomes so familiar as not to need such marking, and accrue where it becomes so infrequent as to welcome extra clues to recognition. Fidelholtz (1975) and Mańczak (1978) are exploiters of the idea. Birkhan (1979) decided that the Germanic weak preterite used both +t and +dh, the latter poaching the former's frequency and so needing simplification – hence Grimm's law.

That frequency means security and stability was noted by Sapir (1921:194) and Martinet (1955:103), amongst others; and Zipf's original suggestion is evaluated by King (1969:200). But in 1936 Zipf tied the need for (just so much) conspicuous recognizability at least partly to the separate principle of 'economy of effort' (on which, see 'Grammont's law(s)'). By *this* principle –

elaborated in 1949 and often quoted as basic 'Zipfism' – the very frequent segments lose complexities of pronunciation not so much because they are so familiar as because, in regular speech, they cost too much in cumulative articulatory toil. That principle was already enunciated by Max Müller in 1864 (176= 1880:193) as "people shrink from the effort of articulating". Counter-examples to this conditioning are easy to find (as by Anderson, 1973:199). What is more to the point is that it really argues for the view that change is essentially dysfunctional and may need counterbalancing, thus in effect opposing Zipf's previous linking of change with the control and correction of over- or under-use.

Zipf produced evidence susceptible to pure statistical analysis, and a frequency formula which has attracted the attention of, and revision by, mathematicians is sometimes called 'Zipf's law' or 'Zipf's curve'. This states that, over a diagnostic length of text, the occurrences of an item of a given frequency rank (or the occurrences of all such items) will be found to vary strictly in proportion to the square of the frequency-index. (As this index is usually assigned with the lowest figure for the rank of most frequent, the occurrence varies by inverse proportion.) This revelation is the major concern of the recent volume of essays edited by Guiter & Arapov (1982). The application is commonly at the level of the word; thus it leads to statements about vocabulary richness, optimum length of text for word frequency measurement, distribution of multiple meaning, and such gross lexical matters.

REFERENCES

Anderson, James M. 1973. *Structural aspects of language change.* London: Longman.

Birkhan, H. 1979. *Das 'Zipfsche Gesetz', das schwache Prateritum und die germanische Lautverschiebung.* Vienna: Sitzungsber. Österreichischer Akad. der Wissenschaften.

Fidelhotz, J.L. 1975. Word frequency and vowel reduction in English. *CLS* 11.200-213.

Guiter, H. & Arapov, M.V., eds. 1982. *Studies on Zipf's law.* (= *Quantitative Linguistics*, 16.) Bochum: Brockmeyer.

King, R.D. 1969. *Historical linguistics and generative grammar.* Englewood Cliffs, N.J.: Prentice-Hall.

Mańczak, W. 1978. Irregular sound change due to frequency in German. *Recent developments in historical phonology*, ed. by J. Fisiak, 309-19. The Hague: Mouton.

Martinet, A. 1955. *Economie des changements phonétiques.* Berne: Francke. (3rd ed., 1970.)

Müller, F.M. 1864. *Lectures on the science of language.* (2nd series.) London: Longman, Green & Co. (Rev. ed., 1880.)

Sapir, E. 1921. *Language.* New York: Harcourt & Brace.

Zipf, G.K. 1929. Relative frequency as a determinant of phonetic change. *HSCP* 40.1-95.

——————, 1932. *Selected studies of the principle of relative frequency in language.* Cambridge, Mass.: Harvard Univ. Press (Note Prokosch's cautionary review, *Lg* 9.89-92 [1933].)

——————, 1936. *The psycho-biology of language: An introduction to dynamic philology.* London: Routledge; Cambridge, Mass.: MIT Press. (Repr., with Introd. by George A. Miller, Bloomington: Indiana Univ. Press, 1965.)

——————, 1949. *Human behavior and the principle of least effort.* Cambridge, Mass.: Addison Wesley.

APPENDIX II

The 'new look' of PIE consonantism.

When Hirt (1931:80) was doubtful as to what sort of phonetic creature to recognize in PIE /b^h/ etc. — the 'voiced aspirate' series (*mediae aspiratae*), a Sanskritocentric reconstruction — he was echoing the disquiet already felt by Whitney (e.g., 1889, §37c) over these segments in Indic itself. Collitz and Prokosch had similar doubts and preferred to posit spirants: see Prokosch (1939: 41 and 304); with reference to articles published between 1918 and 1920). A close sequential combination of voice with (prevocalic) voice-continuation-delay is undeniably curious; and a systematic unitary segment composed of just such a succession of features appears whimsical. Indeed, was the aspiration also voiced (/b^h/)? Freestanding /h/ in Sanskrit *is* so. Quite separately, Martinet (1955:115, 136; cf. also 1952, based on Semitic) and Jakobson (1958:23 = 1962:528) were sceptical of any relevant empirical base. This was particularly true (as the latter influentially remarked) of a reconstructed obstruent system containing a voiced/voiceless unaspirated pair wherein a voiceless aspirate, phonetically an easy concept, was absent or sporadic but the awkward voiced version was present and rife. The laws of typology must have some authority or else PIE will lose credibility. Pedersen (1951) had been suspicious, too.

In 1971 Ladefoged (7-23) regarded 'voiced aspirate' as a terminological blank cheque; he thought no such thing, as described, had ever been encountered. He has, however, effectively recanted since then (1979:905). And Allen first in 1953:34-35 and still in 1977:241), relying on Westermann & Ward (1949), is reasonably sure that a sound can be at once voiced and breathed. He cites *Ṛk-Prātiśākhya* 13.2.4-6, on Skt. *bh, dh, gh* as evidence: *soṣmoṣmaṇāṁ ghoṣiṇāṁ śvāsanādau*, "both breath and voice are properties of voiced aspirates". Support comes from Dixit, whose Texas dissertation (1975) says the same. Rose (1974: 14) finds in a Chinese dialect south of Shanghai an interesting 'breathy voice' release of voiced plosives; but it is limited to co-occurrence with two tones only and cannot operate in a regular opposition. But for early Chinese a case for a system like the traditional PIE version can be made; cf. Colarusso (1981:477) who cites Karlgren. Ladefoged (1971) went so far as to set up a nine-degree analysis of states of the glottis. One extreme is closure (and may include ejectives, so that post-consonantal voicing will go along with a change of air-stream source — see below, on *pibati*). At the other end, degrees 5-9 move through "voice-lax voice-murmur-breathy voice-voiceless (open glottis)".

Such hints as these came upon diachronists in the 1970s when they were susceptible. They were suffering from a long-felt malaise occasioned not only by the very different behaviour of IE voiced and voiceless aspirates (the latter being very sporadic, absent in clusters and resistant to secondary palatalization) but also by the unmotivated rarity of PIE /b/ (but not of /b/ in the known IE languages). Old genetic puzzles and new phonetic and typological scepticism provoked a redefinition of the PIE plosive system. At first the essays were unalike. By using one dorsal as typical of at least five places of stop articulation, one may diagram the range of novelties thus:

	'T'	'TA'	'M'	'MA'
Traditional:	[k	k^h	g	g^h]
Emonds (1972):	[k^h	–	k	g^h]
Gamkrelidze & Ivanov (1972→)	[$k^{(h)}$	–	k'	$g^{(h)}$]
(to which Normier [1977] is close)				
Hopper (1973→)	[k[1]	–	k'	(g̣.)]
Rasmussen (1974)	[K[3]	–	k	g]
Bomhard (1975→; cf.	[k	(k^h)	k'	g^h[4]]
1981b version):				
Vennemann (1979):	[k	k^h	g	g̣]

NOTES

1) Hopper (1983) prefers /kh/.

2) Hopper (1973) has 'murmur' here, but after e.g., comments such as Normier (1977: 177) and Ladefoged's withdrawal of that feature, Hopper (1982:126) has here a plain voiced stop, with aspiration in certain areas.

3) K = any 'emphatic' stop.

4) Bomhard (1975:380) earlier had plain voiced stop here.

To these may be added Butler (1974) who has [g̟] for MA; and Mayrhofer (1983:147n.102) may usefully be consulted for relevant, if less fundamental, input from Birnbaum, Colarusso, Kortlandt, and Ohala. Even the schemata above need to be considered within their authors' (often radical) general PIE phonology: cf. Gamkrelidze (1975), on which also Swiggers (1980).

The title 'glottalicists' may be used to embrace Gamkrelidze & Ivanov, Hopper, and Bomhard (who now uses the 'G-H-I' formula in so far as it is uniform: 1981b:334; cf. 1981a:369; and Colarusso 1981:480 and passim — though his listings at 479 are somewhat different). The 'murmurists' will be early Hopper, Vennemann, and Butler (for later Hopper, see note 2 above). Schindler (1976) is a sort of 'traditional-murmurist'. In the Gamkrelidze-Ivanov bundle /k$^{(h)}$/ appears to be the unmarked form; there seems to be no regular basic item there, unmarked in the Trubetzkoy sense. But Trubetzkoy (see 1969:146, 152-53) allows that /d/ in a bundle containing ejectives ('recursives') may balance /t/ in a bundle which contains an aspirate. For Gamkrelidze (1975) aspirated and glottalized stops were marked; by 1981 he accepts that markedness may possibly be predicated of a plain voiceless stop, as long as its 'strength' rating is relatively low (for the concept of relative strength see Appendix I B, under 'Grammont's laws'). Emonds and Rasmussen are alone in replacing 'old' PIE /g/ by /k/; as Normier (1977:176-77) points out, this means that they cannot explain the morphological absence of g etc., and they must claim that the traditional root shape */deg/ — so sedulously avoided — is really /tek/, a sequence which only a very strange tongue would ostracize. But out of all these rather tangled speculations, which have seemed to some (e.g., Back 1979:184-85) to divorce typological theorizing from contact with the data, and to others merely distasteful, some light shines forth. If PIE really possessed /k'/ etc. many old problems can at least be offered new solutions, and the title of the 'Glottalic Theory' is a reasonable appellation for the most compelling part of this 'New Look'.

The glottalicists, employing MSCs, can explain (1) the rarity — though this does not amount to absence — of PIE /b/ (traditional), which as Greenberg showed (1970:127) is a rather more common gap if its potential filler is a labial ejective rather than a voiced pulmonary labial; even so, Ladefoged (1971: 27) records [p'] as certainly occurring in several languages; (2) the dislike of ejectives for use at the end of suffixes, so that case-forms like -ēd, -ōd are now understandably unusual; (3) the avoidance of root-shapes which would have energy-consuming ejectives at onset and release of the same syllable (i.e. */t'ek'/ = old */deg/) — though Hopper (1983) allows sporadic exceptions. (We bypass here the interesting problem of the impossibility of, e.g., */teg̟/ = old /tegh/ set against the common incidence of, e.g., /steig/ = old /steigh/.)

Reverberations must, then, be felt in any law which functions at some PIE stage: Siebs' law for instance. Here the traditional alternants are word-initial /(s)k-/, /(s)k^h-/, and /g-/, to which Siebs' continuators add /*(s)g-/ and /*(s)g^h-/ as undocumented precursors. If these are re-analysed as /(s)k$^{(h)}$/ and /k'-/ for late PIE, with */(s)k'-/ and */(s)g̈/ as the earlier stage – using a 'murmurist' system – problems soon become obvious. The clusters /sk'/ and /sg̈/ have not been empirically validated even if in Ladefoged's glottal continuum the sequence [sg̈V-] looks like a controlled increase in voicing. Again, if the *g-* which turns up in actuality is from /k'-/, then *either* a change of airstream mechanics attends loss of initial /s/ – which is obscure – *or* the loss of the sibilant results from a glottalization of the whole cluster, as if /sk-/ > ?/s'k' -/ > /k' -/ – and that needs corroboration of its likelihood by comparative fieldwork. If Siebs is correct on the alternations, the glottalicists are on shaky ground; if the glottalic theory receives independent proof, Siebs may have seen a mirage.

Gamkrelidze & Ivanov (1973) are pleased that their revised inventory reduces Grimm's law (plus Verner's) to little more than a redistribution of the breath feature. Lass (1974) opines similarly; and Polomé (1982b) insists on the archaic and conservative character of Germanic. The First Sound Shift can be deleted (so also Normier 1977:186). The PIE segment /g$^{(h)}$/ – and Hopper's counterpart /g/ – is then in Germanic regularly, rather than contextually, realized as unaspirated /g/; hence, Germanic reflects PIE plosives in one simple way while some other IE languages do so in another and more complicated fashion. The glottalic segment is taken over by Germanic as voiceless but normalized by becoming pulmonary. While Greek shifts /g^h/ to /k^h/, and most IE idioms realize /k'/ as /g/ – a fact which needs such explanation as is given to *pibati*, below – Germanic (and Armenian, too) has here made merely minor readjustments. There are objections: for one thing, the worrying degree of shift is simply transferred from Germanic to other parts of the IE world; for another, the Germanic spirantization of /k$^{(h)}$/ etc. is less easy to handle. Gamkrelidze (1975) has ideas on the systemic use of friction; and Normier (1977:198,203) proposes lenition and added sonority for the fricatives deriving from PIE /k$^{(h)}$/ etc. in unstressed syllables (the revision of Verner's law is actually only slight). Even so, the output of Grimm-plus-Verner, however carefully handled, does not entirely corroborate this optimistic picture of a preservative Germanic (as opposed to, say, Greek).

On the voicing of /k'/ etc. elsewhere, Hopper (1981) divides the IE languages into two streams; this split is paralleled in the North-West Caucasus

(Hopper 1982:130). But Greenberg has pointed out (e.g., 1970:125) that a glottalized stop is rarely voiced; certainly, the heavily glottalic plosives of London English never are.

Grassmann's law overtly concerns aspiration. Does it covertly involve murmur (or other degrees of voicing)? Suppose the Indic relation of *dh* to *d* (for example) to be really of $[d^h]$ or $[d]$ to $[t']$. Then the shift is gross on the 1971 Ladefoged scale (from level 5, or 7, to 1); nor can it be handled as a privative feature adjustment. The latter observation is still true if the relation is of $[d]$ to $[d]$ (so Schindler 1976:n.3). The simpler Greek alternation of, e.g., $[t]$ and $[t^h]$ could be left as a totally unrelated phenomenon, and many would prefer it so (see on Grassmann's law). Yet the contexts are sufficiently alike in the two languages, especially in the predominance of the reduplicated root as affected domain, for a strict provincialism not to satisfy everybody. Among the conservatives, Allen (1977:245-46) demurs and links the languages via traditional phonology. Among the radicals, Gamkrelidze (1981:607ff.) presses hard his (and Ivanov's) idea that the 'old' $/b^h/$ etc. were really variant-pairs $/b^h/$ or $/b/$ etc. Then Grassmann's law becomes (1) a mere affair of allophonic distribution – which is very neat – and (2) the same thing in Indic and Greek – namely, a once-for-all fixing of reflexes in similarly differentiated contexts. But then Greek, in, e.g., παχύς versus Skt. *bahu-*, in order to explain the π, has to be credited either with a prior shift of $/g^{(h)}/ > /k^{(h)}/$ or with a later maintained 'global' devoicing of *some* plain voiced stops. Only the former is credible; yet that splits the languages, and gives even classical Greek a transitional system of $/k^{(h)}, g, k^{(h)}/$ ($*κ(χ), γ, χ(κ)$), which is discouraging. (Still, to move from underlying $/g/$ to $/k^{(h)}/$ would be worse.) At least Gamkrelidze offers a better explanation of Grassmann's law in Indic than others can, as it is hardly a matter of of simple voice dissimilation or airstream variation. (In passing, it seems a pity that nobody has encompassed a theory recasting traditional $/d^h/$ etc. (rather than $/d/$) as $/t'/$ etc. – considering how interesting it would be to start with actual but highly unstable vowel-flanking ejectives as Grassmann input.)

If any law seems to require 'mediae aspiratae' it is Bartholomae's: if the output *-ddh-* is taken at face value, then $/-d^h+t^h-/ \rightarrow /-t'd^h-/$, or $/-d+t-/ \rightarrow /t' d-/$, are scarcely credible processes. Even so, the direction of assimilation remains strange. Now Vennemann's (1979) system, using the now less accepted 'murmured' segments, would move the cluster from $/dt/$ to $/dd/$, which on Ladefoged's original glottal scale is $/7+9/ \rightarrow /5+7/$, and at least looks like an overall proportional increase in vocal cord tension. But Gamkrelidze (1981:607ff.) will again assign simply different contextual variants of $/d^{(h)}/$ to the first and second slots in the cluster. Then Bartholomae's law is stripped, but only of the second of its two stages. Actually 'BL proper' (that peculiarly Indic operation) is still there; and (as Butler [1972] points out) its odd rightward assimilatory movement is not found in, e.g., /-g+t-/ (*yukta-*) — from which Miller (1977) improbably deduces a constraint on morphological structure which precludes different voice values across +, and argues for /-g$^{(\hat{h})}$+d$^{\hat{h}}$-/ but /-k'+t-/: a roundabout defence of /k'/ etc. In fact, at least the deaspirating 'coda' of BL ceases to trouble us. But frankly it has not really troubled us since we could put together the Indian phoneticians' analysis of /d$^{\hat{h}}$/ etc. as having 'voice plus breath' and their concept of *abhinidhāna* (non-release of prior segments in clusters); for then [dd$\hat{h}$] is just the outcome we expect (cf. Allen 1953:34-35, 71-72; 1972:235-36.). The murmurists in that case can give BL the revised form /-ḍ+ t-/ → /-ḍ:-/, but must still worry that voicelessness is lost rightwards rather than achieved leftwards.

Winter's law (q.v.) proposes a regular lengthening of vowels in Balto-Slavic before voiced stops. On a glottalic basis, Kortlandt (1978a; 1978b; cf. 1981) proposes that the conditioning stop was, at the relevant period, a voiceless ejective. Hopper agrees (1982:131ff., but see 139n.2). Yet Kortlandt (1978a: 117) goes further and relates these sequences to those involving a laryngeal (and perhaps causing the 'acutes' of Balto-Slavic intonation): but see the comments on Winter's law. Still, Kortlandt's system appears to oppose plain fortis stops to glottalic and aspirated lenes (/t,t',t'/). The full inclusion of laryngeals in the new consonantism comes with Colarusso (1981), although Normier (1977: 180-81) has some ideas here. Compare also Hopper (1982:133), who accepts a multiplicity of laryngeals; and Bomhard (1981b:335), who commendably will not be forced to have more than one.

In this connection arises the famous *pibati* problem. The medial *b* of the Vedic reduplicated present tense form, as of Irish *ibid* (<*pib*-) and Latin *bibit* — as against initial /p/ in Greek πῶμα, πίνω, OCS *piti*, Latin *pōtus*, *pōculum* — has been referred to a voicing *o*-coloured laryngeal (in the Chelsea Flower Show days of laryngealism, days which show signs of returning). In fact, no really secure parallel form has ever been adduced; and for a different explanation see Collinge (1970:81). Hopper (1977a:50, 1978:70, 1982:133) works with the sequences /peʔ/, /pʔ/, being happy with a segmental glottal stop in PIE; and he sees /pʔ/ as reanalyzed as /p'/ and then laryngealized so as to reflect as voiced /b/. These glottalized segments dither, in this theory, between being really glottal (and so voiceless) and vaguely 'laryngeal' (and so theoretically voice-able) items. Normier (177:209n.90) prefers to lose the laryngeal and have /p/ shifted to /p'/

because of finding itself in an unfamiliar environment. So PIE and its laryngeals move nearer to Semitic (after Möller's fashion): cf. *raʔs* > *rās*. With all its faults (the patient's uniqueness still being one) this sort of solution has some appeal. One wonders, no doubt irrelevantly, about the initial item of Latin *bibit* and the medial consonant of Praenestine *pipafo*. 'Mediae' and *H* are also connected by Lubotsky (1981).

Probably more Indo-Europeanists currently welcome *some* version of the 'new look' (in a spirit of relief) than reject it altogether. Mayrhofer (1983:152) sums the position up thus: that the weight of evidence is on the typologists' side and that the traditionalists can produce objection but not counter-proofs. Dunkel (1981) voices a bitter reaction, opining that typology should follow reconstruction. But that view courts the danger of divorcing speculative reconstructions from contact with reality; besides, it is 'extremist' in that it misses a good argument on behalf of free-ranging diachronic suggestion, namely that the empirical control exerted by typology is only a warning light (Mayrhofer 1983: 152) and a flashing yellow light, at that. After all, philologists reconstruct formulae where linguists seek entities; and the more unstable an item the more credible its shifting, so that the typologically suspect can be the more prized starred form. (Compare Mayrhofer's apt citation [1983:146] of Blust's work on Bario-Kelabit.)

Radicals need to be cautious. Even if some laws, especially Grimm's, shrivel if reviewed under the new light, Kortlandt's attempt (1978a:117) to ma lachmann's law a Latin counterpart to Winter's is unconvincing (cf. Mayrhofer 1983: 149n.109). Here *āctus* etc. (*/-gt-/ or */-k't-/ forms) are set against the types *făctus* (*/-kt-/) and *uĕctus* (*/-ght-/). The glottalic feature of their consonant, it is claimed, when it became distinctively voiced, was thereafter credited to the vowel — which is not quite the same process as is assumed in the Winter case. Besides, the rule would generate **pīctus, *strīctus*. True, a simple loss of aspiration plus regressive voice assimilation neatly accounts for *uĕctus*; but one then has flatly to deny *trāctus*, on which the evidence as to length is conflicting.

As Hopper says (1981:137) Grimm's law "will not be ceded without a struggle". Probably every law will have a spitited defence from those of another school of phonology as much as from militant morphologists.

REFERENCES

Allen, W.S. 1953. *Phonetics in Ancient India.* Oxford, Univ. Press.

—————, 1977. The PIE aspirates: Phonetic and typological factors in reconstruction. *Fs Greenberg*, 2.237-47.

Back, M. 1979. Die Rekonstruktion des idg. Verschlusslautsystems im Lichte der einzelsprachlichen Veränderungen. *KZ* 93.179-95.

Birnbaum, H. 1977. *Linguistic reconstruction: its potentials and limitations in new perspective.* (= *JIES monograph*, 2.) Washington, D.C.: Inst. for the Study of Man.

Bomhard, A.R. 1975. An outline of the historical phonology of Indo-European. *Orbis* 24.354-90.

—————, 1977. The 'Indo-European-Semitic' hypothesis re-examined. *JIES* 5.55-99.

—————, 1979. The Indo-European phonological system: New thoughts about its reconstruction and development. *Orbis* 28.66-110.

—————, 1981a. Indo-European and Afroasiatic. *Mem. Kerns* I, 351-474.

—————, 1981b. A new look at Indo-European I. *JIES* 9.332-37.

—————, 1981c. Speculations on the prehistoric development of the Proto-Indo-European vowelsystem. *GL* 21.164-93.

—————, 1984. *Toward Proto-Nostratic: A new beginning in the reconstruction of Proto-Indo-European and Proto-Afro-Asiatic.* Amsterdam & Philadelphia: Benjamins (= *CILT* no. 27.)

Butler, J.L. 1974. A murmured proposal regarding Grassmann's law. *IF* 79.18-30.

Colarusso, J. 1981. Typological parallels between Proto-Indo-European and the North-West Caucasian languages. *Mem. Kerns* I, 475-557.

Collinge, N.E. 1970. *Collectanea linguistica.* The Hague: Mouton.

Dixit, R.P. 1975. (See report at Miller 1977:40.)

Dunkel, G. 1981. Typology versus reconstruction. *Mem. Kerns* II, 559-69.

Emonds, J. 1972. A reformulation of Grimm's law. *Contributions to generative phonology*, ed. by Michael K. Brame, 108-22. Austin: Univ. of Texas Press.

Fisiak, J. ed., 1978. *Recent developments in historical phonology.* (= *Trends in Linguistics, Stud. & Monog., 4.*) The Hague: Mouton.

Gamkrelidze, T.V. 1975. On the correlations of stops and fricatives in a phonological system. *Lingua* 35.231-61 (note earlier and briefer German version, in *Phonetica* 27.213-19 [1963] = Greenberg et al. 1978 II, 9-46.)

—————, 1977. Linguistic typology and Indo-European reconstruction. *Fs Greenberg* II, 399-406.

—————, 1979. Hierarchical relations of dominance as phonological universals and their implications for Indo-European reconstruction. *Fs Szemerényi*

I, 283-90.

——————, 1981. Language typology and language universals and their implications for the reconstruction of the Indo-European stop system. *Mem. Kerns* II, 571-609. (See also forthcoming *P(12)ICL* [Vienna, 1977].)

Gamkrelidze, T.V. & Ivanov, V.V. 1972. Lingvističeskaja tipologija i rekonstrukcija sistemy indoevropejskix smyčnyx. *Conference on comparative-historical grammar of the Indo-European languages*, ed. by S.B. Bernštejn et al., 15-18. Moscow: AN SSSR.

——————, 1973. Sprachtypologie und die Rekonstruktion der gemeinindogermanischen Verschlüsse. *Phonetica* 27.150-56.

——————, 1980a. Rekonstrukcija sistemy smyščeindoevropejskogo jazyka: Glottalizovannye smyčnye v indoevropejskom. *VJa* 1980 4.21-35.

——————, 1980b. Rjady 'guttural'nyx' v indoevropejskom. Problema jazykov 'centum' i 'satəm'. *VJa* 1980 5.10-20.

Greenberg, J.H. 1970. Some generalizations concerning glottalic consonants, especially implosives. *IJAL* 36.123-45.

——————, Ferguson, C.A. & Moravcsik, E.A., eds. 1978. *Universals of human language*. 4 vols. Stanford, Univ. Press.

Hirt, H. 1931. *Handbuch des Urgermanischen*. Heidelberg: Winter.

Hopper, P.J. 1973a. Glottalized and murmured occlusives in Indo-European. *Glossa* 7.141-66.

——————, 1973b. Indo-European origins of the Greek-Sanskrit deaspiration conspiracy. Paper to LSA, December 1973; unpublished.

——————, 1977a. The typology of the PIE segmental inventory. *JIES* 5.41-53.

——————, 1977b. Indo-European consonantism and the New Look. *Orbis* 26.57-72.

——————, 1981. 'Decem' and 'taihun' languages: an Indo-European isogloss. *Mem. Kerns* I, 133.42.

——————, 1982. Areal typology and the early Indo-European consonant system. In Polomé 1982a:121-39.

——————, 1983. Some issues in PIE phonological structure. Collitz Memorial Lecture, Linguistic Socy. of America, (July 1983); unpublished.

Jakobson, R. 1958. Typological studies and their contribution to historical and comparative linguistics. *P(8)ICL* 17-25 (discussion 25-35). (Reprinted in *Selected Writings* I, 523-31, The Hague: Mouton, 1962; 2nd ed., 1971.)

Kortlandt, F.H.H. 1978a. Proto-Indo-European obstruents. *IF* 83.107-118.

——————, 1978b. Comments on Winter (1978). In Fisiak 1978:47.

——————, 1981. Glottalic consonants in Sindhi and PIE. *IIJ* 23.15-19.

Ladefoged, P. 1971. *Preliminaries to linguistic phonetics*. Chicago, Univ. Press.

————, 1979. review of J.C. Catford, *Fundamental problems in phonetics*. Edinburgh, Univ. Press, 1977. *Lg* 55.904-907.

Lass, R. 1974. Strategic design as the motivation for a sound shift: the rationale of Grimm's law. *AL(Haf)* 15.51-66.

Lubotsky, A. 1981. Greek *pégnūmi*, Sanskrit *pajrá-* and loss of laryngeals before mediae in Indo-Iranian. *MSS* 40.133-38.

Martinet, A. 1952. Remarques sur le consonantisme sémitique. *BSL* 49.67-78.

————, 1955. *Economie des changements phonétiques*. Berne: Francke. (3rd ed., 1970.)

Mayrhofer, M. 1983. Sanskrit und die Sprachen Alt-Europas. *NAWG* 1983 5. 121-54.

Miller, D.G. 1977. Some theoretical and typological implications of an IE root structure constraint. *JIES* 5.31-40.

Normier, R. 1977. Indogermanischer Konsonantismus, germanische 'Lautverschiebung' und Vernersches Gesetz. *KZ* 91.171-218.

Ohala, J.J. 1981. The listener as a source of sound change. *Papers from the parasession on language and behavior, CLS* 178-203.

Pedersen, H. 1951. *Die gemeinindoeuropäische und vorindoeuropäische Verschlüsslaute*. Copenhagen: Munksgaard.

Polomé, E.C., ed. 1982a. *The Indo-Europeans in the fourth and third millennia*. (*Linguistica Extranea*, 14.) Ann Arbor: Karoma.

————, 1982b. Germanic as an archaic Indo-European language. In *Fs Schneider*, 51-59.

Rasmussen, J.E. 1974. *Haeretica Indogermanica: A selection of Indo-European and pre-Indo-European studies*. Copenhagen: Kong. Danske Videnskabernes Selskab, hist.-fil. meddelelser 47.3.

Raumer, R. von 1837. *Die aspiration und die lautverschiebung*. Leipzig: Brockhaus. (Repr. Hildesheim: Olms, 1972.)

Rose, P.J. 1974. *Phonology of the Ningpo dialect of Chinese*. Diss., Univ. Manchester. Unpubl.

Schindler, J. 1976. Diachronic and synchronic remarks on Bartholomae's and Grassmann's laws. *LI* 7.622-37.

Swiggers, P. 1980. Glottalization and linguistic universals: A methodological remark. *FoL* 14. 433-36.

Trubetzkoy, N.S. 1939. *Grundzüge der Phonologie* (= *TCLP*, 7.), Prague. (2nd ed. Göttingen: Vandenhoeck & Ruprecht 1958; 5th unchanged ed., 1971; transl. 1949 by J. Cantineau as *Principes de Phonologie*, Paris: Klincksieck;

then 1969 by C.A.M. Baltaxe as *Principles of phonology*, Berkeley & Los Angeles: Univ. of California Press.)

Vennemann, T. 1979. Grassmann's law, Bartholomae's law, and linguistic method. *Fs Penzl*, 557-84. Cf. his discussion, forthcoming, in *PBB(T)* 106. (1984).

Villar, F. 1971. El problema de las sordas aspiradas indo-europeas. *REL* 1.129-60.

Westermann, D. & Ward, I.C. 1949. *Practical phonetics for students of African languages*. Oxford, Univ. Press.

Whitney, W.D. 1889. *A Sanskrit Grammar*. 2nd rev. ed., Boston: Ginn. (1st ed., Leipzig: Breitkopf & Härtel, 1879; 12th unchanged ed., Cambridge, Mass.: Harvard Univ. Press, 1972.)

Winter, W. 1978. The distribution of short and long vowels in stems of the type Lith. *ēsti: vèsti: mèsti* and OCS *jasti: vesti: mesti* in Baltic and Slavic languages. In Fisiak 1978:431-46.

APPENDIX III

Laws of accentuation in Balto-Slavic

It will not have escaped the attentive reader that there is no predictable correspondence between the scope and apparent importance or generality of a historical process (on the one hand) and its success in winning the appellation 'law' (on the other). The title has in recent years been easiest to achieve in one particular field: Balto-Slavic word accent and its history. Shevelov (1964) is a convenient source for beliefs — and conventions of naming — to that date; but later contributions have proliferated. This whole sector perhaps offers the "most complex problem of IE historical grammar" (C.Watkins in *Evidence for laryngeals* (^{2}1965), p. 117). Special comments on each relevant law will be found in the proper place. But it may be useful to underpin these by grouping them together, noting some essential presumptions, and anticipating some confusing arbitrarinesses.

The named laws, alphabetically, are: Dolobko's; Dybo's; Ebeling's; Fortunatov's II; Hartmann's; Hirt's I; Hjelmslev's; Illič-Svityč's; Meillet's; Nieminen's; Pedersen's II; Saussure's; Šaxmatov's; and Stang's.

(Some other laws interact with one or other of these, but are not themselves accentual in essence. They are: Endzelin's; Leskien's; van Wijk's; and Winter's.)

A law ascribed to Georgiev is noticed in Appendix I A. Garde (1976) contains several fundamental rules of accent placing and shifting: these are not named 'laws', but they are sometimes identical with (parts of) those listed here, especially Saussure's and Dybo's.

It is advisable, but far from easy, to remember that:

(1) (a) Dybo's law is sometimes ascribed to Illič-Svityč (as by Garde 1976:16, and even by Dybo himself: see on the law; and cf. also Halle & Kiparsky 1981 passim). It is given both names by Kolesov (1972:8).

  (b) Ebeling (1967:582) calls Hirt's law I 'the law of Hirt and Illič-Svityč'.

  (c) Although Fortunatov's analogous law (II) is treated separately here, Saussure's law is also known as 'the law of Fortunatov and Saussure', and

  (d) Dolobko's law is also called that 'of Vasil'ev and Dolobko'.

(2) (a) Normally, Saussure's law is said to feed Leskien's. But Kuryłowicz (1958:205) bypasses this relationship by holding that (1) the intonation of the final syllable is simply being credited with two separate effects (one on vowel-quantity and one on accent-position), and (2) the quantity change directly accounts for the accent shift. The laws then collapse into one.

  (b) Nieminen's law feeds Leskien's.

  (c) Stang's is fed by Dybo's which is (probably) fed by van Wijk's. (Note that Illič-Svityč's own law bleeds Dybo's, which is ironic in view of 1(a) above.)

  (d) Hjelmslev's law can be seen as a coda to some outputs of Pedersen's Law II.

Kortlandt (1978) perhaps affords the most convenient statement of the interrelation of these ordinances, with supporting bibliography.

(3)   Leftward accent shift ('retraction') is common in Balto-Slavic, if not necessarily so in PIE. It certainly is so in Aeolic Greek (or in Attic, as far as the laws of Vendryes and Wheerler are concerned). It is covered by these Balto-Slavic laws: Ebeling's; Hirt's I; Hjemslev's; Meillet's; Nieminen's; Pedersen's II; and Stang's. (Lehr-Spławiński also suggested such a shift.) Safarewicz offers a Latin parallel (1970 =Fs Stang, 443-47); and a generative rule of the same sort in contemporary English wins from J.R. Ross (Fs Halle, 166-73) the very apt and generalizable label, "Leftward, Ho!".

(4)   Whether each of these laws applies to Balto-Slavic, to Baltic alone, to Slavic alone, or just to one or more languages — on all such issues the debates abound.

(5)   It is equally debatable whether Baltic and Slavic possess at some evolutionary stage a feature of 'metatony', namely an arbitrary reshaping of the tone of a long syllable (on which see 6(b) below). This event (if it occurs) transcends the operation of any named law, most of which have stringent morphological constraints. It may leave a trace in the accent-contours of a later set of reflexes. Saussure (1894:426-27) believes that the direction is normally towards 'rude' (falling) tone; but he can enunciate no principle of motivation (429). A relevant discussion is that by Halle (LI 2.1-29, 1971); for him it is a matter of productive rules of derivation.

(6)   Legitimate input to any law is not easy to diagnose. Some conditioning
factors are:
(a) Whether the paradigm has fixed ('columnar') or mobile accent.
Saussure and his adherents think that the difference reflects a PIE
distinction of barytone from oxytone stems. Stang (1957) is renowned
for establishing three types of declensional accent at least in Slavic:
'*a*' − with fixed stem stress; '*b*' − with stress alternating between the
last syllable of the stem and the first desinential syllable; '*c*' − where
the stress alternates between the first syllable of the stem and the last
syllable of the ending (full lateral mobility). Garde takes some mobile
forms to be entirely unstressed (cf. *Slavic linguistics and language
teaching*, ed. by T.F. Magner, [Cambridge, Mass.: Slavica Publishers,
1976], 3).
(b) Whether the relevant syllable(s) have 'acute' or 'circumflex' intonation (or any other sort); on which, see first Saussure 1894. The intonations − some call them melodies − may not now be precisely definable
(so Garde 1976:5). The syllables should be vocalically long (and not
just 'heavy'); and, by tradition, acute syllables are found where the inherited vowel nucleus is long, not merely diphthongal. Some (e.g.
Watkins, *Evidence for laryngeals*, [2]1965:116) deny any direct link with
PIE /H/; others (e.g. Vaillant, Garde, Lehmann) take the contrary view.

The actual contours (high, rising, rising-falling, etc.) differ within and between Slavic and Baltic: cf. Stang 1957:20-21. The intonational value of an unaccented syllable can only be guessed at; again, some refuse to believe it has any,
as intonation for them entails stress. So Kuryłowicz; see also Lunt (*Word* 19.87,
(1963]); Endzelin disagreed, with Hamp's approval (*IF* 64. 46, [1959]). If
Kuryłowicz was right, Saussure's law is impossible. A high or rising tone may
remain on a shortened vowel (especially if word-final). Nuclei which are short
and nuclei which are long and circumflexed often behave alike, and are sometimes called the 'non-acutes'. 'Neo-acute' signifies a derived, and according to
Stang a left-shifted, stressed and rising syllable (but now see Kortlandt 1983:
37-39). Clearly PIE vocalic nuances are reflected in the intonations, but there is
no agreed opinion as to how: cf. Stankiewicz (1968). Hence vowel duration,
syllabic tune, and word stress are three interlocking systems. Contemporary
prosodic patterns in Slavic figure in Morris Halle's 1974 article.
        Lithuanian is diacritically awkward. The *acute* sign indicates a falling accent
on a two-mora *syllable* (including /VV/ and /VR/); the *circumflex* sign means

the converse, a rise on such a stretch. The Greek (and even the Latvian) usage is precisely the reverse; and Kuryłowicz (1934 = *BSL* 35. 24-34) insisted that Greek and Lithuanian, for all the likeness of their use of mora + pitch-level, were independent both of each other and of PIE, at least as regards the circumflex. (The grave sign in Lithuanian, like the double grave of Serbo-Croat, means a high point on a single mora.) See the discussion and references at Kiparsky 1973: 822, and Garde 1976:3-4.

The relations of scholars' often arbitrary and even obsolete names for accent-contours can be confusing. This display of equivalences may be of service:

Contour	French term*	German term*	Conventional sign	Lith. sign
rising	douce	Schleifton	acute	circumflex
falling	rude	Stosston	circumflex	acute (grave)

Alternative names are 'geschliffener Akzent' (vs. 'gestossener Akzent'). Falling accent is related to glottal constriction (cf. Kiparsky 1973:833). For Latvian – quite unlike Lithuanian – Ekblom (*Die Lettischen Akzentarten*, Uppsala: Almqvist & Wiksells, 1933) offers three equations: ~ for 'Dehnton', ` for 'Fallton', ^ for 'Stosston' (= Garde's 'ton brisé', 1976:385); the separation of the latter pair is a further complexity. Slovenian has, oddly, a long falling tone as a paradigm alternant where congeners alsewhere have a short rising tone; this is the so-called kajkavian 'neo-circumflex' (see Kortlandt 1976; Garde 1976: 240-42; Ivšić 1936:70 = 1971:664).

Finally, everything in this section is controversial, including this sentence.

* * * * *

A full bibliography may be sought elsewhere: notably, Garde 1976: 391-426 has a rich offering up to that date. Even so, there are some authorities on accentuation in general in these languages whose citing of these laws is continual, interwoven and often quoted. In any reference appended to the description of

---

* Although the original application of these informal French and German terms is clear (cf. Saussure, *IF Anzeiger* 6.157, [1896], there has been some casual use more recently. So Georgiev states his law (q.v., in Appendix I A) as normally referring to 'rude' syllables (and cites SC 'pro-circumflex' among the output), but actually marks his reconstructed input with acute or Slavic rising intonation signs.

each named law these selected studies, listed in full form below, are given in abbreviated form and asterisked (as, e.g., Garde 1976*). That they are for convenience set out together here is far from being an indication that they speak with one voice:

REFERENCES

Belić, A. 1914. *Akcenatske studije.* Belgrade: Sl. Akad. Nauk.

––––––, 1925. Zur slavischen Akzentlehre. *ZSlPh.* 2.1-28.

Birnbaum, H. 1975. *Common Slavic.* Cambridge, Mass.: Slavica Publishers.

Diels, P. 1909. Studien zur slavischen Betonung. *ASlPh* 31.1-101.

Dybo, V.A. 1981. *Slavjanskaja akcentologija.* Moscow: AN SSSR.

Ebeling, C.L. 1967. Historical laws of Slavic accentuation. *Fs Jakobson* (2) I. 577-93.

Garde, P. 1976. *L'histoire de l'accentuation slave* 2 vols. (= *Collection de manuels de l'Institut d'études slaves,* 7) Paris: Inst. d'Etudes slaves. (See rev. by Kortlandt, *Lingua* 44.67-91, 1978.)

Halle, M. 1974. Remarks on Slavic accentology. *Slavic Forum: Essays in Linguistics and Literature,* ed. by Michael S. Flier, 17-41. The Hague: Mouton.

––––––, & Kiparsky, P. 1981. Review article on Garde (1976). *Lg* 57.150-81.

Illič-Svityč, V.M. 1963. *Imennaja akcentuacija v baltijskom i slavjanskom; sud'ba akcentuacionnyx paradigm.* Moscow: An SSSR. (Transl. by R. Leed & R. Feldstein, as *Nominal accentuation in Baltic and Slavic,* Cambridge, Mass.: MIT Press, 1979.)

Isačenko, A.V. 1939. Zur phonologischen Deutung der Akzentverschiebungen in den slavischen Sprachen. *TCLP* 8.173-83.

Ivšić, S. 1936. Jesik Hrvata kajkavaca. *Ljetopis jugoslovenske Akad.* 48.47-88. (= *Gesammelte Schriften zum slavischen Akzent* [tr. and ed. by C. van der Berk], 641-82. Munich: Fink, 1971.)

Kiparsky, P. 1973. The inflectional accent in Indo-European. *Lg* 49.794-849.

––––––, & Halle, M. 1977. Towards a reconstruction of the Indo-European accent. *Studies in stress and accent,* ed. by L.M. Hyman. 209-239. Los Angeles: Dept. of Linguistics, Univ. of Southern California.

Kolesov, V.V. 1972. *Istorija russkogo udarenija.* Leningrad.

Kortlandt, F.H.H. 1974. On the history of Baltic accentuation. *HL(A&J)* 2.295-309.

————, 1975. *Slavic accentuation.* Lisse: Peter de Ridder Press.

————, 1976. On the Slovene neo-circumflex. *SEER* 54.1-10.

————, 1977. Historical laws of Baltic accentuation. *Baltistica* 13.319-30.

————, 1978. On the history of Slavic accentuation. *KZ* 92.269-81.

————, 1983. Linguistic theory, universals, and Slavic accentuation. *FoLH* 4.27-43.

Kuryłowicz, J. 1958. *L'accentuation des langues indo-européennes.* 2nd ed. Wrocław & Kraków: Polska AN. (1st ed., 1953).

Lehr-Spławiński, T. 1966. *Studia i szkice wybrane z językoznawstwa słowiańskiego.* 2 vols. 2nd ed. Warsaw: Państwowe Wydawnictwo Naukowe. (1st ed., 1957.)

Lunt, H.G. 1963. On the study of Slavic accentuation. *Word* 19.82-99.

Meyer, K.H. 1920. *Slavische und indogermanische Intonation.* Heidelberg: Winter.

Nonnenmacher-Pribić, E. 1961. *Die baltoslavischen Akzent- und Intonationsverhältnisse und ihr quantitativer Reflex im Slovakischen.* Wiesbaden: Harrassowitz.

Pedersen, H. 1905. Die nasalpräsentia und der slavische Akzent. *KZ* 38.297-421.

Sadnik, L. 1959. *Slavische Akzentuation I. Vorhistorische Zeit.* Wiesbaden: Harrassowitz.

Saussure, F. de 1894. A propos de l'accentuation lituanienne. *MSL* 8.425-46. (Repr. in *Recueil des publications scientifiques*, ed. by C. Bally & L. Gautier, 490-512. Geneva: Sonor; Lausanne & Paris: Payot, 1922.)

————, 1996. Accentuation lituanienne. *IF Anzeiger* 6. 157-66. (Repr. in *Recueil* [see above], 526-38.)

Shevelov, G.Y. 1964. *A prehistory of Slavic: The historical phonology of Common Slavic.* Heidelberg: Winter.

Stang. C.S. 1957. *Slavonic accentuation.* (= *Norske Videnskaps-Akademi i Oslo.* I.1 (*Hist.-fil. kl.*, 3.) Oslo: Aschehoug.

Stankiewicz, E. 1968. The accent pattern of the Slavic verb. *American contributions to the 6th Int. Cong. of Slavists* (Prague), ed. by H. Kučera, 359-75. The Hague: Mouton.

Torbiörnsson, T. 1924. *Die litauischen Akzentverschiebungen und die litauische Verbalakzent.* (= *Series Slavica*, ed. by M. Murko, 9.) Heidelberg: Winter.

Vaillant, A. 1936. Le problème des intonations balto-slaves. *BSL* 37.109-115.

Van Wijk, N. 1923. *Die baltischen und slavischen Akzent- und Intonations-*

systeme. (= *Kon. Ak. van Wetenschappen*, Amsterdam; n.s. 23:2.) (Repr., The Hague: Mouton, 1958.)

Other references are to be sought under the law in question. More general studies of Lithuanian matters are given under Saussure's law.

* * * * *

It may be salutary to close by giving special notice to E. Stankiewicz, *Studies in Slavic morphophonemics and accentology*. (Ann Arbor: Michigan Slavic publications, 1979). This work is largely given over the outright denunciation of precisely these 'contradictory' and 'ad hoc rationalistic' laws. They are declared to be a hindrance to progress in the whole area. This no doubt explains the notable non-mention of most of the named laws in the cursory coverage of Balto-Slavic accent studies at pp.42-47 of vol.1 of E. Stankiewicz & D. Worth, *A selected bibliography of Slavic linguistics*, (The Hague: Mouton, 1976). The predictable storm reverberates (cf. for example, Kortlandt in *Lingua* 52.198 ff., 1980, and the further tussle in *Lingua* 56.179ff., 1982). There is indeed a current sense that modern scholars offer each his own tidying of an older generation's self-indulgence. Yet these ordinances, and their awkward nomenclature, will be about the place for some time to come, to puzzle and provoke.

Dahl's law in Bantu

This law is often paraded, usually by name only, by Indo-Europeanists who are eager to justify their canonic shifts by demonstrating parallels elsewhere. Bantu has been the object of appeal by adherents of Holtzmann's law (q.v.). As to Dahl's law in that group of languages, it has indeed affinities with several IE laws, but seems not unlike Grassmann's to most who quote it. It is used to show that Grassmann's law is quite respectable – because it occurs, in essence, at the other end of the world; or else, that GL does not deserve the status of special law at all – because it occurs, in essence, at the other end of the world. Citations are less varied than motives for citation. Yet it is not really clear what process, with what conditions and with how much regularity of incidence, Dahl meant.

It was Carl Meinhof (1857-1944) on his own admission (1932:15-16), who named the law. He accepted the observations of Edmund Dahl, a missionary, who had been his pupil in 1897. Previous studies from the field had failed to notice certain consonant alternations, to which Dahl drew his old teacher's attention. Meinhof set the law out (1904:299, giving credit to Dahl) in these words: "wenn in einem Wortstamm zwei aufeinanderfolgende Silben mit einer stimmlosen Explosiva beginnen, so wird die erstere stimmhaft". The first problem is whether an 'explosive' is aspirated (where a mere plosive is not); certainly Meinhof says so in 1932 (181-83), speaking of a loss of aspiration. Inherited $*\textit{+pota}$ "twist together" thus becomes (presumably) $*\textit{+}p^{h}ot^{h}a$, whence $\textit{+botha}$; or $*\textit{+kati}$ "in the middle" moves via $*\textit{+}k^{h}at^{h}i$ to $\textit{+gathi}$. This is certainly dissimilatory, and it may be a reduction of incidence of aspiration (although this feature is not original), so that the voicing is not really motivated. The process may be productive both before and after the shift /ph/ > /h/: so $*\textit{+kope}$ "eyelash" > $*\textit{+}k^{h}op^{h}e$ > $*\textit{+}gop^{h}e$, or $*\textit{+}k^{h}ohe$ > $\textit{+gohe}$. For Meinhof (1932:181-83) the position of /+/ is immaterial; in this he seems to agree with Dahl. From $\textit{-}t^{h}w$ "carry", for example, there is derived $\textit{-thw+ala}$ "carry on the head", but $*\textit{-}t^{h}w\textit{+}ik^{h}a$ "load" becomes $\textit{-dw+ika}$ (with deaspiration). Here /+/ stands between the target and trigger stops. The prior stop may itself be in an affix: In Ruanda (Rundi-Ha) there occurs, alongside $\textit{utu+goma}$ "small drums"

(< *utu+*. . . "little"), the affected form *udu+kwi* "some firewood" (cf. *aga+kwi* < **aka+*. . .idem). But there at least the effect is limited to isolated target voiceless obstruents; in a chain they are apparently immune: *tu+ka+ki+mu+ha* "we gave it to him". Meinhof (with Mould's approval at 1979:389) sees /b/ as fricative /β/ but accepts /d,g/. Mould indeed regards the law (as in Logooli) as the only true source of voiced obstruents, which thereafter suffered a Grimm-like shift.

Guthrie (1967:59, §52,82) briefly discusses the process. He notes Nyore as rejecting the shift where the affected stop is /t/ and the trigger slot is filled by /k/ or (curiously) /r/, or where /t/ is preceded by /i/. It was he who divided the Bantu-speaking area of Africa into zones; and the relevant languages are all in his zones E, F, and G (which cover, roughly, a tract running from Southern Tanzania in a north-westerly direction across Kenya and into Southern Uganda). The idioms include Nyamwezi, Dzalamo, Ruanda-Rundi-Ha, Kikuyu (note the local name; it should perhaps be quoted as Gikuyu as the law *did* operate, even if usually with affixes and clitics), Shambala, Bena and Luyia – to name them by groups and with arbitrary spelling. Swahili is not affected. (Cope 1971, or Fivaz & Scott 1977, offer guidance.)

Mould (1979:390) restricts Dahl's law to a purely voicing dissimilation (see above) and has no truck with aspiration; moreover, he limits it to stem-initial consonants in C_1VC_2- stems, where C_2 is a voiceless obstruent. (Also, prior loss of /p/ bleeds the law somewhat.) This holds in Logooli (Luyia) at least:

> Proto-Bantu *ma+tako* "buttocks" > *amadako*
> "   *ma+kuta* "oil, fat" > *amaguta*

(Nyamwezi *mavutha* agrees, aspiration(?) apart, but it apparently derives its friction in -*v*- from Swahili.) Nyamwezi is really supported only by Dzalamo in suggesting that aspiration is involved at all. The recent interpretation of Dahl's law (as simply adding vocal cord movement) frankly makes it look less like Grassmann's law than like Thurneysen's – although the direction of dissimilation is the opposite and accent apparently plays no part in Dahl's law. But Appendix II is perhaps relevant here. Only the Gamkrelidze view of Grassmann's law (that is, of contextually conditioned variant reflexes of inherited /d$^{(h)}$/) comes at all close to 'new look' Dahl's law (which produces /t-g/ but /d-k/). So, as has more than once been said, a comprehensive statement of the exact process, and of the paths of diffusion of Dahl's effect across Bantustan, has yet to be written. Only then can cross-family comparison begin, and be profitably extended across phonemic systems and linkages of shifts.

REFERENCES

Bynon, T. et al., eds. 1973. *Papers on Comparative Bantu.* (Memorial to M. Guthrie, = *African Language Studies* 14.1-114.) London: School of Oriental & African Studies.

Cope, A.T. 1971. A consolidated classification of the Bantu languages. *African Studies* 30.213-36.

Dahl, E. 1915. *Nyamwezi Wörterbuch.* (= Abhandl. Hamburg. Kolonialinstituts, 25 B.) Hamburg: Friederichsen. (Cf. *MSOS* 7.256.)

Davy, J. I. M. & Nurse, D. 1982. Synchronic versions of Dahl's law: The multiple applications of a phonological dissimilation rule. *Journal of African Languages and Linguistics* 4.157-95.

Fivaz, D. & Scott, P.E. 1977. *African languages: A genetic and decimalised classification.* Boston: Hall.

Guthrie, M. 1967. *Comparative Bantu* I. Farnborough: Gregg Press.

Meinhof, C. 1904. Das Dahlsche Gesetz. *ZDMG* 57.299-304.

—————, 1932. *Introduction to the phonology of the Bantu languages.* Berlin: Reimer (Vohsen). (= Translation by N.J. van Warmelo of [author's] revised version of *Grundriss einer Lautlehre der Bantusprachen.* Leipzig & Berlin: W. de Gruyter, 1910. [1st ed., 1899.])

Mould, M. 1979. The Proto Bantu consonants and the feature [voice]. *Language and Linguistic Problems in Africa*, ed. by P.F.A. Kotey & Haig Der-Houssikian (= *Proc. 7th Conf. on African Linguistics*), 389-94. Columbia, S.C.: Hornbeam Press.

Werner, A. 1919. *Introductory sketch of the Bantu languages.* London: Kegan Paul, Trench & Trubner.

APPENDIX V

Latin verbs in *-io, -ere* and *-io, -ire.*

Ever since Remmius Palaemon (see Keil 1868:543) assigned Latin verbs to just four paradigm classes, according to the vowel length in the final syllable of second person singular forms of the present indicative active (*-ās, -ēs, -ĭs, -īs*), the dual membership of the 'third conjugation' has caused difficulty. One group of verbs, represented by *capĭs*, infin. *capĕre*, displays a post-stem prevocalic *-i-*, sporadically but totally predictably, as in *capiō, capiunt*. It is thus as different from the other verbs of its class (*regĭs, regĕre* but *regō, regunt*) as it is from those of the fourth conjugation (*audiō, audiunt* but *audīs, audīre*). Hermann (1923), using arguments familiar from Sievers' law, propounded a phonologically motivated split based on root-final vocalism:

(1) *-VC+yeti* > *-VC+ĭt* (*capĭt*; likewise *capĭs*)
(2) *-CC+iyeti* > *-CC+īt* (**sentīt*, whence *sentĭt* by subsequent change; likewise *sentīs*)

– and type (2) is widened to include first post-diphthongal *audīs* etc., and then even the differently constructed *uĕnĭs, sălĭs*.

On this base Seebold (1972:110-21) speculates as follows: *Four* variants are to be recognised:

(1)	*mitt∅ + is/ont*	>	*mitt-ĭs* ,	*mitt-unt*
(2)	*capy + is/ont*	>	*cap'-ĭs* ,	*capi-unt*
(3)	*audiy + is/ont*	>	*audi'-is > audīs,*	*audi'-unt*
(4)	*ueni + is/ont*	>	*uenīs* ,	*ueni-unt*

Of these (3) is not 'pure Sievers' as *thus* expressed. But no matter: (4) is not, after all, Sievers-Edgerton. Perhaps one could assign some fictitious environmental value of quasi- 'CC' or 'RC' or ':C') to single nasals and laterals, in order to equate (4) with (3) in suffixal exponence. Certainly Latin has no type (2) verbs whose root-final consonant is *m, n,* or *l* – though it has them in *-r* (*părĭs, mŏrĕrĭs*).

But, in (2), why should *capyis* pass to *capĭs*? *Aĭs* is adduced; but there a prior shift of **agy+is* to **ayyis* leads either to a total loss of -*yy*- before -*i*-, or to a loss of a -*y*- which stands before -*i*- and after another -*y*- (itself only graphically lost); and neither case is parallel. It is even worse to appeal to the type *consilī* (as from **consily+ī*, for nominals with nominative in -*ius* or -*ium*). The general Latin shift of -*VCyV*- > -*VCiV*- (as in *medius, alius*) rather supports the actually attested, if restored, *negotiī, imperiī* etc. from the late Republic onwards. A more specific case is that where -*VCyi*- is retained, except that the -*y*- is lost in spelling: so in *abicis* = [´abjikis] etc., as described by Aulus Gellius (*Noctes Atticae* 4.17) and as indicated by classical verse prosody (cf. Catullus 24.9 – although there are counter-cases early and late, as Plautus, *Asinaria* 814 and Juvenal 15.17). Still, this is manifestly *not* exemplified in *consilī*, where the preceding syllable is metrically light (e.g., Horace, *Carmina* 3.4.65). Only two possibilities remain for it: either contraction of -*iī* > -*ī* or complete replacement of the -*iī* formant(s) by the single genitival -*ī* of consonant-final roots in this stem-class. Neither solution helps *capĭs*. The preceding syllable's accent has been cited as a factor, and it is present in *consílī*, by all indications. Yet there (like the retained accent-position of apocopated *adhŭc* etc.) it is a relic of pre-shift days, a phenomenon akin to Bloomfield's 'reminiscent sandhi'. So it seems that Seebold has no valid conditioning factor or shift-parallel in his armoury: indeed, **căpl+is* and **uĕnl+is* are for him structurally indistinguishable. This whole approach is as speculative as is Pariente's (1946), for whom the paths are:

a.   *TVT-y+es(i)* ——   *TVT-y+'s*   (*capĭs*)
b.   *TVX-y+es(i)* ——   *TVX-i(y+)is*   (*uenīs*)

Condition: X =   (i)   liquid or nasal, plus or minus stop
               (ii) single stop in onomatopoeic verbs (like *mūgīs*).

Even then some 'perturbaciones' are acknowledged, like unexplained *amĭcīs*. Yet one clear, rhythmic, fact is that a root sequence of two or more light syllables with short vowels induces the '-*iō*, -*īs*, -*īre*' declension (*ămĭcīs, sĕpĕlīs, ăpĕrĭs*) while active '-*iō*, -*īs*, -*ĕre*' verbs have a single light syllable in the simple root (*căpĭs, părĭs, fŭgĭs* – even the deponents *grădī, mŏrī* follow suit). This fact holds good even if its converse is partially negatived by some forms of *ŏrīrī* and *pŏtīrī*, as well as *uĕnīre, sălīre*.

At this point many will turn back, with cries of alarm, to the safety of the 'traditional' explanation as offered by Exon (1901) and in roughly the same terms by Sommer (1914a II) and Skutsch (1902; 1910:367-69). For them, the long stem-final vowel of the *audī-* type is analogical to that of *amā-, monē-,* and the *căpī-* sub-type then arises purely by 'iambic shortening' (see Sommer-Pfister 1977:105; and for a sophisticated radical explanation of the phenomenon, cf. Devine & Stephens at *CR* n.s.75. 142-57, 1980) — the process which occasions *căuĕ* (as *Cau(e) ne eas* was heard as *Cauneas* by Crassus in the famous story), *bĕnĕ, tŏgă,* and the new stems *dŏmă, mŏnĕ* which underlie the perfect (*+wai*?) formation evidenced in *domui, monui,* spreading elsewhere (e.g., *rapui*). The merits of this line of attack are obvious. We avoid at once a PIE scatter of formatives in *+y, +i, +iy* and *+ī*; the absence of the pattern (-)$C\breve{V}C\breve{i}$-s etc. needs no special notice; and the pattern (-)$\breve{V}C\breve{V}C\bar{i}$-s etc. (in *ămĭcīs, rĕdĭmīs*) is predictably retained. There are some flaws, but probably venial. The *-ā/ē* formants have external origins or models (*+eH₂*, as *nouāre*; *+eH₁*, as perhaps *albēre*), while *-ī* looks to them alone and is yet prehistoric in emergence — but that is scarcely a counter-argument. Iambic shortening is a purely Latin phenomenon, true enough; but the hints of *-i* elsewhere, which are unwelcome, amount to no more than Lithuanian *mylĭme* (sing. *myliu*) and Oscan *factud*, (alongside *fakiiad*) — which may be syncopated from **fakitud*, Latin *facitō*, but could be an unextended root formation, like Skt. (*bhrāmyati* but) *bhramati*, or Latin (*ueniat* but) *aduenat.* Certainly, *uĕnĭs, sălĭs* remain as exceptions (although they could be post-Plautine reversions). But they may have their special reasons (cf. Sommer-Pfister 1977:104) — the analogy of *īre* in the case of *uĕnīre*, or a variable degree of conjugational mixing in the case of *sălīre* (still traceable in its perfect, *saliui* or *saluī*; cf. the paradigms of *orīri, pŏtīri*). Even convenient metrical alternating of the types, like *cupĕret/cupīret* (Lucretius 1.71), may have had an influence.

It is hard to return to a Sieversian solution, for all that the pair *-$\breve{V}C\breve{i}$-/-$\breve{V}C\bar{i}$-* seem to suggest earlier *-Cy-/XCiy-* (where *X* is *C* or # or:); after all, *XCiyC →* *XCīC* is neither Sieversian nor Edgertonian (**/-ktiyt/*). Besides, the *ămĭcīs* type would then require an overall equation, for these purposes, of ∧∧ (two light syllables) with — (one heavy syllable). But even in metrics (with 'resolution' rules) this particular simple equation of phonological timing has been suspect, or rejected as naive, in Greek and Latin prosody — see Allen (1973:165, 169, 255ff.), although he accepts it for this specific verbal patterning (1973:164). Moreover, no metrical motivation is apparent in the problem before us. Dactylic hexameters usually alone induce exigencies of a prosodic kind for Latin, yet *audĭŭnt, ămĭcĭŭnt* display a fine disregard of epic metrical needs. As for an *accentual* identifying of ∧∧ and —, it is simply the case that the relevant classical accent-matrices are (discounting the word-final syllable) $\stackrel{\prime}{-}$, $\stackrel{\prime}{\wedge}\wedge$, $\stackrel{\prime}{-}\wedge$

but not *ʌ n ⌐ (i.e. audīs, ămĭcīs, audĭunt, but ămĭcĭunt and not ămĭcĭunt after Plautus).

REFERENCES

Allen, W.S. 1973. *Accent and rhythm.* Cambridge, Univ. Press.

Exon, C. 1901. Latin verbs in -io with infinitives in -ere. *Hermathena* 11(27). 382-402.

Hermann, E. 1923. *Silbenbildung im griechischen und in den anderen indogermanischen Sprachen.* (*KZ Ergänzungsheft*, 2.) Göttingen: Vandenhoeck & Ruprecht.

Keil, H. 1868. *Grammatici Latini*, vol.5. Leipzig: Teubner. (Repr., Hildesheim: Olms, 1961.)

Pariente, A. 1946. Sobre las diferencias de tipo 'facis : venīs' (una ley fonetica latina correspondiente a la de Sievers). *Emerita* 14.1-81.

Seebold, E. 1972. *Das System der idg. Halbvokale.* (*Untersuchungen zum sogenannten 'Sieversschen Gesetz' und zu den halbvokalhaftigen Suffixen in den idg. Sprachen, besonders im Vedischen.*) Heidelberg: Winter.

Skutsch, F. 1902. Grammatisch-lexicalische Notizien. *ALL* 12.197-214. (Esp. 210-131.)

———, 1910. Literaturbericht für 1908: Italische Sprachen und lateinische Grammatik. *Glotta* 2.361-88.

Sommer, F. 1914a. *Handbuch der lateinischen Laut- und Formenlehre.* 2nd and 3rd ed. Heidelberg: Winter. (4th ed. of vol.1, ed by R. Pfister, 1977.)

———, 1914b. Die indogermanische *iā-* und *io-* Stamme im Baltischen. *ASAW* 30.4.

Thurneysen, R. 1879. *Über Herkunft und Bildung der lateinischen Verba auf -io der dritten und vierten Konjugation.* Diss., Univ. Leipzig.

Iam satis est; ne me Crispini scrinia lippi
conpilasse putes, uerbum non amplius addam.

INDEX OF AUTHORITIES

I: INVENTORS OF LAWS OR MAJOR INFLUENCES

II: OTHER CONTRIBUTORS